THE PROFESSIONAL COUNSELOR AS ADMINISTRATOR

Perspectives on Leadership and Management in Counseling Services Across Settings

THE PROFESSIONAL COUNSELOR AS ADMINISTRATOR

Perspectives on Leadership and Management in Counseling Services Across Settings

Edwin L. Herr, EdD
Dennis E. Heitzmann, PhD
Jack R. Rayman, PhD
The Pennsylvania State University
University Park, PA

LAWRENCE ERLBAUM ASSOCIATES, PUBLISHERS
2006   Mahwah, New Jersey   London

Lawrence Erlbaum Associates, Inc., Publishers
10 Industrial Avenue
Mahwah, New Jersey 07430
www.erlbaum.com

Cover design by Kathryn Houghtaling Lacey

Library of Congress Cataloging-in-Publication Data

Herr, Edwin L.
  The professional conselor as administrator : perspectives on leadership and management
of counseling services across settings / Edwin L. Herr, Dennis E. Heitzmann, Jack R. Rayman.
    p. cm.
  Includes bibliographical references (p.) and index.
  ISBN 0-8058-4957-2 (alk. paper)
  ISBN 0-8058-4958-0 (pbk : alk. paper)
  1. Counseling—Management. 2. Educational counseling—Management. I. Heitzmann,
Dennis E. II. Rayman, Jack R. III. Title.

BF637.C6H524 2006
361'.06'0684—dc22   2005041407
                                                                          CIP

Books published by Lawrence Erlbaum Associates are printed on acid-free paper,
and their bindings are chosen for strength and durability.

Printed in the United States of America
10 9 8 7 6 5 4 3 2 1

For my grandsons, Myles Patrick Herr and Fletcher Edward Hess, their parents, Christopher and Sarah and Alicia and Terry, their Aunt Amber, and their grandmother, Pat. Thanks to all for your love, support, and patience while this book was unfolding.

E.L.H.

My contribution to this volume is dedicated to my wife and partner, Marcia, and our children, Colin, Bryan, and Carolyn—teacher, lawyer, manager, and psychologist-to-be, the composite of their requisite professional skills would portend all of the characteristics required of the complete administrator. Their importance to me, however, transcends that—they make me real. Secondly, my sincere expression of appreciation to Lori Schoch, office manager, and the cadre of staff with whom I've had the pleasure to work for many years. Collectively, they provide the infrastructure from which all good directing emanates.

D.E.H.

I would like to thank my parents, Robert and Harriette Rayman, who taught me about the dignity of work and who, as octogenarians, continue to demonstrate the value of a strong work ethic in their daily lives. I would also like to thank my wife, Barbara, and my two daughters, Jamie and Megan, who believed in me when I experienced self-doubt and who encouraged me to believe that my thoughts and experiences might have relevance and value to others. Finally, I would like to acknowledge my long-time staff assistant and office manager, Teresa Keeler, who reminds me every day that you don't have to be charismatic to be an effective leader and manager, but you do have to be organized.

J.R.R.

Contents

Preface

This book, *The Professional Counselor as Administrator: Perspectives on Leadership and Management of Counseling Services Across Settings*, has several purposes. The first is to acknowledge that counselors, counseling psychologists, and related mental health personnel are frequently promoted to administrative positions because they are excellent counselors, not because they have been trained to be an administrator or have administrative skills. Thus, the authors of this book believe that such counselors deserve a reference work that provides insight into what administrators of counseling services do in various counseling-related settings. These settings include school counseling or guidance programs, university counseling centers and career services, academic programs preparing professional counselors and counseling psychologists, state and national governmental offices implementing counseling legislation, local government-supported agencies delivering counseling services, foundations concerned with the improvement of counseling services, workplaces providing counseling services as part of human resource development, and independent practice.

Against the background of the settings selected for inclusion here, the similarities and differences in what administrators of counseling services do are discussed. A subtext of the book and a second purpose is to explore the contexts in which counseling takes place and the challenges that these context differences present to those who provide leadership and management of counseling services.

A third purpose of the book is to acquaint the reader with three important terms: *administration*, *management*, and *leadership*. The differences in meaning, nuance, and implementation of each of the roles reflected in these terms are explored and applied to different settings. Meeting this purpose essentially provides a mini-primer of fundamental processes with which readers aspiring to be administrators of counseling services, in any setting, need to be familiar. Among the major processes discussed are planning; budgeting; recruiting a diverse staff, developing, and retaining professional and support staff; supervision of staff; the use of technology; and evaluation. Components of these major processes, depending on the setting, include such topics as program accreditation and individual credentialing; advocacy, marketing, promotion of counseling services; grant-seeking; statepersonship; and other important topics.

A fourth purpose of the book is to wed scholarship about leadership, management, and administration in different counseling settings, for which there is relatively little specific literature across settings, with the pragmatic experiences of the authors. Collectively, for almost 90 years, the authors have been administrators, heads or directors of counseling services or counselor preparation programs, consultants to foundations and government units, researchers, presidents of major counseling associations, professional counselors and psychologists, and faculty members. Rather than rely for substance only on a professional literature that is thin and uneven in its discussion of leadership and management of counseling services, the authors have viewed these important processes through their own experiential lenses. As such, the book is intended to provide an overview of the roles and processes used by administrators of counseling services in major organization settings as seen by persons who have administered counseling services in these settings.

From a functional standpoint, the book incorporates 10 chapters in what could be thought of as two parts. The first part consists of chapters 1 and 2. Chapter 1, "Leadership, Management, Administration in Perspective," is an attempt to separate these terms and the tasks associated with each term. A variety of writings, often from the corporate world, are examined to distill what it means to be performing administrative, management, and leadership roles. Chapter 2, "Fundamental Processes of Leadership, Management, and Administration," examines the tools, concepts, and processes used by the professional counselor serving as an administrator. This chapter addresses strategic and other forms of planning; systems thinking; budgeting as it relates to planning and as it can be conceived in terms of such concepts as revenue streams, cost centers, and direct and indirect costs (in this chapter and elsewhere in the book, we talk about budgets as both planning documents and political statements); grant seeking and external funding; staff recruitment, retention, and development; supervision of staff; use of technology and knowledge management; ethics; program evaluation; and cost-benefit analysis.

The second part of the book, chapters 3 through 10, includes a series of chapters discussing the characteristics of leadership, management, and administration in specific settings, and the interactions of counseling services within an array of other institutional purposes. A point made in these chapters is that counseling services rarely are stand-alone structures. Typically, they are embedded in larger institutions—schools, universities, government departments, corporations—that require them to plan in ways that demonstrate counseling's contributions to the larger institutional mission. In these chapters, attention is given to seminal documents, legislation, policies, and professional standards that are highly influential in shaping the provision of counseling, who does it, for whom, under what conditions, and for what purposes. The book ends with chapter 10, which reiterates the main themes of the book and suggests implications for the future.

In conclusion, permit us, as authors, to thank the many theorists and researchers from whose scholarship we have learned about leadership, management, and administration. We also want to thank those administrators who have mentored us in pragmatic situations and those colleagues and staff members who have worked with each of us in our various capacities as we have learned administrative skills. Let us also acknowledge the word-processing excellence and organizational skills of Judy Kauffman, the principal secretary preparing this manuscript for publication, and Christine Andrus, whose keyboarding excellence and attention to detail have added quality to the manuscript preparation. As indicated on the dedication page, we want to thank our wives, children, and grandchildren for their love and understanding during the course of this project. Finally, we want to thank Dr. Mark Kiselica, Professor of Counselor Education, The College of New Jersey, who, in an early review of the prospectus for this book, suggested the title, *The Professional Counselor as Administrator*. We have heeded his advice and valued his insights.

—*Edwin L. Herr, EdD*
Dennis E. Heitzmann, PhD
Jack R. Rayman, PhD
The Pennsylvania State University
University Park, Pennsylvania

1

Leadership, Management, and Administration in Perspective

CONTEXT

In an era of widespread psychological uncertainty, problems in living, stress, and growing complexity in individual career choices, the socioeconomic importance of counseling services has become increasingly evident. Indeed counseling has been seen as a process that is directly or indirectly instrumental in meeting national goals and, as such, is embedded in many policy statements and legislative actions. Legislation in support of counseling takes many forms, but it frequently emphasizes the important role of counseling and counselors in rehabilitating those on the margins of society, maximizing the effective choice of work and the preparation of the nation's workforce, and performing early identification and intervention in the lives of children who are at risk of academic, social, and employment failure now or in the future.

It has been argued that during the evolution of counseling in the United States, because of its importance to national goals, counseling has become a sociopolitical process; it receives credibility and resources from federal and state governments which include counseling as a function that, independently or in combination with other functions, is important to the welfare of citizens as they seek to be purposeful and productive. Such governmental affirmations on behalf of counseling as a vital technique relevant to the achievement—personal, social, economic—of children, youth, and adults are evident in legislation that focuses on emphases of national interest across the life span. Such landmark legislative initiatives include the Rehabilitation Act Amendments that provide counseling for persons with disabilities; the

Wagner–Peyser Act, which established the U.S. Employment Service and its counseling of persons seeking employment; the Work Force Investment Act; the School-to-Work Opportunities Act; the National Defense Education Act; the Elementary School Counseling Incentive Act; the Higher Education Act; and the Social Security Incentive Act, which supports counseling for older Americans. In addition to these major pieces of legislation, which focus on counseling and its social, political, and economic impact, there has been legislation dealing with other categories of national concern: child abuse, chemical dependency, assisting persons to move from welfare to work, and helping persons who have lost their jobs because of the movement of American industries to other nations. Some of these pieces of legislation have dealt with capacity building and the education and employment of counselors for schools, colleges and universities, community agencies, employment services, and other settings. In other instances, legislation has supported the need for counseling to focus on a particular type of social, mental health, or economic problem. Further, in some cases, legislation has identified the qualifications or credentials that counselors need to be certified or licensed to perform particular functions with specific populations.

It might be noted here, although it is not a major focus of this book, that counseling is now a worldwide phenomenon. Many nations throughout the world have established policies and legislation that address the need for, purposes of, training and qualifications of, and resources to be committed to counseling and counselors. As nations experience problems of industrial and social evolution, changing occupational structures, problems of addiction to alcohol and other substances, stress and uncertainty, internal conflicts, and mental health issues, they are developing their own indigenous ways to foster counseling and prepare counselors. In some instances, they adopt models and approaches developed in the United States. In a growing number of situations, countries are designing and implementing their own counseling systems, criteria by which to deploy counselors to focus on specific problems, and decisions about the settings in which counseling should be located (e.g., university clinics, Ministries of Labor or Health, schools, community agencies, etc.). The provision of counseling in nations around the globe has risen so rapidly, at least in part, because the world of the present is an uncertain world. National political structures in many countries have changed from communism to market economies (e.g., Eastern Europe), from apartheid to ethnic and racial inclusion (South Africa), from guaranteed life-long employment to much less linear and predictable employment (Japan), from known health problems to new and mutant diseases (e.g., AIDS, SARS, Monkeypox; China, Taiwan, many African nations), and from stable international relationships to conflict, disruption of social systems, threats, and terrorism. Within such circumstances, trends that were historically isolated within a particular nation or geographic region have ripple effects throughout the world as new alliances are formed and others dissolve. Increasingly global labor surpluses occur that motivate persons to emigrate to where economic opportunities exist, bringing with them cultural traditions not typical of the receiving nations. In such instances, immigrant populations cause new challenges for schools and new stresses on religious, financial, and other social services. Nations are classified into *fast* and *slow* nations depending on their ability to use advanced technology in their industrial, business, financial, and health care systems.

Collectively, these problems of major change—decreases in the quality of life of people, rising unemployment, insufficient resources to provide health care and predictable availability of food, inability to live in peace without life-threatening conflict, danger of exposure to new and untreatable disease, inability to gain access to schooling or other forms of education by which to improve one's ability to compete for resources and jobs—are examples of the content of counseling, of areas in which counselors work and have been successful, and areas about which nations have decided to support the development of counseling and the preparation of counselors as national or regional priorities.

THE COUNSELOR AS ADMINISTRATOR

Against this brief backdrop of personal and governmental circumstances for which counseling is often seen in policy and legislation as a treatment of choice, the purpose of this book is not to explore the process of counseling per se. It is not about theories of counseling or the use of specific counseling interventions, but rather about processes that are much less frequently explored: the administration, leadership, and management of counseling services.

The complex factors that are associated with the delivery of counseling services demand administration, management, and leadership. Whether in a one-person counseling office or a large agency of several score counselors, the delivery of counseling services requires funding, advocacy, marketing, staff supervision, validation of services offered, and outreach to clients and the community, among other processes. Unless such processes have oversight, systematic planning, budgeting, trained support staff, and appropriately credentialed counselors, one has chaos, random behavior, and ineffective delivery of services to clients. In each of these situations, it is likely that some counselor will assume responsibility for managing, coordinating, and providing leadership to these counseling enterprises. The question, of course, is whether the counselor is able to provide the competencies inherent in managing, administering, and leading the particular counseling agency, center, clinic, department, or whatever the configuration in which counseling is provided. Does this person understand the complexity of processes and factors that need to be addressed if one is going to give direction to and manage the provision of counseling?

In far too many instances, counselors are appointed to leadership positions for the wrong reasons—because they are good counselors or because they have the respect of their peers, not because they understand the processes inherent in managing or giving leadership to a counseling organization embedded within larger institutions (e.g., a school, a university) or one that exists on a stand-alone basis.

A basic premise of this book is that in an era of increasing competition among social services, education, health care, and other important social institutions for fiscal and personnel resources, the importance of leadership for and management of counseling services is a critical matter for survival and for the improvement of the services at issue.

A second major premise of the book, and essentially the rationale for the title of the book, is that frequently professional counselors who are chosen to be the director, manager, or administrator of counseling services in a particular setting—schools, universities, communities, government agencies, or foundations—have not been trained to do so. Often such persons are chosen to lead or manage counseling services because they are excellent counselors—they are known as professionals who "do" counseling well. Certainly, such technical expertise gives one credibility with one's peers and, probably, with one's supervisors. Yet in an era when strategic planning; envisioning the big picture; understanding what legislation or policy is relevant, if not definitive, in a particular setting; how to recruit and nurture members of the counseling support staff; how to budget for, acquire, and deploy resources to meet one's mission; and how to incorporate technology into one's program of services have become major ingredients of leadership and management, the importance of understanding these roles and finding the right people to administer and lead counseling programs is critical to their success. A lack of understanding of such elements can make the difference between success and failure in meeting the mission of counseling services in a particular setting and the maximum use of the resources committed to that mission.

Basic to these points is the assumption in this book that persons in leadership positions in counseling services would be better equipped for such tasks if they understood the broad concepts of leadership, management, or administrative processes and the functions that constitute such roles. An additional assumption is that, beyond understanding the basic concepts of leadership, management, or administration, it is also important to understand how these concepts are similarly as well as uniquely applied in different settings in which counseling services are provided. Thus, although a director of guidance or pupil personnel services in a large school district and a director of a career services center in a large university need to know, for example, how to provide leadership to a strategic planning process; the development of a mission statement; which relevant documents shape the boundaries of what they do; the sources of revenues and costs for counselors, support staff, and resources; the recruitment and professional development of counselors and staff; the implementation of grant writing; the ways to use technology as a way to augment counseling; and the importance of report writing and advocacy for counseling services, the likelihood is small that each of these processes will have the same content in a school district, a university, or in other counseling settings. Leadership and management skills need to be tailored to the different characteristics of the settings in which counseling services are implemented.

A further issue of note here is the use of language. Although terms like *leadership, management,* and *administration* are often treated as if they mean the same thing, they do not. Although it can be argued that in an ideal situation these terms are interactive, the fact is that an individual might be an effective manager of counseling services but not a leader. Similarly, one may be an effective leader, but not a good administrator or manager. In a large counseling services structure, it is possible to designate a person as the executive, the leader of the counseling center or the counseling program, and other persons as managers of certain phases of the counseling services (e.g., intake and assessment, outreach, data analysis, follow-up, etc.). In reality, however, many counseling programs are too small to formally divide leadership, management, and administrative roles among several persons. One person may have to assume the roles of leadership and management. In such cases, the person in charge of counseling services, whatever the setting, will likely "wear multiple hats" and be fully engaged in multitasking.

LEADERSHIP, MANAGEMENT, AND ADMINISTRATION

To create a frame of reference for the content of this book, it is useful to consider the similarities and differences between these key words: *leadership, management,* and *administration.* One relevant place to start this differentiation is by consulting dictionary definitions. In a collective sense, such definitions suggest that to *lead* is to guide; to run in a specified direction; to direct the operations, activity, or performance; to go at the head; to tend toward a definite result. A leader, then, is one who engages in such roles. To *manage* is frequently defined as to handle or control, to direct or carry on business, to make and keep submissive, to achieve one's purpose. *Management* involves the judicious use of means to accomplish an end and the implementation of executive ability. To *administer* is to manage, superintend, mete out, or dispense. Reference books often suggest that synonyms for *leader* are *guide, bellwether, director, conductor, head commander,* or *chief,* for *manager,* synonyms are *executive, supervisor, director,* and *boss*; and for *administrator,* one who *governs, rules,* or *controls.*

Clearly these definitions suggest that there is considerable overlap among the three terms and some subtle distinctions. Each of these processes or roles is a position of authority and, perhaps, command; management and administration are seen as having control over people and processes. Leadership employs the term *guide* or *guidance* as well. This definition de-emphasizes control and command and accents the importance of having vision, of seeing the "big picture," being able to create a plan and direction for an organization to move toward, and to motivate or inspire people to carry the plan forward.

Because definitions are frequently quite general in their content and in their synonyms or antonyms, to understand terms such as *leadership, management,* and *administration* it is useful to turn to those who are scholars of such terms or those who have applied these terms in what they do. In doing so, one gets a closer sense of how these terms differ. For example, Covey (1996) argued that leadership is different from management and administration in the sense that,

> Leadership focuses on doing the right things; management focuses on doing things right. Leadership makes sure the ladders we are climbing are leaning against the right wall; management makes sure we are climbing the ladders in the most efficient ways possible. Most managers and executives operate within existing paradigms or ways of thinking, but leaders have the courage to bring those paradigms to the surface, identify the underlying assumptions and motivations and challenge them by asking, "Does this still hold water?" (p. 154)

One sees in such perspectives two important distinctions between leadership, on the one hand, and management/administration, on the other. The first has to do with being a guide, mapping new directions, and keeping an organization current with the trends and issues to which it must be addressed, with the ends it must pursue. Management and administration, in this context, are more concerned with efficiently and effectively applying the means to the ends. One can argue here that the manager/administrator is more concerned with the technical aspects of an organization, whereas the leader is much more concerned with creating a vision, mission, or path that gives the organization and its personnel a rationale for being and achieving. Handy (1996) described this view by saying that, "The task of the leader is to make sure that the individuals or groups are competent to exercise the responsibility that is given to them, understand the goals of the organization, and are committed to them" (p. 5). Kotter (cited in Friedman,

1992) contended that "leadership is the ability to move groups of people toward some objective in a non-coercive fashion" (p. 17).

In such contexts, leadership is to a large extent the opportunity to change the environment, culture, and climate in which services are provided to be specific about the purposes to be achieved, the results, and within what kind of conditions. Within such concepts of leadership, there is room for distributed leadership. In such instances, there may be task leaders—persons who assume roles of responsibility for different aspects of an organization or a program of counseling services. In many cases, managers may be task leaders, team leaders, project coordinators, or committee chairs. In such cases, distributed leadership may accrue across individual counselors and support staff members as they make their collective contributions to the whole. Certainly in an age of competition for resources and for opportunities to make a valued and longer term contribution in a setting, organization, or community, there is the need for leadership to be personalized—to provide the conceptual and personal glue that holds the organization together, to give the counselors, support staff, and other functionaries a common identity and the motivation to do their best. In discharging these responsibilities, the leader is not only a guide, but also a teacher who informs and encourages those who work in the counseling agency or organization about mission, perspective, and other relevant information, as well as advocates and represents the counseling organization to those outside the organization. These perspectives about leadership and management/administration ultimately translate into roles that are tailored to the unique characteristics of the particular counseling setting. Sometimes these roles are created intentionally, and sometimes they evolve over time as the special culture of the organization unfolds.

MANAGER, LEADER, OR BOTH

The differentiation between the terms *manager* and *leader* is relatively recent, emerging primarily in the 1970s. Before that time, scholars of management tended to use these terms interchangeably and to think of leadership and management holistically. For them, managers should be leaders, and leaders needed to do many tasks that others would consider management. Deming (1986), one of the major organizational and management theorists of the latter half of the 20th century, argued that the terms *management* and *leadership* should be remerged, not separated. He used instead the term *managerial leadership*. He proposed 14 Points for Management and a System of Profound Knowledge that defined his view of how leadership and management need to be performed in the contemporary era of changing organizations, intense competition, and the need for longer term thinking and planning about organizational missions and the quality of services. Deming introduced a number of important concepts into the literature of leadership and management.

For example, Deming (1993) viewed leadership as a unifying theme for managerial practices. He stated:

> As I use the term here, the job of a leader is to accomplish transformation of his organization. He possesses knowledge, personality, and persuasive power. How may he accomplish transformation? First, he has theory. He understands why the transformation would bring gains to his organization and to all the people that his organization deals with. Second, he feels compelled to accomplish the transformation as an obligation to himself and to his organization. Third, he is a practical man. He has a plan, step by step.
>
> But what is in his own head is not enough. He must convince and change enough people in power to make it happen. He possesses persuasive power. He understands people. (p. 119)

Aside from the use of sexist language, Deming, his students, and his colleagues (McNary, 1999) believed that the separation of management and leadership served to divorce an organization's administrative tools and techniques from the strategic vision and mission required to achieve effective innovation and adaptation, ultimately harming the organization. In this sense, differentiating management and leadership can be seen as requiring wholly different approaches in philosophy and techniques, although both should be committed to the same purposes of transforming the organization and supporting the employees to provide quality services. This dichotomy of management and leadership in terms of philosophy and techniques is seen by other observers as also requiring differences in style of thinking: Management requires rational, analytical, logical thinking; and leadership requires emotional, intuitive, creative thinking. In Deming's view, what is needed is not dichotomies of philosophy and techniques or styles of thinking, but a synthesis of these in a holistic view of the organization, its mission, and its methods.

Deming, in advancing his theory of managerial leadership, introduced other important concepts. One is systems thinking. In his view, all organizations can be thought of as systems or networks of processes. These systems must all be working toward the same organizational aims, and each system must be optimized so that it can make its maximum contribution to the whole.

Therefore, the aim of managerial leadership, according to Deming, should be to help people, machines, and processes to do a better job. This includes removing barriers that rob people of their pride in their workmanship, their contribution to the whole; instituting a vigorous program of education and self-improvement; helping employees to "work smarter, not harder"; and helping everyone in the organization to view it as a system of integrated processes that requires teamwork to maximize the quality of the system in its progress toward its vision, mission, and goals.

A fundamental concept in Deming's view of management leadership is *quality management*. In this perspective, Deming introduced a variety of processes to improve or address systems issues. Such processes include continuous quality improvement, quality circles, monitoring and reducing variation in quality of services, constancy of aim or purpose to the organization, an emphasis on cooperation and win–win relationships throughout the organization, dependability in the quality of services, and use of statistical and nonstatistical tools and techniques to collect and analyze data to stabilize and improve any process. Deming argued that all of these processes and others need to be embedded in the organization in a holistic way. Using only one process (e.g., quality circles) leads to a segmented organizational culture that is unable to respond creatively or quickly to needed changes. Thus, leadership needs to be proactive not reactive, holistic in its views of the organization, and comprehensive in its use of quality management tools.

Perhaps the most significant point for leadership and management of counseling services from a Deming viewpoint is that these two processes do not need to be split by position. Indeed Deming, as indicated earlier, argued for remerging these concepts in a holistic way. Thus, rather than talking about leaders and managers as separate roles, jobs, or positions, it might be more appropriate within a Deming frame of reference to think about leadership and management as sets of activities that one or more persons would engage in for different purposes or problems. Deming argued that the ideal managerial leader is one who can merge the current dichotomous roles of management and leadership. As we note later in the chapter, other scholars of leadership or management support differentiation or splitting these functions, and they frequently think of them as different positions. We take a middle-of-the-road position in the book, and we argue that, although it is easy to differentiate leadership or management tasks, the reality in counseling is that in many settings, because of the small size of the counseling and support staff, one person is likely to need to incorporate both sets of competencies, activities, or tasks. Kotter's (1999) perspectives help to operationalize such a view.

MANAGEMENT AND LEADERSHIP AS DISTINCT PROCESSES

In Kotter's view, leadership and management are different. Neither is better nor a replacement for the other. "Rather, leadership and management are two distinctive and complementary systems of action" (Kotter, 1999, p. 51).

The term *complementary* means that one person can engage in both leadership and management activities. In practical terms, it is likely that, depending on the setting and specific role one occupies, the ratio of leadership to management activities will differ. For example, the higher the position one occupies in an organization, the more that leadership tasks will be required, compared with managerial tasks. For many positions, perhaps most positions, it is important for the administrator to combine strong leadership and strong management skills as leader-manager.

Kotter (1999), like the other scholars of leadership and management we cite, contrasts these terms in a somewhat different way. He contended that management is about coping with complexity and bringing order and consistency to a program or organization. Leadership is about change, volatility in the program's external environment, and the ways it will transform itself in response to change.

Kotter suggested that, within these two systems of action (management and leadership), each involves "deciding what needs to be done, creating networks of people and relationships that can accomplish an agenda, and then trying to ensure that people actually do the job" (p. 53). These tasks are accomplished differently when engaged in leadership or management.

The major way to manage complexity is by planning and budgeting (setting targets and goals for the future, defining the steps necessary to achieve these targets, and allocating resources to accomplish these plans). In contrast, leadership begins by setting a direction (developing a vision and the strategies needed to produce the change required to achieve the vision). In a second step, management engages in organizing and staffing to carry out the plan and monitor its achievement. Leadership, however, has to do with aligning people, helping them to understand the organizational or program vision, getting people to believe and embrace the alternative future inherent in the strategic vision, empowering staff to take initiatives and engage in problem solving consistent with the vision, and to move with others in the same organizational direction. In this sense, aligning people is to acknowledge that change and program success requires interdependence among the program's personnel as well as among formal and informal networks of people external to the program. Aligning people accents the reality that successful leadership is not primarily an issue of power, but of dependency on one's staff members and on one's network of colleagues and constituents who can help or block progress toward the program's vision.

In summarizing his 10 observations about managerial behavior, Kotter (1999) offered Items 6 and 8 in his list of observations that speak directly to the contrasts just discussed:

> 6. Increasingly, those in managerial jobs can be usefully thought of as people who create agendas filled with plans (the management part) and visions (the leadership part), as people who develop implementation capacity networks

through a well-organized hierarchy (management) and a complex web of aligned relationships (leadership), and who execute through both controls (management) and inspiration (leadership). . . .

8. Because managerial work is increasingly a leadership task and because leaders operate through a complex web of dependent relationships, managerial work is increasingly becoming a game of dependence on others instead of just power over others. (p. 6)

Whichever perspective one takes about leadership and management/administration, there must ultimately be a translation of these terms into roles that are tailored to the unique characteristics of the particular counseling setting.

PERSPECTIVES ON ROLES IN LEADERSHIP AND MANAGEMENT IN COUNSELING

Few perspectives in leadership and/or management have been directed to counseling services per se, although in the ensuing chapters some of those views are cited. Yet perspectives on leadership, management, or administration that have been put forth by scholars or in other settings—nonprofit organizations, business, governmental organizations—are worth considering and extrapolating to counseling. One of these is that of Covey (1996), who suggested that it is possible to break leadership into three basic functions or activities. The first is *Pathfinding*, which focuses on the creation of a "compelling vision and mission." This is a futurist view, the big picture, a large perspective that combines an organizational value system and a vision as well as the needs of those who will consume the service provided (in our case, counselees and others with whom the counselors and counseling services at issue may consult and support). The operational bridge from the vision and mission, which emerges from "path finding" and analysis of the organization's function, is the strategic plan, a process and document, which is discussed more fully in the next chapter.

A second leadership function, according to Covey, is *Aligning*. In essence, this leadership function is devoted to ensuring that the "organizational structure, systems, and operational processes all contribute to achieving" (p. 152) the mission and vision of meeting the needs of those to be served. Basic to such an activity is ensuring that the counselors and support staff truly understand the vision, mission, strategy, and results of needs assessments for which the existing structures and systems have been designed. In such a view, it becomes understood that the most important matter is not the vision or structure of the organization, but the commitment of the staff to accomplish the vision, mission, or strategic plan with quality, empathy, and respect for those persons to be served.

A third leadership function is *Empowering*. This is the impetus and culture that "unleashes the latent talent, ingenuity and creativity [of the counseling and support staff] to do whatever is necessary and consistent with the principles agreed upon to accomplish their common values, vision, and mission in serving customers and stakeholders" (p. 153).

Covey's views about leadership in the future express the need for it to be principle-centered, focused on a mindset of interdependence and a skill set of synergy that yields not just cooperation, but creating better solutions. Leadership, in this view, is more than an emphasis on achieving efficiency and effectiveness; it also includes challenging old paradigms and evolving a set of principles that are values-based and that care for and act in consonance with the needs of the customers, clients, or counselees.

Covey's perspectives on leadership and management are consistent with the views of Deming and Kotter, previously discussed, and those promulgated by Bennis. Bennis, like Covey, made a clear distinction between leadership and management. It is Bennis' contention that, "managers . . . are more involved in the how-to, the short-term, and the bottom line, while leaders must have vision, mission, strategic intent, and dreams" (cited in Bolt, 1996, p. 166). Bennis saw managers as one-dimensional persons who frequently have highly developed quantitative and analytic skills and a narrow functional-technical perspective. Although such persons may be capable of managing, they are often unfit to lead because when they are placed in leadership positions, their style is often traditional and authoritarian, they overmanage, they need to be seen as the expert on everything, and they need to solve all problems, make all decisions, and maintain control.

Such self-absorption and emphasis on complete control is a tenuous way to project and implement leadership. In part this is true because leadership is not only a matter of skills, but is also psychological and emotional—a bond, perhaps a passionate bond, between followers and the leader. According to Bardwick (1996), during periods of predictability, peace, and security, people are often content with management, rather than leadership. However, "emotional neediness, or the desire for leaders, results from the condition of change, crisis, and urgency" (p. 134). In such conditions, "people have an emotional need for a leader, a person whom they can trust and to whom they want to make an emotional commitment" (p. 134). She would argue that the six things leaders must do to create a sense of strong leadership and to achieve success include, in abridged and paraphrased form, the following. Their implications for counseling services are included.

1. *Define the business of the business.* This relates to the earlier observations of Covey, Kotter, and others that a major role of leaders is to help an

organization create a vision, mission, and strategic plan. In this instance the questions are: What should this organization do and not do? What is the focus of what we do? Why do we exist? What are our priorities? What are the goals that motivate us as an organization? What values drive what we do? To make the poignant point that gives these questions significance, Bardwick quoted a now classic story told by Dumaine (1994) describing the mindset of three stonemasons:

> In the days of misty towers, distressed maidens, and stalwart knights, a young man, walking down a road, came upon a laborer fiercely pounding away at a stone with hammer and chisel. The lad asked the worker, who looked frustrated and angry, "What are you doing?" The laborer answered in a pained voice: "I'm trying to shape this stone, and it is backbreaking work." The youth continued his journey and soon came upon another man chipping away at a similar stone, who looked neither particularly angry nor happy. "What are you doing?", the young man asked. "I'm shaping a stone for a building." The young man went on and before long came to a third worker chipping away at a stone, but this worker was singing happily as he worked. "What are you doing?", the young man asked. The worker smiled and replied, "I'm building a cathedral." (p. 196) ·

Those of us who have the privilege of serving as a counselor help our clients each day to clarify whether they see their life as drudgery and hard or as building a cathedral by how they approach their daily tasks, by how they conceive their purposes, and by how they bring motivation to their productivity. One can argue that, in some ways, a leader has an organization for a client and a major role in helping those who work in and create the organization to find a vision/mission that is based on values, principles, and goals that are clear and sound. In doing so, leaders are helping them to develop a sense that they are part of and making a contribution to something larger and more important than the frustrations, stress, and emotional content they experience in the individual lives of their clients. Although they may not be building a cathedral in the work they do, they are, as counselors, providing a safe haven, a protected space, and a place of dignity and respect for clients to examine their problems in living and to be supported in their search for new pathways, for reframing their self-concepts and their possible actions, for being taken seriously, and for receiving care and support. In defining the vision of and rationale for the counseling program, the leader is also defining and shaping the culture of the organization.

2. *Create a winning strategy.* Competition among organizations is not confined to those in business; it is also present among agencies or organizations that provide counseling services. There is competition for resources among nonprofit agencies just as there is among for-profit organizations. There is competition to provide the highest quality services for clients. There is com-

petition to ensure that potential clients can differentiate the value of professional services from those offered by persons who are untrained, but who offer "glitzy remedies" for very serious personal problems of relationships with others, scripting one's life, decision making about marriage and careers, geographic moves, and many other choice options. In essence, a strategy for helping a program of counseling services to be the best that it can be is as important in this context as it is for a winning business strategy.

Strategies are conceptual and they are certainly in part psychological. To be useful, they must accurately and effectively identify what the organization can do better than its competitors and help it become the client's choice. Because the social, political, and economic factors that shape the content of clients' problems are always changing, effective strategies must anticipate, create, and guide change and create commitment in the organizations' members. Such strategies must generate a conviction among counseling and support staff that, although the professional journey on which they are embarked is hard, it is worth taking because the strategies they employ provide a competitive advantage in quality for and marketing to their clients.

3. *Communicate persuasively.* A major role of leaders is to ensure that communications are clear and trustworthy. People trust those who say they will do something and they do it. Thus, trust is in many ways a function of predictability. Leaders must decide what information their colleagues and employees need and how to provide it clearly, simply, and accurately. They need to be sure that the communications sent to employees state what is real, what will happen, and what those affected by the communications can and should do in response. When the communication goals are to reduce anxiety and increase commitment to the program mission, in addition to written communications, personal opportunities for dialogue and face-to-face communication are preferable and, frequently, essential.

4. *Behave with integrity.* In the same sense that leaders' communications must be trustworthy, they must also be persons of integrity in their personal behavior. They need to do what they say they will do, and they must behave in accord with the values they expect of others. They cannot play games with people's emotions and aspirations, be duplicitous in their dealings with others, or play favorites. They need to display consistency in how they treat their employees and how they make choices. In a sense, they need to be predictable and transparent to those who work for or with the leader. Although these comments do not suggest that the leader is a paragon of all virtues, they do mean that leaders should have convictions about the importance of the organization they lead, the values reflected in what is being done, and certainty in the purposes being pursued.

5. *Respect others.* Leaders need to value the experience, intelligence, and talents of those who are employed by their organization. They must be open

to receiving input, including disagreement, from persons at different levels of their organization without feeling demeaned or uncomfortable. They need to be confident enough and sufficiently respectful of others to "hear" them when they provide input or feedback on a particular topic or issue. Hearing others, regardless of whether one accepts and acts on the information provided, is an important form of respect, inclusion, and empowerment of others.

6. *Act*. Certainly it can be argued that the most difficult role of a leader is to act, to decide, to choose. Although others may not agree with the actions taken, leaders must accept the reality that ultimately they are charged with taking actions that enhance the organization's ability to function or that anticipate and respond to change. Taking actions that terminate employees who are not able to perform their roles, closing down a particular unit, opening a totally new initiative, downsizing the organization, and merging with other organizations are not easy choices. If leaders do not act, they are likely to be seen as weak or indecisive; if they do act, others may disagree with the choice and stereotype the action as uninformed, stupid, or worse. Yet it is clear that the leader who does not act on decisions to be made is likely to generate anxiety, insecurity, and feelings of powerlessness in his or her employees. Taking actions that are difficult, complex, or unpopular, but that, after due consideration, the leader believes are right are, in fact, courageous and, typically, inspire confidence that the leader is leading, rather than letting the organization drift with no clear-cut direction or purpose.

AN EMPIRICAL STUDY OF LEADERSHIP

Although there has been relatively little empirical research about leadership, a major example of such research is that sponsored by the Senior Executive Service (SES) of the U.S. government (U.S. Office of Personnel Management, 1998). Given the need to move from passive management to active leadership, the SES, through the U.S. Office of Personnel Management, engaged in a 1991 study of 10,000 supervisors, managers, and executives in the private and public sectors to identify executive core qualifications. Based on this research, the SES qualifications were revised several times through 1997 as a result of the rapidly changing management environment and the need to focus increasingly on leadership and the ability to drive change (Guide to the Senior Executive Service, U.S. Office of Personnel Management, 2003, http://www.cpm.gov/ses/sesguide-staffing.html#executive). As a result of collaboration with many other federal agencies, review of the professional literature, and analysis of the relevant research data from the 10,000 participants, five fundamental executive core qualifications are currently used by a Qualifications Review Board to assess experience and potential—not technical expertise—of all candidates for leadership positions in the SES. The assumption is that successful executives are able to bring all five of these fundamental competencies to bear when performing their strategic leadership. In a collective sense, the execution of these five core qualifications is seen as creating a corporate leadership culture. In an ideal sense, this culture is shaped by visionary leaders who can apply people skills to motivate their employees and apply management skills to produce optimum results with limited resources. The five executive core qualifications include the following (http://www.opm.gov/ses/exqualify.html):

1. Leading Change
The ability to develop and implement an organizational vision that integrates key national and program goals, priorities, values, and other factors. Inherent in it is the ability to balance change and continuity—to continually strive to improve customer service and program performance within the basic government framework, to create a work environment that encourages creative thinking, and to maintain focus, intensity, and persistence even under adversity.

2. Leading People
The ability to design and implement strategies that maximize employee potential and foster high ethical standards in meeting the organization's vision, mission, and goals.

3. Results Driven
The ability to stress accountability and continuous improvement, to make timely and effective decisions, and to produce results through strategic planning and the implementation and evaluation of programs and policies.

4. Business Acumen
The ability to acquire and administer human, financial, material, and information resources in a manner that instills public trust and accomplishes the organization's mission, and to use new technology to enhance decision making.

5. Building Coalitions/Communication
The ability to explain, advocate, and express facts and ideas in a convincing manner, and to negotiate with individuals and groups internally and externally. It also involves the ability to develop an expansive professional network with other organizations, and to identify the internal and external politics that impact the work of the organization. (U.S. Office of Personnel Management, 1998, pp. 13–30)

For each of these five executive core qualifications, a series of competencies are identified as the underlying ingredients of the performance of each major qualification. Each of the competencies is defined in the following Web site: http://www.opm.gov/ses/define.html. As such, the executive core qualifications and the definitions of the underlying competencies represent a metalanguage of the leadership qualifications used by the SES and by extrapolation to leadership and management performance in other contexts.

1. **Leading Change**
   Continual Learning
   Creativity and Innovation
   External Awareness
   Flexibility
   Resilience
   Service Motivation
   Strategic Thinking
   Vision
2. **Leading People**
   Conflict Management
   Leveraging Diversity
   Integrity/Honesty
   Team Building
3. **Results Driven**
   Accountability
   Customer Service
   Decisiveness
   Entrepreneurship
   Problem Solving
   Technical Credibility
4. **Business Acumen**
   Financial Management
   Human Resources Management
   Technology Management
5. **Building Coalitions/Communications**
   Influencing/Negotiating
   Interpersonal Skills
   Oral Communication
   Partnering
   Political Savvy
   Written Communication

CHARACTERISTICS OF LEADERSHIP IN SUMMARY

The competencies and metalanguage of skills that now define those persons serving in the SES of the U.S. government are clear affirmations that leadership requires a complex mix of interpersonal skills, creativity, technical expertise, and ability to anticipate emerging trends of relevance to the organization one leads. One implication of such perspectives is that leadership is not passive, but active; the leader is not aloof and remote, but involved with the persons and dynamics of the organization, and the leader, among other roles, is sensitive to the need to demonstrate an organization's accountability. Most leaders would recognize that the language of measurement has become pervasive in federal and state legislation, in the health care industry, in manufacturing and financial processes, in basic and higher education, and, indeed, in any discussion of the allocation of resources. As the roles of leadership and management have taken on new characteristics, so has the language of accountability. Terms such as *measurement, testing, assessment,* and *evaluation* have become pervasive in the legislation on counseling services and, by implication, a major concern for the leadership of counseling services.

As a reader of this book, it is likely that your professional life in counseling, in virtually any institution, has exposed you to such terms as *data-driven, standards, performance indicators, evaluation, continuous quality improvement, total quality management, management by objectives, PERT, PPBS, accountability, benchmarking, strategic initiatives, strategic actions, competency, certification, accreditation, licensure, high-stakes testing,* and *results-based outcomes-based accounting.* Every one of these terms, in whatever setting it is used, is based on some form of quantification, testing, assessment, measurement, or evaluation. As one anonymous wag suggested: In the Declaration of Independence, we have replaced the elegant words of the Founding Fathers, "We hold these truths to be self-evident," with the less eloquent but socially pervasive words, "We hold these truths to be statistical." One can argue that in a growing number of organizations, leader-managers are immersed in an environment comprised of numbers, trend lines, and other evaluative data monitoring or supporting the organization's accountability. Frequently, it is managers who collect and prepare relevant data for their areas of responsibility; it is leaders who frequently have to interpret the meaning of the various trends that symbolize the quality and impact of the counseling services at issue and, as a result, to institute new program initiatives. Suffice it to say here that neither leaders nor managers can ignore issues of accountability or the measurement tools used to monitor and make conclusions about the comparative values of counseling processes or their contribution to an organization's vision and mission. Subsequent chapters return to the matter of accountability as a leadership/management function.

Although leadership in most organizations needs to pay attention to data and their implications, leaders must go beyond the data available, which usually talk about what is, what has already taken place, and what has been proven. Organizational environments are filled with many diverse factors—political, economic, and social—and the collection of data may not characterize all of these factors. Rather, leaders must be studious and able to think abstractly, philosophize, be creative, and think "outside of the box." They must know their discipline (e.g., counseling), its history, its potential, and its future. Leaders need to use their abstract thinking to build for the future. In one sense, as suggested earlier, managers are technicians: They fix and clean up problems, and they make sure that services delivered are effective and done well. But leaders look beyond these important matters and ask What if? questions. Are the procedures we use the right ones? Are they based on evidence? Are they culturally sensitive? Can they be done more efficiently? What are their benefits as compared with their costs? For whom are these services most important? What if we stopped doing certain procedures and emphasized others? In essence, the leader must be a student of the climate in which his or her program functions and how the services employed relate to the political, economic, and social factors that affect and are affected by what the organization does.

As Handy (1989) argued,

> the leader must recognize that as organizations are changing—downsizing, flattening their organizational structure, changing the composition of their work force—they need to run in new ways. Increasingly, they need to be seen as federations and networks, as alliances and influences that require new ways of leadership, new ways of thinking, less control and more creativity. . . . Anyone who has tried to run an organization has always known that it is more like running a small country than a machine. It was only the theorists who tried to apply the hard rules of number and logic and mechanics to an essentially soft system. (p. 133)

In such a view, "A leader shapes and shares a vision which gives point to the work of others" (Handy, 1989, p. 134). With new organizations emerging, "The vision must be different. A plan or a strategy which is a projection of the present or a replica of what everyone else is doing is not a vision. A vision has to 'reframe' the known scene, to reconceptualize the obvious, connect the previously unconnected dream" (Handy, 1989, p. 134). Whatever the content of the vision, it must make sense to others, be understandable, and relate to the work that people do in the organization so they can see themselves within the context of the vision.

Within such a context, a leader must also be a politician (Friedman, 1992). A leader in counseling services must know that, in almost every setting where counseling operates, it is not a stand-alone organization. As counseling centers occur in universities, schools, or corporations, counseling is not likely to be the principal mission of those institutions. In many cases, counseling can be instrumental in helping an institution achieve its mission goals, but it is not likely the primary mission of the organization. Therefore, the leader of the counseling program must guide the counseling unit's plan to support the larger institutional mission. One can argue that the mission of the counseling unit is to ensure that its contributions to the larger institutional vision and mission are clear and explicit. Thus, the leader of the counseling program must be politically astute in acknowledging the larger institutional mission and ensuring that the role of counseling in that mission is understood and accepted. The leader must be a politician who is not only able to guide planning for counseling, but also an advocate for counseling with institutional-level administrators and other influential (e.g., Advisory Council Member, Boards of Trustees) persons who have the power to allocate resources to and acknowledge the importance of counseling in the larger institutional context. To the degree that the connections of counseling to institutional mission goals are clear, accepted, and valued, the likelihood that counseling will be ancillary or a frill easily dispensed with is diminished. However, it is important to acknowledge that the leader as politician is not an event, but a process. The leader's political sensitivities, advocacy, planning, and insight into institutional trends must be a constant element of the skills the leader uses.

The counseling leader as politician cannot direct these sensitivities only to those who have broad administrative authority in an institution (e.g., the Vice President for Student Affairs, the Assistant Superintendent for Pupil Personnel Services, the Director of Human Resources), but must also be astute about other constituencies who need attention, to be heard, and to receive advocacy. These include the employees, counselors, support staff, as well as the clients. What do they need to be able to function more effectively? What types of improved access or procedures do clients need to address their concerns for more economical services, effective procedures, and culturally sensitive treatment? There are many forces that affect counseling—institutional priorities, institutional administrative personnel, one's staff members, clients, external constituencies such as advisory committee members, legislators, accreditation boards—and each needs political attention in unique ways. Leaders of counseling are going to need to employ outreach efforts that are sensitive to the effects on counseling services that each of these constituencies represent. Such outreach may mean walking the halls in the State Capitol or in Washington to talk with legislators about pending legislation that is not favorable to counseling or could be improved by some judicious modifications; it may mean talking to institutional administrators informally and mentioning some positive feedback from clients about the importance of counseling to them; or it may mean chatting with counselors or support staff about their ideas on how to improve intake procedures or other matters. Regardless, leadership of counseling services requires the leader to be an advocate, a statesperson, and an interpreter of the importance of counseling services to policymakers as well as to internal and external constituencies.

SUMMARY

We conclude chapter 1 with a summary and comparison of leadership and management activities discussed in this chapter. These are portrayed in Table 1.1.

TABLE 1.1
Activities of Management and Leadership

Variable	Activities
Leadership	Shaping visions and goals
	Defining and communicating the organizational culture and management philosophy to current and potential employees
	Shaping the culture and climate of the organization
	Envisioning trends that will affect the future processes of the organization
	Delegating effectively
	Helping groups make decisions
	Building consensus among stakeholders (e.g., Boards of Directors, Employees, Consumers)
	Team building
	Negotiating successfully
	Managing change
	Understanding change
	Planning
	Implementing
	Consolidation
	Motivating employees
	Creating reward structures
	Developing methods of supervision and professional development of employees
	Gaining legitimacy and respect for the agency or organization
	Attracting support for the organization
	Providing advocacy for the organization
	Defending the group
	Stimulating cooperation with other groups
	Coalition building
	Constructing and managing budget
	Overseeing program evaluation, analyzing and interpreting data
	Engaging in cost–benefit analysis
	Securing fiscal and personnel resources for an agency or organization
	Institute and monitor quality management processes
	Continuous quality improvement
	Feedback to counselors and support staff about directions and progress of the organization or agency

(Continued)

TABLE 1.1
(Continued)

Variable	*Activities*
Management	Organizing the staff members to implement the program plan
	Implementing change
	Managing teams
	Budgeting specific resource allocations
	Managing resources
	Consulting with the executive director or administrator on program issues
	Ensuring that procedures used are efficient, effective, and evidence-based
	Orienting and working collaboratively with counselors and support staff
	Managing the use of technology for scheduling, reporting, and evaluative purposes
	Engaging in continuous improvement procedures
	Teach new and current employees about specific procedures to be used for referral or other agency issues
	Organizing teams to examine or implement specific tasks
	Acquiring and organizing information related to continuous quality management and the effectiveness of procedures used in the agency
	Being attentive to the quality of the work environment, the support and resources available to individual counselors, and opportunities for them to engage in self-care
	Being attentive to the psychological reactions of client to the agency environment—whether it is welcoming, helpful, pleasant, and useful
	Applying one's clinical knowledge in supervision of counselors and in making the technical aspects of the program of the highest quality
	Designing training programs that address issues relevant to counselors and support staff
Leadership and Management	Communicating clearly
	Thinking analytically
	Managing time
	Making decisions
	Considering alternative solutions
	Motivating people
	Managing meetings
	Interviewing potential counseling and support staff members
	Providing presentations on program directions, resource needs
	Minimizing stress
	Resolving conflicts
	Ensuring counseling and support staff awareness of ethical issues, laws, and policies affecting the counseling unit
	Problem solving
	Managing the organization's environment
	Exploring with counselors the status of evidence-based practices in areas of concern to the counseling services offered

Note. Management and leadership encompass many potential activities that occur in one or the other function or both. Table 1.1 illustrates such activities. In some counseling programs, it is likely that the executive, director, or administrator will perform both management and leadership activities in varying degrees throughout his or her responsibilities.

The activities in Table 1.1 are not exhaustive of the processes in which leaders and managers in counseling services are likely to engage. Nor do they suggest that every administrator in counseling services will do the same things. The actual inventory of such activities applied in any given setting will vary in intensity and focus as we look at examples of counseling leadership in different organizations (e.g., schools, universities, government) in subsequent chapters.

In chapter 2, we are going to look more explicitly at the tools, procedures, and types of issues that administrators in counseling services need to know about and be prepared to implement. Throughout the remaining chapters of the book, we return to the perspectives in chapter 1 which argue that leaders in any area of endeavor (business, military, government, education, counseling) need to pursue a vision of quality service, influence others and the conditions in which they work to adapt and work toward this vision, and create opportunities for these persons to perform to their fullest potential by maximizing the organizational and personal development of all the employees and clients involved.

Like so many other notions that are sometimes taken for granted, it is important to remind ourselves that "leadership is an ongoing process, not an event, not the implementation of a program, and not simply the articulation of a great idea" (Bornstein & Smith, 1998, p. 283). Thus, leadership must be a constant dimension of what the administrator of counseling services does and thinks. Chapter 2 examines more specifically the definitions and content to which leadership is addressed.

In the subsequent chapters, the term *administrator* frequently is used to mean the person who has administrative responsibility for the counseling program. The actual title of this person may be director, chair, head, executive, or some other term. Whatever the title, it is assumed that this person will have a combination of managerial and leadership skills and be able to use these skills in combination as complements to each other. It is also assumed here that in most institutions in which counseling programs exist, the administrator of the counseling program will be a second- or third-tier administrator reporting, for example, to a vice president, assistant superintendent, head of human resource management, or similar institution-level administrator. Unless noted, the discussion about administrators, leader-managers, and so on in subsequent chapters is directed to administrators of counseling programs and academic departments preparing counselors or community counseling agencies, not institutional-level administrators.

2

Fundamental Processes of Leadership, Management, and Administration

CONTEXT

As chapter 1 discussed, leadership, management, and administration have subtle but important distinctions. Management and administration tend to be more technically oriented, making sure that processes are running well and achieving the results expected. Leadership is more about vision or mission—making sure the organization has the right programs, appropriate directions, and effective use of its resources and that its goals and technical content are related to the skills and aspirations of its professional and support staff.

Although leadership and management/administration functions may be combined in one person or distributed across several persons, it is clear that leadership functions are intended to guide the execution of those systems and processes that are central to a program's existence: in the case of this book, the provision of counseling services. To execute or guide the execution by other people of specific processes, a leader must be engaged in continuous planning: planning for uncertainty, possibilities, contingencies, as well as probabilities. Leadership frequently requires decisions that commit current time and resources in relation to assumptions about the future—changing demographics of the client population to be served, effects of political and economic events on the problems that clients are likely to bring to counselors, increased use of technology in augmenting the work of individual counselors, recruitment of professional and support staff with new skills, and increased needs to strengthen one's fiscal resources.

In these examples, leaders must be futurists—persons who continually analyze trends likely to have an impact on their program or organizational goals and incorporate these judgments into their planning. In doing so, leaders frequently incorporate various paradigms like the classic SWOT analysis into their planning. SWOT stands for strengths, weaknesses, opportunities, and threats as categories by which to assess an organization's current status and its needs for change to cope with the future. In essence, the important questions include: What are our strengths as an organization, as a counseling program? What are we good at? What are our weaknesses? What new strengths do we need to acquire? What opportunities are available that would allow us to expand our service to new constituents or to function in new ways? What threats exist to limit our future opportunities? The answers to these questions may signal the need for policy changes; marketing one's services differently; recruiting counselors who bring unique skills or credentials to the counseling program; assigning counselors to program functions or clients in new ways; increasing the ratio of self-directed client options (e.g., using relevant reading material, engaging in computer-assisted guidance systems) or group counseling to individual counseling; seeking new sources of revenue for the program; and seeking new alliances with other organizations or networking internally with departments or other units in an institution where they are located (e.g., a school district, a university, a corporation).

In essence, a counseling program is a "learning organization" (Senge, 1990). It is compelled by its ethics to engage in continuous quality improvement and, at its core, to be comprised of "knowledge workers," counselors, and technical staff who need to be specialists in human behavior, various types of counseling interventions, assessments, use of technology, use of groups, as well as knowledge of contextual factors—political, economic, social—that affect the counselees/clients who are served. It is within this context that leaders, directors, executives, and administrators in counseling services have multiple functions. One is to inspire, not to command. Another is to make decisions for the organization or nothing will get done. They must lead, initiate, and execute. A further one is to be accountable for the organizational mission and its culture, spirit, performance, and results.

The notion of leadership as other than command is a response to the notion that a counseling program is a learning organization based on various types of knowledge and comprised of various kinds of knowledge workers. Each of these knowledge workers brings his or her own knowledge to the organization and, thus, their contribution to the performance of the counseling program. Unlike perspectives of persons who worked in organizations several decades ago, they are not so much employees who must be told what to do, how to do it, and how fast to do it, but rather are professionals or specialists whose knowledge and training are the capital that underlie the counseling process in its many forms. They must bring their knowledge and training to bear on the problems that the consumers of their knowledge and training bring to them to successfully achieve the results the organization seeks. Therefore, a counseling program is not likely to be successful if conceived of as a bunch of subordinates and a boss; it is rather more closely identified as a collection of equals working as a team to move their combined services forward to meet the accepted mission of their organization and to constantly improve the quality of what they do. This does not mean that the counseling program should be leaderless, but rather that the administrator as leader/manager cannot function from an isolated, all-powerful, command position. Rather, as stated previously, this is a role with multiple dimensions, including the need to articulate a vision that the knowledge workers in the organization accept and internalize and by which they are inspired. It also means that, among his or her other roles, the leader must constantly earn loyalty by demonstrating to the counselors and other specialists in the organization that this counseling program offers them exceptional opportunities to put their knowledge to work within a mission and a set of tasks that are socially valued and important.

Handy (1989) spoke to these points by observing that in the United States in newer and more high-tech organizations, the term *manager* is beginning to disappear. What is appearing, instead of managers, "are team leaders, project heads, coordinators, or, more generally, executives" (p. 153). According to Handy, the term *manager* implies someone to be managed—a stratified society. What is apparent in the current transition from the term *manager* to a word such as *executive* or *team leader* is that "management ceases to be a definition of a status, of a class within an organization, but of an *activity*, an activity which can be defined, and its skills taught, learned and developed" (p. 154). In this sense, management activities have content, processes, and tasks. We described some of these in chapter 1 as we tried to differentiate management from leadership. In that array of activities, three major types of skills can be noted as embedded in both leadership and management activities: conceptual, human, and technical.

In chapter 1, we indicated that leadership is certainly predicated on conceptual skills, the ability to execute planning, understand trends, engage in goal-setting, motivate professional and support staff, and, in general terms, understand the technical processes used in the organization. Leaders have to be credible in the technical skills central to the organization they lead, but actually engaging in such technical tasks as the core of their work is unlikely. As we said previously, management activities tend to be more technical in their orientation than do leadership activities. Thus, the person engaged in management activities is more likely to emphasize technical and human skills, although they must be aware of the conceptual skills that give the organization its direction and vitality, its *raison d'etre*, and that must be linked with the technical and human skills that give it its core identity and validity.

To discharge these important roles of leadership and management, there are a number of important processes with which persons occupying these roles must be familiar and able to use. A discussion of some of the most important processes that the counselor who becomes an administrator, leader, or manager of counseling services must apply follow in the rest of this chapter. The discussion here of these processes is limited. Each of these processes has been the subject of multiple volumes. Hopefully, the reader will pursue further reading on any of the processes about which they need more specific information.

In the nearly 90 years that the three authors of this book have collectively served in administrative, management, and leadership roles in academic units preparing counselors, in units actually delivering counseling services, in state and federal government roles providing technical assistance, in legislative and policy support for counseling services, and in professional organization roles (e.g., elected roles as President, the American Counseling Association, the National Career Development Association, the Association for Counselor Education and Supervision) that advocate for the recognition of counseling in public policy and its funding, planning has been constant. Whatever else these roles entailed, they always included the need to do formal planning of some sort. Over the years, the names of planning techniques have changed from acronyms such as PERT and PPBS to preferred current terms such as *strategic planning*. In fact there are many types of planning (e.g., strategic, comprehensive, long-range, program, and project; Cook, 2001). The professional counselor who has been assigned to a role as administrator, director, or executive of a counseling program would be well advised to become familiar with the various planning models now extant. For the purposes of this chapter, we focus our discussion on strategic and action planning and program planning.

PLANNING

Strategic Planning

Strategic planning is a comprehensive approach to planning, usually at an institutional level, but that can be used at smaller organizational levels as well. Institutional levels at which strategic planning occurs would include a school or a school district, a college or university, a rehabilitation facility, a correctional institution, and a corporation. These are generally large organizations comprised of a number of systems or units interacting, hopefully, in support of the whole enterprise. Strategic plans can be useful in time management to reduce vagueness and wasted effort about the institutional objectives and how any given unit fits into the overarching institutional directions and goals. Strategic plans are also useful in helping to establish the institutional or organizational identity or culture. Such organizations have the responsibility of "creating and nurturing their own culture—the values and vision that lead, guide, and sustain everyone who is a part of the organization" (Cook, 2001, p. 48). Strategic plans are typically linked to budget processes as well. The content and directions cited in strategic plans are often used as the frame of reference in which to acquire and allocate resources. In a sense, strategic plans are like road maps: They lay out aspirations, goals, and directions for the organization's long-term future, typically for the next 5 or 10 years.

Definitions of *strategic planning* vary in their language and comprehensiveness. Typical definitions suggest that strategic planning is basically a process of developing and maintaining a strategic fit among an organization's goals, capabilities, and opportunities. Strategic planning is often referred to as a *coordinated and systematic process* to develop a plan for the overall course and direction of the organization and for meeting its future potential. Inherent in strategic planning are identifying an organization's vision of what it wants to become, its long-term goals, and the best approaches for achieving these goals. The intent of strategic planning is to create a sense of direction that is sound, appropriate, and able to be achieved. Thus, the limitations of resources, both physical and personnel, must be considered as well as how resources can be increased and capacity strengthened.

A strategic plan is not a substitute for leadership. Rather, it can provide concepts, procedures, and tools that can clarify decisions to be made and that sharpen the organization's focus, describing what is relevant or irrelevant to the organization's identity, purpose, and functions. As such, a strategic plan can (a) represent a shared vision of what can and will be an organizational commitment; (b) provide a framework for action that can provide consistency over a specified period of time; and (c) identify the context within which the organization will seek or reject new opportunities and assign its resources to current and future services.

In structural terms, strategic plans typically articulate the beliefs and vision of the organization, its mission, parameters (the boundaries within which the organization operates), internal analyses (strengths, weaknesses, internal organizational design, ways in which responsibility and authority are allocated, how decision making takes place, and nature of the information flow) of the organization, external analyses (predictions about the influence on the organization of social, demographic, economic, political, technological, scientific, and educational trends), competition (other organizations providing the same products and services to the same clients), critical issues (those issues that the organization must deal with if it is to survive or re-create itself), strategic goals (the organization's commitment to achieve specific, measurable end results), strategies (the commitments to deploy the organization's resources—people, facilities, equipment, money toward the strategic objectives), and action plans (detailed description of the specific actions required to achieve each strategic objective).

Action Planning

Action plans typically include reference to a strategic goal or goals that a specific unit (e.g., counseling program) supports within the overall organization strategy; the specific strategic objectives to be achieved by the action plan; a detailed description of each step required to accomplish the plan; allocations of assignments and responsibilities; a time line for the plan; and a cost–benefit analysis (Cook, 2001). Within such perspectives, a typical arrangement is that a specific goal is cited as one to which the counseling program will contribute. Then a set of specific objectives to be accomplished by counseling are identified, and then for each objective benchmarks are identified. Benchmarks usually include a statement of how attainment of the goal or objective will be measured; the benchmark specifies the criterion for success. Frequently the data source is also identified. Alternatives to benchmarks are key performance indicators (KPIs). The KPIs describe a measure of an outcome(s) assigned to a particular organizational performance activity embodied in the specific objective.

In some cases, units that are subsets of the systems that make up an institution create their own action plan that is, in essence, a miniature strategic plan. In such a case, there is a unit vision statement that would succinctly reflect the aspirations and values of the planning unit, a unit mission statement that indicates how the specific activities of the counseling program will complement the institution's mission statement, unit values that discuss the values framework on which the unit's decisions and actions are taken, and unit goals that state broad objectives of the counseling program that supports the purpose, mission, and vision as stated in the institution's larger strategic plan.

Although other approaches to strategic planning may use different language or components of the plan, strategic planning is a wide-ranging analysis of an organization's values, aspirations, and means of getting to its goals. Because counseling programs are not typically autonomous or standalone programs, they usually do not do institutional-level strategic plans per se. Rather they contribute to the institutional strategic plan by preparing an action plan or unit plan as discussed earlier or a program or project plan briefly discussed later. These plans, however structured, must be linked to the strategies and objectives of the institution or organization plan of which they are a part.

Program Planning

As suggested in the previous section, planned programs can serve as a bridge to translate conceptual models, theory, and research into practice. Planned programs not only emphasize important content, but are useful in describing the likely results of counseling, group work, or other therapeutic approaches. Rather than arguing in the abstract that if a school, community agency, or independent practitioner offers a specific defined set of counseling processes or services, the outcomes for counselees will probably be positive, planned approaches that define the outcomes or results, including competencies and other indicators, that translate the program content into behavior to be achieved and indicate the evaluative methods that will affirm that such outcomes have been achieved. The intervention strategies used in such planned programs can vary in relation to the intended outcomes, and these can be evaluated in terms of their impact on the outcomes to be achieved. Such a process yields different and more important evaluative data than data which simply indicate that certain interventions are in place, but not whether these interventions make specific contributions to achieving the outcomes sought. When a planned program has a clear set of outcomes to be achieved, there are likely to be many processes or interventions that can be implemented to achieve selected individual outcomes. Focusing on the content of specific program outcomes and then determining what intervention (or interventions) is likely to be effective in achieving the intended outcomes is different than providing every counselee the same intervention (e.g., individual counseling) or set of interventions regardless of whether they are relevant to the specific needs to be served or to the outcomes sought.

It is important to note here that planned programs of counseling need to include time for unplanned activities. Although such a notion sounds contradictory, it simply means that in any program there will be walk-ins— counselees in crisis or experiencing dilemmas that do not lend themselves to immediately existing groups, workshops, or other planned activities. Opportunities must be available for these counselees to be seen and their needs assessed. Making time available to see such clients is part of a planned program of services and certainly addresses such outcomes as "meeting the individual needs of all students or workers or members of a particular group or setting." After intake and a period of individual counseling, many of these counselees will be matched to selected planned interventions, whether self-directed, group, workshop, computer mediated, or other processes. Thus, although not all interventions with counselees are able to be planned in a specific sense, they can still be incorporated into a planned program of services.

Program planning is usually conducted within the purview of the larger organization of which it is a part. Program planning may focus on initiating a new program of counseling services in a particular organization or planning modifications to an existing program to (a) bring it into better alignment with an organization's strategic plan, (b) renovate an existing program because of new research knowledge or policy mandates, or (c) address changing client demographics or other trends. Program planning is the process of creating a design by which to make a concept of a counseling services program operational, or it may be directed to a subset of such a program (e.g., development of a course in decision making, a series of workshops on job search techniques for students in university dormitories).

Program planning usually consists of stages or phases that take a proposed initiative (e.g., the organization of a program of counseling services for a particular setting), tests the idea against what exists and what is desired, justifies it by identifying the intended outcomes, and describes how to make it work. Often this process uses the creation of hypotheses to guide the implementation and testing of different elements of the proposed program; carries out assessments or evaluations of need for the proposed program; establishes goals and objectives for the program using relevant research, theory, or policy mandates as the conceptual framework; details the relationships among goal objectives, counselor roles, and interventions used to meet the objectives; and describes how a program will be monitored and evaluated using specific processes.

A subset of program planning is sometimes called *project planning, intervention design*, or some similar title. Basically, this process typically focuses on a specific task to accomplish a specific purpose. For example, to ensure that all students know how to manage their anxiety about test-taking, a counseling program might propose a series of brief workshops designed to teach students to understand the symptoms of anxiety, the triggering mechanisms, and the techniques by which to manage anxiety. In this context, it would be necessary to identify the task proposed in specific terms, analyze the current status of such training, develop the objectives to be achieved by the proposed workshops, consider other possible ways to achieve the outcomes sought, specify the obstacles to be overcome in each possible course of action, and then make a decision about the specific action to be taken. Once such a decision is made, many of the same processes used in program planning are implemented (e.g., describing intended outcomes, evaluating needs for specific outcomes, identifying the relationships between goals or objectives, counselor roles, specific interventions used, and describing how the program will be monitored and evaluated).

Inherent in such approaches to planning is the reality that change of any kind must proceed within the institutional culture—the interactive pattern of norms, beliefs, values, and behavior present in any level of organizational setting and its strategic plan. Dealing with such change requires that the professional counselor as administrator must be knowledgeable in pursuing systematic planning processes that accommodate the unique characteristics of and the needs for counseling services within such an organizational culture. As such, systematic planning introduces and accents the concept of systems thinking.

Systems Thinking

As suggested in our discussions so far, counseling services are rarely stand-alone entities or organizations. They are typically part of a larger organization and one of several subsystems that make up the larger organization as a functional system. In its briefest description, a system is a collection of parts (or subsystems) integrated to accomplish a set of overall goals. Although each system has its own boundaries, its particular knowledge and skills, inputs, processes, outputs, and outcomes, the intent is that all of these elements are integrated to accomplish goals that support the mission of the organization of which the counseling program is a part. In overly simplified form, if the counseling program is in a school district that has as its vision to "educate all of the children of a particular community to their fullest potential," then a major goal of the counseling program is "to assist students to learn how to modify the academic and psychological issues that disrupt or reduce their academic achievement." If the counseling program is located in a corporation whose vision is "to create a workforce that is efficient, teachable, and committed to lifelong learning," then a major goal for the counseling program is "to provide interventions that reduce worker inefficiency (e.g., job stress, adjustment to supervision, family difficulties) and help workers develop openness to change and information about in-house and community opportunities for relevant education to increase their competencies."

Systems thinking for administrators of counseling in any setting means that they must be constantly learning about the organization of which counseling is a subsystem and trying to make the two interact in positive and purposeful ways. Thus, they must know the inner workings of both the organization as a whole and of the counseling program, and they must continually attempt to understand the world outside of the organization and the counseling program and its effects on each. Hence, systems thinking for the counseling administrator is a process of continuous learning and inquiry as one tries to balance the relationships of counseling to the other parts of the system of which it is a part. The important underlying point is that the properties or behaviors of each subsystem have an effect on other subsystems and the organization as a whole. Specifically, each subsystem interacts with and affects the organization of the whole (Vailli, 1996).

Systems thinking is not new. Such thinking has been influencing various organizational perspectives or paradigms for more than 50 years. Yet systems thinking has come into its own in management, planning, and organizational development terms in seminal books such as those of Bennis, Benne, and Chin (1961) and, more recently, Senge (1990). The importance of systems thinking as a managerial perspective has, in some ways, paralleled and is now increasingly replacing physics as the preeminent discipline by which to study technological developments. As Naisbitt and Aburdene (1990) contended:

> We are shifting from the models and metaphors of physics to the models and metaphors of biology to help us understand today's dilemmas and opportunities. . . . Physics furnished the metaphor that suggests: energy-intensive, linear, macro, mechanistic, deterministic, outer-directed. . . . Today, however, we are in the process of creating a society that is an elaborate array of information feedback systems, the very structure of the biological organism. . . . Biology is a metaphor suggesting: information-intensive, micro, inner-directed, adaptive, holistic. (p. 24)

One could argue that the paradigm for addressing change and planning speaks to the processes associated with the industrial age; the processes and mechanisms inherent in biology focus on the processes inherent in an information age, in which change is a constant, in which accountability is a prime issue in all organizations, and in which the interactions among system elements pervade the structures in business, government, and social services. Thus, systems thinking is helping managers and leaders look at organizations in broader perspectives and interpret the patterns and events that characterize the organization. It is an affirmation that subsystems (e.g., counseling) do not occur in a vacuum. They occur in particular organizational, social, economic, and political environments to which they respond. Systems thinking helps managers analyze separate functions in isolation, and examine the interactions of structures and functions in achieving desired outcomes. In this sense,

> An entity is not just a collection of parts. It is a combination of related parts, and it is the *specific pattern* of relatedness that gives the entity its individual identity. For example, a collection of pieces of slate and wood, blocks of stone, pieces of metal, wire, and colored glass would be a pile of junk, an accidental grouping of materials in space and time with no connections between them. Relate such parts in one way and a nightclub could be constructed. Relate them in another way and a gothic cathedral could evolve. The key properties of being a nightclub or a cathedral do not lie in the nature of the parts but in the ways they are assembled, and the possibilities thereby created. It is

this pattern of relatedness to which the term organization refers. (Ford, 1987, p. 35)

So it is with counseling programs as their functions are assembled to emphasize crises intervention, career development, assessment, or other goals.

OTHER PLANNING ELEMENTS

Strategic or program planning in counseling services must first be oriented or aligned with the mission of the organization in which counseling services are deployed. Such plans must also reflect the focus of relevant legislation, which may be the primary source of policy and funds for counseling, as is frequently the case in rehabilitation counseling or employment counseling that occurs in the public sector, or such legislation may support only selected programs within counseling services (e.g., career counseling, substance abuse counseling, or child abuse prevention). Such public policy or legislative initiatives frequently give legitimacy to, approve, or fund part or all of the counseling program. Thus, these directions or purposes specified in seminal documents, policy, or legislative, which give the counseling program authority or validity in a particular setting, must be acknowledged and identified. Further, planning documents must reflect the counseling program's attention to trends that affect the counseling needs of the constituents for the program and to the availability of interventions that are likely to enhance the quality or cost benefits of the counseling program.

It is likely that the counseling program administrator will need to go beyond the development of planning documents per se or their simple submission to the executive to whom they report. Indeed in many organizations, the administrator of the counseling program needs to discuss the plan for the counseling program with members of a board of directors, trustees of the organization, advisory board, or other policymaking groups (e.g., possibly including legislators). Sometimes such discussions are held to inform group members about the status of the counseling program, the types of problems with which it is dealing, how many students or adults are using the counseling services, and with what results. However, because counseling services require funds to function, policymakers or advisory groups are required to vote on their support for the counseling program and the budget requested.

In presenting the results of strategic or program planning and requests for funds to a policymaking body or to the executive who has administrative oversight of the counseling program (e.g., in a university, the vice president for student affairs; in a school district, the assistant superintendent for pupil personnel services; in a corporation, the director of human resources management) as well as other programs, the director/administrator of the counseling program must recognize that there are multiple purposes to be served in such a process. These include interpreting the planning results, educating the policymaking group or executive about what counseling does and its important contributions to the organizational mission, and advocacy for the counseling program and its needs. Each of these purposes is extremely important and needs to be taken seriously. The administrator of the counseling program must be prepared to talk about the content of the planning document, the process that was implemented to prepare it, and the importance of the planning recommendations to achieve the maximum contributions of the counseling program to the organization's mission. The administrator must also discuss other areas that represent the history and context for the counseling program (e.g., why counseling has become so important in American society, the need for all counselors to have multicultural competencies and be able to work with counselees whose cultural background is different than theirs, current legislation and public policy affecting counseling, trends in the field, training and credentialing of counselors, values and ethics of counseling, and related topics). Perhaps of most importance, the administrator of the counseling program must be prepared to discuss the costs of the program and the additional funds being requested.

In the last analysis, the administrator of the counseling program must consider her or himself as a statesperson for the counseling program. Being a statesperson means being informed about one's field, its evolution, the issues that the counseling profession has experienced and the ways they have been resolved, the research findings that are pertinent to the interventions and structure of the counseling program, the degree to which counseling programs occur in this particular setting and the purposes for which they exist, major legislation, public policy, and accreditation standards that pertain to the particular program. Boards of Trustees or Directors of the organizational entity in which the counseling program is embedded expect the administrator of the counseling program to be an advocate for the program; more than that, they expect the administrator to be well informed and articulate about the profession of counseling that he or she represents, a professional capable of discussing the "big picture" of counseling programs, a statesperson who understands and can speak effectively about how counseling contributes to the mission of the larger organization it supports, and any available evidence of that interaction. The counseling administrator as a statesperson needs to be able to answer "So what?" questions: Why should we support counseling? What do we receive for our investment? Why is counseling better than some other social service emphasis we might support? How do we know that counseling is effective?

These are not easy questions, but they are consistent with the accountability mentality pervading education and human services organizations that is no longer satisfied with opinion or general answers; the questioners want scholarly, informed, fact-based answers that are focused and pertinent.

Being a statesperson in any setting is not easy. Those whom one is trying to influence as one advocates for counseling are often skeptical, perhaps cynical, and unwilling to be convinced unless the counseling administrator can communicate information that is data-driven, research-based, and affirms best practices and the utility of counseling to clients and the organizational mission. These are often the elements that achieve additional or diminished support for counseling as a corollary to the planning process.

Budgeting

Planning is not only a process of identifying a vision, mission, goals, or objectives for a program—it is also a financial process. To wit, how much is it going to cost to provide for a counseling program that will have particular emphases or capabilities that will be able to achieve the recommendations presented in the planning document? Where will these funds come from? Beyond such planning questions, the director or administrator of the counseling program must be able to manage whatever organizational funds are allocated to the program or that can be acquired from sources external to the organization.

From many perspectives, budgets are political statements. In crude terms, they represent the adage, "Put your money where your mouth is!" To say the same thing more eloquently, budgets are statements of what an organization deems to be important. This is true of any kind of budgeting, whether it is a household budget or a multimillion dollar organization budget. Does the budget reflect an emphasis on things or people, on new facilities or the tools that people need to do their job, on adequacy or quality, on strengthening a program or letting it languish, on acknowledging its important contributions to the organizational systems with which it interacts or is it seen as good to have but not particularly valuable in the total organizational picture? Again the director or administrator of the counseling program will likely be required to (a) advocate for the budget proposal submitted by the counseling program, typically on an annual basis and probably as part of the organizational planning process; (b) explain its rationale; and (c) argue for its value, perhaps in competition with the budget proposals presented by other organizational units also trying to obtain the best funding they can attract.

There are many ways to prepare budgets, and they are frequently organization-specific in their form and content. In some organizations, counseling programs simply receive an allocation of funds without much discussion or planning. Other organizations base budget allocations on detailed plans and comprehensive analyses of costs. However budgeting occurs—whether one is the sole counselor in an independent practice, the head counselor among four or five counselors in a school, or the director of a counseling program in a university that includes 15 or 20 professional counselors and 10 or 15 support persons—the budget available must be understood and managed effectively by the director or administrator of the counseling program. Such management is both a leadership and management skill because the available budget is a tool that must be monitored and allocated within organizational guidelines to provide the "life blood of the program." Indeed in university departments of counselor education and counseling psychology, and in programs delivering counseling services, whatever the setting, the chair of the department, the director, or the administrator of the counseling program is the person responsible for approving expenditures and ensuring the correctness with which funds are received, assigned to fiscal categories, monitored, and expended.

Revenue Streams and Cost Centers

Budgets can be thought of in several ways. We have already suggested that what and how available funds are allocated can be thought of as a political statement, signifying what is seen as most important within a program. Beyond such a perspective, budgets can also be thought of as revenue streams and cost centers. Revenue streams can be thought of as all of the forms of income that a program acquires. For example, a department of counselor education or counseling psychology will likely receive an allocation from the university that is intended to cover operational expenses and the salaries of the permanent professional and support staff. Such allocations are intended to cover the continuing faculty and support staff and some graduate assistants, although some funds may also be provided for work-study students and other temporary assistance. The operational funds provided are intended to cover expenses such as telephones, some professional travel, purchase or maintenance of equipment, printing, postage, and so on. In the first author's 25 years as a university department head (24 as head of a department of counselor education, counseling psychology, and rehabilitation services), he consistently found that the operational funds allocated to the department covered about one third to 40% of the expenditure. Thus, as a department head, it was necessary to find other revenue streams and other types of income. Such revenue streams included income from summer program courses, and money from the credits generated was shared with the department. Money was also obtained from internal sources for which proposals needed to be prepared. Included were monies from the graduate school for recruitment of doctoral students. Another major revenue stream was funds obtained from external grant seeking. Such grants were often written to provide some part of faculty salaries to permit them to do the research or instruction for which the grant was written. Monies from external funds for some portion of faculty salaries essentially released the university support for those faculty members up to the proportion of their time covered by the grant. These released funds could then be used to hire part-time or fixed-term faculty to teach the courses from which faculty on grants were "bought out" or for other program purposes. In some grants, additional graduate students could be supported. In addition, external grants usually have "an indirect rate" that will be described next. In this university, 10% to 12% of the indirect rate generated by a department is returned to the college in which that external funding occurred and then shared with departments that wrote and received the external grant. This is another revenue stream.

Thus, when one thinks about revenue streams or income to support a counseling program, such revenue streams may include the organizational funds allocated to the program for salaries and operational expenses, funds from credits generated by summer courses, internal grants acquired for specific purposes (e.g., recruitment of graduate students), external grants for research or continuing education programs that may provide some portion of some faculty salaries, graduate assistants, and some operating funds. A department might also have a revenue stream from providing and charging for services (e.g., counseling of townspeople who pay fees for services, selling monographs or other reports prepared and published in the department, etc.). These examples of revenue streams for a university department of counselor education, counseling psychology, and rehabilitation services will likely be similar in other colleges and universities. However, in some universities, the budget of a department for personnel and operational expenses is tied to how many instructional credits the department generates. In the university discussed in this section, many of the revenue streams would be similar for the counseling center and the career services center, with the exception of any funds returned from teaching courses and, more specifically, from the credits generated.

Just as one thinks of revenue streams for a counseling program in a university, one finds similar perspectives in other settings. In schools, the amount received for the counseling program is an allocation based on the total annual budget of the school district, although that budget can be augmented by special grants from particular initiatives related to, for example, technology, career counseling, or other emphases reflected in state or federal legislation or other state funds. School counseling programs also can engage in grant-seeking for external funds from foundations or other possible revenue sources. Corporations typically provide funding for counseling services in-house or as a subcontract to community agencies from their own budgeted funds. Income streams for counselors in independent practices tend to come from one of three sources: hourly fees from clients, third-party payments from insurance companies or employers for treatments delivered to clients, or contracted services to state or federal agencies (e.g., assessment of aptitudes, interests, experience related to potential training programs, jobs for clients of a rehabilitation agency, providing an employee assistance program for an employer). Although counselors in independent practice can submit proposals to foundations or employers for funding of specific workshops or other programs, the reality is that most of their revenue is likely to come from direct client service. Corporations are less likely to be the recipients of funds from legislation or foundations. Government agencies (at the state or federal levels) that have offices responsible for counseling services often provide technical assistance, advocacy, or research on behalf of counseling services to legislators. Such offices are frequently charged with managing the funds related to any legislation, state or federal, that deals with counseling services. In such cases, most legislation has provisions to pay for administration of the legislation. Usually such a set-aside provision represents 3% to 5% of the costs of dispersing the funds, securing and reviewing grant proposals, monitoring the use of the funds by recipient agencies, and so on. These funds as well as governmental budget provisions are likely to be the major revenue streams of governmental offices at state and federal levels. At community levels, rehabilitation and employment counseling offices in the public sector are likely to be allocated funds from relevant legislation or other organizational allocations to support their functions.

In this brief sketch of sources of revenue streams used in different counseling program settings, we find a continuum of support from organizational budget allocations to legislative entitlements to other external funding requiring grant-seeking by the counseling program and typically requiring the involvement of the administrator of the counseling program. However, before talking about grant-seeking, it is useful to mention some other terms and concepts associated with budgeting. One of these is cost centers.

Typically, a counseling program budget will include a number of areas to which funds are allocated for expenditure. For example, typical cost centers in an operational budget include faculty salaries, office rent, communications, postage, travel, technology updates, equipment, printing, supplies (e.g., including tests), construction, subcontracts for consultation, or special services. Also included, either in the operational budget or a separate budget, is personnel cost. The latter would contain the salary of each professional or support staff member, including salaries allocated to vacant positions. Depending on the budget format used, the personnel budget would include the funds allocated for graduate assistantships, wage payroll or temporary positions, and funds for contractual services. In essence, a cost center reflects budgeted areas for which expenditures are required and how much money is authorized for each of these budget categories.

Cost centers also assume funding input. In other words, the counseling program administrator needs to know how much it will cost for personnel and program operations as well as where the funds will come from to pay for each cost center. Thus, in some budgets, the revenue sources for each cost center and each item within each cost center will be noted so that funds are properly allocated and deficits in support available can be readily identified. Many budgets will also include the cost of fringe benefits for each personnel position. These are the costs to the organization of such items as health benefits, retirement, workers' compensation, and so on. Although to many recipients these benefits are invisible, they are direct costs to the program or the organization of which the program is a part. Indeed when a director or administrator of a counseling program considers filling a personnel position, he or she has to consider more than salary. The true cost of the position is the salary, fringe benefits, plus such items that the person needs to do the job (e.g., office furniture, computer, specialized equipment, travel support, heat, light, and related resources). Regardless of whether they are apparent, these are true costs of funding a position and enabling the person occupying that position to do the intended tasks.

For those counseling programs that engage in grant-seeking from external sources (e.g., federal or state agencies, foundations, industry), there is another term that is important—*indirect costs*. This term is frequently referred to as *overhead* or *facilities and administrative costs*. In essence, when a director of a counseling program or faculty member in a department of counselor education or counseling psychology engages in grant-seeking for a research project or an instructional program, he or she must prepare and submit a proposal to a possible funding agency (e.g., a foundation or government agency) that is engaged or interested in the content of the counseling proposal. Costs of conducting such a funded project can be classified in two ways: direct costs and indirect costs (overhead or facilities and administrative costs). We previously discussed direct costs as those costs that can be specifically identified with a program or, more specifically, with a particular project potentially to be funded. Indirect costs, as the name implies, are costs that cannot be specifically attributed to an individual program or project. For example, several programs may be housed in the same building or several projects may take place at the same time in the same laboratory. Although it is difficult to determine the amount of heat, light, or other resources that should be specifically attributed to each program or project, various formulas are typically used by funding agencies to identify what are allowable indirect costs for a project to be funded by a specific foundation or governmental agency. These formulae spread the costs of all the programs or projects in a particular building across all programs, labs, or other work areas. For example, in a university setting, a faculty member may propose to do a research project comparing the comparative impact of several counseling interventions on selected outcomes to be sought in persons having specific mental health problems of interest to the agency to which the proposal is being sent. In addition to the faculty member and probably some other professional staff, the proposal requires the review and processing by university accountants and research administrators, the keyboarding time and preparation of the proposal by clerical support staff, postage costs, and, perhaps, some travel to discuss the proposal with persons at the potential funding agency. If the faculty member who submitted the proposal is successful in having it funded, then conducting the project, in addition to its direct costs, will likely involve a variety of university resources that are difficult to calculate specifically, but are nevertheless being used indirectly to support the project. Rather than calculating each of these resources specifically, they are treated in a collective sense as a percentage of the direct costs of the project. Examples of such indirect costs in the indirect formula include such items as accounting staff and research administrators, the utilities cost for the building housing several research projects, office supplies, postage, local telephone service, communications infrastructure, salaries of departmental support personnel, specialized facilities, libraries, equipment (not purchased for the project, but used in it), legal counsel, custodial services, security devices, human subjects protection, and affirmative action monitoring.

The items to be included in a calculation of the indirect costs of a project submitted to a funding agency must be allowable to the funding agencies. Typically, major funding agencies agree on written policies that identify what costs can be included in the calculation of indirect costs. Although the items included in indirect costs are not paid for as direct costs of the project, they are available to support the project and therefore seen as true costs of the project. As such they are considered elements of the university infrastructure necessary and available to support "sponsored" (externally funded) projects.

In summary, depending on the indirect rate calculated to reflect the services available to support research in a given university, the proposal submitted to the potential funding agency lists in detail the direct costs to conduct the proposed research as well as the percentage of direct costs that is defined as the indirect or overhead rate for research projects. This rate differs from university to university and may vary from 30% to 90% or more of the direct costs. Both of these costs are included in the budget submitted to the funding agency.

Grant-Seeking

As implied previously, it is typical for a counseling program or department preparing counselors to receive fewer funds from its parent organization than the administrator or department chair feels are warranted or necessary to achieve the goals the program seeks. Such a circumstance is likely to be more frequent in an age of limited resources, increased client needs, and increased competition for resources among social services agencies. One alternative is grant-seeking. If a professional staff is willing to undertake the additional work that preparing a proposal and then conducting a research study or a special instructional project encompasses, externally funded grants are ways to increase one's resources (e.g., equipment, travel funds, additional professional help, etc.).

The first step in grant-seeking is to identify those research ideas, instructional initiatives, or other activities (e.g., hosting specific types of interdisciplinary conferences) that funding agencies may be willing to support. A second step might be to identify other programs or institutions that would be willing to collaborate in the proposed research or other initiative. A third step is to locate possible funding sources that have interests that match those which are inherent in what is to be proposed. In locating potential funding sources, it is important to understand what the proposal process for them entails. Some foundations, for example, only want a brief 3- to 5-page concept paper that talks about the basic idea or project being proposed. If the foundation program staff determines that they are interested in your idea, they will typically ask for a full proposal using a specific format tailored to their particular needs. In either case, a fourth step is to prepare either a concept paper or proposal that follows the instructions for such submissions that is on their Internet home page or in their written reports of their funding priorities and procedures that are relevant to proposal submission. Sometimes proposals are considered for funding once a year, semi-annually, or each quarter. In either case, the proposal submitted needs to follow the instructions/procedures for grant applications and proposal submissions that are available from funding agencies. Such proposals need to be tightly written, provide a selected review of the relevant literature on the research or other project goal to be pursued, specific and clear research questions, hypotheses and methodology or the instructional goals for the target audience and what the content will be, the intended statistical analysis intended to be used in the research study or project, and the expected modes of dissemination of the results. It is also necessary to provide the timeline in which you plan to complete the proposed initiatives and the budget being requested. Although the elements listed are likely to appear in virtually any proposal format, there may be other elements requested (e.g., the proposer's previous research experience, whether the originating program submitting the proposal will provide matching funds or other contributions to the research study or project).

Once the proposal is funded, it becomes both part of the program's revenue stream and a cost center. The budget as proposed and approved must be allocated precisely and monitored continually to ensure integrity in the

use of the funds for the research study or project purposes. In large measure, the administrator or director of the counseling program is assigned the
responsibility for ensuring that these funds are handled efficiently and in
accordance with the budget allocations approved by the funding agency.

A typical question relative to grant-seeking is: How do I find agencies or
foundations that might be interested in my research or project? There are
many ways to do this. One of them is to identify what keywords effectively
describe what your research or project is about. Then using foundation or
other funding agency databases, attempt to match the keywords associated
with your research or project to the keywords that describe what particular
agencies or foundations are interested in funding. Depending on the type of
organization your counseling program is a part of (certainly if a university or
other educational institution), it is likely that the office of the organizational
research administrator (or whatever the official title) can provide databases
that can be scanned to find potential funding agencies. There are also commercial organizations, as well as learned or professional organizations, that
will provide assistance in locating funding agencies pertinent to your interests. In addition, there are directories of grant-seeking opportunities that can
be purchased. A counseling program can request annual reports or reports
on research themes for the upcoming year from pertinent foundations or
government agencies that can help the seekers of external funding to determine which agencies are a likely match in interest with the proposal under
development. Many grant-seekers constantly scan material that can help
them identify upcoming or active RFPs from government agencies or foundations. RFP is an acronym for Request for Proposals. When funding agencies
want to initiate a research program or provide an agenda of activities that
they want to support, they are likely to distribute RFPs that outline their interests, proposal submission procedures, timelines, amount of money available, and so on. Frequently grant-seekers read, on a daily basis, the *Commerce Business Daily* or the *Federal Register*, which describe upcoming or
active RFPs issued by various federal agencies. Many states have similar directories (e.g., *The Pennsylvania Bulletin*) that list state RFPs or other funding
opportunities. Certainly, as suggested earlier, the home pages of funding
agencies on the World Wide Web (WWW) are extremely valuable sources of
information on research/training priorities of these organizations for the next
year or 3- or 5-year cycles. In addition, once you identify funding organizations, foundations, or government agencies that are compatible in interest
with your proposed research themes or instructional projects or other activities, it is important to visit such organizations to talk with their program officers about possible fundable ideas and to begin to establish a personal relationship with such personnel.

Grant-seeking is a comprehensive endeavor. It is not something that a
director/administrator of a counseling program or department should do

alone. Rather it is important to create an environment in which the professional staff see the value of grant-seeking and are willing to undertake the work involved in identifying possible fundable ideas and relevant funding agencies, and engaging in proposal preparation. Viewing grant-seeking as one of the obligations of leaders in an era of limited resources and being willing to learn the techniques associated with being successful in this process are increasingly fundamental to success in leadership/management activities.

STAFF RECRUITMENT, RETENTION, AND DEVELOPMENT

A major outcome of planning and budgeting in counseling services is the recruitment, retention, and development of high-quality professional and support staff. Such a goal is not always easy to achieve, but it is essential to a successful counseling program. Even with the growing use of advanced technology (e.g., computer-mediated test administration, information resources, scheduling, administration, and the Internet) to augment individual and group counseling or instructional processes in preparing counselors, counseling services in any form are labor-intensive. The relationships between counselors engaged in consulting and their consultees, counselors and counselees, or counselor education faculty and students is intimate, emotionally intense, and personalized. Technology can complement, but not replace, such personal relationships. Thus, a major goal of any counseling service must be the maintenance and nurture of both a professional counseling staff and a support staff (e.g., those who can provide clerical, technological, and administrative support) that provide an environment that is welcoming, respectful, helpful, and competent.

Recruitment of either professional or support staff members is not done by whimsy or on an ad hoc basis. Planning and budgeting processes largely determine how many staff members—either professional or support—can be employed or authorized and for what purposes. In this sense, it is not possible to recruit new professional or support staff members unless there is a vacancy—either because of a resignation, termination, or retirement or because new funds have been placed in the budget to permit hiring of a new staff member. As mentioned in the previous section, each professional or support staff position is actually a cost center; it is not only the salary allocated to a position, but the cost of fringe benefits, furniture, special equipment, travel and communication expenses, and supplies associated with the position.

Assuming, then, that recruitment for a position is authorized and funds are available to provide for the costs of the position, fundamental questions include: What will the person who is hired for the position do? What will be the position description for this person? What specific skills or credentials will they need for the position? With what client populations will they primarily work? What multicultural counseling competencies and experiences will the counselor in this position need? How will we ensure that the recruitment process is an open one that welcomes applicants without bias or discrimination? These are important and, indeed, legal questions that guide the recruitment process. They are important whether the intent is to replace a person who has left a position or add a new person to the staff.

Once decisions have been made about the skills, experience, and credentials of the type of person to be recruited, the questions turn to the recruitment process. Will there be a nationwide search? Will there be a search committee, and, if so, who will serve on it? Will advertisements about the vacant position be purchased and placed in major professional publications? Will telephone calls be made to preparation programs to request nominations of possible candidates? From whom will references be requested, and when? What will be the timeline in which applications will be accepted? How will the applications be logged in and their confidentiality maintained? How and by whom will the applications be reviewed and rated?

The actual steps in the recruitment process will likely differ from one setting to another. The processes used by a university department of counselor education or counseling psychology will differ in some way from those of a university counseling or career center, a school district, a government agency, or a group of practitioners in independent practice. In any case, recruitment is a major responsibility of the person who is engaged in the leadership or management activities on behalf of the counseling program. Although this administrator is not necessarily active in the search process that generates applications for positions, it is imperative that he or she personally interviews the short list of candidates recommended as the most qualified for the available position; monitors the whole recruitment process to ensure that it is following organizational, legal, and affirmative action guidelines; negotiates the employment terms with the applicant selected; and advocates for this person with any organizational authority who has the final word on making an employment offer.

Recruiting either professional counseling or support staff has its challenges. In the case of support staff, training and prior experience with keyboarding, the use of specific software, accounting procedures, organizational guidelines, and ability to get along with coworkers, clients, or students are each important depending on the skills required in a particular position. The latter is particularly important because support staff may be the first contact, via telephone or in person, from the counseling program to the client, to a student, or to a professional in another department or organization attempting to contact a professional in this counseling program to make a referral, consult, or collaborate. Whatever specific tasks individual support staff are required to have for a particular position, in recruitment and retention of such staff, it is important for administrators and professional staff to recognize that support staff are the administrative and communications glue that holds the program together. They typically create and convey the communications that project the image of the counseling program to its various constituents and thereby signal the climate in which it functions.

In recruiting professional counseling staff, as providers of counseling services, university faculty, government specialists in counseling, or in other roles, a first consideration is the professional skills and credibility that they bring to the program. Documented academic degrees, work published in refereed professional journals and books, descriptions of their practicum or intern experiences, their professional reputation as described by persons serving as their references, their ability to work with culturally diverse clients and constituencies, and evaluations of their counseling or teaching effectiveness are each important ways to understand their skills. Increasingly, however, professional counseling staff is expected to have earned credentials that signify their professional skills and commitment to professional growth because such credentials are frequently a function of meeting professional standards established by accrediting agencies or program-approval mechanisms.

The typical credentials sought in professional counseling staff members depend, in part, on the setting in which they function. For example, in counselor programs in university settings, it is likely that professional staff, either in academic or service-delivery roles, will be expected to be licensed by state authorities as a Licensed Professional Counselor or a Licensed Counseling or Clinical Psychologist. Such professional staff in universities, particularly those in teaching or supervisory roles, may have additional credentials. These might include being selected as a Fellow of the American Psychological Association, the American Counseling Association, or the National Career Development Association—awards that are conferred because of their important published theoretical research or professional leadership contributions. In schools, it is expected that guidance/school counselors may be certified by the state in which they work to perform such a role. In a rehabilitation setting, counselors may be expected to be certified by the Congress of Rehabilitation Education (CORE) as a Certified Rehabilitation Counselor (CRC). Any counselor or counselor educator, including those in university settings, may also have additional credentials such as the National Certified Counselor (NCC) conferred by the National Board of Certified Counselors (NBCC). Although there are other credentials for professional counselors or counseling psychologists that could be identified here, those named are probably the most well known and expected in recruiting counselors.

The point of recruiting professional counseling staff members who have earned specific and relevant credentials has several purposes. One, most of these credentials are awarded after the counselor has successfully passed an examination testing his or her knowledge of the theories and practices in counseling or counseling psychology and a review of one's academic training, course work, and practicum to ensure that they meet the requirements for the particular license or certification. In a major sense, these credentialing processes serve as gate-keepers relative to those who can enter particular counseling settings or positions. In this view, these credentials are essentially proxies for possessing or knowing about skills, theories, ethical guidelines, or other material important to being a professional in this field. Thus, persons engaged in recruitment frequently assume that those professionals who hold these credentials have at least minimal skills and knowledge in all the areas pertinent to different counseling roles.

A second purpose of credentialing is to make the professional counselor eligible for third-party payment. Third-party payment typically means that some entity other than the client will pay for some or all of the costs of counseling. Ordinarily, this means that insurance companies or selected governmental agencies will pay some or all of the costs of counseling at a predetermined rate for a specified number of hours per year. Third-party payments, usually under the rubric of mental health insurance payments to the counselor, are the revenue stream that largely sustains the counselor in independent practice. However, in addition, there are growing instances in some colleges and university counseling centers of charging student medical health insurance for counseling services provided to students if treatment needed exceeds a specified number of free sessions. If the counseling centers in such colleges and universities did not have on their professional staff counselors and counseling psychologists who are licensed as professional counselor or psychologists, these counseling centers would be ineligible to receive third-party payments for student mental health services.

A third purpose for the rise in emphasis on the credentials counselors and counseling psychologists have earned is related to accreditation. There are basically two types of credentialing: that which certifies or licenses individuals, and that which approves or accredits programs. In the previous paragraphs, we discussed individual credentialing primarily. In fact, however, in many instances, program accreditation and individual certification or licensure are closely tied together. For example, in many states, it is almost impossible to be licensed as a counseling or clinical psychologist unless you have graduated from a program accredited by the American Psychological Association. Similarly, in a number of states, it is difficult to be licensed as a professional counselor unless you have graduated from a program accredited by the Council for the Accreditation of Counseling and Related Programs. These circumstances are a function of many factors, but certainly one is that the accrediting organizations strongly emphasize certain types of content that must comprise the curriculum of counselor education or counseling psychology programs seeking accreditation. At the individual level, state examinations for licensure tend to assess the candidates' knowledge of content that was required to be in the curriculum of the preparation programs being accredited. The effect is that individual licensing authorities, although they are state entities, frequently link the review of academic preparation of candidates and test their knowledge of counseling theory and practice to that content which must be offered in accredited programs.

A fourth purpose of credentialing programs and individual practitioners is to protect clients from persons who are not competent to practice counseling, consulting, or the teaching of counselors or counseling psychologists. Many observers would argue that this is the most important of the purposes for credentialing, and well it may be. Yet as suggested in the previous paragraphs, credentialing of programs and practitioners serves many purposes, both pragmatic and ethical.

Recruitment of professional counseling staff, then, is a comprehensive process that is subtly, but importantly, affected by a variety of external factors, including as a major issue the credentials held by those recruited. Recruitment of professional counseling is a leadership and management tool by which to change the directions of a program, to strengthen or add new emphases to a program, to increase the capacity of the program to serve diverse constituents, to add credibility to the program as it is rated by external accredited agencies, and to educate organizational-level administrators to the importance of quality staff and to meeting requirements of accrediting agencies.

Retention

Another leadership and managerial responsibility is that of retaining professional and support staff. Retention of staff is the second emphasis in a continuum of processes intended to build the capacity of the counseling program to meet its goals and to change its directions and emphases as necessary.

Retention of staff has many dimensions. Certainly a competitive salary and fringe benefits are essential elements of retention. Yet perhaps significantly more important is creating an environment in which both professional and support staff feel connected and able to make contributions to the counseling program mission. People want to be acknowledged as competent and effective. They want to feel valued, able to make suggestions that will improve the processes for which they are responsible, and able to do so with minimum insecurity, uncertainty, and stress. Clear communications to staff about how the counseling program is meeting its goals and new opportunities that are opening to the program are ways to help staff feel that they are important stakeholders in moving the program forward effectively.

Research by Davenport (1999) indicated that, although many employers assume that workers place "the greatest value on high wages and job security, in reality, employees typically rank these two factors below such factors as having interesting work and feeling appreciated for the jobs they do" (p. 34). Such findings indicate that the investment by an individual of his or her personal human capital (e.g., knowledge, behavior, effort, time) is more than an economic exchange between the worker and the organization. It is also one that emphasizes psychological, social, recognition, and affiliation needs. One's workplace provides a place to obtain a salary by which to purchase goods and services, provide a home for one's family, acquire physical assets, and gratify wants or needs. It is also a place to meet people, develop friendships, feel valued by others for one's ability to perform or produce, be needed by others to get a job done or meet mutual goals, nurture one's self-esteem, self-efficacy, and feelings of mastery or competency, and foster one's sense of identity and commitment. Workers— professional and support staff—are likely to remain in a counseling program where the leadership is concerned with creating a culture that reinforces the ability to meet these economic, psychological, affiliative, social, and recognition needs.

The process of retention really starts in the recruitment process. It is in the latter process, recruitment, when the administrator of the counseling program needs to assess the likelihood of the person–environment fit, ensuring that the needs of the applicant are as congruent as possible with the needs and opportunities of the position for which recruitment is taking place. The greater the degree of individual fit with the position to be filled and with the larger environment in which the position is embedded, the more likely that retention of the individual will follow.

Professional Growth and Development

Recruitment and retention are also products of opportunities for professional growth and development. Growth and development of professional and support staff can take many forms. Among them are opportunities for continuing education, attendance at professional conferences, in-house seminars about topics that build insight and skills among staff members, opportunities for staff to serve as project leaders, on search committees, on a continuous quality improvement team charged with examining a particular program issue (e.g., counseling intake, resource library, time management, outreach) and recommending ways to improve it, to present a particular professional topic at a staff meeting, to be responsible for a particular aspect of the program (e.g., assessment, outreach, group work), and to serve as the resource person in this area for one's colleagues. All of these options acknowledge, increase, and solidify one's value to the program and to one's colleagues. These options also provide learning opportunities by which staff can refine their skills, learn about new topics, demonstrate their dependability and reliability, and work with others for the good of all in the program. As such, professional growth and development is a way for the administrator of the counseling program to nurture distributed leadership within the professional and support staff of the program, demonstrate that each member of the staff has important skills and leadership potential that is valued by program colleagues and by the administrator, and ensure that the counseling program is a learning organization. Professional growth and development and its by-products is a major element of the culture of the counseling program. In this sense, it is both a management tool and a major process that complements recruitment and retention through growth and development.

SUPERVISION OF STAFF

One of the elements of recruitment, retention, and the professional development of staff is the supervision of the staff, the purposes for which it is done, and how supervision occurs. In some settings, clinical supervision is the capstone experience—the culminating opportunity to work with another professional to refine one's skills, to ensure that one is behaving ethically, to learn alternative ways of dealing with specific client-presenting problems, and to assess one's knowledge of theory and interventions. Frequently, such supervision occurs in a graduate preparation program for counselors, typically in a practicum or internship. The supervisor may be a faculty member, and the supervision may occur in the department where the student is learning to be a counselor. Frequently, however, the student in a counselor preparation program may engage in a practicum or internship outside of his or her university department. The site may be a University Counseling Center, a Career Development and Placement Center, another University office in which counseling takes place, or a community agency. In such a case, the student may receive supervision from both a faculty member in his or her department and a staff psychologist or counselor at the placement site. In such instances, students being supervised will likely receive two different emphases in supervision. The faculty supervisor will likely focus on the student clinical competencies and the integration of theory and practice that the department expects the student to acquire and demonstrate, while the on-site staff psychologist or staff counselor may focus on the expectations of the counseling or career center or agency about how counseling in that setting should ensue (e.g., time limits, intake procedures, resources available, likely presenting problems, participation in staff meetings, recording of client interviews) as well as the clinical competencies that the counselor-in-training brings to supervision.

In many ways, supervision of professional counselors in a counseling or career center or an agency setting combines the supervision foci for counselors-in-training discussed earlier. It is important that, from a professional development perspective, professional counselors are provided a regular opportunity to meet with their supervisor to discuss cases, to discuss alternative ways to deal with particular presenting problems, to consider treatment plans and useful intervention strategies (best practices), and to discuss ways to deal with client resistance, multiple dimensions of client problems, or ethical dilemmas. In addition, the supervisor and professional counselor will likely assess procedures by which the counseling agency or center functions (e.g., counselor case loads, communications with clients, case notes, closing out of client cases, the quality of other roles that the professional counselor may carry in the counseling agency).

The intent of supervision in either the clinical aspect of counseling or the procedural aspects of counseling in a particular setting is not intended to be punitive, but rather evaluative. In this sense, a major purpose of supervision is to be empowering; to help the members of the professional counseling staff to be resilient, energetic, and passionate about what they do; to help them improve their skills as a team performer; to feel comfortable with their responsibilities and their opportunities; to help them deal with failure and learn from it; and to be clear about competencies that they need to improve and how that can be done. Although it should be obvious, it is important to reinforce that the intent of supervision is to help the supervisee to succeed, not to fail.

In such circumstances, a supervisor is a teacher, a collaborator in problem solving, a role model, a consultant, and a counselor. These are vital aspects of the professional growth and development of the professional counselor(s) whom they supervise.

In many instances, the amount of supervision provided and its purposes are connected to accreditation standards. The accreditation standards of the American Psychological Association and the Council for the Accreditation of Counseling and Related Programs (CACREP) are quite explicit about expecting supervision each week when counselors-in-training are seeing clients. Accreditation policies related to counseling centers also require the availability of supervision on a regular basis for professional counseling staff.

The term *administrator* has not been used in this section for several reasons. One is that, in a counseling center or an agency devoted to counseling in which 8 or 10 persons are employed as professional counselors, it is likely that a senior member of the counseling staff will be designated to engage in clinical supervision. Thus, the administrator is freed up to provide supervision to the support staff rather than the professional counseling staff. In a smaller group of counselors, as one might find in a school counseling program, the administrator of the school counseling program will likely supervise both the professional counseling staff and the support staff.

Regardless of who does the supervision of counseling or support staff and for what purpose, there are several common and important tasks. They include being prepared for the supervisory session, time management, record keeping, planning ahead, evaluating the supervisees' progress toward expected competencies, ensuring that the supervisee is knowledgeable about clinic policies, including the material found in clinic manuals, accreditation requirements, and so on. In the case of counselors-in-training, supervisors also need to serve a gatekeeping role, representing the counseling profession as to whether a particular counselor-in-training has the personal and professional abilities to be considered capable of serving in an independent professional role.

Because supervision has become increasingly seen as an organizational intervention in its own right and as an important factor in how the organizational or program culture is shaped, both accreditation processes and ethical guidelines have been directed to the importance of supervision. As noted previously, accreditation processes typically make explicit the role of supervision in a preparation program for counselors or counseling psychologists. The same is true in the accreditation standards for university and college counseling centers and other agencies. Further, most individual credentialing processes for licensure or supervision require the candidate to have had supervised counseling experience.

One example of the accreditation processes pertinent to university and college counseling centers is that of the International Counseling Services (IACS). Among its standards for counseling services' roles and functions is the provision of training as part of the professional development of trainees and staff. With regard to the comments in this section on growth and development, the IACS standards state the following: "Counseling centers must provide training, professional development, and continuing education experiences for staff and trainees. Training and supervision of others (paraprofessionals, practicum students, predoctoral interns, postdoctoral psychology resident/fellows, etc.) are appropriate and desirable responsibilities of counseling services" (Boyd et al., 2003, p. 170). These standards further speak to the importance of supervision for professional staff and trainees and the importance of all staff members being afforded regular opportunities to upgrade their skills through case conferences, workshops sponsored by the counseling center, and professional conferences. Specifically, under Professional Development, the IACS standards indicate that,

The counseling service should maintain a continuous in-service training program, the chief features of which are supervision and consultation. Junior staff members should have the opportunity for continuing supervision and consultation from more highly trained and experienced staff members. It is highly desirable that additional in-service training be provided for all staff members, including activities such as case presentations, research reports, discussion of issues, and so forth. It is important that staff members be encouraged to participate in community activities related to their profession. (Boyd et al., 2003, p. 175)

Throughout any set of accreditation standards runs the theme that professional ethical practice is the basis of counseling practice in any setting. Thus, because supervision has become more widely acknowledged as a vital intervention for staff members and trainees in a counseling program, center, or agency, ethical standards have been established that relate specifically to the supervision process. One such set of standards for counselor supervision was developed by the Association of Counselor Education and Supervision and subsequently adapted by the American Association for Counseling and Development (now the American Counseling Association) in 1989. The standards include some 11 core areas of personal traits, knowledge, and competencies that are characteristic of effective supervisors. Among the perspectives on counselor supervision are that professional counseling supervisors should be effective counselors who can demonstrate personal traits and characteristics that are consistent with their role as a supervisor. They must be knowledgeable about ethical, legal, and regulatory aspects of the profession and skilled in using supervision methods and techniques to promote counselor development. Further, they must understand and apply their knowledge of the counselor developmental process and have competency in case conceptualization and management, assessment and evaluation, oral and written reporting and recording, evaluation of counseling performance, and research in counseling and counselor supervision.

Perhaps the overarching issue in these ethical standards for supervision is that supervisors be chosen for this role because they are well prepared to supervise counselors-in-training by virtue of their own skills and experience as counselors, their knowledge of how the professional development of counselors ensures their knowledge and skill in the methods of supervision, and their ability to understand and apply their experience, knowledge, and ethical judgment in the variety of clinical areas in which counselors must function.

Within this context, the administrator of a counseling program, center, or agency, if not serving as a supervisor him or herself, must recognize the importance of this role in producing quality counseling services and, therefore, choose a supervisor who is well prepared to perform this role. Seniority as a counselor is not the standard; competence as a counselor and supervisor of others is the standard.

If the administrator has a large enough staff to designate one or more persons to provide supervision to other counselors, the administrator must be sure that such supervision is done ethically and in accordance with whatever accreditation standards pertain to the particular counseling program for which the administrator has responsibility. In any such program or setting, the administrator is likely to have supervisory responsibility for the counseling support staff. Such persons may include clerical staff, receptionists, paraprofessionals who maintain resource libraries and function in other support roles, specialists in program evaluation, data collection and analysis, specialists in the installation, and repair and maintenance of the technology used in the program. Presumably none of these persons is engaged in counseling per se, but each of these persons may have many interactions with clients, visitors, persons in other organizational units, faculty, parents, institutional-level administrators, potential employers of students or counselor trainees, or referral sources in the community. As such, these support staff members have major roles in projecting the image of the counseling program, agency, or center. They are vital to establishing a welcoming environment to students or clients, whatever the setting. They represent information resources for persons contemplating entrance to a preparation or counseling program. They are frequently the enablers of the professional counseling staff as they schedule intake or counseling appointments, maintain client records, arrange the use of the resource library, provide computer-mediated tests, make appointments with employers for job interviews, and keep the program's technology functioning. In summary, support staff members frequently represent the glue for and institutional memory of a counseling program.

Given the importance of counseling support staff, the administrator's supervisory role includes making sure that these persons are clear about their role in the program and that they have the information, equipment, and training necessary to performing their role. With respect to any confidentiality or ethical issues relevant in a particular staff meeting, counseling support staff members should be included in program administrative staff meetings to reinforce their view of themselves as stakeholders in the success of the program. Indeed it is also useful to the administrator to meet each of these staff members on a personal basis, at least once a quarter for 15 or 20 minutes, in situations where they can set the agenda, personal or program. Such meetings reinforce that the administrator of the counseling program, center, or agency is accessible, invites ideas from support staff members, and provides recognition that these persons are valued and appreciated while being challenged to do their best and strive for excellence.

Within such contexts, the administrator can empower support staff to make decisions, take responsibility for areas that fall within their purview, and delegate particular roles to them that acknowledges their value and knowledge of the program, and nurtures their contribution. Such interactions with staff engender trust, retention, and energy on behalf of the program. If counseling programs, centers, and agencies are to demonstrate the values that undergird what they do, they must offer supportive environments to their professional and support staff members—administrators must work for their staff, not the opposite; listen to their staff members; and find ways to take pressure off, not put pressure on, these persons.

The emphasis on supervision in this section has been focused primarily on clinical supervision, the supervision of students or professional staff who are in direct counseling relationships with clients, in which their interactions are intimate, confidential, and often emotional. Clinical supervision is frequently mandated by accreditation standards for programs that prepare counselors and for programs that deliver counseling services to clients. As such high-quality clinical supervision is essential to attaining and maintaining program accreditation or individual credentialing. Thus, it is vital to recruitment, retention, postgraduate employment, successful grant-seeking, and other areas of administrative responsibility discussed in this chapter.

Focusing on clinical supervision is not to denigrate the reality that professional counseling staff serving in federal or state government bureaus or offices, foundation programs, or professional organizations also need supervision. They do, but if they are not directly providing counseling to clients, they probably do not need clinical supervision. Instead they need procedural or substantive supervision directed to legislative policies; planning; trends in counseling; financial and legal aspects of soliciting, selecting, awarding, and managing proposals for funding; interactions with constituents; collaboration with other agencies; and policies governing each of these role dimensions. Other issues about supervision with persons occupying these roles are discussed in the following chapters that talk about these roles.

In closing this section, it is worth noting that persons in counseling-related offices that do not directly deliver counseling services per se, professional counselors, counseling psychologists, and administrators of counseling offices, departments, agencies, gain credibility by having the credentials—licenses and certifications—that are seen as prestigious and marks of competence in the field of counseling. Within this context, such credentialed persons are seen as being able to act with greater authority and insight as they administer, supervise, or manage legislation and proposals for funding by counselors in other settings.

THE USE OF TECHNOLOGY
AND KNOWLEDGE MANAGEMENT

In a nation that has been called "Wired" and a "Cybersociety" or labeled by many other metaphors accentuating the degree to which advanced technology is pervasive in the workplace, the home, and social institutions, administrators are responsible for giving leadership to the use of advanced technology in their counseling programs. For the last three decades or more, various technologies have been developed to extend or reinforce the counselor's ability to effect behavioral change in clients, and counseling programs have used these technologies to help with administrative procedures. Depending on what point in time one does an analysis, new technologies have included the application of gaming, audiovideo recording devices, simulations, films, assessment centers, problem-solving kits, self-directed inventories, programmed resource material, and, perhaps most comprehensively, computer–person interactive systems designed to facilitate client behavior rehearsal and exploration, information retrieval, assessment, planning, and simulation of likely outcomes of action and treatment. The latest technology to augment counseling, and particularly but not exclusively career counseling, is the Internet.

As the development of computers and the Internet continues to grow, the possible use of such technologies in counseling and counseling programs will expand both in actuality and possibility. In some instances, the computer has been cast as a mind multiplier, as a way of compounding an individual's vision about possible futures in which she or he can engage, or as the pathway to such futures and the risks or investments associated with different behaviors. In other instances, the computer has been conceptualized as a prosthesis—a replacement for a specific individual's disabilities or limitations that enhances mobility, communication, or problem solving thereby expanding an individual's development. Beyond these roles, computers have been conceived of as forecasters of possibilities, organizers of time, schedulers, and information retrieval devices. They have been used for assessment and diagnosis, psychophysiological measurement and biofeedback, behavior observation and assessment, statistical and visual analyses of data, motivation of children, administrative support of counseling programs (billing, financial management, budget preparation, maintaining databases, word processing), telecommunications, consultation on emotional crises, and intervention with psychiatric patients (Herr, 1999).

Within such possibilities, computers have been found useful in extending the capability of counselors in managing client or student development information; monitoring medication usage by psychiatric patients; record keeping; assessment or test scoring; helping people develop a predictive system about opportunities available to them; creating a personal profile of their strengths; and developing job-seeking skills and guiding individual decision making. Among the many applications of computers in counseling and psychotherapy, perhaps three of the most prominent uses are those involving computerized career guidance systems that service thousands of users each day in schools, universities, community agencies, and private practices. This same use is now being multiplied exponentially as multiple Web sites are being devoted to job vacancies, career information, employer information, ways to apply for existing job vacancies, how to build a resume and exchange it with potential employers, online career counseling, and other related activities, including self-directed assessment of interests and aptitudes, their match with existing occupational and educational opportunities, engaging in various decision-making exercises, and other forms of inquiry.

Second, the use of computers and the Internet is growing in personal counseling. Although still quite controversial, in part because of ethical issues and because many observers continue to view counseling as a process that is face to face, one on one, the only way to provide interpersonal respect and understanding of clients, there is increasing evidence of computer-mediated and online personal counseling taking place on the Internet and other venues. Among the possibilities emerging for counseling through the use of the Internet, as identified by Sampson, Kolodinsky, and Greeno (1997), are the following:

- video conferencing as a possible alternative to the traditional face-to-face employment interview conducted on college campuses;
- using e-mail to respond to specific individual questions about a variety of mental health issues; in this case, the individual frames a problem and a mental health professional responds with information, recommendations for action, and possibly a counseling referral;
- facilitating bulletin board discussion groups that allow counselors to consult with other professionals about specific types of client issues;
- marketing counseling services both online and at a geographic site, with an electronic screening interview provided to determine whether counseling should proceed;
- delivering counseling services by two-way videoconferencing processes, e-mail, using computer-assisted instruction, moderated discussion groups;
- delivering self-help psychoeducational resources;
- providing counselor supervision and case conferencing; and
- assisting in research and data collection.

A further common use of computer-mediated processes is psychological testing. Alluded to previously is the use of computers for test administration and scoring. Such processes may occur in immediate conjunction with the process of counseling or psychotherapy or simply as an administrative procedure in support of, but distant from, the actual counseling with a client. In any case, computer-based test interpretations are becoming increasingly important in counseling and psychology. Relatively few of the major tests used in counseling programs do not have computer scoring available. Often tests taken on computers have software that immediately scores the tests. Such applications include computerized adaptive testing that tailors the difficulty of a test to the test taker's ability level. This approach depends on having a large bank of test items to measure a particular psychological trait that are precalibrated to assess people with different ability levels or other characteristics. There are also computer-based test interpretations that rest on systems of knowledge that can be applied to patterns of test scores, thereby providing narratives, profiles, classifications, diagnoses, and suggestions for treatment as well as hypotheses about the client to be pursued in counseling and second opinions that can aid the client and counselor in psychological decision making. These are so-called *expert systems*. Obviously, computer-based test interpretation systems can score tests rapidly, accurately, and in large volume, and, where required, can engage in data reduction important for research purposes and for the creation of new tests or test forms.

In broad terms, *computer-based test interpretation* refers to the automation of a set of prespecified rules for use in analyzing, interpreting, and assigning certain qualities to a response or response pattern (e.g., test score, profile pattern; Harris, 1987). Implicit in this observation, however, are concerns that the quality of the data used in developing software becomes paramount to successful computer applications, as do the training and expertise of test users. Obviously, the latter has much to do with the accuracy and speed of interpretation and validity of explanations to clients of classifications used in the scores provided.

Administrators of counseling programs have a number of obligations related to the use of computer technology in support of career guidance, personal counseling, administration and scoring of tests, among other possible uses. Certainly a fundamental administrative concern is ensuring that the professional and support staff most involved with using computer-mediated systems or the Internet are trained to do so. This is a critical issue when interpreting computer scored tests and when referring clients to some form of computer interaction. The counselor must be sure that the client, student, or other user knows how to use the system. The computer or Internet must not be seen as a replacement for a counselor, but rather as an augmentation of the counselor's skill. This also means that the counselor needs to brief the counselee about how to use the system and why, be available during the client use of the system, and debrief the client after his or her use of the system. This also may mean that counselors need to be selective about whom they refer to a computer-mediated system because the time involved for the client and, possibly, the counselor may be extensive.

Certainly, the administrator needs to help his or her staff see the use of advanced technology as integral to the counseling program, not something that is independent of it. Thus, the counseling program administrator must guide discussions and planning directed to defining how, when, and for what purposes computers and the Internet will be used in this counseling program, who will provide oversight and maintenance of the computer-mediated systems, what data or information will be sought, and how will it be used.

A further issue for the counseling program administrator has to do with ethical concerns generated by the use of computers and the Internet to augment counselor skills or for administrative purposes. Ethical standards are increasingly speaking to the particular ethical issues that need to be addressed when computers or the Internet are being used in counseling programs.

For example, *The American Counseling Association Code of Ethics and Standards of Practice* (1995) directly addressed computer technology used in counseling:

a. *Use of Computers.* When computer applications are used in counseling services, counselors ensure that (1) the client is intellectually, emotionally, and physically capable of using the computer application; (2) the computer application is appropriate for the needs of the client; (3) the client understands the purpose and operation of the computer applications; and (4) a follow-up of client use of a computer application is provided to correct possible misconceptions, discover inappropriate use, and assess subsequent needs.

b. *Explanation of Limitations.* Counselors ensure that clients are provided information as a part of the counseling relationship that adequately explains the limitations of computer technology.

c. *Access to Computer Applications.* Counselors provide for equal access to computer applications in counseling services. (Section A.2.a)

This section, in turn, states that "counselors do not condone or engage in discrimination based on age, color, culture, disability, ethnic group, gender, race, religious, sexual orientation, marital status, or socioeconomic status." It is this language that specifically addresses the issue of equality of access in computer use, but extrapolates to this specific intervention from an ethical legacy that counselors should treat all persons, that they provide access to counseling services to all persons with the caveat that they do so with sensitivity to the characteristics of the client and to his or her potential cultural or gender differences from the counselor.

The International Association for Educational and Vocational Guidance (IAEVG) adopted its first-ever set of Ethical Standards in Stockholm in August 1995. The basic ethical principles that guide the counselor's or career specialist's obligations to clients as seen through international lenses rest on the same fundamental elements as already described in the ACA Code of Ethics and the APA Ethical Principles, but the *IAEVG Ethical Standards* (International Association for Educational and Vocational Guidance, 1996) also explicitly cited the use of computers in several specific contexts. For example,

6. Members of IAEVG . . . recognize that emerging techniques, e.g., computer-based testing or career guidance programs, require periodic training and continuing familiarity with the professional literature in administration, scoring and interpretation . . .

7. Members of IAEVG promote the benefits, to clients, of new techniques and appropriate computer applications when research or evaluation warrants such use. The counselor/practitioner ensures that the use of computer applications or other techniques are appropriate for the individual needs of the client, that the client understands how to use the technique or process involved, and that follow-up counseling assistance is provided. IAEVG members further ensure that members of underrepresented groups have equal access to the best techniques available, to computer technologies, and to nondiscriminatory, current, and accurate information within whatever techniques are used. (p. 3)

The accreditation standards for University and College Counseling Centers as formulated by the International Association of Counseling Services (Boyd et al., 2003) has explicitly discussed Technology in Section C, 10. It stated,

Counseling centers must demonstrate a basic understanding of technology prior to adopting any new technology for use. It is recognized that counseling centers may need to rely on professionals who are not psychologists to provide technical assistance. Professionals providing technical assistance should be given training concerning issues regarding confidentiality. (p. 171)

In attempting to stay current with emerging technology used in counseling centers, these accreditation standards also warn that,

computerized client data and case records must be secured against unauthorized access and clients must be informed that confidential information describing their treatment is stored on the center's computer; . . . that electronic mail (e-mail) is not a safe means to transmit confidential information; . . . if counseling centers use fax machines to transmit confidential information they must secure the faxed material from unauthorized access; . . . cordless and cellular telephone should not be used to communicate confidential information. (Boyd et al., 2003, pp. 171–172)

There are many other examples of standards now providing guidance about the ethical implications of the use of advanced technology in counseling centers. The examples cited here are consistent with such statements applied to different settings and client populations. Yet as Sampson and Reardon (1990) suggested, such ethical or evaluative standards, although important, are effective only when counselors are aware of the ethical and professional issues involved, have an attitude of cautious optimism about the appropriate use of valid software, and are provided with effective counselor training opportunities. Again the leadership of the counseling program administrator is a critical factor in the degree to which advanced technology is used and integrated with the other elements of the counseling program.

PROGRAM EVALUATION

A final administrative tool or process to be discussed in this chapter is program evaluation, including cost–benefit analysis. In general terms, counseling program evaluation is the collection and analyses of information by which to make decisions about the quality and outcomes of the counseling program. Such a process is used to determine how to change the delivery of different counseling services to make them more effective and efficient in their achievement of the counseling program goals.

Henderson and Gysbers (1998) contended that, "planning involves assessing the needs of students and other program clients against the vision and mission established for the program. . . . Evaluation is conducted in the context of the assessed needs, the program design, and the implementation plans" (p. 59). Thus, planning and evaluation tend to be reciprocal. To be successful, evaluation needs to be planned, and planning needs the results of program evaluation to determine whether the outcomes being achieved are consistent with those established by the program.

Evaluation requires a series of logical steps that, with little variability, include the following: identifying goals and stating objectives to be assessed in the evaluation; choosing criterion measurements (what evidence will we accept that the goals and objectives have been met—ratings, expert judgments, follow-up study results, client opinion, observed behavioral changes, scores on standardized instruments?); establishing levels of performance or standards (what will we define as acceptable performance on the goals we are examining?); specifying which program elements will be evaluated or is the intent to assess the impact of the total counseling program? Implicit in this question is whether we are engaged in a summative or formative evaluation. To oversimplify the matter, a summative evaluation has to do with whether the total program is meeting its goals. In such an evaluation, again depending on what evidence is acceptable, it would be helpful to have baseline data on client performance in behaviors of interest before the counseling program was instituted and data about the clients after the program was implemented so that change can be determined from the original point of implementation to the current point of evaluation. Change data on the performance goals for clients then need to be analyzed in relation to their contribution to program goals, to determine whether the changes are sufficient to justify the program, and what the data mean for future program efforts. Summative evaluation is essentially concerned with the aggregate effects of the total program in relation to its goals, rather than how well specific techniques or activities contributed to such outcomes.

Formative evaluation has a different perspective than summative evaluation. Formative evaluation is typically more concerned with the effectiveness or comparative effectiveness of different program elements. For example, within a counseling program, is individual counseling more effective in meeting client goals than group counseling with particular populations? How effective is a computer-assisted career guidance system as a stand-alone treatment or in combination with other interventions? What are the comparative costs of interventions used in the program and their comparative contributions to the counseling program's impact on clients?

The steps typically followed in formulating and carrying out an evaluation include the following:

Designing the evaluation—When it is determined whether the evaluation will be summative or formative in nature, it is necessary to decide what data will be collected, who will be involved in conducting the evaluation, who the target respondents to the data collection will be, the sample from which data will be collected, and the timing of the evaluation;

Collecting the data—How will the desired information be acquired—questionnaires, interviews, focus groups, observations, standardized instruments?

Analyzing data—This process depends on the kind of information you collect. Are the data quantitative or qualitative in form? Are the data ranked or on an interval scale? Do you have baseline data on client performance to compare to posttreatment outcomes to answer your evaluation questions? Do you need to make between-group or within-group comparisons? How these questions are answered and to whom you will be reporting the findings will affect the type of analyses you undertake. For some purposes, simple comparisons by frequency count, percentages, or graphic representations (pie chart, bar graph) will be adequate; in other forms of evaluation, correlations, analyses of variance or covariance, path analyses, and multiple regression may be more appropriate;

Interpreting data—Ultimately the quantitative or qualitative analyses of data collected need to be interpreted. What will be defined as acceptable performance quality? Do the data indicate that client behavior changed as a result of the interventions used? Do the evaluation results point to areas of needed program improvement? These are not statistical questions per se; they are matters of counselor or administrator judgment. Such results need to be linked to the systematic planning for the counseling program and their meaning evaluated, reported as necessary, and, where necessary, an action plan created to make program changes.

Reporting and using data—Beyond an administrator's leadership in implementing program evaluations, it is likely that other forces may be instrumental in encouraging such evaluations. In an era of accountability, accreditation processes, periodic planning requirements at the organizational level, and state or federal requirements may each be the stimulus for conducting program evaluations. In any case, it is likely that institutional administrators where the counseling program is housed (boards of education, trustees, and legislators, among others) will need to be apprised of the results of the evaluation. Therefore, the information collected and the results obtained, no matter how complex, must be put into a form that decision makers can understand. This process of reporting and interpreting the results of the evaluation becomes the task of the counseling program administrator as he or she explains, clarifies, advocates, and places into context the meaning of the evaluation. As this process of reporting is done effectively, it represents a major method of communications, public relations, and accountability to the counseling program's various publics, both internal and external to the program. This process provides the counseling program administrator another opportunity to be a statesperson as he or she identifies the levels of support the counseling program requires in the future, the program changes that need to be made, and the contribution of the program to the larger organizational mission.

Cost–Benefit Analyses

One of the evaluative tasks with which administrators of counseling programs will be increasingly confronted is cost–benefit analysis. In an era of limited resources to meet the growing needs in human services of all types, policymakers, legislators, institutional-level administrators are asking questions about the costs and benefits of counseling programs. They are not only interested in program evaluation results, but also in how much it costs to put in place and maintain a counseling program. They want to know whether the outcomes achieved, the contributions made to the institutional mission, are worth the cost. Implicit in these questions are such issues as: What is the least expensive way to deliver an effective counseling program? Can we limit the use of the program to only those who most clearly need its services? Would outsourcing the counseling program to a community agency save us money and serve our needs at a minimal level? What is the added value of a counseling program in a school, university, corporation, or community? These are not easy questions to address, but they are emerging more frequently. Certainly public policy and legislation are increasingly oriented to accountability and cost–benefit assumptions. Legislation on education, workforce development, and human services has moved increasingly from providing general guidelines for the acquisition and use of funds to specific requirements for performance evaluation of the processes being funded, the cost–benefit ratios, and other accountability expectations.

In one study of the public policies of 14 nations regarding the provision of career development interventions (Herr, 2002), it was found that each of these nations presumed that the socioeconomic benefits of career interventions exceeded the costs of providing such interventions, but none had yet tested these assumptions empirically. The likelihood that the current status of cost–benefit analyses as a presumptive process will in the near future increase the demands for empirical results testifying to the benefits and the ratio of costs to benefits that accrue from support of a counseling program.

In oversimplified terms, cost–benefit analyses of a counseling program in total or of individual interventions within it refer to the ratio of costs of providing such services to various populations for specific purposes compared with the economic and, sometimes, social benefits derived from such services. Such benefits may accrue to individuals who are the direct consumers of such services/interventions or, less directly, to educational institutions, employers, governments, or society at large. Economic benefits to clients may be measured in their ability to secure jobs with increased pay, in shortened periods of unemployment, in obtaining greater congruence between personal interests and abilities in a job chosen, and in the experience of extended tenure in that job. For educational institutions, benefits may be seen in increased retention of students, therefore preserving government aid paid to the institution per student, rather than losing that aid if a student drops out. For employers, it may be reflected in employee fit, increased productivity, extended tenure, less preoccupation with unresolved family issues, and greater flexibility in acceptance of work tasks and in accommodating change, thereby also reducing costs of recruitment and placement of workers. For government, it may be reflected in reducing the amount of money required to pay for unemployment benefits or to persons with disabilities, and thereby increasing the acquisition of taxes from persons helped to return to or enter the labor market. For society at large, a purposeful, productive, teachable workforce may enhance the competitive edge of the nation in competing for market share in a global economy, in being innovative, and in maximizing high-skill/high-pay jobs in the occupational structure. Each of these outcomes can be measured in economic benefits in direct or more complex ways.

Social benefits from counseling programs are typically more abstract and more difficult to measure than economic benefits, typically requiring some form of long-term follow-up study. Nevertheless, there are typically social benefits of note. They include such benefits as reduction in violence, reduced incarceration for crimes, less physical or sexual abuse of children and adults, less chemical dependency, and less social maladjustment. These are each areas in which counseling has been effective in one study or another and offer social benefits to the individual, employers, governments, and society at large. Although each of these benefits can be thought of in economic terms, they also represent social benefits in the form of more positive interpersonal behaviors, more optimistic and purposeful attitudes, safer children and adults, less crime, and more control of one's behavior. Each of these socioeconomic benefits is among the outcomes sought from counseling in different settings and with different populations. Cost–benefit analyses, like program evaluations, are both practical processes and processes that add to clarity about the vision and mission of counseling services. As such the implications and conduct of program evaluation and cost–benefit analyses add fuel to the content of the administrator acting as advocate and statesperson for counselors and counseling.

SUMMARY

Chapter 2 outlined some of the fundamental processes with which professional counselors as administrators need to be familiar and able to apply. In the remainder of the book, these processes are viewed as tools of counseling administrators in different settings. As such these processes tend to appear with different emphases and content in the requirements of administrators of counseling or counseling-related programs in schools, universities, state and federal government offices and foundations, community agencies, and independent practice. The common and unique characteristics of planning; budgeting; recruitment, retention, and supervision of staff; use of technology; and evaluation are discussed in relation to the work of counseling administrators in various venues. As each of these venues is discussed as a setting for counseling or counselor-related functions, it may be useful for the reader to return to this chapter to amplify his or her understanding of a particular process.

CHAPTER

3

The School Counselor
as Program Administrator

CONTEXT

In many ways, the school counselor, who becomes the administrator of the
school guidance or school counseling program in a school district or a
school building, is a prototypical example of the situations discussed in this
book. Whether known as the Head or Lead Counselor, the Director of Guidance, the Director of School Counseling, or by another term, the administrator of the school counseling program is typically a middle manager representing and providing leadership and management to the other school
counselors in the school district or school building. Typically, however, the
administrator of the school counseling program has limited autonomy because other institutional-level administrators (e.g., the principal of the
building, the assistant superintendent of pupil personnel services, under
which school counseling is frequently subsumed) also have general oversight or authority for the school counseling or guidance program. This institutional-level administrator may also hold the budget for the counseling
program or be expected to approve all of the program expenditures.

Depending on how significant the school counseling program is perceived to be, its needs for resources, personnel, collaboration with teachers, or opportunity to reach out to the community may be dismissed as a
relatively unimportant or ancillary part of the school or, in contrast, as a
major part of the school's mission that deserves to share proportionately in
the total budget of the school or school district. Which of these situations
prevails is a function of the credibility, leadership, and management skills
of the school counselor serving as the head or director of the program and

the priorities of those who have institutional oversight for the school counseling program. The division of leadership responsibility and the differing views that may prevail about the importance of the school counseling program among institutional-based administrators, parents, and Board of Education members, among others, poses multiple challenges to the school counselor serving as the Director of Guidance or School Counseling or the Head Counselor.

Paisley and Borders (1995) summarized the issues that face school counselors and, by implication, their direct leadership in the following manner:

> A major issue is the lack of control school counselors have over their day-to-day work activities and the development of their profession. The school counselor's role continues to be either explicitly or implicitly defined (if not dictated) by a number of sources [and people], few of whom have any background or experience in school counseling and who often provide somewhat contradictory direction. School counselors, for example, are [often] directly accountable to school principals and the school system's director of school counseling. . . . These two . . . supervisors may have very different agenda's about the counselor's role in the school (p. 151) [as suggested above, one could also include the views of an institutional-level assistant superintendent, Board of Education members and other persons who have their own experiences with and agendas about school counseling]. . . . The lack of control over one's professional life and destiny probably contributes a great deal to a second fundamental issue: the ongoing confusion and controversy about the appropriate focus for its practitioners (p. 152). [The lack of control also contributes to two continuing philosophical role questions.] The first concerns their role in the delivery of a comprehensive developmental program [although] despite its centrality to the profession . . . such a program has rarely been implemented; and the second philosophical role question being . . . debated is, "What is counseling in the schools?" (p. 152)

These important issues discussed by Paisley and Borders are, in a sense, constantly recurring across the nation and, indeed, in other nations that have school counselors in place. As we discuss in the latter sections of this chapter, in the late 1990s, the American School Counselor Association (ASCA) developed the ASCA National Model for School Counseling Programs (American School Counselor Association, 1998), which is intended to bring greater coherence and focus to the questions about what counseling is in the schools. However, there are several factors that intervene in decisions about school counseling in any given school. One is the reality that, in the United States, the provision of education from kindergarten (or earlier preschool programs) to Grade 12 is essentially defined by local authorities (e.g., Boards of Education and their designated school administrators). State departments of education are also influential, but less definitive than local authorities. State school codes vary in how they address school counseling programs, whether they require schools to have school/guidance counselors, whether school counselors are included among those positions to be funded by state budget allocations to local school districts, and, if so, what ratio of school counselors to students is expected. State Departments of Education also typically define the certification requirements to become a school counselor, the courses to be taken, the experiential learning (e.g., school counseling practica and/or internships) required, and related processes to be offered in Counselor Education programs in higher education institutions approved to prepare school counselors. Through whatever processes are implemented, State Departments of Education generally have the legal authority to certify school counselors to perform the duties that individual states perceive to be important.

The federal Department of Education as well as the Departments of Labor, Defense, and Human Services also can affect how school counselors are valued and the roles that are perceived to be important from a national perspective. Ordinarily, federal views become embedded in legislation that includes some form of financial reimbursements to school districts that implement counseling or guidance strategies that are directly related to a specified set of national goals: for example, the prevention of child abuse, preparing secondary school students to enter the workforce with necessary skills and positive attitudes, ensuring that children with disabilities have access to available educational and occupational opportunities, and early identification and treatment of children at risk of social, academic, or economic failure.

In many ways, national legislation that supports school counselors' functioning with a particular emphasis can be seen as making school counselors sociopolitical mechanisms to accomplish national goals at a given historical point. The prime example of the effects of federal legislation on school counselors is the National Defense Education Act of 1958 (NDEA). This important Act was written in the middle of the cold war, during the period when the United States and the Soviet Union were seen as unrelenting enemies. The NDEA and its amendments that continued into the late 1960s arose because federal government officials were afraid that the United States was rapidly falling behind the Soviet Union in scientific and technical areas vital to national defense. Such perceptions were given credence when the Soviet Union launched the first orbiting satellite, Sputnik, in 1957, before the United States launched its own satellite. As one of many responses, the U.S. Congress passed the NDEA to strengthen the scientific, mathematical, and technical education of American children and included in this Act the need to identify, train, and place school counselors in the schools, originally in secondary schools and, in subsequent amendments, in the elementary schools. The language of the Bill did not view school counselors as altruistic and caring additions to the school faculty, but rather as persons who could identify and encourage secondary school students who had the potential to be scientists and mathematicians to emphasize such courses in high school and to pursue science and mathematics curricula in higher education. This legislation viewed excellent scientific and mathematical education as a vital part of national defense, an important ingredient in winning the Space Race and gaining scientific and technical superiority over the nation's adversaries.

The consequences of the NDEA included a large increase in the number of school counselors employed in the nation's schools, a major expansion in the number and characteristics of counselor education programs in the United States, a strengthening of the content of school counselor preparation programs, and the development of comprehensive K to 12 school counseling programs, including elementary school counseling.

Although the NDEA has been considered the "watershed" legislation that gave impetus to the expansion and growing professionalization of school counselors in the United States, other federal legislation has also had a substantial impact on the role of school counselors and the resources available to them. Examples include the various amendments to the Elementary and Secondary Act, which began in 1965 and continue to the present; the Carl D. Perkins Vocational Education Act of 1984 and, subsequently, the Carl D. Perkins Vocational Education and Applied Technology Act of 1990 and its subsequent amendments; the Career Education Incentive Act of 1976; the Elementary School Counseling Demonstration Act of 1995; and the School to Work Opportunities Act of 1994. Each of these legislative acts has promoted the importance of the role of the school counselor in assisting students with academic and career concerns.

Although many other pieces of federal legislation could be cited here as having a major impact on elementary and secondary school students, suffice it to say that the federal agenda for school counselors, what state governments have supported, and how local communities prioritize the roles and functions of school counselors can be very different. Such multiple sources of expectations of school counselors can both broaden their roles and significance within schools and add so many expectations that the role of school counselors can lose focus. Such expectations also require the administrator of the counseling program to advocate for and clarify the contributions of school counseling with local, state, or federal officials with responsibilities for policies and resources designed to advance counseling programs.

Given the various expectations of school counseling found at local, state, and federal levels, one can argue that school counseling can take on different forms to meet different purposes as different assumptions about its values and priorities exist. In this sense, school counseling has different types of relevance depending on the needs of a particular school, a particular state government's policies, or as federal legislation focuses on specific goals. Thus, as the demographic nature of a school changes or teachers, parents, students, administrators, or others bring their personal agendas to policymaking, or socioeconomic change causes new problems or issues for children and youth, new expectations for school counseling keep emerging. Counseling in any setting tends to be interdependent with socioeconomic problems that become the content of counseling as well as the differing perspectives by parents, teachers, administrators, employers, the court system, family services, and other community agencies about the problems in which counselors should intervene.

There has long been a core of school counseling concerns—academic adjustment and achievement; curricular choice and planning for postsecondary education, the transition from school to work, personal development and growth, career planning, and decision making. Yet there are many other categories of problems thrust on school counselors for identification, assessment, treatment, or support. Examples of more recent areas in which counselors have been expected to engage and provide assistance are children's and youth's adjustment in single-parent and blended families, violence and bullying, chemical dependency and recovery, grief and bereavement, suicide of a classmate or a family member, child sexual abuse, conflict resolution, anger and stress management, dealing with learning disabilities, and cultivating respect for cultural diversity among students.

It is fair to say that, depending on the school district in which they are located, some school counselors get involved in all of these problem areas. In some schools, the emphasis is on crisis intervention; in others, the focus is on learning problems and academic success; in still others, engaging in educational reform; and in other schools, consulting with teachers about students who are having adjustment problems or are seen as at risk for academic, social, and economic failures. The problem for school counselors is not that they cannot be helpful to children, parents, or professionals in other child-related agencies, but rather how to set and clarify their priorities. A further question is how the counseling staff organizes itself most effectively to serve all children in the school with normal developmental concerns and also make provisions to serve those children currently in crisis because of personal or family issues when they most need the support and interventions available through the school counselor. As the priorities of a school counseling program are being considered, there is a need for counselors engaged in planning to be creative in their use of resources, technologies, and community agencies to help them cope with the often overwhelming demands and expectations that are referred to them. Such circumstances lead to efforts to determine whether more group work with students would be preferable to primarily individual counseling; the degree to which they could collaborate more fully with counseling personnel in community agencies to serve as referral or resource persons; and the possibility of reducing some of the time-consuming and more mundane guidance activities through self-directed reading, games, use of computers, adding parental aides or paraprofessionals to the staff to manage certain aspects of the program.

IMPLICATIONS FOR LEADERSHIP
AND MANAGEMENT OF THE SCHOOL
COUNSELING PROGRAM

Inherent in each of these questions is the need for leadership and management of the school counseling program; the planning for priority setting and the most effective deployment of counselors, clerical staff, paraprofessionals and aides, volunteers, resource people, and community assets; the negotiation with institutional-level administrators about the roles and resources of the school counseling program; and communications with students, teachers, parents, community agencies, and employers to acknowledge or solicit their roles in the school counseling program.

Whatever the priorities established for a school counseling program, the program must be systematically planned; stated in terms of goals, objectives, activities, and student outcomes; tied to the school or school district's strategic plan and mission statements; focused on the roles of school counselors as generalists or specialists who use, in some combination, advocacy, assessment, consultation, coordination, and counseling; and collaboration to serve their various constituents. From a school district standpoint, the school counseling program must be designed in a sequential manner that addresses the implications for school counseling processes and psychoeducational or guidance content tailored to the differing needs of children at elementary, middle, and senior high school levels. As plans for the school counseling program are developed and priorities are established to address the large number of expectations and demands that are directed to the program, efforts must be put in place to recognize and resist short-term fads that move it off course. In this sense, the school counseling program needs to be viewed as continually modifying itself in terms of establishing its limits, its immediate and long-range goals, and its capacity for referral or collaboration with other professionals in the school district or the community as need dictates.

There are many other issues that will be dealt with in other sections of the chapter that have implications for the role of the administrator of the school counseling program. Among them is the counselor–student ratio available in this school district. Where does it stand in terms of various national recommendations for such ratios (e.g., at the secondary school level, the recommended ratio of counselors to students varies from 100 to 275 across different sources, but the actual national ratio, which is difficult to estimate from school to school, is thought to average about 513 students per 1 counselor [Erford, 2003, p. 3], with the highest recent ratio of counselors to students being 1 to 1,171 in California [American School Counselor Association, 2000]). The national ratio of counselors to students is more than double the recommendations of professional organizations as indicated previously in this paragraph. An average ratio of 513 students to 1 school counselor restricts the counselor's time to be able to work with individual students, and it does not incorporate elements of a school counselor's workload that are not counseling related or are quasi-administrative (e.g., conducting a school's testing program, lunch duty, bus duty, data entry to student permanent records, writing letters of reference to colleges or to employers for students). Each of these tasks, however important, diminishes the amount of time available for counseling or consulting with students, teachers, parents, or others.

PLANNING

The brief introductory statements made thus far in this chapter have provided a context for planning and why it is important. Clearly, the roles of school counselors and the programs they provide are wide-ranging in the assistance and support offered to students and their parents as they anticipate and attempt to function effectively in a changing society.

Herr (1999) suggested that there are four current challenges that are having significant influence on individual behavior and on the perceptions of how counselors should interact with the settings and populations they serve. These four challenges include the ripple effects of the shifting economy and the transformation of the occupational structure in association with the pervasive effects of advanced technology; the implications of changing family structures, the gender revolution, and childrearing practices; the growing pluralism of traditions, languages, ethnicity, and race in contemporary America; and changing definitions and the increasing magnitude of at-risk populations.

Subsumed under these four categories of challenges to which school counselors must respond are many subissues. For example, as the occupational structure is being transformed under the influence of the global economy and international economic competition, educational requirements for many existing occupations and most new jobs are rising. Because of the central place advanced technology has now taken in industrial and business processes, computer literacy and operational skills are increasingly job requirements, and because of a global labor surplus, U.S. students are now competing with students from other nations for jobs that are rapidly being redistributed from the United States to India, China, Ireland, several South American nations, and other regions of the world. Wide-ranging changes in family structures, including disintegrating families, families in which both parents are working to maintain economic survival, and limited opportunities for parents to spend time with their children and monitor their behavior and growth is in many cases causing schools to become childrearing institutions and virtually surrogate parents. The cultural pluralism in schools across the nation, where minority group members had not traditionally attended, have sometimes led to the need for conflict resolution, for new initiatives focused on improving intergroup relations, to the need for school counselors who focus on improving intergroup relations and who are bilingual or multilingual. The increasing number of children and youth who are defined as at risk for social, economic, or educational failure has led to a pervasive concern for new methods to address the effects of stress, anger, violence, crisis, grief and loss, and other forms of psychological and social vulnerability among many students.

Each of the four challenges and their subissues suggest that, like society at large, schools must change in response to the shifting attitudes, skill needs, family influences, and socioeconomic competitive forces that are rippling through communities. The perceptions and actual affects of such challenges on children and youth comprise much of the content that school counselors encounter on a daily basis. The question is, how will they respond to these challenges, to this content as it affects different groups of students in the school and community differently? A first response lies with planning processes. Many of these processes have already been discussed in chapters 1 and 2. The issue in this chapter is how are these processes applied in school counseling? Clearly, the administrator of the school counseling program needs to constantly be involved in environmental scanning: reading about, talking to colleagues, and anticipating the trends in the larger community, state, or nation that will likely affect the students in the school district for whom the school counseling program needs to be provided. Environmental scanning is not mystical; the four challenges to counselors that were just discussed are examples of the insights environmental scanning provides about changes in the lives of students for which information, support, counseling, outreach, and leadership need to be implemented.

As mentioned several times previously, a school counseling program does not stand alone and does not occur in a vacuum—it operates within the context of the school or district in which it functions and within a local community. It is influenced by state and national mandates, legislation, and guidelines. Thus, the administrator of the school counseling program must frequently negotiate on the nature of the school counseling program and the deployment of its resources with building principals, assistant superintendents, Boards of Education members, and others. Such negotiations might revolve around several pivotal concerns (adapted from Herr, 1999) affecting the nature of the school counseling program:

• the degree to which the school counseling program is to be systematically planned; tailored to the priorities, demographics, characteristics, strategic plan, and mission statement of the school district or a particular school building; and clearly defined in terms of the results to be achieved, rather than simply the services to be offered;

• the degree to which the school counseling program will begin in the elementary or secondary school—the degree to which the school counseling program will be longitudinal and systematically planned around major developmental tasks at different educational levels and the knowledge, skills, and attitudes they require or be confined to crisis intervention activities and quasi-administrative functions such as testing and scheduling;

• the degree to which the school counseling program will be seen as responsible for the counseling (guidance) of all students or for only some subpopulations of students, such as those at risk;

• the degree to which the school counseling program will include the contributions of teachers, other mental health specialists, community resources, parent volunteers, and families as part of the counseling delivery system or be confined to only what the school counselors and support staff can do themselves;

• the degree to which the school counseling program will be focused on precollege guidance and counseling, counseling in and for vocational education and the school-to-work transition, counseling for academic achievement, and counseling for students with special problems, such as bereavement, substance abuse, antisocial behavior, eating disorders, and family difficulties (single parents, stepparents, blended family rivalries) or that one of these emphases will prevail;

• the degree to which counselors will be generalists or specialists, members of teams or independent practitioners, and proactive or reactive with regard to the needs of students, teachers, parents, and administrators;

• the degree to which counselors will employ psychoeducational models or guidance curricula as well as individual forms of intervention to achieve goals;

• the degree to which the roles of counselors can be sharpened and expanded while not holding counselors responsible for so many expectations that their effectiveness is diminished and the outcomes they effect are vague;

• the degree to which school counselors have a reasonable student load (250 or less) so that they can know these students as individuals and provide them with personal attention;

• the degree to which school counselors effectively communicate their goals and results to policymakers and the media both to clarify their contributions to the mission of the school and to enhance their visibility as effective, indeed vital, components of positive student development;

• the degree to which the school counseling program incorporates national models, federal legislation, and state mandates; and

• the degree to which the school counseling program is built on best practices that are evidence-based and on data that indicate how well the school counseling program and its various categories of interventions are serving students, teachers, parents, administrators, or others.

The School Counseling Administrator as Planner

Responses to these questions in conversations with institutional-level administrators are important sources of input to the planning process, whether one is starting a totally new school counseling program in a new school or leading continuous improvement in an established school counseling program that is undergoing change. The pivotal issues outlined earlier address various ways by which counseling content and structure may be viewed by institutional-level administrators, its importance to the school or school district, how it fits into the total array of subsystems that make up the school, the emphases it should pursue, its structure, its content, and its accountability. Such information is vital to developing the program plan for school counseling and linking it to the strategic plan that integrates all of the academic, clinical, and support programs for the school district. These pivotal issues also could be used to fashion content to be explored with groups of teachers or parents in focus groups, needs assessments, or other surveys being used to collect information about the expectations for the school counseling program held by different program constituents in the school and the community. Such information is vital to the planning process as well as to the accountability process for the program.

Undoubtedly, the direct leader/administrator of the school counseling program will be assigned the function of executing the planning process for the school counseling program, linking it to the strategic planning process for the school district as part of a continuous improvement process for school counseling or as a team leader of a data-driven process to monitor the accountability of the school counseling programs. Although the administrator of the school counseling program may not be expected to design the plan and collect and analyze all the relevant information him or herself, the administrator of the school counseling program will need to ensure that such planning takes place and that the results are reported in a form that institutional-level administrators, teachers, parents, employers, students, and others can understand. Depending on the quality and insights with which these planning assignments are carried out, the results may garner support for the program or be seen as insignificant.

At the least, then, the administrator of the school counseling program should understand the various models of planning, including those described in chapter 2, how programs are evaluated, what data are collected and analyzed, what the professional organizations or scholars in the field are describing as best practices and national models of school counseling, what legislation or public policies bear on expectations and goals of school counseling, the differences between results-based, outcome-based, or evidence-based versus process-based or services-based approaches to school counseling, and other trends that are affecting the future of school counseling programs across the nation.

It is likely that the administrator of the school counseling program will need to teach institutional-level administrators and other constituents about school counseling, its history and evolution, national models, trends in the field, examples of effective school counseling models, and other relevant information. Within these roles, for example, the administrator of the school counseling program needs to perform as an advocate or a statesperson for the school counseling program, but also as a source of factual information, not simply opinion, about what is possible for the school counseling program given its current resources or those proposed for the future. To function in these roles, the administrator of the school counseling program must be a life-long learner, immersing him or herself in the important professional literature of school counseling so that its content can be used in an informed and pertinent manner.

Planning Models in School Counseling

In chapter 2, strategic planning and program planning were discussed in general terms, not specific to school counseling. However helpful that information is to the administration of the school counseling program, it is also useful to cite specific applications of planning models in school counseling. Although there are many such applications in the professional literature, two will suffice for our purpose. One is the frame of reference postulated by Gysbers and Henderson (1994) in their book, *Developing and Managing Your School Guidance Program,* second edition. The premise of this book is that school counseling programs or, more specific to the term used in this book, school guidance programs should be established as comprehensive programs, rather than simply a collection of services, "that [are] an integral part of the educational process with a content base of its own" (p. ix). The book is organized around four phases of developing and implementing a comprehensive guidance program. They include planning, designing, implementing, and evaluating. Throughout the book are examples of forms and processes used by specific school districts to implement these four phases of developing and implementing a comprehensive guidance program.

Ripley, Erford, Dahir, and Eschbach (2003) discussed the contemporary need for planning and implementing a 21st-century school counseling program with particular emphasis on the ASCA National Standards for School Counseling Programs (Campbell & Dahir, 1997, p. 9). Their view of planning a comprehensive school counseling program is similar to the concepts of planning discussed in chapter 2. Recognizing that a school counseling program is one of the many programs included in a school system or school building strategic plan, the emphases here are on the planning process specific to the school counseling program's contributions to the larger school or school systemwide strategic plan.

Within this context, it is recommended that the school counseling program begin with a mission statement. In this view, a mission statement identifies the underlying or philosophical aim of a program. A school's or district's mission statement provides the foundation for the school counseling program to become an integral part of the overall school mission and the school community. A quality school counseling program mission statement parallels and supports a school or district's mission statement while bringing a unique "new vision."

The mission statement is intended to provide and express the general direction of the program and its contribution to the institutional-level mission statement of which it is a part. An example of a school counseling program mission statement might read as follows:

> The school counseling program promotes optimal school learning, psychological wellness, and effective student decision-making through comprehensive developmental processes that encourage the academic, personal, social and career development of all students.

A more extensive mission statement has been formulated as part of the national model for school counseling programs. It reads as follows:

> A comprehensive school counseling program is developmental in nature. It is systematic, sequential, clearly defined, and accountable. The foundation of the program is developmental psychology, educational philosophy, and counseling methodology. Proactive and preventive in focus, the school counseling program is integral to the educational program. It assists students in acquiring and using life-long skills through the academic, career, self-awareness, and interpersonal skills. The goal of the comprehensive school counseling program is to provide all students with life success skills. (Campbell & Dahir, 1997, p. 9)

A mission statement might be followed by a brief program definition that discusses the program components, the student competencies to be achieved from the program, the centrality of the program to the school, or the school district's educational program, and it may include directions for program evaluation.

A further planning emphasis suggested by Ripley et al. (2003) is a program rationale that answers questions about the school counseling program asked by students, parents, teachers, or members of the local community. It emphasizes the benefits of the school counseling program and the linkages among the individual program components. In doing so, it also relates the school counseling program to the goals of the school district and discusses how the school counseling program contributes to these goals. The program rationale is a way to clarify the expectation that the school counseling program is not a stand-alone program unrelated to the other activities or goals of the school, but rather is a central component of the school's mission. In another sense, the content of the program rationale can be conceived much as can a list of consumer guidelines.

The mission statement just presented is that which is provided in the ASCA National Model for School Counseling Programs. It also has implications for other theoretical models in its suggestion of the conceptual foundations on which the national model is developed. The national model, although very important in its content and conceptualization, is not the only model that can be derived from current theories. Administrators of school counseling programs come from different theoretical backgrounds and can apply such theoretical perspectives as social learning, constructivist, or cognitive-behavioral theory to the implementation of a particular school counseling program and the reflection of that theoretical perspective in the mission statement. Another feature of the mission statement of the ASCA National Model is its emphasis on the school counseling program being systematic, sequential, clearly defined, and accountable. These words reflect a fundamental change that has occurred in planning for school counseling programs in the last decade or so: the shift from process-based or services-based programs to evidence-based, outcomes-based, or results-based programs. Process- or services-based approaches tend to advocate specific functions or roles to be performed by each counselor in each setting. The emphasis is on the services or functions offered, rather than on the outcomes of these services. The assumption is that if the designated functions or processes are in place, the outcomes of the service or program will be positive. However, if such functions or services are rendered to every counselee in the same manner, there is no assurance that they are being tailored effectively to the needs of the individual clients. Similarly, if counselors do not have specified outcomes or plans to achieve processes or services, it is not clear what results may accrue from their efforts or whether these processes are being applied flexibly and creatively to meet the needs of individual counselees.

In contrast to the process- or services-based approach to planning and implementing school counseling programs, outcomes-, results- or evidence-based approaches contend that, when a clear set of outcomes are to be achieved, there are likely to be several processes that can be implemented to achieve individual outcomes. Focusing on the content of a specific program outcome and then deciding what process or processes will facilitate the counselees' achievement of the outcome sought is different from putting in place a traditional process that may not be relevant to the needs served or the outcomes sought. Unless outcomes for a school counseling program are specified and defined, it is virtually impossible to hold such programs to accountability criteria or to determine their effectiveness.

In line with the increasing emphasis on results-based counseling programs, ASCA has suggested that school success requires students to make successful transitions following high school graduation, and that such outcomes, in turn, involve the acquisition by students of the attitudes, skills, and knowledge essential to postsecondary education and to the competitive workplace of the 21st century. The areas of student development that underlie such student access are also the areas that school counseling programs must facilitate: academic development, career development, and personal-social development. These three broad areas encompass nine standards, each of which includes a list of student competencies and desired learning outcomes that define the specific types of knowledge, attitudes, and skills students will obtain as a result of an effective school counseling program.

The nine National Standards for School Counseling Programs (without the specific student competencies for each standard) by area are as follows:

Academic Development

- Standard A—Students will acquire the attitudes, knowledge, and skills that contribute to effective learning in school and across the lifespan.
- Standard B—Students will complete school with the academic preparation essential to choose from a wide range of substantial postsecondary options, including college.
- Standard C—Students will understand the relationship of academics to the world of work and to life at home and in the community.

Career Development

- Standard A—Students will acquire the skills to investigate the world of work in relation to knowledge of the self and to make informed career decisions.
- Standard B—Students will employ strategies to achieve future career success and satisfaction.

- Standard C—Students will understand the relationship among personal qualities, education and training, and the world of work.

Personal/Social Development

- Standard A—Students will acquire the attitudes, knowledge, and interpersonal skills to help them understand and respect self and others.
- Standard B—Students will make decisions, set goals, and take necessary action to achieve goals.
- Standard C—Students will understand safety and survival skills.

The standards and associated student competencies in each standard suggest that, regardless of the particular emphasis or model of school counseling implemented by a particular school, there is a core of student knowledge, attitudes, and skills that should be basic outcomes of any school counseling program, these can be measured, and they are central to the mission of the school.

A school counseling program plan might include other elements such as descriptions of needs assessments to monitor perceptions of different populations and the perceptions of these groups about what services should be offered and for what purposes. In addition, it is important to include a section in the plan that addresses how the program will be evaluated—how it will meet accountability requirements from the district, state, and accreditation processes or other external groups. It is also important to include affirmation in the plan that the school counseling program is aware of and acts in accordance with federal, state, and local laws as well as relevant ethical codes (e.g., American School Counselors Association; Code of Ethics, 1998).

The program plan should also discuss whether an advisory group or other persons from the community would be used to help the program refine its directions, components, effectiveness, and communication. The plan should also outline the roles, in relation to the school counseling program, of teachers, school psychologists, student assistance program specialists, special educators, principals and assistant principals, community resource professionals, school social workers (in some states called *visiting teachers*), home and school visitors, pupil personnel workers, school nurses, and the support staff of the school counseling programs: secretaries, paraprofessionals, aides, and volunteers.

The program plan should address the school counseling program components, their use, and the expected outcomes (Bowers & Hatch, 2003). Depending on the particular school district, the school counseling program components may differ in name and what is offered. These can be classified in many ways: components that offer direct service to students and those of indirect service to students, including consultation with parents and teachers; outreach to employers on behalf of students' part-time or full-time employment; and conversations with representatives of colleges or other educational opportunities to learn about changing admission standards or financial aid opportunities.

Ripley et al. (2003) identified four components of a comprehensive school counseling program: *guidance curriculum, individual planning, responsive services*, and *system support*. Each of these components includes several methods by which each is operationalized. For example, a *guidance curriculum* might include presentations by counselors in classrooms, workshops offered on particular topics, and regular group guidance sessions tailored to the questions and needs of students at different grade levels. *Individual planning* might include assessment or appraisal of students' aptitudes, interests, values, skills, and achievements; the use of educational, occupational, or social information to help students explore various options or pathways they might pursue; and advising and supporting students as they consider and implement actions related to the school-to-work transition or the school to postsecondary education and training transition. *Responsive services* typically include several types of service delivery: individual counseling, group counseling, consultation, referral, and crisis counseling. *System support*, in general, has to do with the coordination between school counselors or the school counseling program and other groups of individuals or representatives of systems that have significant impact on the lives of students and on whether they avail themselves of the use of the school counseling program. Included here would be such areas as interaction with community and advisory boards; research and development, including program evaluation; professional development, inservice activities, workshops for school counselors, skill updating; and program management that subsumes planning and administrative tasks that "glue together," give continuity and support to the total system-wide school counseling program, the systematic planning of the school counseling program from the elementary, through the middle school, and on to the senior high school; facilitating staffing needs and training; engaging in the development and presentation of reports designed to obtain and allocate needed resources for the school counseling programs; and engaging in public outreach about the school counseling program to relevant advisory groups, Boards of Education members, teachers, parents, and other constituencies.

Although we have lingered longer in this chapter on the process of planning for school counseling than we will for planning in the subsequent chapters and settings, it is absolutely essential that administrators of counseling programs understand the elements of the planning process and their importance. Many of the planning processes identified here as related to school counseling programs, with some modifications, can be adapted to other settings. Planned programs serve as a bridge to translate conceptual models, theories, research, and desired goals into practice. As such they bring into bold relief the staffing needs, resource requirements, professional development for the counselors and other staff, evaluation strategies, and collaborative possibilities. Some of these functions of the counselor as the administrator of the counseling program are discussed in the remaining sections of the chapter.

STAFF RECRUITMENT AND RETENTION

Whatever the plan for a school counseling program is, its ultimate success will only be achieved if the school counselors in the program are able to carry it out. Therefore, one of the most important leadership roles of the administrator of the school counseling program is recruiting school counselors for vacant positions in the program who can add value to the skills already present in the program. It is fair to suggest that if the administrator of the school counseling program is trying to transform a school counseling program, move in new directions, and create new initiatives, one has got to treat the hiring of new counselors as a precious opportunity to bring professional counselors into the program who have the skills and attitudes essential to such transformation.

If the administrator of the counseling program is not able to recruit new counselors, but must achieve new directions for the program with veteran school counselors who have been in the program for several years, the major effort of the administrator of the counseling program must be on professional development. At one level, professional development means assessing the counseling skills that any new initiative in the school counseling program will require and then making arrangements by which the counselors can learn these skills. The preferred format may be workshops or inservice activities that demonstrate the skills to be acquired, the conceptual frame of reference from which they emerge, the evidence of their success in other schools or with other populations, and opportunities to practice these skills under supervision. The administrator for the school counseling program may arrange to have outside consultants conduct such skill development, have the counselors participate in a specific seminar at a local university or attend a statewide or national workshop to acquire the necessary insights, or conduct the professional development activities themselves. It is often more effective for the administrator not to conduct such professional development activities because the aura that sometimes attaches to an outside consultant or a workshop developed by a state or national professional organization may stimulate a greater commitment to learning than that provided by someone with whom one works on a daily basis.

Regardless of whether the administrator of the school counseling program delivers the professional development for the counseling staff, the success of such skill development, information about changes in the program, and opportunities for continuous improvement in the program are related to the enthusiasm and sensitivity of the administrator of the program. Before professional development activities are designed and implemented, the administrator needs to take the time to engage the school counselors in discussions about their needs, skills they would like to acquire, and skills and information necessitated by new program directions to help them become stakeholders in the continuous improvement process. Too often professional development activities for counselors, teachers, and other educational personnel become virtually ritualistic. The participants attend because they have to, not because they expect to gain much of value from the activity. In such cases, it is likely that the school counselors attending have not been asked about the topics or skills of importance to them, the format that would be helpful, or other issues that would make them feel they had an important part in making professional development useful to them.

Professional development activities are obviously not only for veteran school counselors who the administrator of the counseling program is trying to motivate to try new techniques or to accept changes in the program. They are also of importance to counselors new to the program or new to the profession. Depending on the size of the school counseling program in a given school district, there may be several new counselors or, if a small district, perhaps one or two, if any. Whatever the size of the school counseling program, new counselors need to have an orientation to the philosophy, practices, institutional procedures used, and directions of the program. Henderson and Gysbers (1998) included examples of the multiday agenda for new counselor orientation in the Northside Independent School Districts in San Antonio, Texas. Northside encompasses a large number of schools and school counselors in a rapidly growing urban area, in which professional staff members are being added each year as student enrollments grow. In this school district, new school orientation is not a one-time event. It takes place over 6 separate days through the school year (August, September, October, December, February, and May) as different emphases or tasks occur in the school counseling program and as the new school counselors encounter new expectations.

Examples of the agendas (in abridged form) for these days include August (a full day): getting acquainted; the demographics and organization of the Northside School District; the strategic plan of the district; the history of the Guidance Department and its organization; the Director's role; the structure, delivery, and priorities of the comprehensive guidance program; basic resources available; specific information related to each of the components of the comprehensive guidance program (guidance curriculum, individual planning system, responsive services, system support); crisis management, consultation, referral; performance improvement system; changes to anticipate; future meetings; and assignments. In September (a 2-day meeting): beginning of the year reports; system support; calendars; guidance program improvement planning; nonguidance tasks; questions about responsive services; job-related competency standards; and the budget. In October (2-hour meeting): emphases are on the district's standardized testing program, guidance department and testing, parent involvement/ evaluation/consultation, and assignment. In December (2-hour meeting): professional development resources and opportunities, ethical standards, counseling theory, and assignments. In February (2-hour meeting): getting along with students, parents, teachers, administrators, and so on; performance evaluation, supervision, self-evaluation; program evaluation; record keeping; graduate requirements/4-year planning; sample career pathways; and career guidance system. In May (2-hour meeting): end-of-year evaluation and planning for next year, program self-studies/planning, professional development goals, and advice to next year's new counselors (Henderson & Gysbers, 1998).

Although the rendering of the agendas reported here are quite skeletal compared with the material presented by Henderson and Gysbers, several points are of particular importance. One is that orientation for new counselors is comprehensive and planned to answer questions that become sequentially relevant throughout the school year. Second, each of the orientation periods has assignments for the counselors to do for discussion at the next orientation session. These assignments reinforce the continuity of the orientation process. Third, there are emphases in the orientation process about the procedures to be used in the counseling program and the resources available to help if questions and concerns arise.

The emphases included in these new counselor orientations suggest a well-designed and extensive school counseling program with excellent leadership. These emphases also suggest an array of extremely important topics that, with tailoring to the precise characteristics of any school counseling program in the country, are examples of what new school counselors need to know and that need reinforcement with older, more experienced counselors. In small school districts, however, with one or two new counselors, the group orientation meetings with new school counselors are not likely to be feasible. Therefore, such orientation of new school counselors will likely be conducted on a one-to-one basis between the administrator of the school counseling program and the new school counselor.

However it is done in large or small school districts, professional development is critical to developing a team of school counselors who understand the goals and practices that comprise their school counseling program. Such awareness of what the school district and school counseling program aspires to be and its expectations of each school counselor helps to build a culture of achievement among all of the staff members and ensures that each counselor knows what to do, how to do it, and who to turn to if help is needed. Effective professional development reinforces that each school counselor has an important contribution to make to the program and is a person that colleagues, students, parents, and others count on.

Within these perspectives, one can argue that professional development is critical to help school counselors to be life-long learners and to grow in their personal feelings of competence and job satisfaction. In these contexts, personal development opportunities play a major role in both improving the quality of the program and in retaining the professional school counseling staff.

Recruiting the Counseling Staff

As previously discussed, the recruitment of school counselors is a vital ingredient of continuous quality improvement of a school counseling program. Given the ongoing changes in the credentialing of school counselors from state to state, there are a number of issues to consider as recruitment of new staff is being contemplated. Some of these differ from state to state or district to district.

A first step in recruitment is, of course, formulating a position description indicating the functions for which the new school counselor will be responsible, the skills required, the educational level or populations with whom they will work, to whom they will report, and the professional credentials required for the appointment.

Credentials that are appropriate for school counselors vary from state to state. Ordinarily, in any state, the Department of Education certifies any professionals, and sometimes paraprofessionals, who work in schools. Such certification typically includes a review of the academic coursework taken, the supervised counseling training they have had, where they received their training (in state, out of state), whether training was in an approved program, and any relevant experience. In some states, school counselors must first have a degree in teacher education and possibly several years of teaching (typically at least three) before they can be considered for certification as a school counselor, regardless of their specific preparation as a school counselor. In other states, one can be certified as a school counselor without preparation in teacher education or teaching experience. Usually such persons need to have had the preparation required for a school counselor plus an internship experience to acquaint them with the dynamics of the school setting. In some states, there are separate certifications for elementary school, middle school, and secondary school counselors. In some states, school counselors receive certification to function in any grade from

K to 12. In some states, there is separate certification for directors or coordinators of guidance. In some states, there are counselor education programs that have undergone specific approval or accreditation from State Departments of Education to prepare school counselors. Graduates of such programs are typically eligible to receive school counselor certification from the state automatically. Graduates of institutions that have not submitted a proposal for approval by the state may still be eligible for certification as a school counselor, but only after a comprehensive review of their academic and experiential background and its comparison to the state's criteria for school counselor certification. The latter process is essentially the same for out-of-state candidates for school counselor certification.

The administrator of the school counseling program, when recruiting new school counselors, must be certain that the persons to be employed meet the state requirements for certification to function as school counselors. In addition to their professional credentials, most states now require new school counselors to have undergone a security clearance by State Police and the FBI to ensure that they are not a convicted felon, a sexual predator, or involved in substance abuse or distribution.

Although state certification of an individual to function as a school counselor is an essential element of the employment process, which if violated in any way may bring penalties to the individual or the school, there are other related credentials that are sometimes given importance in hiring school counselors in some schools. First, it may be useful to note that when the term *credentialing* is used it can be divided into two emphases: institutional and individual credentialing. Institutional credentialing typically means accreditation or program approval of an entire institution or a program within the institution. For example, the Council for Counseling and Related Educational Programs (CACREP) accredits counselor education programs to prepare school counselors, career counselors, community counselors, counselors in higher education, and supervisors of counselors. The American Psychological Association (APA) approves doctoral programs to prepare counseling, clinical, and school psychologists. Some State Departments of Education grant program approval to counselor education programs that prepare school counselors, supervisors of guidance, or other related personnel. IACS and APA accredit counseling centers.

In addition to accreditation or program approval within institutions, there is also individual credentialing. Ordinarily, this means certification or licensure to provide particular counseling functions. The National Board for Certified Counselors (NBCC) certifies national certified counselors as well as counselors in various specialties (e.g., school, gerontological, supervision, etc.). State Departments of Education certify school counselors, perhaps supervisors/directors of guidance or school counseling, and other educational personnel. Certification at the national level tends to include a review of academic and experiential background and passing a national examination on eight areas of knowledge required to be provided in CACREP-accredited counselor education programs. The result of the credentials review—if the applicants' academic training, supervised counseling, and experience are appropriate and they pass the national NBCC examination—is the eligibility to use the title *National Certified Counselor* or one of the specialties. State certification means that one has met the criteria to perform as a school counselor at a particular educational level (elementary or secondary). The most powerful of the individual credentialing mechanisms is licensure. Licenses to perform as a psychologist or licensed professional counselor are enforced by state statutes that authorize the licensure holder to perform the scope of work defined as appropriate to the particular licensure and to practice in independent practice outside of an institution.

Institutional and individual credentialing processes are not necessarily independent of each other. For example, to be certified as a school counselor in many states requires the applicant to attend a counselor education program that has been state-approved or CACREP-approved. For an applicant to immediately apply for NBCC certification after graduation from a counselor education program requires that the applicant be a graduate of a CACREP-approved counselor education program. If that is not the case, the applicant must wait at least 2 years after graduation to apply for NBCC certification and take the qualifying examination. In many states, applicants for licensure as a counseling, clinical, or school psychologist must have graduated from a doctoral program approved/accredited by the American Psychological Association. In many states that provide for licensed professional counselors, the applicants for this licensure must pass the same NBCC qualifying exam that is used for National Certified Counselors at a score level set by the particular state licensing board.

To return to the administrator of the school counseling program as he or she is determining hiring criteria for school counselors, the administrator of the school counseling program will likely have to answer this question: What difference does credentialing (either institutional or individual) mean? In some sense, the issue is subjective because the empirical data supporting the superior functioning of persons with a given credential, compared with the performance of persons without the credential, have not been collected and tested. Yet as many persons believe, school counselors who pursue credentials beyond those required by the State Department of Education to function as a school counselor in a school are professionals who are committed to life-long learning, to the continuing improvement of their skills, and to being as competent as possible. Such persons are more likely to seek admission to CACREP-accredited counselor education programs that will presumably be teaching state-of-the-art practices, perspectives, and content that are continually under the scrutiny of the accreditation agency to ensure quality preparation. From these perspectives, the administrator of the school counseling program is likely to prefer an applicant who has received certification as a school counselor from the State Department of Education, attended a CACREP-accredited counselor education program, and, perhaps, obtained certification as a National Certified Counselor or state licensure as a Professional Counselor. Obviously, there are school counselors who only meet the criteria to be a certified school counselor, who have excellent skills, but who do not have the time or the desire to pursue additional credentials that may refine or add to their skills. It is within such contexts that the administrator of the school counseling programs and other staff who have interviewed the candidates available must make their decisions.

Supervision of Professional Staff

Another factor that is related to staff retention and professional development of the counseling staff is the quality of supervision provided to each counselor. As suggested in the extended review of concepts and practices of supervision in chapter 2, in many counseling programs, the lead counselor or administrator of the program may serve as the supervisor. This is particularly true in many school counseling programs with a small number of counselors or where there are head counselors or other leaders assigned to each building having school counselors.

Supervision is a process that should be designed to help individual school counselors maintain and enhance their skills in individual and group counseling and related components, assessment, use of technology, presentations in classrooms, or topical workshops, outreach, and other areas of responsibility. Supervision needs to be seen as a process, not an event. As such it should be regularly scheduled and integrated into the activities of the school counseling program. It should not be perceived as burdensome or punitive, but constructive in its goals and implementation.

Supervision of school counselors can take several forms depending on the content to be dealt with. Frequently, emphases in supervision are labeled clinical, developmental, or administrative. In either case, it is important that the supervisor and supervisee jointly assess the latter's development, status, or needs in whatever supervisory emphasis is to be considered. In the supervisory process, the supervisor can often be considered an objective consultant whose experience and training facilitates helping the school counselor being supervised to identify areas of weak skills, understanding, knowledge, effectiveness, as well as strengths. The supervisor, then, intervenes to nurture the supervisees' professional growth and development.

In a unique analysis of a counselor's behavior in a particular school context, Littrell and Peterson (2001) suggested six levels of a supervisory system and the questions each level provides. Such a scheme is, in its own right, a minor planning perspective that could be adapted to supervision as suggested in the following perspective. For example, thinking first of vision, in relationship to larger systems, for whom is the counselor directing his efforts? How does the supervisee see his or her overarching purpose in the school? Second, identity suggests the question who is the counselor within the context? How does the counselor define his or her mission and its relationship to the counselor's beliefs and values? Third, core beliefs and basic values, why does the counselor do what she does within the context in which she works? What is her motivation to apply her capabilities in the various roles she plays? Fourth, capabilities. How does the counselor generate his behavior as a counselor? His capabilities likely provide him the potential to engage in several specific behaviors. What does he choose and why? Fifth, behaviors. What specifically does the counselor do in this context? How do her behaviors and actions interact with the various dimensions of her external context: rules, policies, student needs, demands from other constituents, and so on? Sixth, context. When and where does the counselor perform her job? How does the counselor perceive both the constraints and opportunities that affect her behavior in her current professional context?

Helping the supervisee to examine such questions with his or her supervisor creates a base for viewing the theories and practices in which the counselor engages and their importance. These questions also allow for significant analysis of how and why the counselor chooses to pursue some behaviors and not others.

Supervision of school counselors is not the same as providing therapy or counseling to the supervisee. One outcome of the supervision may be a recommendation that the supervisee seek counseling or therapy from a professional counselor or psychologist in the community or, if the school district has an Employee Assistance Program (EAP), to use such a professional source to obtain whatever psychological interventions might be appropriate. Although in the closeness of interpersonal relationships like supervision it is difficult to avoid dealing with the anxieties, values, stress, and dissatisfaction that school counselor supervisees may be experiencing, the supervision process is not the place to deal with these issues in the depth or psychotherapeutic manner that may be necessary. However difficult it can be, the supervisor must maintain awareness that the supervisory process needs to remain objective, but supportive, and not serve as a substitute for therapy if needed. In this sense, supervision should focus as fully as possible on improving the clinical or process skills of the supervisee, the skills that need to be developed or strengthened more fully, or the administrative policies or guidelines that need to be clarified, learned, or implemented more comprehensively.

It can be argued that inherent in the supervision process is a conflict between therapy and evaluation. In reality, however, the supervisor of the supervisee is likely to be a professional colleague and possibly an evaluator of the supervisee for promotion, retention, salary increases, or other career moves. This is not, then, an environment that emphasizes therapy, but rather an environment in which skill evaluation and learning in assigned areas of responsibility are fostered.

The supervisory environment is a delicate one. Although it is not therapy, the relationship between the supervisor and the school counselor being supervised must be positive and safe. This frequently requires nurturance of this environment by the supervisor before entering into professional criticism, constructive or not. In this context, it is important that the supervisor be seen as credible by the supervisee—as a person who is a competent school counselor with experience and training that can help the supervisee to be a more effective school counselor. The school counseling supervisor should be knowledgeable about theories, purposes, and processes of supervision as well as knowledgeable about counseling theories and process skills, case conceptualizations, referral and crisis intervention policies, professional standards, ethical codes, and school district policies that affect the work of school counselors. They should be quite knowledgeable about the most recent editions of documents such as "Standards for Counseling Supervisors" (Association for Counselor Education and Supervision, 1989a, 1989b) or Ethical Guidelines for Counseling Supervisors (Association for Counselor Education and Supervision, 1995).

Supervisors of school counselor supervisees need to demonstrate a commitment to professional excellence and encourage their supervisees to be knowledgeable about new ideas and techniques, to keep current with the professional literature, and to get involved with professional development activities as they become available in the school district or other professional forums. In many instances, the supervisors are helpful in expanding the professional range of insights possessed by the supervisees. This might include broadening supervisees' knowledge about the needs and interactions with a range of constituents (e.g., students from different population groups, parents, teachers, building and district administrators) and different processes they can use with these constituents. In many cases, supervisors do not critique a colleague's techniques as wrong or inadequate, but rather as one among several ways to address the issues at hand. For example, when working with a supervisee who is developing a case conceptualization of a particular student, the supervisor might offer an alternative set of hypotheses about the problems the student is experiencing, alternative uses of theory to understand these problems, and alternative techniques or processes that may be useful to help with the counseling goals established for the student. Supervision, in this sense, is committed to increasing the supervisee's behavioral repertoire of conceptualizations and interventions available for use.

There is a large volume of literature about the types of supervision that take place in different settings and different styles of supervision that are used by different supervisors. Ladany, Walker, and Melincoff (2001) defined *supervision styles* as the "distinctive manner of responding to supervisees" as well as "the different approaches the supervisors use" (p. 263). A central theme in much of the literature on supervision is that *support* and *direction* are two concepts that pervade the styles of supervision observed.

Hart and Nance (2003) included the concepts of support and direction to characterize different styles of supervision. Specifically, they have developed measures of four major styles of supervision in their instrument, the "Supervisory Styles Inventory." Their measure identifies Style A as a "directive or expert teacher" who provides high direction and low support. High direction focuses on "the supervisee's conceptualization of the client and the counseling techniques used by the supervisee to help the client" (p. 199). Style B is designated as a "supportive teacher" who would provide high support and high direction. In this role, the supervisor is concerned both about the supervisee's feelings about the client and the use of client conceptualization and the supervisee's feelings about the client and the use of client conceptualizations and techniques. Style C would be conceived as a "personal growth style," in which the supervisor would provide high support and low direction, focusing primarily on the supervisee's feelings and thoughts about clients, and give little emphasis to techniques or client conceptualizations in counseling. Style D has been identified as a consultant or integrative role in which the supervisor provides low support and low direction. "The focus is on the supervisee's integration of his or her existing skills with a caring but not intrusive or directive manner" (p. 149). The research of Hart and Nance suggests that different supervisors tend to prefer different styles and that supervisees also differ in their preference for supervisory styles. Further, this research suggests that some supervisors change either the style of supervision they employ or change styles across supervisory sessions based on the initial developmental readiness or the changing readiness of their supervisees. Among the 90 supervisors and 168 supervisees who participated in this study, supervisors typically professed to prefer using a style that would provide high support and low direction (Style C) or both high support and high direction (Style B). In general, however, supervisees preferred to be supervised using a style that would provide high support and high direction (Style B).

Although the purpose here is not to explore supervision in school counseling or supervision, in general, in depth, suffice it to say that the administrator of the school counseling program needs to include the process of supervision in his or her repertoire of leadership or management tools.

Regardless of whether the administrator actually does the supervision, he or she must understand the process, perceive its likely styles and outcomes, and create a culture in which supervision becomes an integral part of the growth and professional development of the counselors in the program.

The administrator of the school counseling program also needs to determine how supervision will be done and the nature of the facility or equipment, if that is a relevant issue. For example, if the school counselor receiving supervision is expected to bring to each supervisory session the session notes and a case study of a student client with whom the counselor is having particular difficulty or resistance, there is no need for a special facility or equipment. In this case, supervision is primarily a matter of oral problem solving about possible alternative conceptualizations of the student, his or her resistance to counseling, and various techniques that might be useful in improving the counseling process and outcomes. However, if the focus on the school counselor supervisee is primarily on the quality of the interaction between the school counselor and student clients, then it may be necessary to periodically audiotape or videotape selected sessions so that the dynamics of the school counselors' relationships and practices with student clients can be looked at quite closely and constructive criticism can be targeted to particular counseling interview segments that could be done better or differently. If taping (audio or video) is being used in the school counseling program, there are both facility and ethical issues at hand. In the first instance, there needs to be available a room or office equipped with audio or video playback equipment so that the tapes of the school counselors' working with student clients can be heard or seen and then analyzed. In addition, depending on school district policy, it is likely that parents will need to be asked for permission to have their child taped while in counseling, and ethical guidelines pertinent to the confidentiality of the tapes and their security must be observed.

Supervision, then, is a significant element of leadership and management for the administrator of the school counseling program. Because styles of supervision often reflect the particular counseling theories that a given supervisor embraces, and because such styles are located on a continuum of primary attention to a supervisee's feelings and concerns about his or her student clients to an almost total focus on teaching the supervisee how to improve particular skills in individual or group counseling, assessment, the use of technology in counseling, or other processes, the administrator needs to have understanding of the supervisory literature, the differences and similarities between counseling and supervision theory, and the purposes that supervision should serve in his or her specific school districts.

As discussed in chapter 2, supervision takes time, requires that records of the length and contents of the supervision must be kept, and supervision sessions planned for the school year just as other aspects of the school counseling programs are planned. In terms of both time management and quality controls, both the supervisor and school counselor must come to each supervision session prepared with relevant information, case studies, tapes, and questions that are relevant to the guidelines under which the supervisory process is to be conducted. However it is conceived, the supervision process needs to be a professional, growth-producing experience.

Not all supervision in school counseling will focus on clinical or developmental emphases. There is also likely to be an emphasis on administrative supervision. The emphases here may take many forms: the supervisees' professional goals; the quality of their report writing; their work habits; their commitment to the counseling profession as a career pathway; their understanding of and compliance with rules and regulations about crisis intervention, suicide threats, violent behavior, contact with parents, and contact with outside agencies; the fit of their assigned responsibilities that are noncounseling in nature with their competencies and interests; their understanding and implementation of ethical guidelines; and their interpersonal relations with students, teachers, parents, administration, and community representatives.

When administrators of school counseling programs are engaged in the supervision of administrative elements of their supervisees' roles, the supervisor may take on a mentoring role in some cases, an evaluative role in still other cases, and a problem-solving role as various topics unfold.

Supervision of Noncounselor Support Staff

Neither clinical, developmental, nor administrative supervision is confined to the school counselors in a program. Paraprofessionals, clerical support personnel, volunteers, and others who contribute directly to the school counseling program also need administrative supervision. Whether these persons are involved in the program as data-processing clerks, career technicians, receptionists, secretaries, bookkeepers, or in other technical assistance roles, they, like school counselors, need to be specifically informed about their roles in the program; the standards for performance in these roles; the mission of the program; ethical guidelines and dilemmas; and the ways they are to interact with students, teachers, and administrators, visitors, and persons telephoning the program. Because it is likely that most of these persons will work in relatively close proximity to the administrator of the school counseling program, their presence needs to be acknowledged in friendly, but professional, ways. As school counseling program meetings are conducted, these persons in support roles should be included whenever possible, with the exception of personnel actions or confidential, personal information. If appropriate, the administrator of the school counseling program should convene periodic meetings with the support staff to listen to and address their questions. In the interim, brief chats with individual support staff members about how their tasks are going, any questions they might have, or issues that concern them likely would be welcomed and add much to reinforcing a culture of decisiveness and joint direction toward meeting the goals of the program.

Performance Evaluation of Counselors and Others

In many school districts, the administrator of the school counseling program may be expected to complete for each school counselor a performance evaluation form that has been designed by a school district, State Department of Education, or professional association. In other instances, the administrator of the school counseling program may need to develop and complete a performance evaluation system that includes data about school counselor performance in assigned responsibilities from supervision sessions, student feedback, teachers with whom the counselor has consulted, and the counselors. Whatever form the performance evaluation of counselors takes, it requires consideration of a number of salient points.

The performance evaluation of school counselors must begin each school year with the job description assigned to each counselor. These data should constitute much of the content of an evaluation instrument, if used, and any judgments made by the administrator about the school counselor. Thus, performance evaluation is not an abstract and ambiguous process, but one that compares and contrasts relevant data about the individuals' performance with standards for job performance set by the school district or, indeed, the school counseling program.

In a major way, the job description for each counselor is the basis for quantifying or giving relative weight to each function the counselor is expected to perform. In this context, the evaluation of the school counselor is focused on individual professionalism as expressed by the quality with which they function in each role assigned and the quantity of their performance in these roles. Thus, in a performance evaluation form, objectives can be defined that measure the individual counselor's role and indicators of quality at different performance levels identified. The point is that the bases for performance review of a school counselor's role should be objective and measurable on a scale that can be summarized and interpreted in relation to judgments about the quality and intensity with which the school counselor has completed his or her assigned roles. Often such indicators can be related to the percentage of time a counselor or other staff member expends in discharging a particular role and whether there is evidence that the counselor has demonstrated specific competencies relevant to the roles they are assigned (e.g., classroom guidance, crisis counseling, individual student planning, system support). Both time and competency evaluations can be related to those expected to occur in the roles assigned (Ripley, Erford, Dahir, & Eschbach, 2003).

Examples of these elements of a school counselor performance review are reflected in the Program Audit section of the ASCA National Model for School Counseling Programs. They include such selected items as (under Use of Time): "The counselor's total time spent in each component of the delivery system has been compared to the ASCA National Model recommendations" (p. 118); (under Counselor Performance Evaluation): "The school counselor's performance evaluation contains basic standards of practice expected of school counselors implementing a comprehensive school counseling program. These performance standards serve as both a basis for counselor evaluation and a means for counselor self-evaluation." "Criteria. 16.1 is written to assess the school counselor's ability to understand and implement the foundation of the comprehensive school counseling program based on ASCA National Standards . . ." "16.2 is written to assess the counselor's ability to implement the delivery system (i.e., guidance curriculum, individual planning with students, responsive services, system support) . . ." "16.4 is written to assess the school counselor's use of professional communication within the school community" . . . "16.7 is written to assess the school counselor's ability to be a leader, student advocate, and systems change agent" (p. 120). The data available about each school counselor's performance must be summarized, analyzed, and placed into feedback that can be provided to the school counselor in oral and written forms. Such evaluation feedback needs to be discussed in terms of the assigned responsibilities of the counselor, the criteria used to assess different levels of job performance, implications of the job performance review for continuation in the position, for salary recommendations, if any, as well as identifying goals for improvement of skills or knowledge and ways to achieve such goals. Both the administrator and school counselor must be clear about what is being evaluated and the results.

Job performance evaluation typically has multiple goals. The primary purpose is to engage in continuous quality improvement of the school counseling program by periodically assessing school counselors' performance and providing feedback designed to help them improve that performance. If each counselor and each support staff member is helped to identify areas in which their performance can improve and they execute plans to incrementally achieve such goals, then the aggregate effect of such individual performance reviews is to improve the total school counseling program. As such, evaluation results can be used as a framework for creating staff development and technical assistance programs for the school counselors.

A further purpose for school counselor performance review, however, is to have a mechanism that can identify and provide evaluative data relevant to the termination of a counselor who continues to demonstrate unsatisfactory performance. The latter performance review outcome is the most difficult for counselors who become administrators to implement, and it is difficult for any school counselor or support person to accept. Therefore, the performance review system must be as transparent as possible. Those being evaluated must know what is being evaluated, why, for whom, and how the results will be used. School counselors being reviewed must know that the process of evaluation is as fair and objective as possible. It must be as clear as it can be made that the performance review process is not discriminatory, arbitrary, or capricious, and that it adheres to the ethical and legal guidelines that pertain to such processes.

PROGRAM EVALUATION

Although performance review of school counselors and other support team members can be considered as independent from program evaluation, it is important to acknowledge that program evaluation is also, at least indirectly, an assessment of the effectiveness of school counselors in conducting the functions or interventions that comprise a given school counseling program. Unlike performance evaluation, program evaluation is not focused on the performance of individual counselors, but rather on the effectiveness of the interventions used and the impact of the total school counseling program on the goals assigned to it. Thus, in an evaluative sense, program evaluation can be crafted to evaluate one or both of two general themes. In technical terms, these two themes can be described as *summative* or *formative evaluations*.

In an oversimplified sense, *summative evaluation* is designed to assess whether the total program of school counseling is achieving the student behaviors, attitudes, knowledge, and skills that are expected to result from the school counseling program. *Formative evaluation* asks more refined questions about whether each function or intervention is contributing to the total impact of the program or are some interventions being undertaken, but not yielding the results expected? Formative evaluation can be conceived as a way to reduce the interventions in a school counseling program to those that are most powerful and effective. Depending on the design of either a summative or formative evaluation, it can be determined whether a school counseling program or specific interventions used (e.g., individual counseling, group guidance, assessment, job shadowing, specific support groups, computer-assisted career guidance systems) are equally effective for all student populations or more effective with some groups and not others. For example, one evaluation of an elementary school program was designed to determine whether elementary school students who were referred and received school counseling improved and in what ways

(Lavoritano & Segal, 1992). Improvement of counseled students was assessed by pre- and posttest score differences on a self-esteem instrument measuring self-evaluation of competence/adequacy in academics, social acceptance, physical appearance, athletics, behavior, and overall self-worth. A second component of the study was designed to determine whether there were differences between students referred for school counseling and those who were not. The research results indicate that students referred for counseling were significantly different in their characteristics than those who were not referred for counseling. It was found that more males than females were referred for counseling, and significantly more children from single-parent homes, retained students, underachievers, and those who had been suspended were referred for counseling. Change related to counseling was found in both behavioral conduct and scholastic competence variables. In particular, the perceptions of counseled children of their scholastic competence were significantly changed. Several implications of this research study were useful to consider. First, it demonstrated that school counseling does have the potential to affect students' perceptions particularly in relation to scholastic competence. From a management view, however, the study demonstrated which groups of students were being referred to counselors and for what reasons. Further, it was concluded that the school counselors should emphasize helping students make a satisfactory school adjustment, rather than try to have an impact on all aspects of a child's life. In summary, this research helped demonstrate to school counselors that they could have and were having a positive effect on the lives of referred children. Further, the results provided information about the efficacy of the school counseling program's behavioral techniques and how the program could be shaped to be more effective with particular groups of children in the future.

Administrators of school counseling programs need to manage the conduct of program evaluations regardless of whether they actually execute the evaluations or consult with external evaluators whose expertise is purchased to help design and implement the program evaluation. In any human service organization, the terms *accountability*, *efficacy*, and *management* have become constants. In an era of limited resources for education, social services, and health and psychological services, policymakers and institutional or system-wide administrators want to be sure that the funds allocated to the programs within their organization are being used effectively and the impact of these programs can be demonstrated. It typically falls to the administrator of the school counseling program to ensure that appropriate data, analyses, and summarization of the program evaluation results are acquired, compiled, and reported.

Within school counseling programs, it has become widely accepted that a program evaluation plan for establishing and maintaining an effective school counseling program that is ongoing, monitored, and periodically revised is essential. Accreditation bodies, State Departments of Education, legislative support for school counseling, public policy, as well as the mandates of individual school systems increasingly require that school counseling programs provide evaluative data about their contributions to a school district's mission and to the success of students in their adjustment, planning, and achievement.

Particularly in schools, but in other settings as well, the methodology and foci of program evaluation, in historical terms, typically consisted of reports describing the services offered, percentage of time each counselor spent on each assigned activity, and how many students, parents, teachers, or others were served by the school counseling program. As we have discussed in chapter 2 and elsewhere in this book, an increasing crescendo of theorists and researchers have argued that the evaluation of counseling programs, in any setting, should focus on program results, not simply on describing program services offered to students and other constituents. Programs that are results-based or competency-based tend to wed theory, practice, and evaluation in an integrated way that allows for summative and formative results and useful management information. In addition, they are planned programs that identify the domains for which the school counseling program is expected to make a contribution. For example, in the ASCA National Model for School Counseling Programs (1997) previously cited, the three major domains are academic development, career development, and personal-social development. There are three standards for each domain, and in the full report, the competencies and indicators that underlie these standards and domains that shape the content and responsibility of the school counseling program are described. Thus, in planned and comprehensive school counseling programs, planned programs define the outcomes or results, including competencies and other indicators that translate the program content into student behavior to be achieved and indicate the evaluative methods that will affirm such outcomes have been achieved. In a formative sense, the intervention strategies used in such planned programs can vary in relation to the intended outcomes, and these can be evaluated in terms of their impact on the outcomes to be achieved. Such a process yields different, more important, evaluative data and more evidence of accountability than data which simply indicate that certain interventions are in place, but not whether these interventions make specific contributions to achieving the outcomes sought (Herr, Cramer, & Niles, 2004).

Borders and Drury (1992) outlined this process effectively:

> The first step in a student-competency driven evaluation plan consists of writing specific competency statements for various learning domains (e.g. educational, career, personal, social) and learning goals (e.g. knowledge, skills, self-

awareness, attitudes). Student competency statements are consistent with the mission statements of the school and the counseling programs and reflect developmentally appropriate tasks.

Subsequent steps in an evaluation plan are based on the student competency statements: (a) conducting needs assessments to determine student strengths and efficiencies, (b) writing program goals, (c) setting priorities, (d) choosing and implementing program activities, and (e) evaluating program effectiveness. Finally, to complete the sequence, evaluation outcomes are "recycled" through program renewal efforts. Thus, the formulation of student competency statements provides the initial structure for program goals and activities, whereas evaluation of targeted student competencies and related program activities drive further program development. (p. 493)

Cost–Benefit Analysis

In addition to managing personnel and program evaluation, there is a further element subsumed under program evaluation that is becoming an increasingly important management role: the analysis of costs and benefits for the program. In general, in any setting, institutional-level administrators or policymakers expect two things of school counseling or school guidance programs. The first is for the school counseling program to be instrumental in achieving specific goals that contribute to the school or school district's mission or strategic planning statements. For example, if the school strategic plan specifies that the major goal of the school district is to ensure that each student is "learning ready" and "achieving to capacity," then clearly the school counseling program must embrace this mission as a major emphasis in its responsibilities and include functions likely to promote such goals: provide group instruction in study skills, work individually with students who are experiencing academic adjustment problems, and help students see the interactions between achievement in academic subjects and requirements in different occupations or postsecondary educational pathways. Similarly, if the school district includes in its mission statement and strategic plan the need for major attention to the early identification and treatment or better integration into the life of the school of different student groups (e.g., minority and majority, children with disabilities), more effective communication with parents, the need to create new initiatives that will reduce school dropouts or classroom misconduct or bullying, the school counseling program must address and act on these goals as part of their mission and be clear about how they will contribute to these larger institutional issues.

The second expectation of institutional-level administrators and other policymakers is that the school counseling program will be cost-effective, returning more in economic and social benefits than they cost. Such an expectation for positive cost–benefit ratios is not always well articulated and always tricky in its execution. Nevertheless, institutional administrators who see the school counseling program as only a cost center, an expense, a consumer of resources, rather than a benefit that exceeds its cost, are likely to be prone to keep the program as small and inexpensive as possible and often as a target for cuts. However, an institutional administrator who understands the added value of a school counseling program (e.g., in retaining students who might otherwise drop out of school before graduation, reducing vandalism or damage to school property, achieving the academic standards required of their coursework rather than needing to attend summer school or being held back [failed], requiring a repeat of the same school year) realizes that each of these outcomes has both a dollar figure and a social benefit attached to them.

The example of school dropouts illustrates the point well. Across the states and local areas of the United States, schools receive thousands of dollars in school aid from state allocations for each student enrolled in the school. When a student drops out of school, the aid for that student stops. Let us assume that 20 students drop out of the school each year, and each of these students would have brought $5,000 per year to the school's budget if these students remained in school until graduation. The cost to the school budget would be $100,000 lost from these dropouts in a given year. If the students drop out in 10th or 11th grades, the school would be losing $5,000 for each of the years they are no longer part of the school population. However, if the school counseling program, through referrals or other mechanisms, had been instrumental in identifying and counseling these students about the issues that were motivating them to consider dropping out and, in the end, supporting them to remain in school, not only would the school and larger society enjoy social benefits from having these students remain in school and graduate, but the school would have the tangible benefit of the state allocation of $5,000 per student remaining in its budget. Certainly, the aggregate financial benefit from helping 20 students to stay in school is larger than the salary of one or two school counselors per year, suggesting that the school counseling program is not a consumer of resources, but rather a generator of resources.

One can draw similar parallels in situations where aggressive and angry students have vented their frustration and rage on school property, causing thousands of dollars in damage to equipment, furniture, or building. A school counseling program that works intensely with students who have been identified as potentially violent or destructive may provide anger management, stress management, or conflict negotiation groups that may reduce vandalism and the costs to the school for property damage that has occurred in previous years.

The issues involved in cost–benefit analyses related to the school counseling program is first being clear about the costs of the program—the aggregate cost of salaries of counselors and support personnel, resources (tests, book, films, and other materials), inservice, computers, and other equipment. The second issue is how we put a dollar value on the outcomes that accrue from our work and what data need to be collected to validate the economic or other benefits that result from the school counseling program. What functions have been most powerful in achieving these results, and how do we compare these approaches in their costs and impact when different types of intervention are compared as to their impact on particular counseling goals (e.g., changes in particular knowledge, attitudes, behaviors)? In one sense, a step-wise regression question is being asked. In this formative question, the question is how much change in knowledge, attitudes, and behavior can be explained by each intervention, and which intervention makes no impact on such variables? As such questions are asked and assessed, it is possible to provide the budget allocated to the school counseling program to be focused on those interventions that are least expensive and most effective in attaining the outcomes desired from the school counseling program. It is worth noting here that cost–benefit analyses can also serve as the bases for management decisions. For example, in the area of career interventions, research suggests that individual counseling is the most powerful for hour of intervention, but it is also more expensive than other group-oriented interventions. In such a situation, if individual and group career counseling were both under consideration for support and the outcomes they produced favored individual counseling, but group counseling was also found useful and productive of many of the same outcomes as individual career counseling, it is quite possible that an administrator of the school counseling program might decide to support group counseling as a primary intervention rather than individual counseling. Such a decision might hinge on the view that one can simultaneously provide career counseling to multiple clients (perhaps 6 to 8 or 10 or more) in groups much less expensively per hour than is true of individual counseling. In such a situation, group counseling could be seen as the most economic way to reach the largest number of clients, although some power of the intervention would likely be lost. In such circumstances, the provision of individual counseling would likely be much more restricted to only the neediest of students, rather than to every student.

For the administrator of a school counseling program, the need for a new and different vocabulary and mentality is associated with cost–benefit analyses. At base, such a concept has to do with "the return on investment" or the "added value" that can be claimed for a school counseling program or, indeed, a counseling program in other settings. Positive empirical effects about the impact of school counseling interventions on desired student behavior, knowledge, or attitudes imply costs and benefits that need to be more fully explicated. As they are, it is likely that the administrator of the school counseling program, in his or her advocacy role for the program, can confidently contend that the school counseling program is not simply a budget expenditure. It also generates important benefits for individual students, for the learning environment, and for the school system at large.

SUMMARY

The professional school counselor as an administrator of school counseling programs in a particular building or in a school district has a challenging assignment. This is true for several reasons. One of these is likely to be the tension in many schools between the administrator of the counseling program and the principal of a building or another district-level administrator about who should supervise the individual school counselor and what they do. This problem may be exacerbated across a district with several buildings, in each of which the principal may want counselors to perform specific tasks rather than engage in a seamless, fluid school counseling program from K to 12. Beyond these issues, the administrator of the school counseling program may need to ensure that the school counseling program plan, as a subset of the district strategic plan, is clearly defined as contributing to the school district goals. Thus, the professional school counselor as administrator needs to be a planner, an advocate, a recruiter and supervisor of staff, an integrator of technology, and a stimulus to program evaluation, particularly with an emphasis on the added value of the school counseling program as defined by such techniques as cost–benefit analysis.

In many ways, the professional school counselor as an administrator of a school counseling program must be an interpreter of the school counseling program—indeed a statesperson in its behalf. This means that the administrator, as both a leader and manager, must be able to discuss trends in the field, national models of school counseling, evidence-based interventions, and approaches to the deployment of school counselors that tailor their strengths and emphases to the particular characteristics, demographics, and needs of individual school buildings or the district at large.

CHAPTER

4

Leadership and Management
of University Counseling Centers

CONTEXT

> *If your son or daughter is in college the chances are almost one in two that*
> *he or she will become depressed to the point of being unable to function;*
> *one in two that he or she will have regular episodes of binge drinking; and*
> *one in ten that he or she will seriously consider suicide.*
> . —Kadison and DiGeronimo (2004, p. 1)

The message in Kadison's chilling quote, although shocking to most, has become all too familiar to administrators of counseling centers and their staff. For well over a decade, this message has emerged as the formidable challenge, at times daunting, for counseling center staff as they attempt to meet the needs of university students. At the center of the maelstrom, the center director is charged with navigating a course of responsive action, often in a context of restricted staffing and marginal budgets, and an ever-changing student/campus landscape.

In the early days in higher education in the United States, the "counseling service" consisted of a responsibility usually assigned to one person—psychology faculty member, health service physician, nurse, or some other logical campus-based official. In a vintage letter dated January 2, 1934, Health Service Director J. P. Ritenour advanced an appeal to Pennsylvania State University President R. D. Hetzel reflecting the clarion call for a more formalized mental health service: -

During these days when because of a great variety of factors there is so much turmoil, unrest, uncertainty and indecision in the minds of mature individuals,

103

it is not at all surprising to find the reactions to their perturbed state of mind imitated by some of the vacillating members of the younger generation, many of whom are in our colleges. Because of the enigma some of the youths on the campuses of our colleges turn out to be, there is a distinct tendency on the part of those in authority to provide some agency to whom the perplexed may go for guidance and aid in the solution of their mental problems.

Since our campus is no exception and undoubtedly has its share of boys and girls who are groping in the dark, as it were, for help in answering their mental problems, it seems to us that consideration should be given to the matter, with the idea in mind of securing, a member of the health service staff to devote services primarily to assisting students in making proper mental adjustments and adapting themselves more readily to the training for which they are best fitted. It seems to us that such a man [sic] would be of almost incalculable value to the students and to the college, and would place the college among the leaders in this line of endeavor. (p. 1)

Contained within Dr. Ritenour's tortuous sentence structure was the clear recognition of the presence of mental illness and maladjustment within a segment of the student body, and one administrator's seminal appeal to mobilize a university's response to the same.

More recently, the lone voice of Dr. Ritenour has been replaced by the clang of media reports on the challenges to university counseling centers in responding to the needs of today's students. From the *New York Times* (Duenwald, 2004), *USA Today* (MacDonald, 2004), and the *Chronicle of Higher Education* (Hoover, 2003), to alumni news magazines, radio, and TV, one need not look far to see the keen interest in the role of the counseling center in responding to increasing numbers of students at risk. The plethora of articles—primarily revolving around high-profile cases of suicide, violence, and alcohol abuse—have elevated the profile of counseling centers that heretofore have been quietly embedded in the array of university student services. Unfortunately, the attention paid to the more dramatic, headline-grabbing incidents belies the true strength and importance of a comprehensive counseling center; that is, to provide not only remedial services and crisis intervention, but also to provide developmentally oriented activities such as psychoeducational outreach programming, developmental counseling, teaching, training, and research.

Over time the mission of the counseling center has evolved to the point where service to many students goes beyond the provision of supportive counseling to deal with developmental concerns or the "transient situational disturbances" most prevalent in the student population. Whereas many students still seek assistance for mild and predictable problems, the trend, as consistently documented by annual surveys of counseling center directors (Gallagher, 2004), is toward an increasing number of students with more entrenched, serious emotional concerns. As Levine and Cureton

(1998) observed in their book, *When Hope and Fear Collide*, students remain frightened. In fact the results of their national survey of undergraduate students underscored the prevalence of student fears ranging from family disruption to emotional and financial problems. The same year, Archer and Cooper (1998) noted that,

> compared with students in the past, students arrive on campus with more problems as a result of dysfunctional family situations, with more worries and anxieties about the future and about the serious problems facing them in modern society, with an increased awareness of their own personal demons, and with a greater willingness to seek psychological and psychiatric help. (p. 6)

The prevailing world climate of instability, violence, and mistrust only serves to increase the prevailing quality of vulnerability felt by many students. Be that as it may, centers have worked hard to continue to provide a variety of programs in addition to crisis intervention and treatment for the more seriously disturbed. Thus, most counseling centers strive to retain their rich tradition of providing psychoeducational programs, developmental activities, consultation, training, and research as vital parts of their program offerings.

To be sure, counseling centers have come a long way from the early days and have taken a variety of forms in service to "the boys and girls groping in the dark," although all typically endeavor to provide certain basic functions and services:

- Individual counseling and psychotherapy
- Group counseling and psychotherapy
- Consultation with staff, faculty, students, and campus units and organizations
- Educational outreach programs (including Web-based)
- Psychodiagnostic testing
- Teaching and training (including practica, graduate assistantships, and internships for psychologist and social work trainees)

Finally, some counseling centers are mandated to provide more comprehensive services including career counseling and advising, educational enhancement and learning support services, human resource development and counseling, nationally standardized testing programs, student disability services, and other responsibilities as dictated by campus climate, need, and the preference of the administration.

At the nexus of the student in need and the resources designated to meet those needs is the counseling center director. As a result, the challenge to any director is to anticipate and/or react to the changing student culture while maintaining and improving the broad range of services, programs, and activities that have traditionally been part and parcel of university counseling center offerings. The counseling center director at any institution must juggle a variety of roles, maintaining organizational stability and confidence among staff members while catering to the broader university constituency, which looks to the center for leadership in enhancing student mental health. Moreover, counseling center directors are called on to be ever mindful of the institution's mission, ensuring that the goals for the counseling center are in accord with the intentions of the institution as articulated by immediate supervisors, chief student affairs officers, and the administration at the highest levels. To be sure, directing a university counseling center on today's college campus, given an increasingly complex and multicultured student body and an ever-changing campus context, is a formidable challenge. In addition to the technical demands on the counseling center director, there are personal demands best expressed by Bennis (1989):

> Leadership is first being, then doing. Everything the leader does reflects what he or she is. (p. 141)

THE ROLE OF THE DIRECTOR

What Mark Schoenberg (1978) observed nearly three decades ago remains true even today: "It is curious that the position per se of the director of the college or university counseling center has not been the subject of extensive investigation. The position has not been studied in any detail at all or the position doesn't lend itself to generic investigation" (p. 134). As a rationale for the absence of research related to the role of the director, Schoenberg suggested that the variation of the director's role from institution to institution defies categorization. Be that as it may, today the role may be more identifiable as counseling centers become increasingly specialized and, in some manner, narrowed in their focus on service to the clinical needs of students. In any case, most would agree that certain commonalities among directors apply. For instance, chief among the director's responsibilities is to build relationships, promote the value of the service to its campus constituency, capitalize on opportunities to consult with a broad range of members of the administration, articulate the emotional climate of the campus and the needs of the students, and be available in the forefront as a point person in times of crisis and campus upheaval.

There is no doubt that a center's best asset in times of fiscal retrenchment is a strong director with an enduring reputation for service to the campus community. To accomplish the same, the director needs both credentials and credibility. Internal to the center, the director must have the clinical grounding to demonstrate knowledge and leadership in the primary domains of activity, including individual and group counseling, consultation, training, teaching, and research. Moreover, in the public arena, he or she should be viewed as knowledgeable and articulate on clinical matters, a good consultant who works easily and efficiently with individuals in need of assistance, a leader who understands the politics of the institution and is politically savvy, and an informed and reliable manager of the budget. Unfortunately, save for the clinical domain, the balance of requisite director qualities is almost never addressed in one's training as a psychologist or counselor. Thus, the essential qualities listed next are absorbed primarily through study, mentoring, and on-the-job experience.

The essentials of the director's role are briefly described by the following:

Leadership—To develop, articulate, and engender support for a common vision and mission.

Administration—To develop the center's policies and procedures; to justify, generate, and maintain a budget; and to seek, hire, and retain qualified staff.

Supervision—To establish an administrative structure and assign supervisory and coordinative responsibilities, to promote the value and maintenance of continuous performance review, and to provide for a program of staff development.

Campus and Community Relations—To establish and validate the importance of the counseling center function vis-à-vis the academic mission of the institution, to provide ongoing education to the campus community regarding the scope of services offered by the center, and to develop strong working relationships with members of the university administration and key colleagues in academic and staff positions.

THE ASSOCIATION FOR UNIVERSITY AND COLLEGE COUNSELING CENTER DIRECTORS

Although it may be "lonely at the top," arguably the most valuable resource for counseling center director support and management skill development is the collection of administrators comprising the primary counseling center directors' organization: The Association for University and College Counseling Center Directors (AUCCCD). A review of typical programs offered at the AUCCCD annual conference offers testimony to the organization's focused effort to meet the need for training that has been critical for any professional counselor's move into the director's role: "Time Management Strategies for Directors," "Administrative Power: Who's Got It?," "An Administrator's View of Counseling," "Counseling Center Leadership and

Management: Developing a Management Style," and "Visions, Values, and Skills: Leading Counseling Centers in Changing Times." In response to the need for management skill development, in 1996, AUCCCD formed a director training and development task force entitled "Elements of Excellence." The mission of the Elements of Excellence task force has been: "To provide impetus and structure for the organization to address leadership development, management skills development, and creative thinking about current and future issues affecting counseling centers in a coordinated, consistent and collaborative fashion" (AUCCCD, 2005). An important outcome of the task force's work has been the establishment of the Annual Administrative Institute, which provides an opportunity to enhance learning in planning, resource development, budget, personnel, politics, campus environment, and related professional issues.

Illustrative of the resources offered at the Annual Administrative Institute is a Self-Assessment Questionnaire designed for new or relatively new directors, which itemizes the salient issues faced by counseling center directors who are new to their roles and responsibilities (see Table 4.1). The Elements of Excellence task force generated a list of director competencies and administrative checkpoints that promote effective counseling center management. The Management/Competency Checklist (see Table 4.2) outlines the questions and qualities to be satisfied for the effective management of a center (AUCCCD, 2005). Although the items serve as a comprehensive goal set for the administrator, suffice it to say that progress within each of the management/competency domains, all other things being equal, will ensure a quality counseling service while separating the best administrators from the rest.

RELATIONSHIP TO THE UNIVERSITY ADMINISTRATION

As discussed throughout this book, counseling programs or centers rarely operate in an insular fashion. On the contrary, the counseling center administrator strives to ensure that the center is embedded in the larger institution, thus inspiring the pursuit of planning, program development, budgeting, and staff recruitment that is consistent with the institutional mission and policies. At most universities, the counseling center director will report to the chief student affairs officer, typically a vice president, but occasionally the dean of students or another administrator in direct line to the chief student affairs officer. Directors may expend considerable energy seeking to understand and interpret the actions and intentions of administrators, with a view toward developing a unit strategic plan that addresses departmental needs and goals while remaining supportive of and related to the university mission. Whereas in previous times it might have been argued

TABLE 4.1
AUCCCD ADMINISTRATIVE INSTITUTE:
Survival Tools for Director—Sponsored by Elements of Excellence Task Force

Self-Assessment Questionnaire

Participants: Please complete this self-assessment questionnaire prior to attending the institute. This exercise will enable you to focus on specific administrative skills, acquaint you with the various components of the institute, and provide you with a global sense of what you can gain from the institute experience.

A. LEADERSHIP DEVELOPMENT
   1. Why I became a director (include in your brief statement the values that you embrace that are important for you in being a director):
   2. Identify a leader whom you admire. What characteristics or qualities do you admire in that person?

B. MANAGEMENT SKILLS

	Strongly Agree	Agree	Disagree	Strongly Disagree
1. Budget				
My center's budget is adequate.	1	2	3	4
I understand the institutional budget documents I receive.	1	2	3	4
I know how money is formally allocated in my institution. Describe briefly:	1	2	3	4
I know how to seek new funds. Describe briefly:	1	2	3	4
I am expected to generate or raise funds for my center beyond my institutional budget.	Yes	No		

   2. Personnel
   What are your three most pressing personnel concerns (professional, support and trainee staff):
   Describe a personnel dilemma you have had:

	Strongly Agree	Agree	Disagree	Strongly Disagree
I am satisfied with current staff morale.	1	2	3	4
I am satisfied with the rate of turnover of staff.	1	2	3	4
I have the ability and/or resources to deal with difficult staff.	1	2	3	4
I have difficulty managing conflict among staff members.	1	2	3	4

C. CREATIVE VISIONING

Our center has a strategic plan/goals and objectives, etc.	Yes	No
Our mission is embedded in the institutional plan.	Yes	No

   What are the three biggest challenges your Center faces?

D. AFTER REVIEWING THIS SELF-ASSESSMENT, THE AREAS OF GROWTH TO WHICH I SHOULD ATTEND INCLUDE:

TABLE 4.2

Elements of Excellence Task Force Management and Competency Checklist

1. What Do We Do?
   - *Accountability*
     - Productivity
     - Cost per program
     - Cost per unit of service
   - *Tracking Systems* for all functions or "product lines"
     - Client data, outreach contacts, workshops, self-help, training
   - *Data Systems*
     - Client demographics
     - Client problems—symptoms, diagnoses
     - Appointments by type—individual, group, urgent/crisis, intake
     - Appointment status—kept, no show, cancel, reschedule
     - Staff productivity—staff time by program or task
     - Contracts/goals for staff allocation of time/effort
2. How Well Do We Do It?
   Do we do what we say we do? Can we measure what we do? How do we measure it?
   - *Quality Assurance*
     - File review—complete, timely entry, location/security of files
     - Written policies and procedures that insure consistent actions
     - Staff manuals, training manuals
     - Procedural checks
   - *Client Satisfaction*
     - Survey students "customers"
     - Survey "external customers"—linkages to campus/community
   - *Outcome Research*
     - Problem/symptom reduction
     - Connection to larger institution's "success goals" (e.g., retention/academic success)
     - Target populations or issues: Differential impact of service
   - *Environmental Assessment*
     - Atmosphere of safety and security for all "customers" (i.e., clients and employees)
3. Are We Doing What We Should Be Doing?
   - *Needs Assessment*
     - Survey, focus groups, specific targets
     - Multiple customers
   - *Contextual Mapping*
     - Competitive threats
     - Financial factors
     - On and off campus customers, allies, threats
     - Internal and external linkages
     - Institutional characteristics
     - Administrative characteristics
   - *Benchmarking*
     - Who are our comparative groups, aspirational peers?
4. Who Knows What We're Doing?
   Who should know? How do we tell them?
   - *Marketing to multiple customers and funding sources*
     - Scan environment to understand client and campus needs
     - Develop marketing plan
     - Create communication strategies
     - Identify and articulate client satisfaction/success

(Continued)

TABLE 4.2
(Continued)

---

5. How Can We Improve What We Do?
  ◆ *Continuous Quality Improvement*
    • Continuous process looping back to point #1—not static goal
    • Fluid process allowing flexibility to shift priorities, functions and technologies
    • Create and provide "cutting edge," "just in time," context relevant service
  ◆ *Strategic Plan*
    • Assess and align agency and institution values, missions and goals
    • Determine current strengths, weaknesses and challenges
    • Develop action plan and set priorities
6. As the Director, What Do I Need to Know?
  What strengths do I have? What competencies do I need to develop?
  ◆ *Leadership Qualities*
    • Vision for future
    • Managing for change
    • Ultimate accountability
  ◆ *Staff Management Skills*
    • Clinical staff
    • Training program
    • Clerical and support staff
  ◆ *Quality Management*
    • Assess relevance and needs in #1–5 above
    • Ensure organizational, legal and ethical responsibility
  ◆ *Resource Management Skills*
    • Budgeting; developing funding sources
    • Deployment of staff
    • Physical plant maintenance and improvement

Source. Elements of Excellence Task Force. The Association for University and College Counseling Center Directors (2005).

that counseling centers were "left alone to keep students out of trouble," today's counseling centers are increasingly called on to be integrally involved at a variety of levels in the student affairs operation. Thus, it is typical for counseling center directors (as well as designated staff) to be present on university task forces and work groups, in consultative relationships, and as advocates for satisfying the mental health needs of students.

While forging a mission for the center, it is clear that the director must be mindful of the mission and goals of the university. For instance, one institution's stated mission is:

> To help students make a successful transition to and through college by providing a select array of quality educational programs and support services that meet common and unique student and institutional needs.

Generic goal statements such as this would appear to offer the counseling center director much latitude in setting forth a mission and a set of goals for the center. The truth is, however, in most cases, the university goals are filtered and spun through the administration, and it behooves the director to know the true mission, intent, and emphases of the current administration to advance feasible proposals and plans. One thing is clear: The chief student affairs officer is the information conduit from the president's office to the departmental level. An effective chief student affairs officer has his or her finger on the pulse of the institution and is in regular contact with the university president and provost to better understand where he or she is in terms of the overall advancement of the institution. As a result, a well-informed chief student affairs officer is in a pivotal position to provide the necessary support to ensure that the center is well positioned to pursue its mission. Thus, the astute director learns to manage up as well as out. To know the ambitions, interests, values, and experiences of the senior student affairs administrator is invaluable in generating the agenda most likely to be endorsed, the initiatives most likely to be supported, and the resources most likely to be sustained when retrenchment becomes the order of the day.

A far too common mistake with untoward consequences has been for the director to express a narrow goal set that may suit a center's purposes, but fails to match the mandates of the institution. For example, to tout the value of symptom reduction in terms of pre- and postclinical measures may be highly valued by the more narrowly trained deliverer of psychological and psychiatric services, but is it considered to be of singular importance to a president who is concerned about the retention of students to the institution? To the budget officer who wants to know that the dollars spent for counseling services are yielding a return in the fiscal sense? In this case, managing up becomes the elegant process of doing what you do best, but articulating it in terms that are easily understood and that fold neatly into the prescribed patterns of the existing student affairs and university operational paradigm. This does not mean that counseling centers should simply "fall into the party line" with reactive, rule-bound approaches to student service delivery. It does mean, however, that developing a cooperative stance toward the administration goes a long way toward ensuring the viability and health of any counseling operation. To firmly establish a set of working relationships, develop trust and confidence, cultivate the image of "counseling center as team player," and embed itself into the fabric of the institution is to ensure a counseling center's resilience during times of challenge and threat.

CONTEXTUAL MAPPING—
PLANNING IN PERSPECTIVE

Although there are obvious commonalities across centers, each campus has a unique set of circumstances and challenges, and consequently each center must key off the context in which it operates. The director must seek answers to critical questions as they relate to the university context. Such questions include the following:

1. What are the competitive threats to the center?

   Are there other organizations on or off campus that could compete for the counseling service function (e.g., campus mental health training clinics, medical school, health service, private practices, community outsourcing agencies)?

   What is the history of the center's presence on campus? Is it ensconced or marginal?

2. What are the unique institutional characteristics that may dictate service offerings?

   Is it an urban or rural campus? Commuter or residential? Large or small?

   Does the counseling center contribute to the mission of the division and the university?

   What are students' expectations regarding services and entitlements?

   What are parents' expectations regarding services and entitlements?

   To whom are you compared? Against which institutions would your administration benchmark your center?

   Is the center demonstrating its impact on student retention?

3. What financial/budget considerations need to be accounted for?

   What is the current funding formula for generating the counseling center budget?

   What is the financial health of the institution at large?

   Are there creative budget options available in times of fiscal restraint?

4. What is the on- and off-campus nature of relationships/allies/customers?

   Has the counseling center established solid working relationships with the academic departments? Other departments in student affairs?

   Does the director and members of the staff strive to create one-to-one relationships with key stakeholders on and off campus?

   Is there a working relationship with and support from community agencies and other providers of services?

5. Does the counseling center live up to its promise versus the reality of its function?

   What are our strengths and vulnerabilities?

   What data do we need to demonstrate our value to the institution?

   Have we cultivated a favorable cost–benefit index?

Have we developed sophistication in marketing our services to the university community?

Have we developed visibility on a national scale to underscore our contribution to the integrity and reputation of the institution?

6. What are the characteristics of the prevailing administration that may impact on the viability or vitality of the center?

What is valued by higher administration?

What do top administrators want and what are their outcome goals?

How are decisions made and by whom?

What is the power base of the student affairs division on campus?

Is the director in a position to be at "the big table" where higher level administrative decisions are made?

The astute counseling center administrator will seek answers to each of these questions; correlate the center's agenda accordingly; and monitor, update, and recalibrate service and program delivery as circumstances require. A working knowledge of the prior questions allows the director to anticipate changes in the campus climate, leveraging the center's position to neutralize threat and capitalize on opportunities.

BUDGET AND FINANCIAL CONSIDERATIONS

In their chapter on financial issues affecting counseling and health services, Keeling and Heitzmann (2003) underscored the budget implications resulting from the need to provide counseling services for increasing numbers of students. The problem, of course, is that, as counseling centers record regular increases in the number of students served, costs rise concomitantly. While acknowledging the need to respond to the burgeoning numbers of students seeking counseling, university administrators must answer to myriad requests for funding from the array of valued student services reporting to them. Moreover, during periods of fiscal exigency, even the most deserving departments are not immune to budget reductions.

Traditional Forms of Funding for University Counseling Centers

The most common funding formula for counseling centers yields an allocation carved from the university's education and general budget that supports a circumscribed set of counseling center services. This plan establishes an annual budget for the counseling center that is consistent from year to year, given reasonable stability in the university's budget. It is the director's job to provide staffing and a scope of services that remain within the budget limits. The second most common plan for funding counseling centers involves assessing all students a surcharge (typically referred to as a health or counseling fee) above and beyond tuition, the proceeds from which generate the counseling center annual budget. Of the 339 institutions responding to the National Survey of Counseling Center Directors (Gallagher, 2004), 46% reported that they are fully or partially supported by mandatory health fees—up from the previous year and reflecting a trend that has continued for many years. Irrespective of the funding formula, given a relatively fixed annual budget, it is incumbent on the director to carefully consider the range of services needed while setting service limits. It is the director's role to prioritize the need for expanded services in the best of times while remaining at the ready to set reasonable limits in times of fiscal retrenchment.

Creative Funding Sources for Counseling Centers

In addition to the traditional funding of university counseling centers, several creative funding sources are getting increased attention as ways to keep a center solvent in times of need. It comes as no surprise that discretionary dollars tend to be designated in support of academic programs and classroom instruction. Thus, in the lean budget years, some centers may find themselves without the support they had come to expect. Keeling and Heitzmann (2003) cited several alternatives for generating departmental operating expenses that provide flexibility and balance, given the vagaries of institutional budget cycles and formulae. They are outlined from the original in abbreviated form next:

• *Fee-for-service*. Traditionally, counseling centers have provided services without cost to students in need. Increasingly, however, over the past several years, counseling center administrators (and the university officials to whom they report) have become increasingly comfortable with charging modest fees for certain services under certain circumstances (e.g., excess visit fees after a certain number of free sessions or for specialized services such as psychiatric services, psychological assessments, and alcohol assessments and treatment).

• *Grants and contracts*. Many institutions offer funds targeted for creative ideas or research, or in pursuit of diversity efforts. Outside of campus-based funding, the director may seek opportunities for funding through governmental resources, private foundations, and professional associations. Moreover, national organizations, state and federal governments, and private funding sources offer rich resources to enhance and expand current center offerings.

- *Specialized services to on-campus units.* Some colleges and universities may offer a variety of opportunities for counseling centers to provide exclusive specialized services to certain university units. Organizational consultation with administrative departments, enhanced services for student athletes, employment screening, and classroom instruction may generate funds that can be recycled in support of counseling services.

- *Fundraising.* Many counseling centers are discovering the value in accessing the expertise and resources of the university development office. Whereas all universities have a unit assigned to soliciting private gifts and bequests, traditionally the mission of the office has been primarily to serve the academic units. Counseling centers are in an awkward position when it comes to seeking donations and financial support from satisfied customers. Ethical considerations and the requirements for anonymity and confidentiality interfere with the usual ways of tapping into this resource. However, those centers with training programs can legitimately appeal to former trainees who have gone on to successful careers. Moreover, the Development Office, through its various comprehensive campaigns, can highlight the center's importance as a valued student affairs unit in need of support.

- *Collaborative partnerships or consortia.* Counseling centers may have an opportunity to join with parallel service providers on campus and in the community to establish service consortia. For example, partnering with existing on-campus training facilities in the clinical, counseling, and school psychology academic programs could yield broadened service delivery options while reducing administrative costs.

- *Additional funding sources.* The enterprising center director is aware that there are opportunities to complement a budget by offering licensing and certification exams, publishing and selling self-help brochures, developing and selling videotape workshops or Web-based courses, and charging fees for off-campus consultation or workshop presentations.

- *Outsourcing.* The threat of outsourcing, essentially contracting for counseling services by providers outside of the university, has been minimized after several unsuccessful attempts to outsource by select universities. Despite these failed attempts, a university administration could find its interest in outsourcing piqued during time of fiscal exigency, especially if there is an impression of cost-inefficiency attributed to the counseling center.

Although it is tempting to become increasingly entrepreneurial in pursuit of discretionary dollars to drive counseling services, the director is cautioned to consider that success in entrepreneurship may lead to a university administration that assumes that the counseling service can be fiscally self-reliant. Given the unreliability and variability of the many creative solutions outlined earlier, it would be a serious error for a director to convey that image. On the contrary, as observers of the political and economic climate, directors must be at the ready to seek creative solutions under certain strictures, but to resist facile, short-term solutions that may jeopardize the claim to the more durable, traditional forms of funding. Ultimately, in times of fiscal exigency, the director must remain at the table with other student affairs directors to ensure that the center's legitimate needs are given due attention and properly addressed. While offering short-term funding alternatives during the lean times, the director must persist in reminding that counseling services have played and will continue to play an integral role in pursuit of the mission of the institution and are deserving of their share of continuing university funding.

ORGANIZATIONAL STRUCTURE
OF THE COUNSELING CENTER

The determination of centralized versus decentralized counseling services defies a formulaic response. It could be argued that a larger campus would profit from a certain degree of decentralization if only to ensure that all relevant constituents' disparate needs are accorded due attention. Thus, in addition to the primary student counseling service, the larger, more comprehensive institutions are likely to spawn separate psychological counseling centers (typically associated with the doctoral training programs in counseling, clinical, or school psychology), career services, academic support programs, mental health clinics (traditionally associated with a health service or medical school), and the like.

Irrespective of size, the most common counseling center organizational structure provides for the standard broad range of clinical and ancillary services, including individual and group counseling, outreach, drug and alcohol services, research, technology, consultation, training, and, increasingly, psychiatric services. In one form or another, someone must be responsible for each of these areas if the center is to be comprehensive and internally consistent in its offerings. In the larger centers, this typically translates to coordinative assignments, with each senior staff member ensuring that attention is paid to each functional area. For small centers, however, each member of the staff may need to be responsible for more than one of these areas. Obviously, there are limits as to what can be done in a smaller center. Yet given the interests of the staff and the mission of the center, and in service to the institution, each area needs to be carefully considered and factored in or out of the counseling center operational paradigm. Figure 4.1 provides a typical administrative structure for a counseling center with a training program and standard areas of coordination.

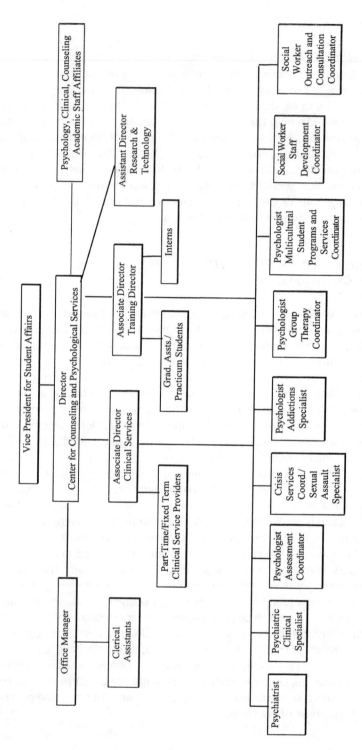

FIG. 4.1. Center for counseling and psychological services.

STAFF RECRUITMENT, RETENTION, AND PROFESSIONAL DEVELOPMENT

Beyond exquisite mission statements, careful planning, and full university support, a counseling center's ultimate success is contingent on the selection, development, and retention of well-qualified, dedicated, and ambitious professionals. Although there are many available professionals from reputable training programs, it is the director's responsibility to design screening processes that yield the right match of skills, interests, personality, and dedication to student services.

In regards to size of staff, the accreditation standards of the International Association of Counseling Services (IACS, 2000) suggest a ratio of one professional staff person (excluding trainees) for every 1,000 to 1,500 students. Moreover, the results of the 2004 Annual Survey of Counseling Center Directors (Gallagher, 2004) indicate that the current average of full-time equivalent professionals to students is 1 to 1,574. Be that as it may, staffing needs may vary depending on the range of services offered by the center, its mission, and its purpose. Traditionally, hiring staff with terminal professional degrees (PhD, MD, MSW) has been the standard for staffing at counseling centers. Over the past decade, however, counseling centers have become increasingly multidisciplinary in nature, now including specialist counselors (e.g., sexual assault counselors, addictions counselors), psychiatric nurse practitioners, and counselors from varied educational training programs. Although it is not imperative that staff professionals be fully licensed and credentialed to practice on a university campus, directors emphasize the importance of the same for quality of care, professional development, liability risk reduction, and the image of the center. Moreover, it is important to keep in mind that the campus looks to counseling center staff to be the experts in mental health matters as they relate to the student body. For all these reasons, having less than fully qualified and certified individuals on the staff should be considered with caution.

Most directors would agree that recruiting good staff is easier than retaining good staff. Many staff, if held to narrow, rigid, and inflexible work responsibilities, would find attractive alternatives in many other settings. Thus, it is incumbent on the director to seek institutional support and incentives for staff that cannot be duplicated in other settings. Fortunately, the counseling center, with its broad service mandate, offers an impressive array of professional and personal opportunities that, if managed properly, may result in the best insurance for staff retention. A decided advantage of university life is the offer of intellectual stimulation, the ambience of campus life, cultural incentives, and, most important, a variety of ways in which to express oneself as a professional. From clinical service to outreach, consultation, funded professional development, teaching, and research, a university counseling service offers the best opportunities to staff members aspiring to becoming complete professionals. These incentives need to be highlighted and packaged in the best interest of each staff member. To retain staff and enhance their productivity, a director needs to provide regular opportunities for professional development internal to the setting, and to ensure that there are adequate funds for off-site professional development as well. Moreover, the availability of supervision and consultation to deal with the myriad clinical challenges experienced by staff must be a built in that cannot be compromised. Finally, in addition to a differentiated workload and opportunities for professional development, a few centers have developed graded salary structures, providing salary increments for such things as licensure, tenure, length of service, and specialty training. In the absence of a career ladder that extends to any degree, artificial ladders of this sort need to be considered wherever possible to cater to a professional's need to be recognized and rewarded for expertise and service.

STAFF MORALE

It is incumbent on any director to set the tone for good morale among the members of the staff. Suffice it to say, no matter how finely tuned a structure for counseling administration might be, it is valueless in the absence of a team of professionals who are committed to what they are doing, who believe in their value, and who care for themselves in ways that allow them to thrive as professionals. There is no worse feeling for an administrator than to work diligently to put together a structure that is designed to provide efficient and effective services, only to have it undermined by unhappy, burned-out, or angry staff. To forestall that eventuality, the director needs to be adept at providing short- and long-range programs of morale enhancement that contribute to the health and vitality of the staff. Depending on the size and structure of the center, either a team may be developed to attend to this important element or a member of the staff may be appointed to generate programmatic opportunities designed to boost and maintain morale. Among the creative solutions to this vexing problem have been staff newsletters; celebrations of anniversaries, birthdays, and other life events; staff process meetings; "fun and games"; retreats; social events; tailgates; picnics; and the like. By no means are staff events intended to replace what is incumbent on all staff members to provide for themselves (i.e., to have a life of their own outside of work). Be that as it may, the creation of a supportive, social, fun, and intellectually stimulating atmosphere on the job goes a long way toward making the workplace a pleasant, friendly, and uplifting place to be. It certainly pays dividends during those times when the seemingly endless line of students seeking services fatigues even the most energetic staff member.

At times, adding a novel program that serves students as well as staff is in order. One director spoke of the value of having a movement therapy intern join the staff for the academic year. In addition to providing adjunct services for students in treatment, the intern also sponsored several movement experiences for the staff, which loosened things up, prompted some spontaneous laughter, and staved off the onset of dour and somewhat pessimistic stances at key points throughout the semester. If the director is not naturally drawn to creative responses to morale issues, it is important that he or she seek to hire (or consult with) individuals who have the qualities and skills to address these concerns.

TRAINING/SUPERVISION

One of the advantages of working on a university campus is the opportunity to provide training and supervision for students in local, regional, or national graduate programs in clinical and counseling psychology, social work, and psychiatry. Most staff persisters in college counseling centers note that the opportunity to train professionals-to-be is an important incentive and a form of diversification of responsibilities that they find challenging and stimulating. Moreover, it is a way to give back to the profession that influenced them because they can directly foster the growth of future colleagues.

Training may take several forms—from doctoral internships in psychology, preferably approved by the American Psychological Association, to paid graduate assistants or practicum students from local or regional programs. Internships are typically 1-year, full-time, supervised experiences. Graduate assistants are up to half-time paid positions, and practicum experiences are course-related, with students carrying a caseload of generally less than six clients per semester. Recently, select centers have established postdoctoral fellowships, largely clinical in nature, for individuals who want to specialize in the delivery of counseling center service or who want an additional year of supervised experience for licensure purposes. Beyond trainees in psychology, some centers provide supervised training experiences in social work, psychiatry, and related fields, capitalizing on the presence of varied professionals who find satisfaction in supervising and mentoring colleagues-to-be.

In addition to the obvious implications for staff morale and professional development, the director is aware that incorporating a cadre of trainees may be a cost-effective way to extend services. Trainees under supervision can provide many hours of clinical service delivery that would go wanting without their involvement. Be that as it may, some administrators question whether the center gets a good return on its investment in training opportunities. Some would argue that the senior staff time spent in supervision, training, and other activities in service to the trainees is only marginally returned in the direct services that trainees provide to student consumers. Thus, it is the director's responsibility to ensure that the ratio of clinical service to training and supervision is adequate to justify the expense, and then to articulate the benefit accurately and convincingly to the administration.

USE OF TECHNOLOGY

Perhaps the most rapidly accelerated change in the past 10 years has been the proliferation of technology solutions to clinical concerns such as scheduling, note taking/record keeping, data management, and communication. It is not unusual for psychologists today to be trained not only in clinical services, but also to have cultivated a working knowledge of the language and application of computer technology. The fact of the matter is, there are many efficiency-oriented improvements in the offing if a center is able to capitalize on available technology. There are currently a variety of tailored programs of benefit to scheduling, note taking, and data management in university counseling centers. With a wide array of options, it is incumbent on the director to understand the needs of the center vis-à-vis the available software. Ultimately, it is the director's task to remain aware of emerging technology solutions, identify value added enhancements, advocate for the same, and secure funding for installation and maintenance fees.

DIVERSITY ISSUES

One of the most vexing challenges for any counseling center is to formulate a response to the needs of a diversified campus population. The range of diversification now incorporates an increasingly broad spectrum, including race, ethnicity and culture, gender, sexual orientation, age, and disability. A manager cannot be content with simply offering one-size-fits-all services to the campus at large. On the contrary, the administration of a counseling center comes with a mandate to reach out to historically underserved student populations, generate contact points, and provide creative services to meet the growing, unique needs of our diverse campus population. Although counseling centers have been known to lead the way in promoting services to those most in need, it is increasingly important during these challenging times to keep diversity issues in the forefront. Such issues must be a priority item in the director's planning and in the recruitment of professional staff dedicated to addressing the needs of a diverse student population.

ASSESSMENT AND EVALUATION

As noted by Schuh and Upcraft (2001), "the pressure on student affairs to demonstrate its effectiveness, for whatever purpose (survival, quality improvement, accreditation, enrollment management, affordability, strategic planning, policy development and decision making, local political contexts) still exists and is growing" (p. xi). Thus, no service should be without regular assessment of services and evaluation of programs. On a more practical note, it is the wise director who elects to evaluate programs and services before the chief student affairs officer mandates it. Nonetheless, experience has proved that counseling centers are often in the forefront of student affairs units that endorse regular evaluation of services.

Surveys of student satisfaction, but also rigorous clinical research, are indexes of the impact that a given service is having on its constituency. Program planning, modification of services, staff development, budgeting, and allocation of resources are all better served by a program of regular evaluation. For the most part, student consumers of counseling services tend to be complimentary of the services they receive. In addition to high ratings on a variety of dimensions, directors relish open-ended items where students talk in glowing terms of how counseling "changed their life," how they "wouldn't have continued at the university if it weren't for counseling," or, more compellingly, "It saved my life." Sharing these personal observations from satisfied consumers is a sure-fire way to touch the heart of the administration in a director's pursuit of a broad-based campaign for support.

Among the available resources for assessment and evaluation, the Counseling Center Village (http://ub-counseling.buffalo.edu/ccv.html) has a number of survey instruments online that have been successfully applied in various settings. A comprehensive model for assessing counseling services has been offered by Heitzmann and Nafziger (2001) and is outlined in abbreviated form next:

• *Tracking client demographics.* Most centers have a wealth of information on the presenting characteristics of students who seek assistance for various concerns. The retrieval of aggregate data, including gender, age, racial and ethnic background, nationality, marital status, class standing/college/major, and source of referral, allows the center director to articulate to interested parties a demographic picture of students who seek counseling.

• *Assessing types of problems and clinical needs.* A system of categorization of client problems and concerns provides rich clinical data that are particularly useful in analyzing trends, thereby informing the director in deploying staff and in the development of programs and services in response to the trends. Moreover, the availability of comprehensive clinical data is advantageous when defending against challenges to the center's budget.

• *Assessing student satisfaction.* Every director should be attuned to how well the services are received by the student consumers. With a captive audience of student service users, it is relatively easy to get satisfaction data at critical moments. Items representing length of wait for services, treatment duration, self-reported improvement ratings, reception services, ambience of the waiting room, and ratings of the counselor provide valuable documentation for how successful a service is in meeting the needs of its constituency.

• *Assessing campus climate and environments.* Universities have an investment in assessing the learning environment as a way of ensuring that the conditions for optimum learning are present. Counseling center directors must avail themselves of opportunities to influence the design and analysis of such campus-wide efforts in ways that provide information useful to the center. Moreover, a well-designed campus environment survey that includes items relevant to counseling center need and function can send important messages to the administration about the importance and value of a center.

• *Benchmarking with other counseling centers.* Perhaps the best method for determining the strengths and limitations of a center is to compare it to other centers at comparable institutions. Fortunately for counseling centers, the College and University Counseling Center Directors Data Bank (Boyd, 2004) and the National Survey of Counseling Center Directors (Gallagher, 2004), along with some regionally-based surveys (e.g., Big Ten University Counseling Centers Annual Survey), provide benchmark data across many dimensions that are easily accessed and interpreted. Salaries by position, budget allocations, workload, size of staff, novel programs, and the like are laid out before the director and serve as an important source of comparison. Needless to say, delivering up these same comparative data to the administration can provide a compelling rationale for improving, maintaining, or enhancing support for the center.

• *Assessing cost-effectiveness.* One thing directors know is that there will be continuing pressure to provide cost-effective services and demonstrate the value-added quality of center functions. Various methods can be employed to determine the cost of the service (see Kennedy, Moran, & Upcraft, 2001) vis-á-vis its perceived value. Most would agree that you are better off anticipating and providing this information before you are put in the defensive position of defending your service when asked by the administration during periods of financial exigency.

PROGRAM ACCREDITATION

The two primary sources of accreditation standards used by counseling centers are those developed by the International Association of Counseling Services (IACS, 2000) and the Council for the Advancement of Standards in Higher Education (CAS, 2003). For those centers that qualify, the IACS has for decades been the standard by which counseling centers assess their ability to meet professional guidelines that hold them to the highest level of professional development. The IACS standards outline areas of importance such as the relationship of the center to the university or college community, service roles and functions, and ancillary activities such as consultation, referral, research, and training. In addition, the standards address ethical standards, the credentials of the professional staff and director, and related guidelines incorporating professional development, staff practices, size of staff, diversity of staff, workload, compensation, and physical facilities.

The CAS provides standards for service delivery in 28 functional areas of student services, including counseling services. The counseling center is assessed in view of its mission, set of programs, leadership, organization and management, human resources, financial resources, facilities, technologies and equipment, legal responsibilities, equity and access, campus and external relations, diversity, ethics, assessment, and evaluation. Although the CAS standards were not promulgated for accreditation purposes, these increasingly differentiated guidelines provide any center with the elements for ensuring the safe, efficient, and effective delivery of counseling services.

Whereas the CAS standards provide a useful guide for virtually any center wishing to pursue self-study vis-à-vis a set of national standards, the rigorous and recurrent requirements for IACS accreditation appear to be more suitable for seeking external validation of the quality of program efforts. In brief, the IACS accreditation process requires an extensive initial written application, followed by an evaluation of the same by a panel of accreditation members, an onsite in-person review, regular annual reports to IACS, and periodic re-accreditations. The receipt and maintenance of accreditation provides an ongoing vehicle for the review and continuing development of the counseling service. Full accreditation provides testimony that the services offered have been scrutinized by a professional agency whose sole responsibility is to enhance high standards of service to the campus community. Accredited counseling centers recognize the value of accreditation and its correlation to service and funding enhancements and the positive attention and recognition it brings to the center. Suffice it to say that it is the director's role to ensure that the center is in conformance with state-of-the-art and existing standards for service. Finally, directors who pursue the accreditation process speak highly of its value in increasing staff morale because all staff participate in the accreditation effort.

Applying IACS or CAS standards to one's center serves as a template for determining the gaps in quality and service and points the way toward future iterations of the center. Indeed if accreditation through IACS is not pursued, it is recommended that, from time to time, external evaluations employing consultant reviewers be considered for insights that may elude the director's view.

DATABANKS AND SURVEYS

The savvy administrator takes full advantage of the annual national surveys emanating from the counseling services at the University of Pittsburgh and the University of Maryland. For over two decades, the Annual Counseling Center Survey, established by Thomas Magoon, director emeritus of the University of Maryland Counseling Center, has been providing comparative tabular data across many dimensions of interest to counseling center administrators and staff. The National Survey of Counseling Center Directors, established and maintained by Robert Gallagher, director emeritus of the University of Pittsburgh Counseling Center, provides a complementary survey that addresses common questions of interest to counseling center directors and their staffs. Among other things, a key value of the annual surveys is in providing benchmark data through which a center can compare itself to other counseling centers. Directors have utilized results of the surveys to consider program enhancements, to seek funding with which to make the center comparable to other centers, and to find sources of support. Then again, many directors have found comfort in knowing that the issues of concern to them were likely to be concerns to other directors as well. Moreover, at their best, the surveys offer rich information and ideas that point toward resolutions to vexing center problems.

SUMMARY

It may be argued that the value of the counseling center to the university administration and campus community may be directly tied to the efforts and profile of the center administrator. Indeed one typically finds that the more prominent centers have a legacy of venerable directors who have well-established records of creative leadership, high visibility, and a proven record of garnering the enduring support of key administrators. The trust and esteem the director cultivates with the administration, together with the sensitivity and awareness of the administrators, have allowed counseling centers on many campuses to grow and flourish in the best interest of generations of students.

The counseling center has not only gained broad acceptance at colleges and universities, but for innumerable students it may be difficult to cite an institutional influence that may have had a more direct or lasting effect on their personal well-being and the quality of their lives. Be that as it may, it is rare that a director would not cite his or her staff at all levels and functions as largely responsible for the successes of the center. Indeed although it is advisable for institutions to seek the most prominent and qualified individuals to fill counseling center leadership positions, it is clear that a leader is only as good as his or her ability to fill staff positions with the very best our professions have to offer. The presence of three critical components—an enlightened university administration and charismatic center leadership, together with creative and skilled staff professionals—bodes well for offering quality counseling services for the campus community. The impact on the institution at large, in terms of the student who is retained by the university, the enhancement of the predisposition to learn, and the contribution to the establishment of a healthy living environment, is palpable.

The counseling center administrator must be mindful of the restrictive definitions applied to its function. At worst, it remains a low-profile agency dedicated to "preventing a headline" about the suicidal, combative, or psychotic student wreaking havoc on campus or in the community. If we see no evil and hear no evil, all is well in the ivory tower. Surprisingly, this narrow mandate has allowed some centers to persist at the university, although on the periphery, even in the face of sweeping budget cuts. At best, however, a center is recognized and supported for its broader mission of treating not only the most seriously disturbed, but also those mainstream students who are seeking to negotiate their way through normal developmental stages. Moreover, the counseling center's contribution to the climate for learning, and its emphasis on civility and the promotion of diversity at all levels, is essential for any campus that claims to be truly interested in educating the whole person.

This chapter has outlined a number of the requirements and expectations for the senior administrator of the university and college counseling center. These positions are typically held by professionals whose training is ordinarily limited to practice and research in their discipline. Nonetheless, despite the limitations to training and preparation, counseling center directors as a group tend to enjoy and appreciate the extension of their professional pursuits into administrative areas. Indeed many discover that the qualities that drew them to the helping profession—typically sensitivity to others, the study of human relations and change, and an abiding belief in the value of their professional domain—are, after all, compatible with the role of director. Administration is not for everyone, but for those select members of our professional groups who aspire to the same and who diligently pursue the learning required for the role, most would agree that there is no position more rewarding than the opportunity to direct a counseling center.

5

The Administration of University Career Services

CONTEXT

The leadership, administration, and management of a college or university career center may be one of the more challenging functions within the counseling community (Rayman, 1993). Career center management is more complex than most counselor management/administrative positions because of the diversity of the constituencies served and the diverse functions performed. Most counseling service units have a relatively focused mission that involves serving a narrow constituency of clients. If the clients' needs are met and the administrator to whom the unit reports is satisfied, the enterprise is seen as being successfully managed. In contrast, career centers serve multiple constituencies and must be multifunctional. In addition to meeting the needs of clients (principally students), career centers must also meet the needs of employers, faculty, administrators, parents, and often alumni and employees as well. Although the delivery of career counseling services is a primary function, career centers must also manage recruitment and employer relations, provide counselor training, maintain massive informational resources, serve a consultative function, and deliver an elaborate array of outreach programs that include the management of large-scale events like career fairs, which often involve thousands of dollars in revenue management.

A second challenge confronting the manager of a university career center results from the diverse functions and associated staff members that must coexist within a comprehensive career center. On the one hand, the career counseling and planning function requires a staff with what might be characterized as typical counselor values and skills—strong counseling and interpersonal skills, strong process orientation, nonjudgmental character, and a relaxed interpersonal style that creates a safe and comfortable environment for personal growth. On the other hand, the staff required to manage the employer relations, on-campus recruiting, and outreach programming functions must be strongly goal-oriented, possessed of excellent organizational skills, judgmental, entrepreneurial, and extraverted with a high energy level. In short, the director of a career center must manage two functional areas staffed by individuals with very different, almost antithetical, skills and values. Promoting staff collaboration and teamwork within such a bifurcated organization represents a challenge not faced by the director of most counseling agencies or counselor education units.

A third challenge stems from the fact that college and university career centers operate on the margin between two very different cultures. On the one hand, career centers function within the safe learning environment of educational institutions, where the major mission and emphasis is on the process of learning rather than on the delivery of a finished product or service. This is a forgiving environment where students are encouraged to take risks because the consequences of wrong decisions are not serious. It is the environment in which the career counseling and associated educational programming functions take place—a safe, protected environment conducive to personal growth and learning. On the other hand, the placement function takes place in an unforgiving business environment. When employers travel a great distance to visit the career center to conduct interviews with previously identified employment candidates, there is little margin for error. The staff must get the right student in the right interview room at the right time with the right employer. This aspect of the career center operates by a different set of rules—those of business and industry. Managing staff, students, and employers on a day-to-day basis as they attempt to function effectively in these two different environments is a daunting challenge, but one the director of a career center must meet on a continuing basis.

Finally, the placement function in most colleges and universities inevitably becomes intertwined, with the development function leading to petty jealousies and destructive competition between the career center and key academic departments (most often the colleges of business and engineering). This competitive, sometimes acrimonious relationship usually occurs because faculty and college administrators believe that if career services staff are allowed to control the placement relationship with corporate America, they will influence corporate representatives to channel corporate gifts, grants, and other forms of support to other than the academic units they represent. Indeed it is not uncommon for Deans of business to insist that they control the placement function and remove it from the central career center even in the face of overwhelming evidence that central services are more efficient, more employer-friendly, and more student service-oriented. Further, Deans of business traditionally have little interest in the career counseling and planning functions and place their focus almost entirely on the single-purpose placement function, driven as they are by the desire to demonstrate high placement rates and to achieve high ratings in the business education ratings game. The management of this ongoing and pervasive challenge to the efficient operation of a centralized career center is one that occupies a considerable amount of most directors' time—especially in large AAU–type universities. Put simply, it is the tendency of the academy to fly apart rather than pull together. An overriding principal objective of the career center director is to get these multiple constituencies to pull together in the interest of serving the career development and placement needs of the entire university community, and to discourage the splintering of career services into independent, uncooperative, and destructively competitive college or departmentally based units.

PLANNING

In the *Handbook for the College and University Career Center* (Herr, Rayman, & Garis, 1993), it was pointed out that planning for career center management must take place on at least two levels. First, one must plan strategically for the long run based on factors that are universal and relatively unchanging, yet be responsive to those factors that change from year to year or even month to month. There is a whole series of strategic factors that impact on career center planning. These are factors like mission of the institution, institutional philosophy, beliefs about human nature (career development theory), professionally developed standards, and so on. These factors tend to remain fairly constant over time, and many are beyond the control of the planner, but all have a significant impact on the planning process and its implementation. Clearly there is overlap between strategic factors and short-term changing factors, but for purposes of discussion, we deal with them as if they are independent of one another. We begin with strategic factors and their implications for leadership and management.

Strategic Factor #1: Mission of the Institution

The management of a career center may vary significantly depending on the mission of the institution. For example, land-grant institutions continue to enroll relatively large numbers of first-generation college students, and a disproportionate number of those students enroll in agriculture, business, science, and engineering. Similarly, a high percentage of undergraduates from Ivy League universities tend to go on to graduate and professional schools, and a high percentage of undergraduates from the AASCU-type (American Association of State Colleges and Universities) institutions go into teaching or business. Institutional mission and career services needs also vary depending on whether the institution is secular or religious, public or private, comprehensive or specialty focused. The critical point here is that the career service emphasis in a land-grant university must be quite different from that of an Ivy League university or a regional university of the type that would be a member of the AASCU. Similarly, the career development needs of students in a community college would be far different from those of an exclusive private liberal arts college.

Leadership Implications. To a considerable degree, the nature of services being offered in a college or university career center is determined by the goals and mission of the college or university. A viable career services management plan must be consistent with and supportive of the goals and mission of the institution. If the center director is not committed to supporting these core goals, the probability of success is significantly diminished.

Strategic Factor #2:
Career Development Theory

It should be evident from the introductory chapter that the authors hold a certain conception of the career development and counseling process and that this conception provides a basis for planning a comprehensive array of services that are the core of the modern career center. The management of these services must in turn be guided by these fundamental theoretical conceptions as outlined in Herr, Rayman, and Garis (1993).

Career Development Is a Life-Long Process (Herr, Cramer, & Niles, 2004; Super, 1957). If one accepts this basic premise, then a comprehensive career center must provide services across a considerable span of an individual's life. The bulk of the services offered in a college or university career center will be targeted toward the needs of enrolled students, and at most institutions many of these students will be between the ages of 18 and 22. Of course one must also consider that, among the 18- to 22-year-olds, there are considerable individual differences in terms of career maturity and needs depending on socioeconomic background, ethnicity, gender, and demographic variables. Additionally, universities by definition have a significant enrollment of graduate and professional students, most of whom are in different stages of career development than the average undergraduate.

Beyond services for enrolled students, there is increasing pressure from alumni and alumni associations to provide for the long-term career development needs of alumni. Alumni career services has become a hot topic at nearly all colleges and universities, and most are taking active steps to develop an array of services to meet the life-long career development needs of their alumni. At the other end of the continuum, it has become increasingly important for career centers to provide at least informational services, if not counseling services to potential students, often in collaboration with the admissions office and the adult learner center. These initiatives are based on the premise that the choice of a college or university is often viewed by potential students as a career decision. Indeed several colleges and universities, in the interest of assisting parents with financial planning for college (which is clearly seen by many parents as a form of career planning), are providing college cost-planning brochures at obstetric and pediatric clinics throughout their service areas. In a real sense, college and university career centers are being asked to provide comprehensive career services "from cradle to grave" in response to the growing conviction that career development truly is a "life-long process."

Leadership Implications. The conviction that career development is a life-long process dictates that career centers must be more than job service-oriented placement offices. No matter how career services are configured, they must be comprehensive and flexible, recognizing the developmental and demographic differences that exist within an increasingly diverse student body. An underlying commitment to meeting student career development needs across the lifespan must drive the planning and management processes. If the director does not share this commitment, the "placement tail is likely to end up wagging the career development dog."

Career Development Is an Integral Part of the Educational Process. This assumption has significant implications for planning in terms of (a) the geographic location of career services on the campus, (b) the position of career services within the organizational structure of the university, and (c) the relationship of those services to the academic programs of the various colleges and the academic departments within them.

Leadership Implications. If career development is viewed as an integral part of the educational process, a strong case can be made for ensuring that career services are housed centrally on campus where access is ensured for the broad mass of students. Given this assumption, locating the career center on the periphery of the campus in a substandard structure is not acceptable. Similarly, sharing facilities with mental health or psychological service units is inappropriate because of the stigma that is unfortunately often associated with such units. Incorporating career services as a component of some other unit within the student services organizational structure often obscures the identity of career services and is likely to create confusion in the minds of students, faculty, staff, and employers. Beyond this, the staff of the service must have credibility with, and must integrate and interact positively with, faculty from all the academic units of the institution. In brief the geographic location and quality of the physical facility in which the career center is located must communicate to students, employers, and faculty alike that the service is a valued and integral component of the educational mission of the institution and that it is not some type of remedial service or marginal office operating on the fringe of respectability with little or no relationship to the core mission of the institution.

Finally, there must be formal linkages between academic units and the career services office to ensure the uninterrupted and direct flow of information in both directions. This critical, interdependent relationship will not exist accidentally or naturally. It must be planned and carried out intentionally with the full support and leadership of the career center director.

In the end, it is the responsibility of the career center director to provide the leadership necessary to ensure that the career center assumes a prominent place within the college or university, in terms of the quality of the physical facilities, the center's geographic location, and the center's position within the organizational structure of the institution.

Career Development Is an Important (Perhaps the Most Important) Component of Human Development. Throughout this chapter, we have assumed that career development is a significant component of human development and that, as expressed eloquently elsewhere, it takes place over the lifespan (Herr, Cramer, & Niles, 2004). As such it is an important element of normal human development, perhaps one of the key elements that lead to identity formation and a source of purpose and meaning in life. Its significance should not be trivialized by thinking of it as "getting people jobs." Although job placement is important, it is just one small element of the career development process.

Leadership Implications. In planning for the college or university career center, care must be taken to ensure that the focus remains on the broader goal of meeting student and alumni career development needs, with equal emphasis and resource allocation to all 4 (or 5) years of college, rather than placing the primary focus on seniors and the achievement of a high initial job placement rate.

The "Four Critical Years" During the Undergraduate Experience May Be the Most Critical Years of the Life-Long Career Development Process. If one accepts Super's (1957) conception of life stage career development, the years from ages 18 to 22 are among the most turbulent and yet the most critical years to satisfactory career development and self-concept implementation. Although career development is a life-long process, some portions of that process are more critical than others. The stage that Super referred to as *exploration* and that Astin (1977) labeled *four critical years* offers a window of opportunity for young adults to transcend their environment and take control of their career destiny.

Leadership Implications. Because of the critical role that the undergraduate years play in the career development process, career services must be "saturation-loaded" on students during this brief 4-year period. Students must graduate with competence in the career development curriculum. In a sense, career development is to placement what a liberal arts education is to vocational education. In parable form, "Give a man a fish, and he'll eat for today; teach him how to fish, and he'll eat forever." A worthwhile paraphrase might be, "Give a student a job, and he or she will be satisfied for today; teach her or him the career development process, and she or he will be satisfied for a lifetime." Career services, if properly managed, must provide an array of services to support this most critical of life's career transitions.

Career Development Is the Undergraduate Experience. Although we believe that the modern career center has an obligation to provide a comprehensive array of services in support of healthy career development, some form of career development will take place with or without those services. In fact we believe career development *is* the undergraduate experience. Everything a student does, every experience a student has during his or her undergraduate years, will have an impact on that student's career destiny. It is the responsibility of the career center to enhance the value of that undergraduate experience as a vehicle for personal career development—to show students how decisions they are making, activities in which they are engaged, and courses in which they are enrolled affect their career destiny. Thus, planning for student career development requires an understanding of the academic curriculum available and an array of career center-sponsored services that integrate with the curriculum (and the extracurriculum—those out-of-classroom activities, programs, and events that are such an important part of college life) to ensure that the undergraduate experience is also a unifying career development experience.

Leadership Implications. Planning for career services must take into account the undergraduate curriculum and provide an array of services that integrate with and enhance it. To borrow an often-used term, career development theory and services must be *infused* into the curriculum. In our experience, that infusion will not happen without its being carefully planned, and the impetus for it must come from the career center under the leadership and administrative direction of a strong director.

Strategic Factor #3: Professionally Developed Standards

Planning for the career center must also take into consideration certain professional standards that have evolved within the profession and that have been codified by professional associations external to the college or university. In the case of career services, the appropriate professionally developed standards are those of the Council for the Advancement of Standards in Higher Education (CAS). This consortium of student affairs professional associations includes five associations with particular relevance to college and university career centers: The American Counseling Association (ACA), the American College Counseling Association (ACCA), the American College Personnel Association (ACPA), the National Association for Colleges and Employers (NACE), and the National Association of Student Personnel Administrators (NASPA).

The CAS Standards and Guidelines for Career Services (2003) represent an external benchmark that career services practitioners and career center directors may use as a cornerstone for college and university career services planning. Readers interested in reviewing the standards are referred to *The Book of Professional Standards for Higher Education* (2003) and the appropriate *CAS Self-Assessment Guide for Career Services* (2003). Key topics addressed in the standards are: (a) mission, (b) program, (c) leadership and management, (d) organization and administration, (e) human resources, (f) financial resources, (g) facilities, technology, and equipment, (h) legal responsibilities, (i) equity and access, (j) campus and external relations, (k) diversity, (l) ethics, and (m) assessment and evaluation. Those unfamiliar with the work of CAS may access the CAS Web site at: http://www.cas.edu/members.cfm.

Leadership Implications. Although it will be clear to the reader that the CAS standards are necessarily generic, with many of the flaws that committee-developed standards exhibit, they provide a fundamental basis for planning that has evolved within the profession. The danger with any set of minimum standards is that they sometimes foster a sort of minimalist mentality. That is, rather than providing a model of excellence to which career centers might aspire, they may be misconstrued to provide a license to get by with the minimum. This mind-set can be particularly destructive to career center quality if it is embraced by the director of career services and/or university central administration. Professionals involved in planning for the career center must be mindful of this possibility and take steps to ensure that the role CAS standards play in the planning process is a positive one. In the end, planning must be driven by aspirations for excellence, rather than by compliance with minimum standards, and the director must be the driver.

Strategic Factor #4: Ethical Guidelines

There are five chief reference documents that guide the ethical behavior of career center professionals. The first four present guidelines for those engaged principally in the counseling and assessment aspects of the profession are: (a) *The American Counseling Association Code of Ethics and Standards of Practice* (1995), (b) *The American Psychological Association Ethical Principles of Psychologists and Code of Conduct* (2003), (c) *The National Career Development Association Ethical Standards* (Revised 2003), and (d) *Standards for Educational and Psychological Testing* (American Educational Research Association, 1999). These documents are too lengthy to include here, but copies of each should be kept on file in the professional library of the career center. Professionally trained counselors will have had exposure to these ethical standards in their academic preparation and should retain copies of the standards in their personal professional files. A key way to stay abreast of critical ethical issues in counseling is continued membership in at least one professional counseling association.

The other important ethical reference document for all career centers is entitled *Principles for Professional Conduct for Career Services and Employment Professionals* (National Association of Colleges and Employers, 1998). Developed by the Board of Governors of the National Association of Colleges and Employers (NACE) as a "framework within which the career planning, placement, and recruitment processes should function," these principles offer ethical guidelines for the interactions between and among colleges and universities, employers, and students. A copy of these guidelines is available on the NACE Web site (http://www.naceweb.org/principles/principl.html). Hard copies of the *Principles*, an annotated version of the *Principles*, and consultative assistance on ethical issues are all available as benefits of membership in NACE.

Leadership Implications. The practice of service delivery within a comprehensive career center is wrought with ethical issues that must be dealt with on a regular basis by the administrative/management staff. Ethical standards and principles as well as consultative assistance available from professional associations like those cited earlier are key resources for the career center director. Most important, in the case of ethical issues, it is imperative that the director leads by example.

Strategic Factor #5: Position of Career Services Within the College or University Structure

The position that career services occupies within the college or university structure is a crucial factor in planning. Although there are an almost infinite number of ways in which the career services unit might fit within the university structure (Bechtel, 1993), the major issues related to this strategic factor have been summarized well in Herr, Rayman, and Garis (1993).

Issue #1: Reporting Lines. Most college or university career service offices report either to the vice president for student services, the provost, or the chief academic officer of the institution. Whatever the reporting lines, it is critically important that the strategic goals of the career center align with those of the division to which it reports. According to the 2002 Career Planning and Placement Survey conducted by the National Association of Colleges and Employers, the most common structure is for career services to report to the vice president for student services (74.5%). The typical alternative to this approach is for career services to report to the provost or chief academic officer if the service is centralized. In cases where career services are decentralized, the most common reporting line is to individual academic deans.

Advantages of reporting to the vice president for student services

• Career services is often one of the larger and stronger student service units, and is thus likely to compete successfully with other student service units for resources.

• The vice president for student services is more likely to be sympathetic to the service nature of career services and embrace a "student development point of view."

• Most student services vice presidents view career development as a developmental process and are more supportive of the costly counseling and programming functions that are critical to a comprehensive approach to career services.

• Reporting to the same vice president as other student services units enhances the probability that quality communications will exist between career services and other related student services (e.g., financial aid, student counseling service, residence life, etc.). It also enhances the likelihood of appropriate and expeditious referral of students between and among student service agencies.

Advantages of reporting to the provost or academic dean

• The academic side of the college or university invariably receives top priority when it comes to resources and facilities. Being allied with an academic department can be helpful in maintaining the career services resource base and is likely to enhance credibility with the faculty.

• When career services is seen as part of an academic unit, it often enhances the quality of the communication and cooperation with faculty and may lead to stronger faculty support for the service.

• In most universities, the provost has more political clout than the vice president for student affairs. As in any business or enterprise, the closer you are to the central power structure, the more control you are likely to have over your destiny.

Issue #2: Centralized Versus Decentralized Services. The debate over whether career services should be centralized or decentralized has raged for years and is likely to always be an issue. In most cases, career services have evolved based on the historical development and unique character of the particular institution in which they are located. For example, the University of Illinois has a long history and commitment to decentralization. It seems inconceivable that a centralized approach to career services or any other service would be successful there. In contrast, other universities (e.g., Penn State, North Carolina, Michigan State, Texas A & M, Florida, Florida State, UCLA, etc.) have histories of strong central management and control. Clearly centralized career services are more likely to be successfully implemented in such institutions. Our experience suggests that high-quality career services of both the centralized and decentralized variety exist; however, each has certain advantages.

Advantages of centralized career services

• Centralized career services are less confusing to students, faculty, and employers because everything is located in one place and everyone knows where.

• There are significant efficiencies and economies of scale that occur in terms of interview room utilization, career resources, placement library, copy facilities, clerical support, audiovisual services, and others.

• A centralized service is more likely to achieve a critical mass in terms of professional staff size, which allows individual staff to achieve higher levels of specialization and skill to the benefit of all staff and students.

• The administrative overhead will be lower because fewer people will hold the position of director. Some large universities have as many as 20 directors of career services.

• Long-standing relationships with employers who traditionally seek technical students (engineers, scientists, and business majors) can be exploited to create opportunities for nontechnical students (arts, liberal arts, humanities, and social science students).

• Because a centralized career service draws a heterogeneous and diverse student population, it creates a more vibrant, challenging, and interesting environment for students and staff alike.

Advantages of decentralized career services

• The service is likely to be perceived by students as being more personal because the career services staff are likely to interact more frequently with students and in a more focused way.

• The facilities are likely to be located much nearer to the students who actually use them, thus enhancing convenience and utilization and reducing the probability that students in need of services will fall between the cracks.

• Because the facilities are typically located within the college they are serving, it is much easier to secure faculty involvement with the staff of the service and with employers. Decentralization usually enhances faculty–employer relations as well as faculty–career center staff relations, with resultant higher faculty participation in the career development process.

One common compromise to the issue of whether to offer centralized or decentralized career services is to implement some combination of the two, whereby certain functions are centralized (e.g., on-campus interviewing or career information center), whereas other services are decentralized (e.g., career counseling, credential services, and programming; Babbish, Hawley, & Zeran, 1986).

Issue #3: Comprehensive Career Services Versus Specialized Placement Services Alone. Despite that many placement offices have changed their names to career development and placement services or career services, many career centers are still functioning as narrowly defined placement offices where little programming beyond resume preparation and interview skill building is done and where nothing vaguely resembling career counseling occurs. When we use the term *comprehensive career services office*, we are talking about an office that offers career counseling and assessment to freshmen as well as upperclassmen and alumni. Such an office must have a well-developed career resource center as well as a placement library, and it must offer a comprehensive array of career counseling, programming, and placement services.

Advantages of a comprehensive career service office

• Career counselors get continuous exposure to employers and the place-ment function. This contact brings a reality base to their counseling that does not often exist when career counseling is provided through a university counseling center.

• A comprehensive service can offer one-stop shopping for all career needs and minimize the tendency for students to fall through the cracks as they are ping-ponged around the college or university from one office to an-other.

• Combining career counseling, programming, and placement functions allows the director to draw on corporate contributions (external resources) that flow principally from the placement function in support of the often underfunded counseling and programming functions.

• When career counseling is combined with the placement function, it is more likely to be perceived by students and faculty as an integral part of the educational mission of the institution, rather than a remedial one, as is often the case when career counseling is combined with psychological counseling. Hopefully this will remove the stigma sometimes associated with seeing a counselor and result in a larger number of students seeking and utilizing ca-reer counseling services.

Advantages of single-purpose placement services

• A single-function placement office is less likely to be confused in the minds of students, faculty, staff, and employers.

• A career service that offers placement only is easier to staff and manage because of the clarity of its objectives and the simplicity of its mission.

• The placement office can utilize all external corporate contributions for the purpose of enhancing placement facilities and services without sharing those resources with counseling and programming staff. Such an arrange-ment can lead to placement offices with elegant physical facilities.

It should be obvious to the reader that we favor the comprehensive career service office over the single-purpose placement office, which we regard as an anachronism.

Issue #4: Relationship to Other Student Service Units. Although there are a number of different models, most colleges and universities choose to deliver career counseling and assessment through the counseling center, rather than through the career service office or career center. Indeed recent reports still suggest that the case load in most college and university counseling centers consists of approximately 50% career counseling and 50% personal counseling. That is, the career counseling is done in the counseling center and not in the career center. There are certain advantages to this arrangement, which we have enumerated next, but in general we favor the separation of career counseling and assessment from psychological counseling.

Advantages of career counseling and assessment being delivered through the university counseling center together with psychological (personal) counseling

• Students get one-stop counseling service. Because career issues are often intertwined with personal issues, an integrated career and personal counseling service has the potential to ensure that students get the counseling support they need without being referred multiple times.

• Certain economies are likely to exist with respect to clerical support, copy service, reference materials, waiting area, and so on.

• Career counselors and psychological counselors benefit professionally through day-to-day association. They develop a better understanding of the similarities and differences in their counseling techniques and strategies and more appreciation for each other's profession.

Advantages of career counseling being provided through career services, rather than the university counseling service

• Career counselors are first-class citizens in a career services office, whereas the career counseling done in counseling center settings is often regarded as being of secondary importance to psychological (personal) counseling. The perception of second-class citizenship is a frequent source of morale problems for career counselors functioning in counseling center settings.

• When career counseling is done in a career center, it is more likely to have a strong reality base because of the day-to-day interactions with employers and placement staff. Career counseling done through a counseling center is often client-centered and may lack this desired reality base.

• External resources that usually flow from the placement function are available to support the career counseling and programming functions.

• When career counseling is provided through career services, it is more likely to be perceived as an integral part of the educational process. When career counseling is combined with personal counseling, students often perceive it as less of an integral part of the educational process and tend to associate it more with pathology and therapy. This association has the potential to create an environment that can be a deterrent to student utilization.

Other student services units that sometimes have a formal relationship with career services are cooperative education, internship programming, and student employment. Each can be and is often legitimately incorporated into a comprehensive career service, where they seem to present few problems. In our experience, student employment is increasingly seen as a student aid function and, as such, is most often housed there. However, cooperative education and similar experiential education programs seem to be a logical extension of the career service function, involving many of the same processes as on-campus interviewing and educational programming. Similarly, the occupational exploration and personal career growth aspects of experiential programs are an integral component of the career development process. Therefore, we advocate that cooperative education and internship programs be at least partially administered through career services.

Leadership Implications. The position of career services within the college or university structure, including reporting lines, degree of centralization, degree of comprehensiveness, and relationship to other student service units, has significant implications for the planning process and for the effective leadership and management of a career center. More comprehensive centers present a broader range of management challenges and clearly require a greater range of leadership and management skills. Directors who enjoy excellent success in one organizational configuration may fail badly in another. It is important that the skill level, philosophy, and leadership style of the director be simpatico with the organizational structure of the college or university.

Strategic Factor #6: Behavioral Expectations (Learning Outcomes)

Perhaps the single most important strategic factor that must be taken into account in planning for the successful management of a career center is the establishment of behavioral expectations (objectives) or learning outcomes. We believe that behavioral objectives should be developed for the several constituencies served by the career center, but we have limited our discussion here to the two principal constituencies: students and employers. Although it is important for each career center to develop its own behavioral objectives, we provide here a fairly generic set of behavioral objectives for each of these two important constituencies:

Expected Behavioral Objectives for Students
  1. Increased exploration and understanding of career information and options

2. Increased self-understanding in terms of values, interests, skills, and abilities and how those personal characteristics relate to a variety of careers

3. Increased awareness of the need to plan and take responsibility for one's own career destiny

4. The development of greater understanding of oneself, occupations, and the relationship between self and occupations

5. The development of a realistic, appropriate, and congruent occupational choice

6. Increased knowledge of available career options and an understanding of the means of attaining those options

7. Increased knowledge of appropriate job-search strategies and job-seeking skills and experience utilizing those strategies and skills

8. Placement into a job, acceptance into further education or training, or some client-accepted alternative

9. The development of an awareness that career development is a life-long process and the development of a set of skills to ensure the successful navigation of that process

Expected Behavioral Objectives for Employers

1. An understanding of the array of employer services offered by the career center

2. Equal and easy access to students from all academic fields

3. A comfortable professional relationship with staff of the career center that includes open and direct communication

4. The opportunity to participate in the full array of career center offerings

5. Consultative advice from career center staff regarding the vagaries of the academy

Leadership Implications. Nothing is more important to the successful accomplishment of goals than the explicit definition of those goals in behavioral terms. The practice of career counseling within a college or university career center must be guided by a set of carefully developed and explicitly stated behavioral objectives. These objectives must be developed for each set of constituents served, which in the case of a career center would include students, employers, faculty, staff, alumni, and parents, among others. Directors who aspire to management success need to be skilled in the process of rigorously identifying behavioral objectives and the related learning outcomes. Those without these skills may wish to enroll in a course in instructional design.

Strategic Factor #7: An Office Management Philosophy

One of the most important things a director can do to enhance the professionalism and productivity of the career center is to commit to writing a management philosophy, communicate that philosophy to potential and current employees, and make every effort to live by that philosophy. The concept of a codified management philosophy is based on Ouchi's (1981) Theory Z of management. It is predicated on the notion that every organization or office has a certain set of values and expected behaviors that create a characteristic culture. Persons who share the core values of the culture are likely to be successful, productive, and satisfied staff members, and those who do not will be better off elsewhere and should be assisted to migrate there. Put simply, this is a person–environment fit approach, and it involves committing the organization's management philosophy to print, but doing so succinctly in less than two pages so that it can be easily shared with every employee and potential employee. Such a document serves as a philosophic compass that can guide the day-to-day behaviors of the entire staff of the career center, but most especially the director.

We have included an example of such a philosophy for the purposes of illustration.

PENNSTATE
Career
Services
CAREER PLANNING FOR LIFE

OFFICE MANAGEMENT PHILOSOPHY

Office Objective

Our office objective is to perform and be recognized as the best, the leader, number one in student service among all departments and agencies at The Pennsylvania State University and throughout the nation. If as an office we achieve this objective, then it will clearly reflect positively upon us as individuals. It is assumed that it is not possible to be an outstanding success as an individual if the office is mediocre or average. Our ego is strongly tied to this aspect of our philosophy.

Innovativeness, creativity and above all quality are stressed in all our programs and services and in our approach to the delivery of these programs and services. We must continuously strive to improve in every way. "You don't have to be sick to get better"—no matter how well we do it, we can always do it better.

It should always be our practice in working collaboratively with any individual (student, staff member, faculty member, recruiter or anyone else) or any other office or department to display a willingness to go "more than half way" to insure the success of such collaborative efforts.

We are sensitive to our image with students, the business and university communities. Commitments to students and other clients are considered sacred and we are upset with ourselves when we do not meet our commitments. We strive to demonstrate to the entire university and business community on a continuing basis that we are credible in describing the nature of our programs and services and that we are well organized and in complete control of all things that lead to the successful delivery of those programs and services.

Management Style

Career Services is an office of individuals each with their own personalities and characteristics. And while this is true, certain general characteristics of the management style will allow us to achieve our objectives.

1. The staff is self-critical. Everyone must be capable of recognizing and accepting mistakes and learning from them.

2. Open, constructive confrontation is encouraged at all levels, and is viewed as a method of problem solving—conflict resolution. Hiding problems is not acceptable. Covert political activity is strongly discouraged.

3. Decision by consensus is the rule. Decisions once made are supported. Position in the organization is not the basis for quality of ideas. Decisions are encouraged to be made at all levels within the organization, wherever the facts are. What people help create, they support.

4. A highly communicative/open management approach is part of our style. People want to know as much as possible about their work environment, and not knowing hurts. It hurts their pride, insults their intelligence, arouses their fears, and results in counter-productivity. We must have "enough" meetings. Problems must be discussed in an open forum; decisions must be made in an open forum and so on. Staff members at all levels must be accessible.

5. A high level of organizational skill and discipline are demanded. Consistent with our office objectives, staff are expected to be organized in their approach, and a high degree of planning is required. The relationship between performance and commitments should be closely monitored and viewed as a key indicator of an individual's overall performance.

6. Staff members must be ethical. Decisions and actions must be consistently beyond question from an ethics standpoint. By telling the truth and by treating everyone within and without our organization equitably, we establish our ethical credibility.

7. Trust in relationships is important. Without trust, any human relationship will inevitably degenerate into conflict. With trust, anything is possible.

8. Staff must face up to difficult work-related decisions, whether they are professional, organizational, or personal.

9. The responsibility for individual development rests to a considerable degree with the immediate supervisor. To behave in an ethical manner here means that time

and effort must be put into the professional development of subordinates. This means "pushing" subordinates and encouraging continued improvement in both skills and performance while creating an environment conducive to professional development.

Work Ethic

It is the general objective of our office to arrange individual work assignments that are consistent with individual career objectives.

Further, we must work to create an environment that allows each employee to enjoy his/her work while achieving his/her career goals.

We should strive to provide an opportunity for personal career development. This implies the necessity for a strong commitment to training but does not imply that the sole responsibility for this training lies with the supervisor.

Our office is results oriented. The focus is on substance vs. form, quality vs. quantity.

We believe in the principle that hard work and high productivity are things to be proud of. A high degree of discipline is to be expected and admired. Timeliness is a key element of our work ethic. It is not good enough to deliver a quality product - the quality product must be delivered on time.

The concept of assumed responsibility is accepted. If a task needs to be done, assume that you have the responsibility to get it done and do it.

We desire to have all staff involved and participating in their relationship with this office. We want the staff to care about their office. To aid in achieving this end, we stress good communications in the hope of establishing a sense of identity and closeness.

Student Service Orientation

Students are:

. . . the most important people on the campus, without students there would be no need for our office or this institution.

. . . not cold enrollment statistics, but flesh and blood human beings with feelings and emotions like our own.

. . . not people to be tolerated so that we can do our thing. They are our thing.

. . . not dependent on us. Rather, we are dependent on them.

. . . not an interruption of our work, but the purpose of it. We are not doing them a favor by serving them. They are doing us a favor by giving us the opportunity to do so.

Office of the Vice President for Student Affairs

Short-Term Factors

Finally, there are a number of short-term factors that must be taken into consideration in the management of a career center. These factors may or may not come into play depending on current circumstances. Examples of such short-term, rapidly changing factors are the economy; changing student demographics; staff strengths, weaknesses, and vacancies; social and political issues both locally and nationally; and unexpected administrative directives. Depending on prevailing conditions, these short-term fluctuations sometimes present a greater management challenge than do strategic factors, which are more likely to be anticipated. Often the management of short-term factors is thought of as crisis management, or as one management guru characterized it, "management as white water rafting" (Vailli, 1989). As crucial as planning is to the management of a career center, the ability to remain calm in the face of crisis and to deal effectively with that crisis remains a crucial asset that will serve any director well.

BUDGETS AND BUDGETING

Budgeting within a modern-day career center has become increasingly complex for a number of reasons. First, most college and university career centers have come to depend more and more on fees-for-service. Because of the tight controls that regulate the establishment of student fees in most institutions of higher education, a great deal of effort and energy must be expended to secure permission to establish fees. Once established, efforts to increase fees to reflect increased costs over time also require the negotiation of an extensive approval process. Second, the establishment of fees requires rather elaborate systems for fee collection (including the acceptance of credit and debit cards), money handling, storage, and accounting. In larger centers, this may mean the addition of a staff position just to manage the business aspects of the enterprise. In brief, many career centers have taken on the character of small businesses in terms of the necessity to estimate the resources that will be generated by fees, the collection and management of revenue, and the establishment of accounting processes necessary to ensure the expedient and secure management of financial resources. Third, most career centers have become increasingly dependent on fees charged to employers for participation in career fairs and other center-sponsored events. These fee interactions with employers add yet another level of complexity because now the center is receiving resources from external sources, creating the need for additional transaction and accounting procedures. These changed budget circumstances have had a significant impact on all aspects of the budget process in the modern career center.

Expenditures

The operating budget of most career centers consists of two key components: personnel salaries and departmental allotment. Like most service agencies and educational institutions, personnel salaries in career service centers comprise between 75% and 90% of the total operating budget. Thus, a large portion of total expenditures is fixed, leaving the budget manager with little budget flexibility. The fact that personnel salaries are fixed should not deter a budget manager or director from scrutinizing these salary expenditures carefully with a view to ensuring equity while providing salary-based performance incentives. Typically, individual personnel salaries are governed by some form of human resource classification system that specifies salary ranges by grade. Within the constraints of such a classification system, efforts should be made to establish creative ways to provide high-performing staff with merit increases. Without such an incentive system, the largest portion of the career center budget (personnel salaries) is likely to be appropriated on a flat, across-the-board basis, which ultimately becomes a disincentive to performance and deterrent to productivity.

The departmental allotment at most college and university career centers comprises approximately 10% to 15% of the total budget. In actual dollars, most university career centers that serve approximately 10,000 undergraduates or more had operating budgets that averaged $149,901 in 2002. In the entire nation, only a small number of institutions (presumably large universities) with enrollments in excess of 20,000 had operating budgets of greater than $250,000. The clear trends in career center operating budgets in recent years have been: (a) institutional support in the form of budget increases has been minimal, (b) career centers have been forced to supplement their operating budgets through the introduction of fees for service, and (c) there has been an expectation that operating budgets will be supplemented by corporate gifts, grants, and other forms of external funding. This emphasis on the acquisition of external resources has fundamentally changed the management of the career center by requiring that the director spend a greater percentage of his or her time generating external funds and accounting for these funds. In effect a larger percentage of the director's time must now be spent as a development officer and business manager.

There is no typical career services operating budget, but the sample operating budget provided here for purposes of illustration is reflective of the major operating expenses incurred by most college and university career centers. For the sake of simplicity and to aid comparative analysis, this sample budget (Table 5.1) is based on an annual departmental allotment of $100,000 and excludes salaries. Column 1 provides a description of the budget item, Column 2 indicates the estimated annual expenditure, and Column 3 indicates the percentage of the total operating budget that each item represents. It can be quickly deduced from this sample budget that nearly 50% of the typical career center operating budget is devoted to five key areas: office supplies, telephone and fax services, postage and mailing services, printing and copying services, and capital equipment—principally computer hardware and related technology. Column 3 serves as a convenient per-

TABLE 5.1
Sample Career Services Operating Budget

Description	Amount	Percent of Total
Work study and wage payroll	3,000	3
Office supplies	8,000	8
Catering and food supplies	1,500	1.5
Miscellaneous supplies	2,000	2
Supplies and materials for resale	500	0.5
Telephone and fax	8,000	8
Postage and mailings	10,000	10
Conference registrations	600	0.6
Group meals	700	0.7
In-state travel	2,000	2
Out-of-state travel	6,000	6
Publications	6,000	6
Subscriptions	2,000	2
Building rentals	300	0.3
Equipment rentals	400	0.4
Equipment maintenance	7,000	7
Repair or maintenance of building	1,000	1
Honoraria or consulting fees	1,000	1
Professional services	400	0.4
Unemployment compensation	1,000	1
Tuition and fees	1,500	1.5
Auxiliary enterprise charges	400	0.4
Freight charges	300	0.3
Purchased services	1,000	1
Photographic services	200	0.2
Printing and copying	12,000	12
Advertising	1,500	1.5
Software	1,500	1.5
Memberships	500	0.5
Noncapital equipment (under $1,000)	1,000	1
Promotional printing	500	0.5
Other miscellaneous	200	0.2
Capital equipment (computer & related)	15,000	15
Lease/purchase agreements	1,000	1
Videotapes/films	1,000	1
Total	100,000	100%

centage benchmark against which career center directors can compare their own expenditures.

Revenue

Resources in support of most college and university career centers come from three principal sources: (a) the general operating budget of the institution, (b) fees for service, and (c) external sources. Although personnel salaries and some portion of the departmental allotment to cover operating expenses are normally covered from the institution's general operating budget, it is becoming increasingly common to expect that all or most of the career center's operating expenses will be covered by fees and external resources. Indeed it is not uncommon that some portion of personnel salaries be covered by external resources.

Supplementing the Career Service Budget

As identified in the prior section, one of the keys to balancing a career center budget is the director's willingness to seek resource support from alternative sources. This strategy is sometimes referred to as using OPM (Other People's Money)! Over the years, successful career center directors have become quite adept at securing resources from a broad range of different sources. Here are the most common techniques used by career center directors to supplement their budgets.

Advertising. Many career centers solicit advertising revenue from employers. The most common source of advertising money is the placement manual. Most career center placement manuals are supported totally from advertising dollars. Similarly, electronic message boards, career center bulletin boards, various targeted publications, and career center newsletters are increasingly supported through advertising. At large university career centers, advertising support often accounts for up to $100,000 in additional operating funds.

Shifting Operating Costs to Employers. Many career centers have made arrangements to shift the cost of parking, phone calls, fax transmissions, Federal Express charges, and other mailing/shipping costs to employers. Although most career center directors regret having to resort to these techniques, such cost-shifting measures may save the career center thousands of dollars in just a year's time, and these nuisance charges have come to be expected by employers, if not always cheerfully accepted.

Contracted Services. External vendors are increasingly willing to provide services on behalf of the career center and then charge employers for access to those services. Examples are Web-based job listing services, on-campus recruiting and scheduling systems, coin-operated copy services, and so on. Although most directors resist subscribing to these types of services, they do represent yet another way to supplement meager operating budgets.

Corporate Sponsorships. Many college and university career centers have established corporate sponsorship or corporate associate programs. The essence of such programs is that corporations contribute an annual sum to the career center in return for public recognition in the form of having their corporation's name and logo appear prominently in the foyer of the career center on a plaque. Such corporate sponsorships often provide thousands of additional discretionary funds in support of career center programs. Sometimes specific employers become permanently associated with certain career center programs. An example might be the "ABC Company Mock Interview Program." Such sponsored programs are often seen as a win/win because they bring positive recognition to the sponsoring corporation and they allow the career center to deliver services that would otherwise be cost-prohibitive. Corporate sponsorships of this sort can represent a significant source of revenue for career centers at large universities with prestigious engineering and business colleges, but they have enjoyed less success elsewhere.

In recent years, there has been a trend toward corporations sponsoring capital projects, including the building of career center buildings. This generous corporate support has led to the naming of career centers in much the same way that athletic stadiums and facilities are being named. Although career centers and their clients have been the benefactors of this corporate largesse, there are some downsides. Relying on external funds shifts a certain amount of control to those who provide the funds. Ethical dilemmas sometimes develop as contributors seek favors in return for contributions (Goodman, Rayman, & Ferrell, 2001). Of perhaps more concern is the tendency to develop a dependence on soft money that may dry up in hard times, leaving the career center without the necessary operating budget to deliver expected services. Despite these disadvantages, career centers, because of their long-standing close relationships with the corporate world, are likely to look increasingly to corporate sponsorship as a means of supplementing their budgets.

Fees for Service. As mentioned earlier, many career centers supplement their meager operating budgets through user fees charged to student, alumni, and community clients. Such fees usually take two forms: general fees for service (registration fees) or specific fees for specific services. Data from recent NACE (2004) surveys suggest two trends with respect to fees for service. First, general fees are uncommon for any of the user types mentioned before, and there does not seem to be a trend toward increasing such fees. Second, more than one third of all career centers charge students, alumni, employers, and community clients for specific services, and there is a clear trend to increase such fees.

In general, we are opposed to user fees for two reasons. First, we believe that quality career services are an integral part of an undergraduate education and, as such, should be available to all students free of charge. Second, fee collection is a costly, time-consuming activity that drains staff time away from the delivery of career services. Nevertheless, if financial exigencies dictate that some form of fee be charged, we regard fees for specific services to the alumni and the general public as being far preferable to general fees or fees for enrolled students.

Capital Fundraising Campaigns. Beyond the budget supplementing techniques suggested earlier, most large career centers have become engaged in full-fledged capital fundraising drives to support specific projects. Such fundraising drives often target corporations with which the career center has developed long-standing relationships. This seems like an obvious strategy because most successful development efforts are based on long-standing positive relationships—it is simply a matter of tapping into the good will that has been built up over the years. Unfortunately, fundraising of this type has never been easy for student service units because of an often-held perception by central administration that such efforts siphon off funds that would otherwise go to academic units. Therefore, it is suggested that any capital fundraising campaigns be closely coordinated with the university development office.

Leadership Implications

In summary, current trends require that career center directors spend an increasing portion of their time functioning as development officers, accountants, and financial managers. The positive reward for skillful financial management is often a modest increase in autonomy within the university community—if you play an active role in generating the resources, you are often given greater liberties in how you spend them. The unfortunate side effect is that central administrators sometimes interpret your ability to generate your own resources as a license to cut institutional support—in effect, the more you raise, the more you are expected to raise.

STAFF RECRUITMENT, RETENTION, AND PROFESSIONAL DEVELOPMENT

Nothing is more crucial to the success of a career center than the careful selection, training, and professional development of staff. A comprehensive college or university career center requires a staff with a wide range of interests, skills, abilities, academic backgrounds, and experience. In addition, all staff should be skilled in the areas of customer service, counseling, and the effective use of technology. Such a staff is likely to be comprised of at least seven different types on the basis of function.

Administrative Staff

The administrative staff will normally consist of the director, one associate director, and an administrative assistant/office manager whose primary responsibilities are to maintain the resource base, the political battles within the college or university, handle all budgetary and personnel matters, represent the office to the greater university and the outside world, and generally provide leadership for the office. In smaller centers, these individuals may also be involved in several of the other functional areas, including the provision of some direct service, whereas such direct service is unusual in a large center.

Placement Staff

The placement staff consists of an associate or assistant director and an additional professional staff member whose primary responsibilities are to supervise and conduct the placement-related services of the center, including employer relations, on-campus recruitment, credential services, placement library, placement advising, and programming in support of the placement function. This associate director normally has a master's degree in Counselor Education, Student Personnel Administration, or Higher Education and 5 to 10 years of closely related work experience.

Counseling Staff

The counseling staff consists of an associate or assistant director and a number of counselors with specialized training in career counseling and/or counseling psychology. Their primary responsibilities are to conduct, supervise, train, and evaluate individual and group career counseling sessions; teach career development courses for credit; and prescribe and interpret assessment devices and other standardized treatment modules, including computer-assisted career guidance. All members of the counseling staff will normally have at least master's degrees in Counselor Education or Counseling Psychology and be licensed or certified career counselors.

Programming Staff

The programming staff should consist of an associate or assistant director and one or more professional staff who deliver a wide range of outreach programs, including seminars, workshops, training sessions, lectures, and career fairs. Some of the programming staff are likely to be counselors, placement staff, and administrators because few career centers have the luxury of single-purpose programming specialists. All members of the programming staff should have excellent presentation skills and an interest in and flair for creatively delivering and managing a wide range of career programs.

Systems Analyst/Programmer

The pervasive use of technology in all aspects of the career center has dictated that most large centers employ a full-time professional to manage information technology. This staff member should have a BS in information science, management information systems, computer science, or related field with a strong commitment to the utilization of technology to enhance the work of a service agency.

Graduate Assistants

Graduate assistants are likely to be of two principal types: master's-level student personnel administration students interested in programming, placement, management, and administrative tasks; and master's- and doctoral-level counseling students with an interest in individual and group career counseling, assessment and research, and the teaching of career development courses.

Support Staff

Each of the professional classifications enumerated earlier require quality clerical and administrative support. This includes receptionists, scheduling clerks, word processing/data entry clerks, and administrative assistants among others. In all cases, support staff should be well versed and experienced in the use of technology.

For reader convenience, we have included here a fairly detailed example of a position description for Director of Career Services. Practitioners seeking benchmark position descriptions for other key career center staff are referred to Herr, Rayman, and Garis (1993).

Title of Position: Director

Classification: Professional

Department: Career Services

Function of Position:
Responsible to the Vice President for Student Affairs for the direction and management of university career services. Has overall responsibility for and authority over

planning, organizing, developing, administering, budgeting, and directing career-related programs and delivery systems for the university.

Principal Duties and Responsibilities:

1. Responsible for overall administration of Career Services including:
   a. Overseeing the operation of established services and programs, including evaluation, improvement, policy enforcement, and change
   b. Establishing long-range plans for the office
   c. Developing and administering the budget
   d. Developing and assessing the effectiveness of day to day management and communication procedures, policies and forms
   e. Assessing, maintaining and improving office physical environment including equipment, furnishings and facilities
2. Responsible for staff supervision including:
   a. Developing and maintaining staff patterns as office needs dictate
   b. Developing and overseeing the hiring process for all staff including selection and/or approving selection of all staff
   c. Developing and conducting and/or overseeing training and development of all staff (professional and clerical)
   d. Conducting ongoing supervision and evaluation of staff
3. Responsible for representing the career center to the university and public including:
   a. Publicizing office programs and services to faculty, staff, and students
   b. Serving on university committees
   c. Representing the center on consortium institution committees and programs
   d. Representing the center to employers locally, regionally, and nationally
4. Responsible for representing the career center and the university to the profession including:
   a. Attending, participating in, and presenting at professional conferences and communicating relevant information to center staff and university faculty and staff
   b. Staying abreast of the professional literature as well as contributing to it on a regular basis
   c. Integrating information and knowledge gained through (a) and (b) above into office planning and practices.
5. Participate as a management team member in student affairs including:
   a. Attending all appropriate meetings and communicating information about career services to other departments and from other departments to career services
   b. Participating in student affairs decision-making, planning and problem solving as appropriate
   c. Working with other student affairs unit directors and collaboration as appropriate
   d. Maintaining of high quality two-way communication with the Vice President for student affairs.
6. Interpret university policy and government (state and federal) rules and regulations to students, faculty, executive staff, governmental officials, and representatives

from business and industry in all matters pertaining to career development and professional employment. Ensure that the university adheres to current national and state guidelines on equal opportunity and affirmative action insofar as career services activities are concerned.

7. Serve as spokesman for the university to media for articles, forecasts, quotes, and appearances (radio, TV, and business/civic groups) as expert on the job market for graduates, employment data and trends, and related research.

Supervision:
Duties and responsibilities are performed under general direction and through the interpretation of university policy based on general objectives. Thorough knowledge of university policies and procedures is required in their application to cases not previously covered. Work is performed independently toward general results and requires the ability to devise new methods or modify existing procedures to meet new conditions. Problems are rarely referred.

Minimum Qualifications:
An earned doctorate in counseling psychology, counselor education, higher education, industrial psychology or related field plus a minimum of 8 years effective administrative experience in higher education, career services or related area. Excellent interpersonal and communication skills, strong theoretical and practical knowledge of the career development field and proven ability to translate ideas/concepts into successful career programs/services. Must be qualified for immediate affiliate faculty rank in counseling psychology, counselor education, industrial psychology, or other academic department.

USE OF TECHNOLOGY

The use of technology in career centers is perhaps more pervasive than in any other counseling-oriented office. Nearly all of the functional units within career services now depend heavily on technology for their operation. Here we discuss several of those functional units and comment on the state of technology as it relates to them.

On-Campus Recruitment

All career services offices now utilize some form of software to manage their on-campus interviewing process. Historically, many offices attempted to develop their own software, but the enormity of that task has ultimately led to most offices adopting one of several available commercial software packages. At this writing, there are about four surviving commercially available on-campus recruitment software packages. These are (listed here alphabetically): Experience, MonsterTrak, NaceLink, & Symplicity. Through consolidation and the test of time, these four systems have survived and now dominate the market. All provide similar functionality, but each offers certain unique features, and each is based on a different business model. Experience and MonsterTrak are most similar to each other. Both are privately owned and operated, and both rely heavily on revenue from employer vacancy listings. NaceLink is a partnership between a private company (Employer Direct) and the National Association of Colleges and Employers (the professional association). NaceLink provides similar functionality to the other two systems, with the added benefit that comes from being associated with NACE. Symplicity is a private company that produces enterprise software. They provide the most sophisticated and customizable system, although the cost of their system is substantially greater than the other three systems.

It seems probable that one or two of these systems will ultimately survive and dominate the market. Until clear winners and losers emerge, career center directors will need to evaluate these (and possibly other yet-to-emerge systems) on a continuous basis. One thing is certain: All career centers must utilize technology to perform the on-campus recruitment and vacancy listing functions because it is far more efficient and both student and employer clients demand it.

Counselor Tracking

Another function that lends itself to solution via technology is the maintenance of counseling client demographics and counseling case notes. Commercial software is available for this purpose, but many career centers have developed their own software, which is customized to their specific needs. One system of which we are aware is CounselorTrak. This system allows counselors to store an extensive array of client information via the use of customizable drop-down menus and also provides the capability to store unlimited narrative progress notes. Perhaps most important, from the perspective of the director, the system offers an elaborate summary-reporting capability so that counseling activity can be monitored by client type, presenting problem, counselor, age, college, major, year in school, gender, and a nearly limitless number of other criteria. Such systems offer the capability to store and instantly retrieve massive client data files, offering maximum counselor and administrator convenience while maintaining absolute confidentiality.

Events Management

Most colleges and universities now offer Career Fairs, Graduate School Fairs, Professional School Fairs, Multicultural Career Fairs, and a broad range of other large-scale events that can only be managed effectively through the use of technology. These Web-based systems manage nearly every aspect of event management, from registration and fee payment to program production, space assignment, and participant census-taking. These types of events management software are available commercially, although most are quite expensive. The most widely used Career Fair management system at this writing is Symplicity (2004).

Integrated Database Management Systems

As described earlier, many sophisticated software packages have been developed to enhance the efficiency of various functions within the career center. Unfortunately, most of these are stand-alone systems that do not integrate readily with each other. In the future, it is desirable to develop systems that "talk to each other" and utilize shared or integrated databases. The clear trend is in this direction, but at this writing career centers are forced to use a grab bag of different unrelated software packages to support the numerous career services functions.

Computer Assisted Career Guidance and Counseling Systems

Nearly all career centers employ computer assisted career guidance systems. The two most widely used, highly developed, and carefully researched such systems are DISCOVER and SIGI-Plus, although other less well-known, computer- and Web-based systems are available. The challenge for career center directors is to integrate the use of computer assisted guidance and counseling systems in a way that supplements and supports more traditional delivery systems without threatening the integrity and existence of those systems.

Career Center Web Information Systems

All career centers have found it necessary to develop a Web presence. These vary from relatively simple sites consisting of little more than an online office brochure to highly sophisticated sites with literally thousands of pages of information and text, including online assessment devices, complex navigation systems, and multiple linkages to commercially developed sites.

Leadership Implications

Few counseling agencies are more dependent on the use of technology than are career centers, and no other counseling-related agencies have exploited the power of technology as extensively as career centers. The successful management of a university career center is critically linked to the effective utilization of technology, and directors who do not embrace this reality are not likely to be successful. Most large career centers employ at least one systems analyst/programmer, and many employ additional technical staff as well. Perhaps the greatest challenge facing career center directors is how to generate sufficient resources to become and remain technically current. As valuable as technology has proved to be to the career services enterprise, even software developers are reluctant to develop career center software because it is not a profitable market niche. As a profession, career services must find the financial means to support emerging technologies that will carry the profession into the future.

INTERNAL ORGANIZATION OF STAFF/ PROFESSIONALS

In general, college and university career center organizational structures are of three types: (a) centralized and hierarchical, (b) centralized and flat, or (c) decentralized and flat. Because career center staffs are usually not large, the structure is normally fairly flat. We believe that a flat structure is generally superior to a more hierarchical one because it encourages direct communications between and among all staff, and it shortens turnaround time (Townsend, 1970). The organizational structure of career services at most universities is dictated, to a considerable degree, by the structure of student affairs and the greater university. Clearly the structure of career services must be compatible with the institution in which it operates. Our experience suggests that excellent career services often exist despite, rather than because of, a particular organizational structure, and although the choice of a structure is not trivial, it is seldom critical. In the handbook for the College and University Career Center, Rayman (2001) summarized the advantages and disadvantages of the three structures cited before.

Centralized/Hierarchical Structure

In this type of organizational structure (Fig. 5.1), the director has full responsibility and authority for career services university wide. Under this model, most large university career centers will have a professional staff of 10 to 25 persons and a clerical staff of 5 to 10. Such a structure will probably have at least four levels or grades of professional staff and perhaps four clerical grade levels as well. Depending on the size of a college and its student affairs staff, it may be necessary to collapse these levels to three or even two.

Advantages of the Centralized/Hierarchical Structure
1. A hierarchical structure provides a career ladder for staff. Entry-level professionals can aspire to a progression up the ladder with concomi-

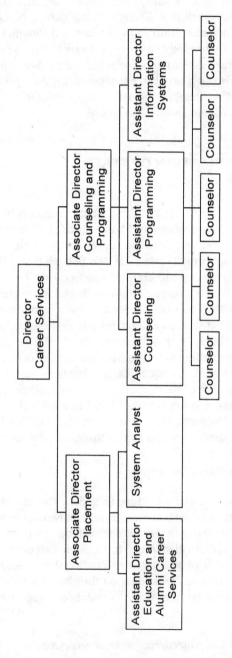

FIG. 5.1. Centralized hierarchical structure.

tant increases in responsibility, authority, and salary. (This is a corporate model.)

2. Centralization allows for more specialization of function and provides the flexibility to better draw on the special skills and talents of staff.

3. It recognizes that certain functions are more crucial to the operation of the center than others, and it rewards persons performing those functions with appropriate authority, responsibility, titles, and salary.

4. Reporting lines are clear, and if the organization functions in accord with the reporting lines, responsibility should follow authority.

Disadvantages of the Centralized/Hierarchical Structure

1. If the structure is rigidly adhered to in terms of communication within the organization, turnaround time on decisions can be time-consuming and decision making can become inefficient.

2. Specialization can lead to boredom and perceived lack of variety in work assignments.

3. Staff at the lower levels of the hierarchy can feel as if they are isolated from the decision-making process and thus feel uninvolved and uninvested in the goals and mission of the center.

Some examples of institutions employing the centralized/hierarchical model are:

Arizona State University
The University of Florida
Florida State University
University of Maryland
New York University
Penn State University
Stanford University
UCLA

Centralized Flat Structure

In this type of organizational structure (Fig. 5.2), the director has full responsibility and authority for career services university wide. However, nearly the entire professional staff reports directly to the director. The staff may be just as large as in the centralized hierarchical structure, but all professional staff have similar titles (e.g., assistant director or career counselor) and are at approximately the same level in terms of salary, responsi-

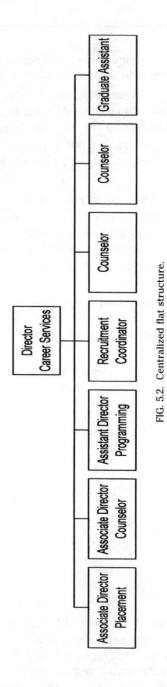

FIG. 5.2. Centralized flat structure.

bility, and authority. This model is more likely to occur in a college than in a university structure.

Advantages of the Centralized Flat Structure

All professional staff are at the same level, and thus ideally a collegial atmosphere exists. (This is an academic model.)

1. Because in theory all professionals are interchangeable, work assignments can be rotated and shared, enhancing variety of work tasks and minimizing the burnout that is sometimes associated with specialization.
2. There is less compartmentalization and specialization of work tasks. Thus, staff coverage in the event of sick leave and vacation leave is more easily arranged. In theory, any staff member can cover for any other staff member.
3. Such a system may be in place to ensure that all professional staff within the career center are regarded as management as a means of dealing with staff unionization.

Disadvantages of the Centralized Flat Structure

1. The director's job may be more difficult because she or he must direct and supervise such a large number of employees.
2. Rarely do all professional staff contribute equally, and this structure limits options available to the director to reinforce high productivity and discourage poor performance.
3. The lines of authority and responsibility are often vague, leading to confusion about who has the authority to direct certain functions and who has the responsibility for those functions.

Some examples of institutions employing the centralized flat structure are:

Bradley University
Carnegie Mellon University
Indiana University of Pennsylvania

Decentralized Flat Structure

In this type of organizational structure (Fig. 5.3), there are several (and may be as many as 10 or 15) directors of placement and/or career development. Generally, such directors run one- to three-person operations affiliated with individual colleges or schools within the university. There may also be a director of the career development center, which may serve all colleges (the University of Illinois and Cornell University model). Another variation on this

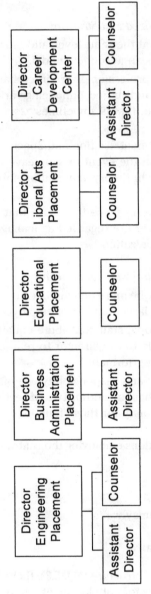

FIG. 5.3. Decentralized flat structure.

theme is the centralized career development and placement service with individual assistant directors affiliated with, and housed in, the individual colleges, but with joint reporting lines to the central director of career services and the dean of their particular college (the University of Virginia model).

Advantages of the Decentralized Flat Structure

1. Placement staff are located close to the faculty of their respective college and presumably can give more specialized service and attention to both students and faculty of the college.
2. Day-to-day involvement with the faculty and staff of a particular college or school enhances the probability of faculty involvement in both career development and placement functions.
3. Individual college staff size is small, and thus there is more variety in the workload and staff feel they have more individual autonomy.

Disadvantages of the Decentralized Flat Structure

1. Communication between and among staff of the separate colleges often becomes difficult, and geographic separation exacerbates it.
2. Destructive competition often develops between individual college offices for access to employers at student expense.
3. Duplication of services and facilities is almost inevitable.
4. Students and employers may become confused about which office to use and where they are welcome.
5. Colleges of engineering and business administration generate a great deal of interest, large numbers of interviews, and financial resources, whereas liberal arts and other nontechnical colleges with fewer natural linkages to business and industry struggle to survive.
6. Such systems often result in conflicted loyalties on the part of staff. If a student's interests, values, and abilities suggest a better fit in another college, staff members are likely to be reluctant to encourage a transfer because of their vested interest in maintaining enrollment in their own college.

Some examples of institutions employing the decentralized flat structure are:

Cornell University
University of Illinois
Iowa State University
University of Virginia

Finally, some institutions have endeavored to combine various aspects of both centralized and decentralized approaches, claiming to achieve the efficiencies of a centralized career planning and placement operation with the ease of communication and more personal approach of a decentralized operation (Babbish, Hawley, & Zeran, 1986).

OUTREACH TO THE UNIVERSITY COMMUNITY

One characteristic that distinguishes career centers from most other counseling agencies is their strong commitment to outreach. Historically, many counseling agencies have been reluctant to aggressively market and promote their services because of the pervasive philosophical influence of the medical model. It is not thought to be professional to advertise or actively market your services—better to let those who need assistance seek you out. Career centers have broken from this view and have become increasingly adept at aggressively reaching out to a broad range of constituencies. The following section describes specific outreach initiatives that have become the trade in stock of the modern career center.

Placement

The roots of the career center derive from the placement function and especially the on-campus interviewing programs (OCR) offered by most large colleges and universities. It has become common practice to advertise OCR and other placement-related services aggressively to students (and their parents) via college and university newspapers, local radio and TV spots, Web sites, as well as targeted e-mail messages. Nearly all of the office–student interactions that transpire prior to an on-campus interview take place via the Internet, thus the process has been pushed out to the customer, allowing interactions from nearly any geographic location 24 hours a day, 7 days a week. Similarly, resume referral services, vacancy listing services, and other related placement services are now routinely delivered online 24/7.

Interactions With Employers

Interactions with employers have also been transformed by the Internet. Much of the communication that necessarily takes place between employers and the staff of the career center takes place via e-mail or Web-based transactions, including the scheduling of interviews, choice of interview candidates, announcement of employment opportunities, and scheduling of on-campus information sessions. The use of technology now allows career centers to reach out and touch employers anywhere in the world.

Career Counseling

Most career centers aggressively advertise their counseling services to students via the mass media and via the Internet (see later section on marketing and public relations). Similarly, many college and university career centers now offer career counseling to faculty and staff, alumni, local area employees, and other general members of the community. This aggressive outreach reflects the recognition by most career centers that career development is a life-long process and a recognition by the general public of the benefits of career counseling. Through the use of technology, computer-based career counseling and assessment are increasingly being made available to the greater society as part of the service mission of many colleges and universities.

Career Courses

Most career centers now find it beneficial to offer career development courses to their enrolled students as part of normal classroom instruction. These courses often include a structured curriculum involving self-assessment, utilization of formal assessment tools, comprehensive study of the world of work, introduction to strategies to assist in career implementation, and even group and individual counseling sessions in many cases. Similarly, a significant component of career development theory and practice is increasingly being imbedded into freshmen seminar courses that have gained great popularity on most college campuses in recent years. The introduction of these types of career courses is a clear example of the way in which career centers are reaching out into the classroom with their career development agenda.

Workshops

Career development workshops and seminars have long been an important element of the service menu provided by career centers. It is often the case that more actual client contacts are made through the vehicle of structured workshops and seminars than through traditional counseling. Indeed the conduct of workshops and seminars can be thought of as a significant element of the marketing strategy that attracts potential clients to the career counseling process. In the past, most of these workshops were conducted within the career center with significant marketing efforts being made to draw clients into the center to participate. The recent impetus toward outreach has caused a significant change in that strategy. At many campuses, the majority of workshops and seminars are now conducted off premises in residence halls, fraternity houses, at club and professional meetings, and in classroom situations at the request of the recipients. This strategy not only has the advantage of reaching out to the customer, but also ensures an attentive audience because the host organization assumes responsibility for attendance. The current environment favors those career professionals who are prepared to aggressively take their seminars and workshops to the participant.

Yet another way that career professionals are reaching out to customers with educational programs and workshops is through the use of technology. Angel software and other similar instructional software packages are now being used to deliver a broad range of online workshops, including resume preparation, interview skill building, job-search strategies, networking, and many others to clients in the comfort of their dormitory rooms and homes. Active outreach initiatives of this type now make career assistance available to clients 24/7 anywhere in the world.

Assistance to Special Populations

As in other areas, career centers have been at the forefront in reaching out to special populations, which have heretofore been underserved by career services. The key here has been initiatives that specifically identify special populations, target them with direct invitations to utilize services, and go the extra mile to create a comfort level that ensures their participation. An example of this type of program is the Spanish-language Intake Counseling program offered by Career Services at Penn State University. A Spanish-speaking counselor holds special hours during which Spanish-speaking students are invited to address their issues in Spanish. Once the counselor establishes a relationship with the client, the client can be referred to the mainstream services offered to all students. Similar programs have also targeted lesbian, gay, bisexual, and transgender (LGBT) students, disabled students, returning adult students, international students, and graduate students—all resulting in increased participation by these special populations.

Assistance to Alumni

Perhaps the strongest indication of the degree to which society has acknowledged career development as a life-long process has been the recent surge of support for alumni career services among the nation's colleges and universities. Many of the outreach techniques described earlier are now being utilized to deliver a comprehensive array of career services to alumni throughout the lifespan. It can be expected that this trend will continue as alumni associations seek to maintain life-long relationships with their alumni through the provision of career services. Such services meet a growing need among alumni, and satisfied alumni are generous alumni.

DIVERSITY ISSUES

The first and foremost diversity issue for any career services director is to ensure that the programs and services of the career center are meeting the needs of its diverse student and employer clients. The more diverse the student population, the more effort must go into ensuring that programs are in place that reach all students, and that a comfort level is created that assures students that they are welcome.

The director of a modern career center must take active steps to ensure that the career development needs of various minority groups are fulfilled. The first step in meeting those needs is to be fully aware of what the minority population is. That is, what percentage of the student body is African American, disabled, gay, international, in graduate programs, Asian American, and so on? Knowing this is not always as easy as one might think because some minority groups choose not to self-identify, others cannot be identified by visual inspection, and still others are understandably reluctant to participate in special programs. Once the difficult task of identifying the various minority populations and their relative numbers has been achieved, there are a number of steps that must be taken to ensure effective program delivery.

1. Staff must receive multicultural sensitivity training and multicultural counseling training to minimize the effect of long-standing institutional bias against certain subpopulations.

2. An effort must be made to create an environment that is attractive and comfortable to all clients. The goal here is to create an environment that is perceived by all students as being inclusive.

3. Special targeted advertisements must be utilized to ensure that various minority groups understand that the career center serves people with their background and that the career center is not only safe for them, but is possessed of specialized skills to serve their special needs.

4. Special programs must be developed to meet the unique needs of certain populations. Examples might be Spanish-language intake counseling or multicultural internship programs. The purpose of such programs is not to create separate but equal approaches, but rather to draw minority clients into the center and create a comfort level that ensures that they will utilize all of the center services.

5. Finally, an accurate online record must be maintained of minority utilization of center services. The minimum acceptable goal should be that all identifiable minority groups utilize all career services in percentages that are equal to or greater than their percentage of the total enrollment. Thus, if the institution's enrollment of African Americans is 8%, one would expect

that at least 8% of those using career services would be African American. These utilization statistics must be continuously monitored to ensure that appropriate rates of minority utilization are sustained.

Diversity of Staff

Although university career center professional staff generally work in the functional areas described previously, it is necessary to ensure diversity along a number of key dimensions that cut across these functional areas. The dimensions of staff diversity that we regard as most important at this point in the historical development of university career centers are enumerated here and are consistent with those identified by Herr, Rayman, and Garis (1993).

Gender. In coeducational institutions, it is desirable to maintain as close to a 50/50 balance on the basis of gender as possible. This gender balance should cut vertically through the hierarchy of the professional and clerical staffs. That is, it is important to have both women and men at all levels of the organization. Too often women are concentrated in the entry-level positions, whereas men are concentrated at the upper management levels. With the undergraduate student gender ratio in most co-educational institutions being nearly 50/50, it is important to maintain a similar gender ratio among staff. In recent years, it has been increasingly difficult to recruit men into entry-level positions within career centers. At this point in the history of the profession, an affirmative action initiative to recruit males seems indicated.

Ethnicity. As the ethnic diversity of university enrollments grows, so too does the need to ensure appropriate ethnic diversity among the staff of the career center. At most modern university career centers, it is reasonable to expect that at least some of the professional staff will be African American, Asian American, and Hispanic. The degree and nature of the ethnic diversity within the student body should dictate the degree and nature of the ethnic diversity of the career services staff, and a good-faith effort must be made to achieve that degree of ethnic diversity.

Academic Background. Although it is natural for career center staffs to be dominated by individuals with degrees in education and counseling, it is highly desirable to ensure some diversity in terms of academic background. Where possible, the disciplines of engineering, science, liberal arts, education, and business administration should be represented on the university career center staff. Such diversity of academic background not only allows for specialization, but enhances the richness of staff and staff–student interactions and ensures the probability that a variety of viewpoints will be represented in the delivery of career services. Few diversity issues are as critical to the successful delivery of career services to the multiple colleges of a comprehensive university as academic background of the staff, and yet this is one area of diversity that receives little attention.

Experience Background. Just as it is desirable for staff to exhibit considerable diversity in terms of academic background, diversity of work experience is also important. All too frequently career services staff have little or no work experience outside of the educational setting. Where possible, the previous work experience of staff should complement their academic backgrounds to ensure that career counseling and advising have a strong reality base. In brief, it is not desirable to employ career counselors who have never held employment outside an educational institution.

Sexual Orientation. Diversity in terms of sexual orientation has taken on increasing importance as the general population has become more aware of the issues confronted by gay, lesbian, bisexual, and transgender individuals. Although it may not be possible to hire staff who embrace a range of sexual orientations, the director of a career center must, at a minimum, (a) acknowledge sexual orientation as an important issue in career development, (b) reach out to clients with varying sexual orientations and create a comfort level for them at the career center, and (c) sensitize counselors and other staff to the wide range of career issues related to sexual orientation.

Age. Diversity along the age dimension may be more important in the career center than in other student service offices. On the one hand, undergraduates may find it easier to relate to young staff who have recently graduated from master's programs. On the other hand, young staff with limited life experience may lack the credibility to provide effective career counseling to returning adult students, graduate students, postdoctoral students, and alumni. To some degree, the nature of the student body and the relative mix of graduate to undergraduate students should dictate the age range of the staff, but clearly an attempt should be made to maintain some balance.

Disability. One of the most difficult minority groups to reach with career services is the population of individuals with disabilities. Employing a staff member with an obvious disability is one way a career center can demonstrate its commitment to serving members of the disabled community.

There are obviously other dimensions of diversity that we have not addressed here, but that may be of greater or lesser importance depending on the nature of the student body and the mission of the institution. The important point here is that the career center director must maintain a high level of awareness regarding staff diversity, and this awareness must be translated into action every time a hiring opportunity exists.

EVALUATION OF PROGRAMS

Evaluation and assessment are essential aspects of all counseling agencies. In his list of 10 imperatives for the career services profession, Rayman (1999) stated,

> We have entered an era of accountability never before experienced in higher education. If we wish to survive this era, we will need to do a better job of advocacy, and we will also have to become more efficient and innovative in our use of existing resources. We must work smarter AND harder. We must develop and utilize valid and reliable assessment tools and techniques so that our requests for resources are data driven. (p. 182)

In the career center, evaluation and assessment tend to take two forms—formative and summative. Formative evaluation results are used to assess program quality and improve performance, whereas summative evaluation provides a means to estimate the aggregate or total impact of a program, service, or individual or group activity on some predetermined set of criteria (Kuh & Andreas, 1991). In brief, formative evaluation helps us improve our services and performance, whereas summative evaluation helps us justify our existence and secure adequate resources.

Formative evaluation techniques vary in terms of their formality, complexity, and convenience, but a wide range of techniques must be employed in the effective management of a career center. Several of the more common formative evaluation techniques are described here.

Advisory Boards

Advisory boards are not often thought of as elements of an evaluation strategy, but if they are effective they will perform that function. Student advisory boards are the most important of such mechanisms, but many career centers also employ faculty and employer advisory boards. The key characteristic of advisory boards is that they are usually made up of consumers (of one sort or another) of the services of the career center. As such their members interact with and relate to their peer consumers frequently, and are thus in a position to represent views beyond their own about the quality and appropriateness of career center services. Because of their dual role as both consumer and advisory board member, individual members usually take a positive approach to providing feedback to center staff. Their vested interest in ensuring that the center provides the very highest quality career service makes them a key source of feedback to the director and other members of the administrative staff.

Program Evaluation Forms

Another useful method of securing formative evaluation data is through the continuous and ongoing use of program and presenter evaluation forms. Such forms can be used for nearly any type of center-sponsored program. Our experience has shown that high percentages of program participants will respond via such forms if the programmer implores them to do so at the beginning and again near the end of the program. We find that between 90% and 95% of program participants complete and submit evaluation forms when the programmer presents them as a means to improve both the quality and relevance of future programs. Forms are collected by the presenter and reviewed immediately. Then they are forwarded to the assistant director for programming, who collates the information and provides feedback and suggestions to all presenters at the end of the semester. The purpose of such forms is not to evaluate individual presenters. Rather, they are to be used developmentally to assist presenters to improve the quality of their programming efforts.

Employer Evaluation Forms

Employers represent a crucial source of feedback about the quality and character of various elements of the on-campus recruitment process. Key among these elements are: (a) number of students who do not show up for interviews (no-shows), (b) students who might benefit from assistance with interview skills, (c) suggestions pertinent to placement services, staff support, and accommodations, (d) suggestions pertinent to the relevance of the curriculum of various academic programs to the employers' needs, and (e) general comments and suggestions. Feedback from such forms provides useful support for planning change in training programs, the curriculum, placement policies and procedures, as well as university parking policy.

The Suggestion Box

One should never overlook or undervalue this obvious and perhaps simplistic means of securing user feedback. In our experience, some innovative and useful ideas result from the placement of a suggestion box in high-traffic areas within the career center. We have found that moving the suggestion box from one service area of the center to another week to week or month to month has a tendency to stimulate user input.

Spot Evaluations

From time to time, it is useful to identify a random sample of service users and send them service evaluation forms via direct mail or e-mail. Such spot evaluations can be extremely useful in evaluating the effectiveness of various existing services and in modifying and improving services in accordance with client perceptions and expectations. These one-shot, random surveys are easy and inexpensive to administer and, if well designed and carried out within 2 weeks of the date service was rendered, typically result in a high response rate.

Written and Verbal Complaints

Often complaints about service are regarded as a nuisance, and some of them are; but nearly every complaint contains a kernel of truth that can provide context and insight that will be of value to the planning process. Clients should be encouraged to express their complaints, comments, and suggestions both verbally and in written form, and every such complaint, comment, or suggestion should be acknowledged and taken seriously. Such a policy is not only good for public relations, but just good business.

Evaluation by Walking About

Peters and Waterman (1982) and others have advocated that a key to excellence is getting close to the customer. We know of few better means of formative evaluation than for the director and other key staff members to get out on the front line, mingle with the customers (students, employer representatives, and alumni), and listen to what they are saying. Often the best front-line position for feedback is that of the office receptionist or clerk. Few experiences provide greater insight for enhancing office policies and procedures than a short walk in the shoes of the customer or the front-line service purveyor.

Summative evaluation has become easier and more efficient with the advent of computer software programs that facilitate the capture, storage, and rapid retrieval of client/user census data and allow for the rapid generation of reports for planning and management. One particularly useful tool in the capture of client data has been the advent of the ID card swipe reader that allows career centers to register students for counseling, placement, and programming with the simple swipe of each student's ID card. Combined with swipe card registration, Web-based survey software allows career service centers to push evaluation forms to client users via e-mail 2 or 3 days after the program or service being evaluated. This technological advance not only eliminates paper, but also allows program participants and

service users time to process their experience before rendering an evaluation, often leading to more thoughtful and relevant evaluations.

PROGRAM ACCREDITATION

Although the topic of program accreditation is much debated within the career services profession, to date no formal program of accreditation or certification exists either at the state or national level. It is the case that many
career centers evaluate their programs against the CASS standards as described earlier in this chapter, but these evaluations are either self-
evaluations or done by informally established external review committees.
The National Association of Colleges and Employers (NACE) board continues to debate the merits of accreditation even as many of the regional
NACE-affiliate associations have established formal external review committees. These review committees are made available for formal visitations
on request, and they have had a considerable positive impact on career
center quality both regionally and nationally. It seems likely that NACE will
continue to move toward formal accreditation in the near future.

MARKETING/PUBLIC RELATIONS OF SERVICES

A major distinction between career centers and counseling agencies is the
open and direct way in which career centers market their services to their
various constituent groups. Unlike agencies, which focus on personal counseling and embrace the medical model, career centers are perceived by
most constituencies as being an integral part of the educational process
and, as such, promote and advertise their services openly and aggressively.
One of the most difficult challenges most career centers face is that of "rais-
ing student awareness to the need to take responsibility for their own career destiny." Most centers devote a substantial portion of their operating
budget to advertising and promotion, and if they don't, they probably
should. Survey research at Penn State University indicates that more than
half of the student body never graces the career center with their presence.
Although an extensive discussion of various marketing and public relations
strategies is beyond the scope of this book, the reader may wish to refer to
the *Handbook for the College and University Career Center* (Herr, Rayman, &
Garis, 1993) for a more thorough discussion of marketing-related issues. In
our experience, it is not sufficient for career centers to offer a quality product; that product must also be marketed effectively in an increasingly competitive and sophisticated multimedia environment that includes the use of
Web ads, direct e-mail, promotional brochures, advertisements in the col-

lege/university newspaper, radio and TV spots, flyers, give-aways, bribery with food, raffles, and just about any other marketing ploy used in the goods and services marketplace. A number of large career centers have even established full-time marketing and public relations assistant directorships. Clearly an effective career center director must devote considerable time, effort, and energy to the marketing function. The strategies that work for McDonald's, Nike, and Mazda also work for career services.

ADVOCACY FOR PROGRAMS

The directors of all service agencies must spend a certain amount of their time and energy advocating for resources and constituent support. Career services directors are no exception. Although the central administration of most colleges and universities recognize the importance of career services and the value that it adds to the educational enterprise, their lip service does not always translate into the resources necessary to provide for the complex career development needs of today's students. Accordingly, the director and other senior members of the career services staff must work diligently to ensure that central administration understands the mission and goals of the career center and has an appreciation for the value that a quality career center adds to the educational programs of the institution. This often begins with a quality *annual report* that is circulated to central administrators, including deans and department heads. It also includes what some refer to as a *placement report* that surveys the postgraduation activities of all students at all degree levels and demonstrates the effectiveness of various academic programs as preparation for careers or graduate and professional education. This type of postgraduation survey is particularly important in the professional schools of business and engineering, where an important accrediting criterion is the school's placement rate.

Beyond these once-a-year reports, many large institutions find it desirable to publish quarterly or semi-annual newsletters (hard copy or e-mail) directed to faculty, administrators, trustees, and parents to keep these stakeholders apprised of the activities and services offered by career services because resource support for all college and university units is controlled to some extent by these key stakeholders in the educational process. One particularly powerful form of advocacy is to arrange to give a presentation before the institution's Board of Trustees at least once each year if possible. Because Boards of Trustees wield ultimate power within academic institutions, there can be no better advocates.

Similarly, consideration should be given to providing some type of formal update on career center activities to employers on a periodic basis. Not only are employers powerful advocates for career centers vis-à-vis central administration, they are often key sources of direct supplemental financial support to career centers. Keeping employers apprised of center goals, objectives, and achievements is an important aspect of the director's role. To this end, many career centers have established employer advisory boards as a means to formalize this important advocacy relationship.

PARTICULAR LEADERSHIP/MANAGEMENT ISSUES

The management of a career center has certain similarities to that of managing any counseling agency or enterprise. Perhaps the most intriguing and challenging aspect of career center management is bridging the differences that exist between the business and educational/counseling cultures straddled by the career center. In this chapter, we have endeavored to point out the similarities and differences between career center management and that of other counseling agencies, and we have attempted to emphasize those similarities and differences in terms of their implications for leadership. We close with a series of thoughts/issues on the leadership and management of career centers, some of which have been drawn from the chapter entitled "Management of the Career Center" from Herr, Rayman, and Garis (1993).

1. Use technology to improve the quality of career services. Don't let technology dictate office policies and procedures. The pervasive use of technology has had a greater impact on career center management than on any other counseling-based service agency. Too often career centers change what were sensible, meaningful procedures because those procedures cannot be carried out conveniently on existing software or hardware. Do not be seduced by technology, which is often a cheap and inferior solution to human service problems. Technology must be used to free professional staff time so they can perform those functions that require human sensitivity.

2. Eliminate the obstacles. A director must devote a significant amount of time to eliminating the obstacles that stand in the way of staff member productivity and professional development. It is important for a director to use his or her relationship with those administrators above him or her to liberate the staff from bureaucratic, political, and procedural obstacles and the frustrations that accompany them.

3. Cultivate a can-do bias for action among the staff. Many counseling agencies seem to cultivate a "we're overworked and ain't it awful" attitude. A core value in virtually all of the best-run organizations, whether they are businesses or educational institutions, manufacturing or service organizations, is a strong bias for action (Kuh, 1985; Peters & Waterman, 1982). We believe such a bias for action will serve the director of career centers well. In

our experience, there is a tendency for professionally trained counselors to have a strong process orientation that often deters them from moving to the action phase of leadership and management.

4. The feminization of the profession. In the past 10 to 15 years, the career services profession has come to be dominated by women (NACE Survey, 2004). On the one hand, this would appear to be a positive trend because it suggests that women are entering this profession (and other professions) in greater numbers, signaling the end of gender discrimination. There are, however, several disturbing aspects to this trend. First, the ratio of male–female clients seeking assistance in career centers is almost 50–50. Does it really make sense that nearly all the staff in career services are now women? It would seem that the domination of any field by either gender is not desirable from the perspective of those being served. Second, nearly every profession that has become dominated by women has experienced declines in average salary levels. It is a sad, but true, fact of American life that the feminization of a profession often leads to a loss of prestige and reduced average income. Finally, the domination of any profession by either gender tends to create an unbalanced work environment—a subculture that may not be in the best interest of clients, the profession, or society.

5. The sacred nature of the performance appraisal process. It is our belief that a quality performance appraisal process is one of the most critical tools for effective leadership, management, and staff development. Too often in our experience, administrators steeped in counselor training are reluctant to engage in performance appraisal with the rigor that is necessary to ensure superior staff performance. Indeed one of the major obstacles to appropriate performance appraisals is the confusion between clinical supervision and performance appraisal. Often the deeply held counselor commitment to being nonjudgmental interferes with the absolute necessity to critically distinguish between excellent and mediocre performance and to rewarding differential performance. This reluctance to discriminate is pervasive throughout educational institutions, but is particularly pronounced in counseling agencies.

6. Leadership is serious business. It is important to recognize that leadership and management take time and are very complex—they are difficult human processes that are easily as difficult as teaching or counseling. This is one of the premises that underlie the need for this book. Effective career center directors work at leadership and management every day. They are students of leadership, and they are constantly on the lookout for more effective methods and means of leading and managing. Effective leadership is not something that can be done on a part-time basis from one's hip pocket. It must be lived every minute of every day.

7. The importance of leading by example. It seems trite to say it, but "Do as I say, not as I do" just never works for long. Effective career center direc-

tors become involved in the day-to-day business of the career center and demonstrate on a daily basis that no aspect of the work done in the center is beneath their dignity. Directors who demonstrate skill in the broad range of tasks performed within the career center and the willingness to become involved in performing those tasks are more likely to be respected and accepted as leaders. They earn their credibility to lead every day.

8. Organizational skill and persistence will often make up for a lack of charisma and brilliance. Some directors are effective leaders because they have natural charisma, but most must also have solid organizational skills and a strong work ethic to be effective. Nearly all productive and efficiently run organizations are led by hard-working individuals with well-developed organizational skills. Preparation and perspiration are more important than inspiration.

9. High level of awareness of what is going on around you. One characteristic of effective leaders is a high level of awareness of what is happening in the workplace. This often involves what some management gurus have called Management by Walking About. Directors who notice who works hard, who arrives at work on time, and who maintains a good balance in both their work and personal lives are more likely to be effective leaders and managers.

10. Genuinely care about all members of your staff and be willing to go the extra mile to get them to perform at a high level. Over the years, we have found that directors who care about what others think about them, those who care about their employees' personal lives, and those who care about morale in the workplace are the individuals who become the most successful leaders.

11. Hire the highest quality staff you can and support them with quality professional development opportunities. You can only be as effective as the people you surround yourself with. You never go wrong hiring the best, most-qualified individuals into your organization. Excellent employees are productive while they work for you, and because they are productive, they have opportunities to move on, which gives you as a manager the opportunity to hire other excellent employees. Marginal employees perform poorly while they work for you, and they never leave because they have limited marketable skills and few career opportunities. To this point, Andrew Carnegie wanted the following inscription carved on his tombstone: "Here lies a man who attracted better people into his service than he was himself."

12. Set the tone and values of the organization by providing an office management philosophy and living it by example. An example of an office management philosophy was presented earlier in this chapter.

13. Faculty rank. To ensure the credibility necessary to function effectively within the increasingly credential-oriented university community, a

doctorate and at least affiliate faculty rank in an appropriate academic department are almost a necessity for the director of a university career center. Other key career services professional staff are also likely to benefit from such affiliate relationships.

SUMMARY

Chapter 5 described the multiple management and leadership challenges confronting the modern-day career center. It describes the crucial strategic factors in planning for successful career center management and highlights the related leadership implications. It then describes and details the essential topics of: budgets and budgeting; staff recruitment, retention, and professional development; use of technology; organizational structures; outreach to the university community; diversity issues; evaluation of programs; program accreditation; marketing/public relations; and advocacy for programs. Throughout the emphasis is on managing and leading counselors in the rather unique environment of the college or university career center. Finally, a summary of timely leadership/management issues is provided together with suggestions for action.

6

Chair, Department of Counselor Education, Counseling Psychology, or Both and More

CONTEXT

The role of head, chair, or administrator of a university or college department, which includes or is solely focused on counselor education or counseling psychology, is a complex job requiring multitasking. In some respects, it is difficult to talk about the organizational configuration in which programs of Counselor Education or Counseling Psychology are located because there are so many variations in such structures across the nation. The first author of this book was an administrator of a Department of Counselor Education, Counseling Psychology, and Rehabilitation Services for 24 years at the same institution. During that period, the organizational structure that he headed began as part of a Department of Educational Leadership. Then the Counselor Education program was pulled from that structure and became an autonomous Department of Counselor Education. Subsequently, a new dean decided to organize the college into divisions. In that case, the division became the Division of Counseling and Educational Psychology. A further reorganization renamed that division and increased the programs it housed and it became the Division of Counseling and Educational Psychology and Career Studies. At that point, the division included programs preparing elementary school counselors, secondary school counselors, directors of guidance, rehabilitation counselors (and undergraduates in rehabilitation education), college student personnel specialists, educational psychologists (specializing in learning, measurement), vocational teachers, vocational administrators, industrial trainers, and school psychologists. After 10 years in this structure, with the arrival of another dean, the divisional structure was abolished and a departmental structure was re-instituted; to wit, the Department of Counselor Education, Counseling Psychology, and Rehabilitation Services. In each of the configurations cited, the chair or administrator of the department or division remained the same, but the programs grew or receded in number and complexity.

Shifts in the organizational structures in which Counselor Education or Counseling Psychology are located are not unusual. The restructuring varies in rationale from saving fiscal resources by combining programs under one administrator, thus saving the administrative and operational costs of three or four separate departments, to putting programs most alike in purpose together (e.g., clinical programs, teacher education, psychology programs, foundations programs, etc.) to reinforce communications and collaborative activity among such programs.

Shifts in the organizational structures in which Counselor Education or Counseling Psychology are located are often driven by other external or internal factors. External factors include accreditation criteria. For example, it would be difficult to get a program in Counseling Psychology accredited by the American Psychological Association if the program's name were not prominent in a department title and in university documents that separate the curriculum, faculty, and resources of Counseling Psychology from those for Counselor Education or Rehabilitation Services if they are in the same department or division. In some cases, organizational shifts are motivated by such dynamics as the changing prestige or importance of certain programs, the potential student demand for entry into such programs, the credentialing circumstances related to program accreditation, or the licensure or certification of graduates of programs. Internally, deans of colleges in which programs are located prefer specific organizational structures (department, divisions, individual programs), and they create those structures as a method of easing the administration of such entities or primarily for the sake of change. Some deans of colleges would make such organizational changes as a way to foster new mixes of faculty members working together in research projects, seeking externally funded contracts or other collaborative initiatives. Other internal dynamics sometimes operate within universities. It is not unusual to experience or know of colleges in the same university with overlapping purposes to raid programs from other colleges. For example, a college that has been assigned responsibility for Allied Health programs may try to argue that Rehabilitation Services or Counseling Psychology should be seen as health care providers and should be moved from their current department or college location to a new location in the college assigned the Allied Health programs. In some cases, programs are moved to another college or eliminated because they are not seen as central to the mission of the college in which they are currently located; in other cases, programs are moved because institutional-level administrators decide that all psychology programs should be in the same department or for some other reason.

DEPARTMENT HEADS AS PERSONS OF MANY ROLES

In any of these cases, the administrator of the department or division in which the counseling programs are located must be a buffer, an advocate, a facilitator, a statesperson, and a leader of *all* of the programs for which he or she has administrative responsibility. The administrator is likely the person financially responsible for all of the funds that come into the department and the expenditures that take place. Therefore, the administrator must work diligently to allocate resources fairly across programs, to avoid favoritism, and to be as transparent and clear about the criteria by which funding or other decisions are made as is possible.

The administrator of the department or division must be credible in the areas where he or she judges faculty members or expects performance. For example, the administrator should have a solid history of excellent teaching, of scholarship and research, of publications, of grant-seeking, or of outreach and statespersonship in his or her area of specialization. If he or she does not have such a background, one becomes vulnerable to faculty claims that the administrator, chair, or head does not understand the implications for the faculty member of what they are being asked to do or how to do it. Thus, to the degree possible, the administrator of the department or division would be well advised to continue to teach a course, publish, and engage in other professional activities that give evidence to the faculty that the administrator values these functions, can execute them, and, as a result, can serve as a mentor and give relevant advice to faculty members. In a sense, the perspective advanced here is part of the old adage that, "Leaders never ask anyone to do anything they can't or won't do." Such an expectation places a substantial burden on administrators to demonstrate their capability in the professional areas they expect of others as well as in the leadership and administrative roles they are also obligated to perform.

The playing out of these sets of professional and administrative roles is delicate in several ways. For one, administrators of a department or division must come to terms with how they want to be seen: as an administrator first and a faculty member a distant second, as a faculty member who also has major administrative responsibility, as a professional colleague or a person who transcends the faculty role and is somehow more important than faculty members, or as a servant, a facilitator, of faculty members to empower them to be the best they can be, or as their boss.

How one makes these decisions and converts them into action is a critical issue for most administrators. It is compounded in situations where the administrator or chair of the department or division is elected on a rotating basis (e.g., serving 3 years and then returning to the faculty). How one performs in such a role has much to do with the colleagueship one may experience when one returns to a faculty role and how the subsequent administrator of the department treats the now former department administrator. Again, probably the overarching principle that the administrator of the counseling department can work to optimize is fairness in the treatment of individuals and programs. Once faculty members believe that the administrator of a department "plays favorites," "strikes deals," "manipulates decisions," and does not keep his or her word, passive resistance and undermining of the administrator's credibility, among other dynamics, can result.

One of the factors that can affect a department administrator's credibility is an unwillingness or inability to understand the differences in the programs for which one has responsibility. Individual academic disciplines have cultures that are different. For example, programs in Counselor Education, Counseling Psychology, and Rehabilitation Services teach similar techniques and intervention procedures. However, they frequently function in different settings, have different values, work with different populations, experience different histories and roots, have different resource bases, and have different accreditation policies. To briefly illustrate the point, programs of Counselor Education are accredited by the Council for the Accreditation of Counseling and Related Programs (CACREP), programs of Counseling Psychology (doctoral programs only) are accredited by the American Psychological Association (APA), and programs of Rehabilitation Services are accredited by the Council on Rehabilitation Education (CORE).

Although these are the major accreditation bodies for each of these programs, there are other less important accreditation bodies that deal separately with programs for clinical mental health counselors, with programs preparing counselors or psychologists for educational settings or other specialties. These programs of accreditation have different expectations for curriculum content, for faculty–student ratios, for the amount of supervised counseling with live clients required, for practica and internships, and for the professional identity that students in the program are expected to acquire. Although there may be some overlap in coursework or supervised experiences across these accreditation processes, the reality is that there is little such overlap, and each of these accreditation processes is fundamentally a stand-alone process that expects the program accredited to be capable of standing alone, being independent in its ability to meet the accreditation criteria that are relevant to it alone. From the viewpoint of the administrator of the department, each of these separate accreditation processes has substantial costs in faculty and support staff time and energy as well as in fiscal expenditures to pay an accreditation fee, for the preparation of self-study and other documents, and the costs for transportation, housing, and per diem for the visiting accreditation team. In the case of the Department of Counselor Education, Counseling Psychology, and Rehabilitation Services with which each of the authors of this book has a faculty role, each of the three major programs identified are accredited, must pay an annual fee to maintain their accreditation, and periodically be reaccredited with all of the costs involved.

The point is that the administrator (head) of the department must budget for and allocate resources to each of these accreditation processes. In addition, he or she must understand the accreditation process, facilitate the analysis of required information about the program seeking accreditation, ensure the completion of the self-study for the program being accredited, and promote the ability to interpret it to the visiting team members as they ask questions about procedures, student identity, placement, and other matters of relevance to the accreditation process.

It must be added here that, in addition to the matter of accreditation, the administrator of a department must also be knowledgeable about the individual credentialing of graduates to perform the functions for which they are being trained in a specific program—Counselor Education (and its specialties in elementary school counseling, secondary school counseling, college student affairs, chemical dependency counseling), Counseling Psychology, and, perhaps, Rehabilitation Services. Typically, the credentialing of individuals is a process independent of the accreditation of programs. Credentialing of professionals—either certification or licensure—is usually a state government matter rather than a national accreditation organization matter, with the exception of the National Board for Certified Counselors, discussed in chapter 3 and elsewhere. The issue is that, although accreditation of programs and credentialing of individuals may have some interactive dimensions, they are distinct processes. Thus, to ensure that graduates of a program are eligible for certification or licensure in a particular state may require something more or different than that incorporated in the accreditation process. The administrator of the department must provide leadership in faculty understanding of these different processes and lead the systematic execution of the required curricular content and emphases, supervision of the clinical experiences of students, or whatever is necessary.

Although thus far we have talked about accreditation of programs and credentialing of individual graduates of specific programs, it is useful to acknowledge that department administrators must also be cognizant that a department or division they lead is likely to include undergraduate, master's degree, and doctoral students. Each of these educational levels incorporates issues about which administrators have responsibility. They include differentiation of curriculum content related to the professional level of a given program and the expected roles that graduates of the program are being prepared to assume. Sometimes all three levels of preparation are under the influence of accreditation processes that effectively define curriculum content. This is more typical of graduate programs than of undergraduate programs, but that is not always the case. For example, the Council on Rehabilitation Education (CORE) accredits both undergraduate and graduate programs in Rehabilitation. The American Psychological Association (APA) accredits only doctoral programs in Psychology (e.g., Counseling Psychology, Clinical Psychology, etc.), not master's degree or undergraduate programs. The Council on the Accreditation of Counseling and Related Programs (CACREP) accredits both master's and doctoral programs in various counseling specialties. The department administrator needs to be aware of these general processes, where the department programs fall short of accreditation criteria and how to shore them up, how to pay for the required instruction or accreditation processes, and how to facilitate the quality of programs at each educational level and in each discipline.

THE DEPARTMENT HEAD AS COLLABORATOR

Another important and related role of the department administrator is communicating with other department administrators in which students take courses. For example, in virtually any undergraduate, master's, or doctoral program, students take a large portion of their academic subjects from departments other than their home department. Many foundation or specialized courses in psychology, sociology, statistics and measurement, learning, and human development are taught by faculty who are not counselors, nor do they apply the content they teach to counseling problems per se. They also may prefer not to have large numbers of students in their classes, particularly if comprised of students not in their own departmental majors. This leads the administrator of the counseling program to several communication issues. For example, it is important for him or her to advise other department administrators about the courses that counseling students would like to take in the other administrators' department, how many students are likely to enroll in a given semester, and the importance of these resources to the counseling department and to its ability to achieve or maintain accreditation.

Such communication avoids many problems between departments. For one, it allows the receiving department time to plan how many course sections or instructors are needed to meet these student demands from other departments in the college or university. It also allows them to determine how to pay for such course sections. Further, it allows the administrator of the counseling department to talk with other department administrators about accreditation procedures and how important the receiving department's instruction is in meeting such goals. In some instances, potential receiving departments do not want to or cannot accommodate the needs for course instruction that emanates from the counseling department. If the coursework offered by the potential receiving department is really essential for the undergraduate or graduate students involved, the administrator of the counseling department may have one of several choices: help the administrator of the potential receiving department pay for the courses it can offer to the students in the counseling department; in collaboration with the other department administrator, put together a proposal to the dean of the college housing the counseling program indicating how important the additional sections of this coursework are to the quality and, perhaps, the accreditation of the program in counseling; and request some funds to help pay for the instructional costs of those courses or teach these additional required courses in the counseling department per se. The latter action is likely to be particularly problematic because other departments may object to "their courses" or "competing courses" being taught by the counseling department, thus violating their instructional turf. In addition, however, teaching these courses in the counseling department also requires additional funds for faculty, part time or full time, to teach these courses and, perhaps, reduces the opportunities to fund other departmental initiatives that are seen as potentially more important then teaching courses, which, at least theoretically, can be taught more effectively by other departments in the college or university.

What these illustrations demonstrate is that, although departments or academic programs appear to be autonomous or to stand alone, in fact they are not. They need to have student access to selected courses taught by faculty in other departments or colleges as well as the availability of these faculty to serve in such roles as members of interdepartmental committees or as outside members of students' master's or doctoral committees. To an increasing degree, then, given limited resources in colleges and universities and increasing student demands for courses and faculty involvement across programs, such resources do not come for free. Someone has to pay for this teaching, consultation, or faculty time. The payment made may be "in kind"—your students can take these courses from our department if our students can take x courses in your department—or by directly sharing fiscal resources for access to courses or other expertise.

We have lingered on some of the pragmatic examples to reinforce that the administrator of an academic department in counseling needs to blend management and leadership skills in working with the heads of other units or institution-level administrators in the university or college as well as in working with organizations outside of the university: accreditation groups, professional organizations, state and federal government agencies, foundations, and other relevant entities. Such interactions will be reiterated in the other sections of this chapter and elsewhere in this book.

THE COUNSELING ADMINISTRATOR AS FUTURIST

Implicit, if not explicit, in these prefatory comments for this chapter is the expectation that the administrator of a counseling department is able to manage a wide range of resource and interpersonal challenges as well as be a visionary, a futurist, if you will. We talk more fully about the latter in the next section of the chapter, but suffice it to say here that being a visionary or futurist requires constant monitoring of both the external and internal environments in which one functions. Thus, the administrator of a counseling department needs to be attentive to external and internal trends. From an external viewpoint, the department administrator needs to be sensitive to ongoing political, economic, and social issues that are likely to affect the provision of counseling in different settings and with different populations; how government agencies or foundations are reacting to these issues with legislation or new initiatives funding counseling or research in counseling; how program accreditation or individual credentialing processes are changing in their standards or ethical guidelines; and the conceptual themes and practices that are evident in the professional literature. From an internal standpoint, the administrator of a counseling department needs to develop points of contact with administrators of departments or agencies (e.g., the counseling center, the career services) that are complementary in their instruction or research to that of the counseling department as well as other institutional-level administrators who have administrative oversight or decision power that directly affects the counseling department.

The administrator of the counseling department also needs to learn about such major internal policies as promotion and tenure guidelines; student conduct policies; budgeting and expenditure policies; selection and assignment of graduate assistants, temporary employees, and adjunct or affiliate professors; union rules related to custodial, physical plant, or clerical staff; use of technology; scheduling classes; grading students; processes related to external grant-seeking and management of such funds; and internal program reviews. Although the department administrator does not need to be an expert in each of these internal dynamics, he or she must be attentive to them, ensure that they are complied with, know where to find information about them, and otherwise reflect their importance in his or her planning and management.

PLANNING

As is true of the other settings in which the professional counselor may become an administrator or have administrative responsibilities, the administrator of an academic department preparing counselors does not operate autonomously. He or she acts within a web of relationships, policies, and trends that are constantly churning, changing, and requiring responses.

Indeed planning in a Department of Counselor Education, Counseling Psychology, Rehabilitation Services, or any or all of the above is subservient to the strategic plan of the university or college in which the department is located. Although the department's plan must complement the institutional mission and contribute to its goals, in fact the department's plan is at the confluence of several types of input. Certainly, the department's plan must reflect and show the department's interaction and support of the institution's stated goals. It must also reflect a variety of professional factors that give it credibility within its own discipline. Therefore, the accreditations it has or aspires to; the roles for which it is preparing students and how; and its demonstrated successes in contributions to the larger professional community in teaching, publications, external funding, and professional leadership must be reflected in the plan for the future. The elements of the planning process are reflective of many of the steps identified in chapters 1 and 2, but certainly the seminal documents and factors influencing the program's directions need to be analyzed and interpreted in the planning process.

There are many seminal documents of importance to an academic department preparing counselors. Which specific documents are most important depend on which educational levels (undergraduate, master's, doctorate) and counseling roles students are being prepared to undertake. The seminal documents also depend on the type of college or university setting in which the counseling department is located: an environment that emphasizes teaching primarily, research and publication, grant-seeking and external funding, professional leadership, or all of these.

LEGISLATION

Any administrator of a graduate Department of Counselor Education or Counseling Psychology wants to be cognizant in planning of any active or impending legislation that provides funds for counselor training or performance in particular settings, counselor certification or licensure, and target populations for which counseling is one of the preferred treatments. Although there may be few legislative statutes currently active that focus primarily on providing support for building more counseling capacity, there are a sizable number of legislative pieces that talk primarily about critical social problems and secondarily about the needs for counseling and the roles that counselors can play in addressing such problems. Examples include legislation dealing with child abuse, violence, and bullying; school-to-work transition; unemployed persons; populations with disabilities; older workers, and so on. Each of these pieces of legislation tends to include counselors as professionals who can assist in helping persons affected by the problems identified to move beyond the trauma, anxiety, confusion, information, or skill deficits they may experience to greater purposefulness and productivity.

It is in this sense that, in the preparation or practice of counseling, one can argue that counselors and the various techniques they employ are sociopolitical instruments given credibility by governmental statutes. Such perspective means that there are few examples of counselors in any settings, including counselors in independent practice, who are not touched by regulations or legislation that frames what they do, monitors it, and identifies the national or state goals that counselors in schools, rehabilitation agencies, employment agencies, mental health, or other settings serve and affect. Ordinarily such legislation or regulation does not address all that counselors do or could do, but they nevertheless express the importance of counselors in achieving legislative goals related to certain social, economic, or personal problems. Such information is vital to departments because it gives relevant information to be included in planning for counselor preparation in different program emphases and as possible sources of external funding for research, instruction, and outreach.

POSITION PAPERS AND COUNSELING MODELS

A second category of planning documents is position papers and models of counseling advanced by professional organizations (e.g., The American Counseling Association, the National Career Development Association, The American School Counselors Association, the American Rehabilitation Counselors Association, American Psychological Association and its division of Counseling Psychology, the Council for the Advancement of Standards in Higher Education). Examples include the American School Counselor Association (ASCA) National Model for School Counseling Programs cited in chapter 3. In chapter 5 and elsewhere, we mentioned what are commonly called the CAS standards (Miller, 2003). These standards embrace general and specific standards related to both the higher education curriculum and the co-curriculum, the interaction between academic affairs and student affairs or student support practitioners. The CAS standards and the organization that created them exist to promote quality programs and services for college and university students. The standards and guidelines incorporated by the Council for the Advancement of Standards in Higher Education are, in fact, the amalgamation of standards and guidelines crafted by representatives of some 32 professional organizations that individually represent some function or activity that has to do with the effects of college on student learning and development, including academic advising, admission programs, career services, college health programs, counseling services, financial aid programs, housing and residential life programs, international programs, minority student programs, religious programs, and so on.

Although CAS is not an accreditation organization per se, the standards and guidelines, including the standards for preparation programs of master's-level graduate programs for student affairs professionals, are extremely influential in planning and evaluating the variety of counseling and student affairs processes now extant in higher education. Indeed for each set of standards and guidelines, CAS provides a SelfAssessment Guide (SAG) that includes a self-study process for program evaluation. The seven basic steps proposed by CAS to use a self-assessment guide are quite relevant to initiating a broader program planning process: (a) establish and prepare the self-assessment team, (b) initiate the self-study, (c) identify and summarize evaluative evidence, (d) identify discrepancies between the assessment criteria and actual practices, (e) determine appropriate corrective action, (f) recommend special actions for program enhancement, and (g) prepare an action plan.

The use of CAS standards and guidelines by higher education or an academic department preparing counselors or student affairs professionals in higher education confers a level of credibility on such programs, suggesting that they are seeking to implement best practices in specific function areas or preparation programs. As such the standards and guidelines can be used for staff development—as content in courses dealing with the organization and functions of student support programs and their relation to student learning and development.

In addition to the university or college strategic plan, governmental legislation or regulations related to counselors, and models and standards from professional organizations, academic departments preparing counselors must pay particular attention to accreditation standards relating to the mission, context, curriculum, supervision, practica, and internship standards required to be accredited. We discuss three major accreditation processes to which Counselor Education, Counseling Psychology, or Rehabilitation Services refer for their planning. Although these three accreditation organizations have already been identified earlier in this chapter, here we focus on their substance.

ACCREDITATION STANDARDS

Council for Counseling and Related Programs (CACREP)

CACREP, although an independent council, was created by the American Counseling Association in 1981. It received recognition as a nationally recognized accrediting agency in 1987. CACREP's primary mission is to develop standards and procedures that reflect the needs of a complex society, provide leadership, and promote excellence in professional preparation in Counselor Education and related educational programs. (Council for the Accreditation of Counseling and Related Education Programs, 2001). As of 2001, the scope of CACREP accreditations include:

1. Master's degree programs preparing individuals for roles in:
   Career Counseling
   College Counseling
   Community Counseling
   Gerontological Counseling
   Marital, Couple, and Family Counseling/Therapy
   Mental Health Counseling
   School Counseling
2. Doctoral-level programs
   Counselor Education and Supervision

Each of these programs, housed within an academic unit (e.g., department), is expected to be a structured sequence of curricular and clinical experiences for which accreditation is sought. The CACREP standards for each of the programs, several of which may be in the same academic unit, are considered to be minimal criteria for the preparation of professional counselors, counselor educators, and student affairs professionals. The master's degree programs, considered to be entry-level programs, are, at the time of an accreditation visit, to be comprised of a minimum of 72 quarter hours or 48 semester hours of graduate studies, with the exception of mental health counseling and marital, couples, and family counseling, which must have a minimum of 90 quarter hours or 60 semester hours of graduate studies. Doctoral programs must have a minimum of 144 quarter hours or 96 semester hours, which include entry-level preparation.

CACREP standards require for entry-level programs a minimum of three core faculty members whose academic appointment is in counselor education; doctoral programs are required to have a minimum of two full-time equivalent faculty positions in addition to the three required of entry-level programs.

For students pursuing any of the programs that CACREP accredits, they must have curricular experiences and demonstrated knowledge in eight common core areas. These eight core areas include:

• Professional identity
• Social and cultural identity
• Human growth and development
• Career development
• Helping relationships
• Group work
• Assessment
• Research and program evaluation

In addition, the programs to be accredited must require supervised experiences, including practicum and internship for all students. Supervised practicum experiences require a minimum total of 100 clock hours that can be dismantled into 40 hours of direct service with clients in individual and group work, weekly individual supervision of an average of 1 hour, 1.5 hours per week of group supervision, and evaluation of the student's performance during and at the end of the practicum. In addition to the supervised practicum, the CACREP standards require a supervised internship of 600 clock hours after successful completion of the student's practicum. It is expected that the student will, during internship, have an opportunity to perform, under supervision, a variety of counseling activities that are typical of those performed by a professional counselor. More specifically, the internship experience is expected to include 240 hours of direct service with clients appropriate to the program of study (e.g., elementary and secondary students for those counselor trainees in school counseling, college students for those counselor trainees in college counseling, etc.); an average of 1 hour per week of individual supervision; an average of 1.5 hours of group supervision; opportunities to perform duties of professional counselors that go beyond direct service, including such things as record keeping, in-service and staff meetings, and so on; opportunities to record, using audio- or videotapes, their interactions with clients for supervising purposes; supervised experiences in the use of various professional tools and resources such as assessments, technologies, directories and print resources, research, and so on; and formal evaluations of their experiences during and at the end of the internship.

Although there is much more to say about the standards applied specifically to each of the programs accredited by CACREP, suffice it to say here that the visiting teams examine the academic unit in which counselor preparation programs are administered and are concerned about issues such as faculty–student ratios by program and selected courses, cooperative relations with other departments and clinical performance settings (e.g., practica and internships), budgets, teaching loads, financial assistance, student recruitment and admissions processes, library and data processing resources, research support, and program identity.

As is true in most accreditation processes, the CACREP accreditation process requires a formal application for accreditation to be submitted with an application fee and a self-study of each program being considered for accreditation. Documentation of a program's compliance with the standards required for that program and validation by an onsite visiting team of the accuracy of the self-study and related information submitted to CACREP are essential components of the accreditation process. Then accreditation decisions are made by the CACREP Board based on the written self-study, onsite team report, institutional response to the team report, and interim and other reports periodically submitted to CACREP to monitor the program's compliance with specified standards.

National Board for Certified Counselors, CACREP, and State Counselor Licensure

Although the National Board for Certified Counselors (NBCC), like CACREP, was originally spawned by the American Counseling Association, both CACREP and NBCC are now independent corporations functioning as standalone organizations, rather than as units of the American Counseling Association. Similarly, CACREP and NBCC are independent of each other as organizations. Practically, however, the examination that NBCC uses as one of the elements of credentialing individual counselors for certification as a National Certified Counselor is comprised of items that assess the candidates' knowledge of the eight core curricular areas required to be provided by CACREP accreditation process. In that sense, graduates of CACREP-accredited counselor education programs may have an advantage over graduates of non-CACREP programs when taking the NBCC examination because their curriculum would have covered the knowledge bases required by CACREP.

Further, many of the 50 states that now license professional counselors interact with CACREP, NBCC, or both. For example, some states require the NBCC examination results and scores at a particular cut-off level as part of the academic and experiential process they use to review individual counselors for award of state licensure as a licensed professional counselor. Some states also expect that counselors who apply for licensure as a professional counselor will have covered the eight core knowledge bases as defined by CACREP regardless of whether they were trained in CACREP-accredited counselor preparation programs. State licensure boards assess whether applicants have met the curriculum requirements for licensure by evaluating the course transcripts of applicants to match courses taken with the knowledge bases required by the state licensure policies. Some state licensure boards require both NBCC examination scores that meet a cut-off score criterion and core knowledge requirements as defined in CACREP curriculum standards as core knowledge bases for counselors working with any population or within any setting.

It is worth noting here that some states require more credits for licensure as a professional counselor (60) than CACREP requires for a 2-year program being accredited at the master's level (48). This means that, in some states, students can graduate from CACREP-accredited programs with excellent grades and pass the NBCC examination with excellent scores, but be 12 credits short of the course credits required for licensure. In such instances, many counselor education programs have found a new market for outreach and service provision to counselors seeking to become licensed professional counselors and to meet the state requirements of some states that licensed professional counselors engage in continuing education, acquiring some defined number of credits each 3- or 5-year period after licensure.

The implications for the administrator of an academic department preparing counselors are several. Although we have lingered here on CACREP, NBCC, and state licensure of professional counselors as representative credentialing processes, the implications are essentially the same for the American Psychological Association (APA) program-approval process and state licensing boards of psychologists, as well as for the accreditation of rehabilitation counselors by the Council on Rehabilitation Education (CORE) and boards that grant the Certified Rehabilitation Counselor designations.

APA and CORE are discussed next, but we return to the implications of these processes for the administrator of academic departments preparing counselors for different settings. First, these accreditation processes largely define the content of the preparation programs that need to be offered if these programs are going to be successful in recruiting students and placing them following graduation. Second, participation in accreditation processes signals that a given academic program is consistent in its preparation with national trends in the field and prepares its graduates to obtain individual credentials increasingly important to employers. Third, accreditation of Counselor Education, Counseling Psychology, or Rehabilitation services programs is not free; the initial application fees and the expenses of preparing self-studies, hosting visiting teams, and paying yearly maintenance fees are considerable, particularly if a department is involved in all three—CACREP, APA, and CORE—accreditations for its programs. The department head must ensure that the annual expenses devoted to accreditation are provided for in the annual budget and are seen as important in the budget as are other routine expenses of telephone, salaries, and so on. Fourth, successful completion of accreditations appropriate to the counselors being prepared in a particular department arguably results in more highly qualified applicants for available places in the program. These persons, in turn, graduate and distinguish themselves with firmer professional identities, better clinical skills, and a more comprehensive knowledge of counseling and settings than students who do not graduate from accredited programs. Fifth, academic departments that successfully participate in accreditation of their counseling programs signal to internal institutional administrators that the counseling programs are among the best in the nation and in a constant state of continuous improvement. Sixth, accredited programs of counselor preparation are likely to gain new market niches for outreach, in-service, and the provision of coursework of value to individual counselors who are seeking state licensure or other certification or maintaining these credentials. Thus, although administrators of academic departments preparing counselors need to clearly understand and operationalize in their planning and budgeting that accreditation processes are cost centers, they are also sources by which to enrich the quality and image of the department. As such they become important priorities in the leadership and management roles of the department administrator.

The American Psychological Association

It is not unusual for Counselor Education programs at the master's and doctoral levels to be housed in the same academic department. In some colleges or universities, it is assumed that Counselor Education programs preparing counselors for multiple settings and programs preparing counseling psychologists or school psychologists are a natural fit. In some places this is true, whereas in others there is a tension between Counselor Education programs and Counseling Psychology programs because the differences in their accreditation processes argue for independent identities for each of these programs and for little, if any, overlap in courses, clinical experiences, or other program aspects. These tensions can be handled effectively by administrators who are able to treat each program fairly, without favoritism, in allocation of resources, psychological support, and valuing of program goals and students.

In comparison to the CACREP accreditation process just discussed, the APA only accredits doctoral programs in "professional psychology that part of the discipline in which an individual with appropriate education and training provides psychological services to the general public" (Committee on Accreditation, American Psychological Association, 2004).

The accreditation process as defined by APA is a process that involves "judging the degree to which a program has achieved the goals and objective of its stated training model" (p. 1). In Counseling Psychology, there are several training models, but perhaps the most common one is the scientist-practitioner model, which webs in emphasis the science and practice of psychology. The accreditation processes employed by the APA are intended to allow a preparation program "broad latitude in defining its philosophy or model of training and to determine its training principles, goals, objectives, desired outcomes (i.e., its mission), and methods to be consistent with these." That being said, however, APA expects a program seeking accreditation to be clear, coherent, and well articulated in its description of the principles directing its training philosophy or model, its goals and objectives, and the resources, methods, and processes by which it proposes to attain its intended training goals.

The APA accreditation process places emphasis on the outcomes or products of the training program. Of particular concern is the quality of the training experiences for students, the ability of the program to attain its goals, and the likelihood that the quality of the program can be maintained.

Rather than a checklist of criteria for accreditation, the APA accreditation approach is to identify general domains of activity that are considered essential to the success of any training program in professional psychology. Selected examples from these domains are provided next to demonstrate these domains.

Domain A has to do with the eligibility of doctoral programs to prepare students for the practice of professional psychology. Some specific eligibility requirements include that the program offering doctoral education and training in the practice of professional psychology be sponsored by an institution that is accredited by a nationally recognized regional accrediting body.

> The program is an integral part of the missions of the academic department, college, school or institution in which it resides. It is represented in the institution's operating budget and plans in a manner designed to enable the program to achieve its goals and objectives. The program must have students in sufficient number and the facilities necessary to ensure meaningful peer interaction, support, and socialization. (p. 3)

The program requires a minimum of 3 full-time years of academic study and completion of an internship prior to the award of the doctoral degree. The program engages in actions that indicate respect for and understanding of individual and cultural diversity. "The program adheres to and makes available formal written policies and procedures that govern academic admissions and degree requirements; administrative and financial assistance; student performance evaluation, feedback, advisement, retention and termination decisions and due process and grievance procedures for students and faculty" (p. 3).

Domain B. "The program has a clearly specified philosophy of education and training, compatible with the mission of its sponsor institution and appropriate to the science and practice of psychology. The program's education and training model and its curriculum are consistent with the philosophy" (p. 3).

Domain C. "The program demonstrates that it has resources of appropriate quality and sufficiency to achieve its education and training goals and objectives" (p. 3).

Domain D. "The program recognizes the importance of cultural and individual differences and diversity in the training of psychologists" (p. 4).

Domain E. "The program demonstrates that its education, training and socialization experiences are characterized by mutual respect and courtesy between students and faculty and that it operates in a manner that facilitates students' educational experiences" (p. 4).

Domain F. "The program demonstrates a commitment to excellence through self-study, which assures that its goals and objectives are met, enhances the quality of professional education and training by its students, and contributes to the fulfillment of its sponsor institution's mission" (p. 5).

Domain G. "The program demonstrates its commitment to public disclosure by providing written materials and other communications that appropriately represent it to the relevant publics" (p. 6).

Domain H. "The program demonstrates its commitment to the accreditation process by fulfilling its responsibilities to the accrediting body from which its accredited status is granted" (p. 6).

A second set of domains has to do with the internship experience required in all APA-accredited programs. Several of the domains are essentially repeats of those already described under program eligibility. A few specific domains illustrate the internship domains. Domain B: "The program has a clearly specified philosophy of training, compatible with the mission of its sponsor institution and appropriate to the practice of professional psychology. The internship is an organized professional training program with the goal of providing high quality training in professional psychology. The training models and goals are consistent with its philosophy and objectives. The program has a logical training sequence that builds upon the skills and competencies acquired during doctoral training" (p. 7) ... (b) Training for practice is sequential, cumulative, and graded in complexity. Domain E. "The program demonstrates that its education, training, and socialization experiences are characterized by mutual respect and courtesy between interns and training staff and that it operates in a manner that facilitates interns' training and educational experiences" (p. 9).

These selected items representing the principles and values of accreditation by the APA are like neon signs flashing *plan, plan, plan*. Like the CACREP standards, APA expects the accreditation process visiting team to a Counseling Psychology program to validate the intentions, processes, context, resources, identity, and outcomes of the professional psychology program.

Pragmatically, the process of accreditation includes an application, payment of an application fee, and a self-study document including tables, appendixes, and supporting information relative to the domains identified as relevant to the accreditation process. Subsequent to receipt and positive determination of the eligibility of a counseling program to be considered for accreditation, the Committee on Accreditation of the APA contacts the program head to set up an accreditation visitation. Typically three professionals selected by the Committee on Accreditation with consultation with the program comprise the visiting team, which spends approximately 2.5 days on site assessing the status of the doctoral program. It examines supporting documents and talks with students, faculty, the department administrator, and institutional-level administrators to ascertain the validity of the observations made about the program in the self-study document. Following the onsite visit, a report is sent by the visiting team to the Committee on Accreditation, which makes the final decision about the program's accreditation status. If that decision is positive, the accredited program is revisited in 3 to 7 years depending on the visiting team's concern about areas that need to be strengthened or monitored.

Unlike CACREP, which is independent of the American Counseling Association, to manage accreditation of counseling programs, the APA Committee on Accreditation is integral to APA and its Education Directorate. Unlike CACREP, APA does not accredit master's degree programs of professional psychology, only doctoral programs. This posture reflects the APA's decision that the appropriate level of preparation for psychologists rendering independent, direct service to clients is at the doctoral level.

State Boards of Psychologist Examiners

APA and CACREP are alike in that neither is a licensing body. As mentioned earlier, the licensing of psychologists or professional counselors for independent practice is a function of state governments. Ordinarily state governments create what is typically termed a *state board of psychologist examiners,* which carries out the individual assessments and makes recommendations for or against awarding licensure. The review of individual applications for licensure includes the individual's academic and clinical preparation, internship, formal professional experience, scores on a written examination, and recommendations from doctoral-level supervisors. In some states, it is difficult for an applicant to be judged eligible for review for licensure unless he or she has been prepared in an APA-accredited program of professional psychology. In other states, the accreditation is not used to bar candidates for licensure, but certainly their experience, academic coursework, clinical experience, internship success, test scores, and recommendations are given intense scrutiny.

Each of these dimensions of program accreditation and individual licensure become of importance to the administrators of an academic Department of Counselor Education and/or Counseling Psychology. Their importance derives from the planning and budgeting required to accommodate each program and to meet the separate criteria that are associated with program accreditation. Although the department head may not and probably should not be the sole planner and creator of documents, self-study or other, that are required for accreditation review, the administrator of the department must understand the processes of accreditation, the pros and cons of such processes, the costs involved, and the policies and facilities required to implement accredited programs. Again within discussions with faculty and students about either initiating or maintaining such programs, the department administrator moves among being a leader, creating a vision of how such programs will fit into and benefit the department, and being a manager who supports the development of the self-study process and identifies or obtains the resources and facilities required to implement the program.

Council on Rehabilitation Education (CORE)

Again, depending on the size and mission of the academic department in which the preparation of counselors or counseling psychologists occur, there may be a single program (e.g., Counselor Education or Counseling Psychology) and one accreditation or there may be several programs, each eligible for accreditation. If the counselor preparation takes place in a College of Education, the department may be expected to prepare counselors for schools or for higher education. As such these programs will probably be involved in accreditations by the National Council on the Accreditation of Teacher Education (NCATE) or by state departments of education, which may have approved programs to prepare students for certification as school counselors. Much the same accreditation process—self-study, visiting team—ensues as was described under CACREP or APA. Rather than discuss these accreditation processes more specifically, we discuss one other national accreditation process that may be included in academic departments preparing counselors. Because the three authors of this book serve together in a department that has CACREP, APA, NCATE, State Department of Education, as well as CORE accreditation, such examples do occur.

In some colleges and universities, the training of rehabilitation counselors occurs in a separate Department of Rehabilitation Psychology or Services, in some cases in schools of Allied Health, or, in other instances, in Departments of Counselor Education, Counseling Psychology, or Rehabilitation Services or Rehabilitation Psychology. In some instances, the preparation of rehabilitation counselors is seen as part of Counselor Education, although most faculty members who specialize in Rehabilitation Counseling, Rehabilitation Psychology, or Rehabilitation Services prefer to maintain their primary identity in rehabilitation. At any rate, in the department in which the authors of this book reside, the third major program to be accredited is Rehabilitation Services. The Council on Rehabilitation Education (CORE) is the accrediting agent.

Although there is considerable overlap with CACREP and APA in the steps of the accreditation of Rehabilitation Counselor Education programs, the content of the CORE accreditation is on the training of students to provide the effective delivery of rehabilitation services to individuals with disabilities. Within CORE, the evaluation of Rehabilitation Counselor Education programs is handled by the Commission on Standards and Accreditation, which handles communications with programs wishing to be considered for accreditation, receives self-studies, sponsors visiting team members, and makes recommendations about accreditation status. The application to CORE consists of an application form, an application fee, and specified program information (in a sense, a self-study). The review process consists of three elements: a self-study document, data collection from CORE questionnaires, and the site visit. The unique aspect of the CORE accreditation review process is the CORE questionnaires, which are (a) distributed to second-year students, recent graduates, and employers of the program's graduates, and (b) provide evaluative ratings about various aspects of the program's operations, the quality of students, and the performance of graduates. These data are statistically analyzed and provided to the site visit team.

Programs applying for CORE accreditation must meet several eligibility criteria:

- Be part of an educational institution that is accredited by an appropriate regional accreditation body and that offers graduate degrees in areas other than that being evaluated;
- Provide for 2 years of full-time graduate study; like CACREP, this means 48 semester hours;
- Have institutional approval for courses and degrees offered;
- Have a person designated as coordinator or equivalent who is a Certified Rehabilitation Counselor; and

- Have a written statement of the program's mission, objectives, curriculum, and criteria for student selection.

CORE's Standards for Rehabilitation Counselor Education Programs are quite comprehensive and include specific expectations for program performance in each of the following categories:

Mission and Objectives

Program Evaluation

General Curriculum Requirements, Knowledge Domains, and

Educational outcomes, including study units or courses in the following:

    Professional Identity

    Social and Cultural Diversity Issues

    Human Growth and Development

    Counseling and Consultation

    Group Work

    Assessment

    Research and Program Evaluation

    Rehabilitation Services and Resources

Clinical Experience

    100 hours of supervised counseling practicum with at least 40 hours of direct service to persons with disabilities and

    600 hours of applied experience in an agency approved by the RCE coordinator, with at least 240 hours of direct service to persons with disabilities.

Administration and Faculty

Program Support and Resources

Rehabilitation Counselor Education programs that successfully obtain accreditation undergo a brief annual review to monitor changes in the program, if any.

In most states, rehabilitation counselors are able to be considered for designation as a licensed professional counselor (LPC). Obviously they must meet the academic and clinical experience requirements of the state for LPCs, perform successfully on any examination used by the State Board that administers the license, and have positive recommendations. Within the field of Rehabilitation Counseling, graduates of CORE-accredited or other rehabilitation programs may find the designation Certified Rehabilitation Counselor to be more important than the designation of LPC. Of course, many Rehabilitation Counselors and Rehabilitation Counselor Educations hold both designations.

Certified Rehabilitation Counselor

As is true in CACREP and NBCC, APA and state licensing boards for psychologists, the accreditation of Rehabilitation Counselor Education by CORE, and the credentialing of Certified Rehabilitation Counselors by the Commission on Rehabilitation Counselor Certification (CRCC) are separate processes conducted by separate organizations. In general terms, to obtain the credential as a Certified Rehabilitation Counselor, applicants must document their compliance with coursework in rehabilitation counseling, 600 hours of internship in a rehabilitation facility under the supervision of a CRC, or acceptable employment under the supervision of a CRC.

There are a number of categories of coursework, internship, or acceptable employment that allow an individual to become eligible to take the Certification Examination and, if successful, receive the designation of CRC. The most efficient way to become a CRC is to obtain a master's degree in Rehabilitation Counseling from a Rehabilitation Counselor Education program that is fully accredited by CORE and complete a 600-hour internship in a rehabilitation facility supervised by a CRC. There are additional eligibility requirements, including specific courses required and various lengths of acceptable employment for persons who did not graduate from a CORE-approved program, from a program in counseling, but not rehabilitation counseling in emphases, from a different discipline, or for applicants with a doctoral degree.

Once applicants are found to be eligible (by meeting the academic, internship, or employment standards), their eligibility allows them to take the 300-item, multiple-choice certification examination, which covers 12 knowledge domains that would be present in the curriculum of CORE-accredited Rehabilitation Counselor Education programs. These 12 knowledge domains include:

Vocational Consultation and Employee Services
Job Development and Placement Services
Career Counseling and Assessment Tech
Mental Health Counseling
Group and Family Counseling
Individual Counseling
Psychological and Cultural Issues in Counseling
Foundations, Ethics, and Professional Issues

Rehab Services and Resources

Case and Caseload Management

Health Care and Disability Systems

Medical, Functional, and Emotional Implications of Disabilities

Following successful passage of the certification examination and the eligibility requirements, the person will be designated a CRC and obligated to renew his or her certification every 5 years by accruing and documenting a minimum of 100 hours of continuing education or passing the current version of the certification examination.

NATIONAL TRENDS IN COUNSELOR PREPARATION

It can be argued that national trends in counselor preparation are reflected in the content and procedures of the various accreditation processes examined in the previous section. Because a major goal of any academic department or other unit preparing counselors is to know about and implement state-of-the-art programs for quality instruction, clinical experiences, and supervision of counselors-in-training, one can argue that meeting and maintaining accreditation standards is fundamental to the planning of the department administrator. In fact, however, there are a large number of subissues that must be considered when such plans are made. Some examples make the point.

Supervision of clinical experiences is an area in which a variety of decisions are required. For example, by whom will supervision be conducted: by regular faculty, part-time faculty, professional staff where the students' clinical experiences will take place, off-campus or on-campus? If several different supervisors are involved from different clinical settings, how will their work be coordinated? What will be the modes of recording student counselor–client interactions that will serve as the content for supervision: case studies, typed transcripts of counseling sessions, student-generated case studies, reports on critical incidents, audio or video recordings?

With regard to curriculum content and opportunities for clinical experiences, how will multicultural counseling competencies be developed and assessed? How will the developing competencies of counselors-in-training be assessed, and what criteria will be used in different skill areas to judge that individual competencies are adequate? How does a program ensure that counselors-in-training who do not meet standards for progress in the program or who are at risk for termination be provided due process as well as legal and ethical treatment? How often and in what form should all students be apprised of their progress in the program? Who should provide that appraisal? What are national models of such procedures?

A further issue has to do with how the program can recruit and admit the best possible students. How should the program plan to recruit ethnic minority and international students? What are the incentives that can be offered to support students who have been chosen for admission? How can the program recruit ethnic minority counselor educators or provide Counselor Education programs with other characteristics or skills that are needed by the program to provide diversity and reflect the characteristics of the student population?

Another national trend that is important in planning within a department preparing counselors is the emergence of counselors for new settings. A basic planning question is, "Are we preparing counselors or counseling psychologists for the right specialties?" If we are not, do we have the skills, knowledge, and experience among the faculty to prepare counselors for other settings or does this require additional faculty to be employed? Do we have the resources to do so? Will we have sufficient student demand to launch new specialty preparation options? Because counseling has become more comprehensively applied to a larger proportion of the population or to persons who have not been adequately served in the past, new skills, knowledge bases, research studies, and specialty areas continuously emerge and demand for such training intensifies. Recent examples of such specialties include counselors working with (a) senior citizens (gerontological counseling), (b) individuals who have substance abuse problems (addictions counseling), (c) changing families and a myriad of issues within family systems (marriage and family counseling or therapy), and (d) multicultural clients or gays, lesbians, and transgendered individuals. As immigration to the United States continues to grow and the national origins of such populations continue to change, the demands of these populations, when added to the shifting proportions of indigenous ethnic populations (e.g., African American, Hispanic, Asian, Native American) for counseling, raise important planning questions for academic programs preparing counselors: How do we train counselors effectively to address the needs of new or growing populations of clients? How do we expose counselors in training to experiential learning opportunities that will equip them to understand and be competent to serve such populations? If we, as a counselor preparation program, are located in a university situated in a rural area, how do we train counselors-in-training to deal with clients experiencing problems that are essentially found in urban areas?

For counseling psychology trainees, as well as for LPC students, there are additional national trends to those already identified. Many of them are in the changing health care marketplace. They include providing prevention and wellness programs in many different venues, hospital privileges to work with clients who have major mental health disorders and must be hospitalized for intermittent periods of time, professional privileges to write prescriptions for psychotropic medication, and participating in multidisciplinary group practices requiring significant amounts of collaboration with persons having different specialty skills.

Although there are many other examples of national trends that could be cited here as having affects on the content and practices that counselors are taught to execute in institutional settings or independent practice, the examples given suggest the range of questions and decisions that need to be addressed in planning. These are the types of issues about which the department administrator must be aware and about which he or she can lead discussions and initiate planning processes. It is in this sense that the department administrator must be a futurist, constantly scanning political, social, and economic factors; public policies; and professional trends that are likely to affect the recruitment, preparation, and placement of counselors-in-training, whatever the specialty.

The department administrator as the leader in planning must also manage the facilities and fiscal resources that are implicated in whatever planning decisions are made. However attractive, ideal, or appropriate possible directions for the program may be, they must be fitted within the realities of the facilities and resource bases available.

FACILITIES

Departments preparing counselors or counseling psychologists need three major types of facilities: offices and meeting rooms for faculty members, graduate students, and support staff; and classrooms for didactic purposes and for both small- and large-group instruction. Increasingly, these classrooms need to be provided with technological capabilities to support the use of computers for Power Point presentations, data analysis, and so on. The third type of facility includes counseling rooms, observation sites, and related areas to support the experiential learning or clinical experiences in which students are to engage under supervision.

These three categories of facilities required to support counselor preparation are rather gross descriptors of the resources involved. For example, although faculty, support staff, and usually graduate assistant offices need to be available, these offices typically need to be equipped with desk or laptop computers so that, in the case of faculty, course syllabi, course notes, assignments, management of student data and grades, analysis of research data, preparation of manuscripts, and correspondence can be accomplished. To the degree that such tasks can be done by individual faculty members, computers in faculty offices reduce some of the pressure on support staff for clerical work. Even so, support staff typically require individual computers to record and manage program data, student admission information and correspondence, instructions about program procedures, and many other forms of administrative information. Typically, graduate assistants may share offices and, rather than be supplied with an individual computer, are required to share access to a computer.

Although it is desirable to have faculty offices near didactic classrooms, space and room availability frequently cannot achieve such a goal. Classrooms may be in an adjacent building or across campus. In some universities, they are assigned from a central office on campus to individual departments on a first-come, first-served basis. Thus, department support staff, under the guidance of the department administrator, must request the number and types of classrooms they will need for subsequent semesters 9 months or so ahead of time. Having such needs pinned down and specified as to location, equipment available, and allocation to a particular faculty member for a particular class is important to faculty morale. In some departments, where classrooms are in the same building or in buildings in close proximity to faculty offices, departments have created carts on which a computer system, screen, and other peripheral equipment are located so that they can be moved to classrooms where they are needed. Increasingly, as universities renovate their buildings or construct new buildings, they are creating multipurpose rooms that can be quickly configured for small- or large-group instruction and with portals to provide power for computers and access to the Internet. Again it becomes a continuing management function for many department heads to oversee the access and scheduling of classrooms that are configured and equipped as fully as possible for individual faculty needs.

The third area of faculty needs of particular importance to departments preparing counselors or counseling psychologists are those supporting clinical experiences and supervision. Some university departments have their own counseling centers or clinics in which counselors-in-training provide counseling to university students or townspeople under supervision. Such clinics or counseling centers are superb opportunities to socialize counselors-in-training to the policies, forms, and ethics that occur in any agency or counseling center in which they are likely to work after they graduate. If an academic program is fortunate enough to have its own clinic, it needs to be configured to provide offices for intake supervisors (possibly doctoral-level students who do intake and attempt to match counselors-in-training to clients whom they judge to be appropriate for individual counselors), receptionists, and for counseling. In the clinic that the first author of this book designed many years ago, there are four counseling offices, a reception area for clients, a group counseling or play therapy room, a central core with one-way vision windows with cameras to make videotapes of each counseling session if the client signs a permission form to tape, and a utility room by which to control all of the cameras and audio recorders in the facility and to do split-screen videotapes and other types of recordings. The department counseling clinic is capable of providing clients for first-year doctoral students and master's students and the intake forms, lecture notes, and videotapes of counselor-in-training–client interaction as the basis for supervision.

Although the department clinic began as a resource to students in the College of Education and to townspeople referred to it, more recently the clinic has become a satellite of the University Center for Counseling and Psychological Services. As such it systematically receives referrals and backup support if clients demonstrate suicidal ideation or related phenomena.

Clinical facilities must be designed to maintain confidentiality for clients in records kept and in interactions within the facility. Counseling offices need sound-proofing, and the entrance to the facility can be built to reduce client exposure to passersby who may know them.

At the university in which the three authors of this book are located, doctoral students in counseling psychology are in practice in the University Counseling Center (the Center for Counseling and Psychological Services) in the first semester of their second year in the program and in the University Career Services in the second semester. Both of these facilities have excellent offices and equipment by which students can engage in supervision with both staff psychologists/counselors and with department faculty.

Many academic programs preparing counselors do not have the luxury of their own clinic, therefore plans must be made to have practica and internships off campus. Indeed for school counselors and rehabilitation counselors-in-training, regardless of whether they have access to a clinic on campus, they need to engage in experiential, clinical training in an elementary or secondary school or in a rehabilitation agency so they gain exposure to the types of clients—children, youth, or adults—with whom they will work following completion of the program.

The administrator of a department having its own clinic or one that must use other university or local sites as locations for counseling practice and socialization will likely have oversight responsibility for the policies and support that govern the department clinic and that are relevant to off-campus sites. Often formal agreements need to be created and signed by all parties when off-campus sites provide opportunity for counseling and supervision of its students or adult clients. Again, although the running of a department clinic or the development of off-campus or on-campus sites is delegated to particular faculty members, the department head will likely be identified as the responsible party to sign such agreements and to ensure that the interactions of all parties are ethical, professionally sound, and protect the clients being served. In addition, the administrator of the department will be responsible for any financial arrangements that are made with either other campus units or off-campus sites to provide opportunities for counseling and supervision.

BUDGETING

Each of the elements of planning, staffing, and implementing the processes to which a department preparing counselors and counseling psychologists is committed ultimately is reflected in a need for resources—human, material, and technological (e.g., equipment). Each of these resource needs is also fiscal. A department administrator needs to pay salaries and benefits for professional and support staff, graduate assistants, part-time faculty or staff to be hired when a teaching or other workload is too heavy for available faculty or staff to manage, operational expenses (e.g., telephone, postage, supplies), faculty travel and per diem support when they attend professional conferences or are seeking external funding for some project, resource materials (e.g., tests, directories, books, journal subscriptions) used in classes, equipment and advanced technology (e.g., computer, recording equipment, Internet access, Power Point equipment, copiers, and related equipment) used in instruction, department management, and research. The actual quantity and form each of these items will take varies depending on the mission of the department, its size, the programs included, the number of students served, the research projects underway, and related factors.

In budgeting parlance, the needs for fiscal resources just identified can be considered investments in the people and resources needed to accomplish the mission (Brinckerhoff, 2000). Among other characteristics, they include expenditures of funds or cost centers. For example, each faculty member may be considered a cost center. In essence, then, such a concept asks, What is the total cost of maintaining each faculty position? Included in such a cost center would be such things as the salary allocated to the position, the health and retirement benefits paid for each position, the funds needed for furniture, computers, or equipment for each faculty member, the costs for professional travel, and the costs of supplies and instructional materials needed by each faculty member. Some administrators and faculty or support staff believe that the cost of faculty is their salary (let's say $50,000). In fact the salary is only one element of the real cost center for each faculty position. Thus, rather than the cost center for Professor X requiring $50,000, when the actual costs are added together—benefits, equipment, furniture, travel, and so on—the real costs to employ Professor X may be $100,000 or more. Indeed some administrators would add into cost centers for each faculty member the additional costs from the percentage of time a staff person provided clerical support and the costs of recruiting the faculty member, which of course would elevate the amount of funds required in a cost center to recruit, support, and staff a position. In a similar way, cost centers can be created to address the costs of recruiting students, constant updating of computers or other equipment, supporting department research initiatives, or myriad other endeavors inherent in the department's mission.

Again, although each of these cost centers express requirements for expenditures of funds, they can also be seen as investments in the people and things that allow the mission to be accomplished.

A major issue for any department administrator is, where are the funds coming from to support the initiatives that undergird our mission statement? One way to think about such funding is revenue or income streams. These are examples of the several ways by which to fund cost centers or other investments to which the department is committed. Revenue streams take many forms. Examples are an allocation for the department from the general funds budget of the university or from a specific college. The amounts that accrue to departments through such general funds budgets obviously vary depending on the type of institutions, its priorities, its fiscal reserves, the amount of tuition revenue received from students, annual budget allocations from state government, if the institution is public, and from other sources. One can also include external funds that universities receive from donors and development campaigns, although these are not typically considered general funds, nor are they typically used to fund operational budgets. They tend to be more focused on funding student financial aid, special and endowed chairs for professors, graduate assistantships, special research equipment, and so on.

At any rate, from a revenue or income stream standpoint, the department administrator needs to obtain funds from a variety of sources. As suggested earlier, the starting income or revenue stream is typically the funds allocated from the college or university to support the operational expenses of the department. Unfortunately, such revenues are often able to accommodate only 30% to 50% of the actual department costs. Thus, other sources of revenue are necessary. Some examples are to probe any special grants that might emanate from specific university offices for particular purposes (e.g., graduate assistantships) or perhaps from the University Office of International Relations, which provides grants for faculty to travel abroad to conduct research or create new programs. In some universities, summer schools are separately funded, allowing department heads to obtain bonus funds if they meet or exceed target numbers of student credits in courses offered in the summer. In some cases, summer tuition received by a college is shared with the departments that generated the instructional credits. Some departments offer counseling services to clients or organizations for a fee. For example, some counseling departments test and evaluate children at risk for school districts and provide a recommended behavior treatment plan for a fee. Some counseling departments offer a counseling clinic for clients from the surrounding communities that provide master's and doctoral staff to do the counseling under faculty supervision for a fee. In some departments, faculty members write books or other publications that they sell to consumers and share the royalties with the department. Any one of these approaches can be construed as an income or revenue stream; in business parlance, they would be considered profit centers.

Another important source of funding in many academic departments engaged in the preparation of counselors is the seeking of grants or contracts from external organizations, frequently called *sponsored projects*. Three classes of external funding sources tend to be most apparent: state or federal governmental agencies, foundations, or industry. For example, many governmental agencies exist to purchase training or instruction for a particular group of employers from an academic department. Some governmental agencies are interested in funding research that ultimately can be translated into more powerful or cost-effective treatments for particular groups of persons experiencing behaviors that put them and others at risk: those who engage in sexual abuse or violence, have difficulty with stress management, are dependent on various illegal chemical substances, and are undereducated and unable to build a positive work history.

Many governmental agencies (e.g., the National Institutes of Health, the National Institute of Drug Abuse, the U.S. Department of Labor, the Rehabilitation Services Administration, etc.) at both federal and state levels annually publish brochures describing their research priorities. Such agencies also publish Requests for Proposals (RFPs), which describe a particular research study for which they are willing to provide grant funds. RFPs typically include the conditions and timelines under which the grant will occur, the research problem, the techniques or methods they are interested in evaluating, the funding available for individual projects, and other pertinent details. Essentially, then, the agency is using an RFP process to solicit interested researchers from academic departments or other research groups to prepare a proposal indicating how they would undertake the research problem, who would be involved, and how much it would cost. All proposals submitted by persons or departments interested in pursuing an RFP are then placed under a competitive review process, which frequently is made up of invited researchers from academic or research programs who have not submitted a proposal to address the problem posed in an RFP, but are knowledgeable about research design and the knowledge base related to the RFP focus and guidelines. This competitive process focused on evaluating the worth of the proposals submitted for funding eventually results in a rank ordering of the quality and viability of the proposals, and those who prepared the proposals that are selected are invited into a negotiation process to finalize the award by the government agency that issued the RFP.

The process of publishing research priorities and publishing RFPs to obtain proposals from researchers or other specialists is not only typical of governmental agencies, but also of foundations and industrial groups offering grants or contracts for specific projects.

Ordinarily RFPs tell potential researchers how to format their proposals and about the information elements that need to be included in the proposal, including the specifics of the budget (e.g., what the contracting budget would pay for and what costs would be excluded). When annual brochures about upcoming research priorities are published by agencies, they also frequently include information about the expected format of proposals. Different agencies use somewhat different formats for the proposals they consider for funding. Some agencies give a page limit for proposals (e.g., 25 pages plus appendixes). In other cases, particularly in the case of some foundations, rather than asking for full proposals, they request a brief concept paper or a 3- to 5 -page letter explaining the researcher's experience, previous publications related to the RFP topic, and, in general, how they would structure a research study in the topical area at issue. After screening the concept papers or brief proposals for research, these foundations or governmental agencies request full proposals from a smaller group of researchers whose concept papers are considered promising in their methodology and approach. These proposals, like the concept papers, then undergo a competitive peer review before selections are made about grant or contract awards.

Before returning to the budget implications of external grant-seeking for a department, it is useful to note that administrators of departments need to become acquainted with the agencies, foundations, or other organizations that provide support, grants, or contracts for counseling-related research or training. It is typically useful to actually travel to selected agencies or foundations to discuss with relevant program officers in those agencies their plans and goals and, in general, to become acquainted with them as fellow professionals to whom questions can be addressed and information about funding priorities secured. It is also important that the department administrator be aware of sources of information about funding opportunities and their focus in governmental agencies, foundations, and other sources. Publications such as the *Federal Register* and the *Commerce Business Daily* provide information on RFPs that have been or soon will be published, the timelines for proposals, where to obtain the RFP, and other pertinent information. These information sources are primarily addressed to federal government agency RFPs or other fundable contracts. Many states have parallel sources of information on state agency funding processes (e.g., The *Pennsylvania Bulletin*). Information on foundations is available in directories that are focused on particular types of funding, research, or consulting projects.

Many academic departments have a support staff member or a faculty member reviewing the *Federal Register* or *Commerce Business Daily* to identify any funding opportunities that are pertinent to the emphases or goals of the program. In many universities, there are central offices devoted to facilitating faculty or departmental external grant-seeking. These offices usually have their staff examining such publications as the *Federal Register* to flag any RFPs or other information about funding possibilities that are relevant to particular departments. Frequently, such offices have computer software by which they can convey the information they have acquired directly to a particular department or researcher. These offices are often involved in doing searches on various governmental or foundation databases by which they can match the researchers' interests or areas of expertise to funding opportunities in specific government agencies or foundations. In summary, there are now available many services as well as Internet Web sites (e.g., Grants Information Service [GIS], Office of Federal Programs [OFP], The Sponsored Programs Information Network [SMARTS], The Federal Information Exchange [FEDIX], Grants Web) that can link a department or specific researcher to a variety of information bases on funding opportunities.

The budget implications of external grant-seeking by academic departments are many. Although successful acquisition of grants or contracts from government agencies, foundations, or other funding sources does not imply free money that comes into department accounts without any conditions, externally funded grants and contracts are still able to be considered a revenue stream and it may be so for several reasons. Many grants or contracts are funded and contracted over a 3- to 5-year period as long as annual progress reviews indicate that the department or researchers are making satisfactory progress toward the goals they were funded to achieve. Thus, to obtain a funded grant or contract, the department or specific researchers must do the research study or perform other activities required by the grant—in other words, they must do the work they have contracted to do. In so doing, however, the grant will likely support some graduate assistants, offer some portion of faculty time, provide travel funds, purchase necessary equipment, and fund supplies, communications, and other items necessary to complete the project. Such contractual provisions increase the department's ability to recruit new high-quality students who are assured of a focused graduate assistantship for the duration of the funded grant, provide faculty the support they need to conduct research in the area of their professional expertise, provide funds to travel to and present at conferences they might not otherwise have an opportunity to attend, have their ideas tested and refined in a competitive grant-seeking environment, and obtain equipment that department funds may not have been able to provide. In a pragmatic sense, the funds for many of the possibilities just described actually release funds in a general department budget for travel, supplies, equipment, graduate assistantships, and other elements that no longer need to be paid for from general funds, but are contained in the externally funded grant.

Inherent in externally funded grants is another potential revenue stream that may be shared between a university or college and the department that initiated a funded proposal. To explain this revenue stream requires clarification of two additional terms: direct costs and indirect costs. In a sense, whether operating a department or conducting a research study, there are two general categories of costs. *Direct costs* are those costs (personnel salaries, supplies, equipment, etc.) that can be specifically identified with a particular function (e.g., teaching) or a mission of a department or research study. These are necessary costs to achieve the mission or goals of a department or project, and they can be identified with a high degree of accuracy. However, for a university, department, research study, or other sponsored project to function, there are also indirect costs. *Indirect costs* are referred to by the federal government as *facilities and administrative* (F & A) costs. Sometimes these costs are known simply as *overhead*. Indirect costs are those that tend to be spread across departments or projects and cannot be specifically attributed to a specific project. Indirect costs are usually defined by a formula that tries to calculate all of the costs that contribute to a department or project, but are not readily visible or considered. These include institutional resources that are considered to be part of the overhead rate used by the university for each externally funded project. Examples of these institutional resources are laboratory space, office space, specialized facilities, libraries, equipment, telecommunications infrastructure, utilities costs (heat, electricity, etc.), insurance, custodial services, research accounting, sponsored programs offices, legal counsel, and building maintenance.

Universities charge different rates to external funding organizations or sponsors depending on the factors they include in their indirect cost or overhead rate and the focus of the externally funded project—research, instruction, continuing education, whether the project is conducted on or off campus, and negotiations with the federal agency (e.g., office of Naval Research) that may help to establish or accept the official university indirect cost rate, which is then applied to all research projects across the university regardless of college or discipline or department. In essence, then, an administrator of a department must understand the budgeting of external projects and the current university policies regarding such budgeting. Often a department administrator must be able to explain to faculty why budgets for externally funded projects include the direct costs of the project and the indirect costs associated with university provision of heat, light, advisement and processing of projects, project space, and other possible resources that a department does not have to pay for, but are vital to the department's ability to propose and conduct an externally funded research study or instructional project.

The department administrator will need to explain to faculty members who are proposing externally funded studies or projects why, in addition to the direct, department-based costs of a project they are also required to add to the cost of the projects, indirect costs that may vary from 40% to 110% of the direct costs. Thus, in such situations, the indirect costs may add as much as 50% to 100% of the direct costs. Faculty members need to understand that these are real dollars that need to be recovered to maintain many important activities in the university—that if nonexistent would likely mean there would not be a structure that could support research studies or other projects in the university.

In addition to the funds available from direct costs of projects, that within certain limitations can be considered a revenue stream, the way universities treat the indirect costs that are obtained from funded projects can also constitute a revenue stream. For example, many universities return to the college or department a percentage (often 10%) of all of the indirect funds that have been received in a specific fiscal year. Let us assume that a department has been awarded $5 million in grants that are being conducted in a given year, and 40% of the $5 million is overhead. In essence, those projects would yield $2 million in recovery of overhead. If the university shared 10% of those funds with the college and the department where these projects are conducted, this could mean a return of $200,000 that could be used for a variety of research support needs, matching funds for new projects, equipment, consultation, and so on.

In summary, budgeting includes both the expected income or revenue streams likely to be available, when the funds will be available, the sources of funds (and any restrictions on their use), as well as the budgeted expenditures or costs of the department for salaries, supplies, communications, and other cost centers. Most department budgets reflect direct costs and income, rather than indirect costs, unless one is implementing externally funded projects or the department is required to pay specific overhead rates on its regular department activities. The latter is not typical, although having separate ancillary budgets for each cost center, including externally funded projects, may require one to monitor the return of overhead to and from the university.

One of the good things about serving in a department in a college or university is that the college or university will likely have a centralized financial system that will track all expenditures and income pertinent to the department. The department administrator will likely view constantly updated information about how the budget for the year is unfolding. In addition to the more sophisticated financial systems used by a university or college, the department administrator may wish to keep a simplified version of a projected budget for the current fiscal year against which to compare projections of actual income and expenses with the projected income and expenses that drove the current year's department planning. Such a simplified budget worksheet may look like Table 6.1.

Table 6.1 is a fictitious budget created to illustrate that information such as is illustrated can be helpful in monitoring an administrator's planning. Although there are many ways to design such financial worksheets to identify the information of a particular utility to a given administrator, Table 6.1 would provide quite a bit of information. For example, the revenue streams are identified as those from the general funds budget allocated to the department by the college and the additional funds acquired from competitive and externally funded projects beyond the basic general funds budget. Even so, according to the column entitled "% of Total Budget," the general funds allocated to the department is about 91.3% of the total income budget. We note in the column entitled "% of General Funds Budget" that the allocation to the department is comprised of over 95% committed to salaries for tenure-track faculty, support staff, temporary faculty and staff, and graduate assistants. The specifics of these expenditures are seen in a somewhat refined manner in the first two columns of the expense worksheet.

In both the income and expenditure workshops, we find that we spent $3,750 less per month for graduate assistantship stipends than were budgeted for because these assistantships were not filled under the general funds allocation, but rather were paid for by a special university project. As a result, some $22,500 was saved from the General Funds Allocation for the first 6 months of the budget year that could be allocated to areas where the expenses exceeded budgeted commitments. For example, on the Expenses worksheet, the costs of temporary faculty, telephones and postal rates, and faculty travel exceeded the amounts budgeted for such expenditures. These rising costs may require the administrator to increase the next year's budgeted expenses to ensure that such costs are covered.

In comparing the income and expense worksheets, in terms of monthly, 6-month, and annual projections, it is clear that the income for the department exceeds its expenditures. This outcome is largely a result of obtaining the graduate assistant stipends from agencies external to the department and college. The other revenue streams from such sources as counseling clinic fees, charges for some client assessments, and selling some publications help the financial picture, but add little to the total income of the department. The administrator may decide to initiate ways to dramatically increase such revenue streams or seek other revenue sources. It seems clear that if it were not for the released faculty salaries from externally funded re-

TABLE 6.1

Income and Expense Work Sheet (as of June 30, 200x)

Income (Projected Revenue Streams)	Monthly Actual Income	Monthly Budget Income	Monthly Difference	% of General Funds Budget	% of Total Income Budget	Year-to-Date (YTD) Actual Budget (6 months) for Income	YTD Difference at 6 Months	Total Annual Income Budgeted
Allocations from college general funds								
Faculty salaries	70,833	70,833	0	72.4	66.1	424,998	0	849,996
Support staff salaries	15,166	15,166	0	15.5	14.2	90,996	0	181,992
Grad assistants stipends	3,750	7,500	3,750	7.7	7.0	22,500	22,500[1]	90,000
Department allocation for operational expenses	4,500	4,333	(167)	4.4	4.0	27,000	(1,002)[2]	51,996
Total general funds	94,249	97,832				565,494		
Summer school tuition bonus	1,250	1,250	0		1.2	7,500	0	15,000
Released faculty salaries from externally funded projects	2,000	2,500	(500)		2.3	12,000	(3,000)[3]	30,000
Special university competitive projects								
Graduate assistantships	3,750	3,750	0		3.5	22,500	0	45,000
International travel	500	583	83		.05	3,000	498	6,996
Department fees								
Counseling clinic	300	208	92		.19	1,800	552[4]	2,496
Assessments	150	166	(16)		.15	900	(96)[5]	1,992
Publications sold	125	125	0		.12	750	0	1,500
Return of overhead	667	667	0		.62	4,002	0	8,004
Total income	102,991	107,081	3,242			617,946	619,452[6]	1,284,972

(Continued)

TABLE 6.1
(Continued)

Expenses (Projected Expenditures and Cost Centers)	Monthly Actual Expenses	Monthly Budget Expenditures	Monthly Difference	% of Total Budget Expenditure	Actual Expenditure Year to Date (YTD)	Differences from Budget at 6 months	Total Annual Budgeted Expenditures
Salaries							
Tenure-track faculty	69,433	69,433	0	71	416,598	0	833,196
Support staff	15,166	15,166	0	15.5	90,996	0[7]	181,992
Temporary faculty and staff	1,400	1,250	(150)	1.3	8,400	(900)	15,000
Graduate assistantships stipends	3,750	7,500	3,750	7.7	22,500	22,500	90,000
Department allotment (operational expenses)							
Office supplies	900	900	0	.92	5,400	0	10,800
Communications							
Telephones	1,700	1,500	(200)	1.5	10,200	(1,200)[8]	18,000
Postage	500	400	(100)	.4	3,000	(600)[9]	4,800
Equipment	0	0	0	0	0	0	0
Maintenance/repairs	400	500	100	.5	2,400	600	6,000
Travel	1,500	1,000	(500)	1.0	9,000	(3,000)[10]	12,000
Miscellaneous	100	200	100	.2	600	600	2,400
Total expenses	94,849	97,849	3,000	99.3	569,094	18,000	1,174,188

[1]Released tuition from graduate assistant stipends paid from external research grant.
[2]Operational expenses over budgeted amount at 6 months.
[3]Released faculty salaries from external grants not expended at 6 months.
[4]Counseling fees received that exceeded budget at 6 months.
[5]Assessment fees less than budgeted at 6 months.
[6]Surplus of income at 6 months.
[7]Temporary faculty and staff cost more than budgeted.
[8]Rises in telephone rates cost more than budgeted.
[9]Rise in postal rates cost more than budgeted.
[10]Increases in travel by faculty exceeded budgeted amounts.
[11]Expenditures were less than budgeted by $18,000 at 6 months into budget year.

search projects and the released department allocation to the department, covering expenses for the year could require substantial restraint of expenditures. With the funds that accrued from the released salaries for some faculty and graduate assistants, the department was able to project a significant surplus of income over expenditures that, if university policy allows it, can be carried into the budget for the forthcoming year or expended for new initiatives not anticipated at the beginning of the fiscal year.

This worksheet is a primitive example of the type of line item budgeting information a department head needs to monitor on a monthly or more frequent basis to ensure that the department is getting the income anticipated and not expending funds beyond those projected to be expended. This type of worksheet would likely be backed up with separate worksheets for specific cost centers, externally funded projects, or specific revenue streams. Unless the department has a lot of cost centers or complex projects to monitor, the information on the worksheet is probably adequate. The worksheet used as an example here might also be shared with faculty members and staff as a way to help them understand how the department operates. Such sharing of general budgetary information, not individual salaries, is likely to engender more ownership by the staff of budget issues and their complexity. The information on this type of worksheet can also be used as the basis for discussions with institutional-level administrators to show overall costs for the department and the funds being obtained to offset the differences between the general funds allocations to the department for operating expenses and the real costs to operate the department. However, as a particular budget is conceived and formatted, it must be considered a planning document that supports the mission of the department and provides a lens on the revenue streams available and the expenditures taking place. If expenditures are seen as investments, these worksheets provide the information by which to assess whether the department is getting the most mission out of its resources and whether the investments (expenditures) being made on people, equipment, or other costs centers are the appropriate ways to use available resources.

COLLABORATION WITH OTHER FACULTY IN THE UNIVERSITY

In addition to the leadership and management of the planning process and the stewardship of the budgeting of income and expenditures in which the department administrator must play major roles, there is also an outreach role for the administrator in communicating with other departments or organizational units and their faculty members or professional staff.

Given the complexity of preparing students in a Counselor Education or Counseling Psychology department and the growing interdisciplinary nature of research and scholarship in Counselor Education and Counseling Psychology, there are many reasons for the department administrator to reach out to other departments or service units to engage in collaborative activities. In the first instance, it is unlikely that any department alone can or should teach all of the courses the graduate students in that department need to take to fulfill accreditation requirements or prepare them for the professional positions they aspire to enter. Typically, foundation courses in psychology or sociology or methodology courses in statistics are among the courses taught by departments other than the department preparing counselors. Such a situation is important for several reasons. For one, in many departments preparing counselors, there are no faculty whose expertise lies in teaching foundations courses in such disciplines as psychology, sociology, or the intricacies of statistics. However, even if such faculty do exist in a counseling department that is focused on applying the knowledge found in psychology or sociology, the emphasis is on using such insights to better understand the internal and external factors that comprise and trigger human behavior and, in particular, the clinical interventions that target particular psychological or sociological issues.

Depending on faculty from other departments to teach foundation courses in particular disciplines or methodologies keeps the counseling faculty from treading on the responsibilities assigned to other departments, signals that they value the faculty in these other departments, identifies faculty who might serve as outside members on master's or doctoral thesis committees, and frees the counseling faculty to teach courses central to the clinical and professional activities, which are at the core of their department's mission.

There are also other reasons for collaboration between counseling faculty and faculty in other departments. A major one has to do with joint research initiatives. To an increasing degree, government agencies and foundations expect research studies to be conducted by interdisciplinary teams. In such cases, it is sometimes assumed that no one discipline (e.g., psychology) has the knowledge base to fully comprehend and find evidence-based practices that are adequate to the complexities inherent in many major social problems of the day. Therefore, an interdisciplinary team of faculty from several departments or colleges is expected to be more effective in conducting complex research studies that can profit from the insights and perspectives found in more than one discipline. Similarly, inviting a methodologist in statistics, measurement, or research design is likely to add more precision and tighter controls to a research study than would otherwise be true. Although virtually all faculty members who teach graduate students and supervise their research are competent in particular statistical processes, they are unlikely to be as competent to compare statistical and research design alternatives and choose the one that best fits the available data as a specialist in that area.

Collaboration among faculty members from different departments can be informal or formal. For example, if a faculty member from a different department has expertise that is particularly vital to the counseling department, he or she may be offered a joint appointment in both departments, requiring both departments to contribute to the faculty member's salary and benefits. Joint appointments may occur for faculty members whose expertise is of a special quality that would be attractive to accreditation groups or would enable a department to develop a special option (e.g., gerontological counseling, counseling in urban areas, counseling Hispanics, etc.).

Formal collaborations often exist between departments preparing counselors and specialists in counseling in university counseling centers, career services, or community counseling agencies. The latter counseling specialists may teach a particular course, supervise counseling practica or internships, or otherwise make significant contributions to the preparation of counselors in the department of counseling. In such cases, the counseling specialists will likely have a doctoral degree and appropriate training that is parallel to that of academic faculty in departments preparing counselors, but their role in a university or community is devoted primarily to delivering counseling services to students or clients, not to teaching students to become counselors. Their relationship to the academic program preparing counselors may be paid or unpaid. For example, such persons may be named clinical professors of counseling or adjunct professors of counseling. The former designation often means that they are not in a tenure-track position requiring research and scholarly activity, but they are teaching or supervising counselors-in-training about the applied aspects of their preparation. Clinical professors may be delivering counseling services in a unit in the university or outside of it. Sometimes the designation *adjunct professor* is used for persons who meet the criteria to be a faculty member, but whose principal employment is outside the university in a counseling agency or research organization and they bring their expertise and experience to the counseling department through teaching a course periodically or supervising students interning in their facility. Another designation sometimes used by academic counseling departments is *affiliate professorships*. Again these positions may be paid or unpaid, but most likely the latter. Like clinical professorships, these positions signal that the affiliate professor has met the criteria for a faculty role, but they are employed by the university as a counseling psychologist, a career counselor, or an administrator of a counseling unit. Because of their full-time role in the university as other than a faculty member, they are permitted to serve in an affiliate professorship with the academic department to facilitate collaboration between the two groups, teach or engage in joint research, serve on graduate student committees, or otherwise engage in professional activities that will enhance their skills, use their expertise, and promote their active learning in both their full-time staff or direct clinical service position and as an important contribution to the preparation of counselors in the academic program.

As suggested here, collaboration among the department preparing counselors and other departments or clinical units in and out of the university can be a win–win situation for all concerned. Such collaboration can (a) improve the quality and reality base of instruction that counselors or counseling psychologists in training receive; (b) stimulate research studies that are interdisciplinary and methodologically sound; and (c) provide opportunities for academic faculty and clinical professionals to interact, learn from each other, and complement the skills and contextual understanding each brings to the teaching and supervision of students. It is likely that holding a clinical, adjunct, or affiliate professorship will add to the prestige of a clinical professional who has been selected for his or her expertise to serve in such a role.

In the last analysis, regardless of whether collaboration across departments and clinical facilities will occur, the results are functions of the leadership provided by the department administrator. Collaboration is a culture that must be nurtured; it is seen as providing an adequate return on investment for those who provide their time and energy to it, and it is valued as a major ingredient of the success of the department in preparing top-flight counselors or counseling psychologists. The department administrator must understand that collaboration can be more complex and difficult than not collaborating with others, but that its rewards can accrue to the benefit of the faculty, clinical professionals, students involved, and the department at large as its outreach efforts are consistent with its mission and seen as an exemplar of scientist–practitioner interaction.

RECRUITMENT OF FACULTY AND STAFF

As an organization devoted to learning and transmitting the knowledge it gains through research and scholarship to counselors-in-training and other professionals, an academic department preparing counselors has as its major assets the brainpower, commitment of effort, and social behavior of its professional and support staff. Thus, it becomes essential that the department administrator provide leadership to the processes by which staff members are recruited, retained, and professionally developed. In most academic departments, vacant or new positions are limited in number and precious resources in the effort to continuously improve the quality of instruction and scholarship and the social environment in which learning takes place.

Cultural Diversity in Recruiting

Of major importance in the recruitment process is meeting needs for cultural diversity among the faculty and staff. It is quite clear that if the academic program hopes to attract excellent students from underrepresented groups, it is necessary to have faculty members and support staff with whom these students can identify—staff who are culturally sensitive and possessed of multicultural sensitivity and multicultural counseling competencies. Although it is true that many White and heterosexual faculty meet such criteria, it is important to provide faculty and staff who reflect the characteristics of the student population to be taught and in sufficient numbers that neither faculty members, staff, or students of color, alternative sexual orientation, or disability feel isolated, a token, a person hired to meet a minority quota. Thus, the department administrator must ensure that qualified candidates for faculty or support staff positions are provided interviews, encouragement, and employment to the fullest extent possible. In many universities, to create a critical mass of minority faculty members on a support staff, the central administration will provide funds for opportunity hires. In such cases, the central administration may provide funds to pay half or more of the salary of a position for which a minority faculty or support staff qualifies to facilitate the recruitment of that person.

The Recruiting Process

The process of recruiting faculty and support staff begins with clarifying the duties of a vacant position. What will the person employed be expected to teach, and what will be the expected workload of research and scholarship, student advisement, and service commitments (e.g., committee membership)? For support staff, it is important to identify what responsibilities they will have in providing information to students, engaging in clerical tasks, handling budgets, supervising other staff members, and so on. Such position descriptions need to identify the skills required to fulfill the functions needed by the department, by whom one will be supervised, and the general mission of the department to which the new employee will be expected to contribute.

Because academic departments are comprised of faculty holding different academic ranks—instructor, assistant professor, associate professor, professor, distinguished professor—and conditions of employment—tenured or serving in tracks leading to potential tenure, nontenure-track appointments, full-time temporary, part-time, or joint appointments—position descriptions for faculty appointments must be individualized in the ranks, roles, and expectations of each person recruited. The processes of recruitment and employment should be devoted to finding the most qualified person who best fits the skill profile and role expectations designated for the position. In an important sense, the future quality of a department rests on present decisions about whom to employ.

Recruitment of faculty takes many forms: requests to other departments preparing counselors for nominations of persons who might meet the criteria for available positions, announcements in newsletters of relevant professional organizations of faculty positions available, and identifying potential candidates at professional conventions and following up on their possible interest in a position through telephone calls or letters. These efforts and others are intended to create a pool of candidates from which the search process will ultimately yield the best candidates for the position vacancy.

The search process for faculty is ordinarily carried out by a committee of current faculty in and out of the department doing the hiring. Most universities have specific policies by which faculty searches are to be conducted. These policies include legal and ethical guidelines that define the search process and include policies that preclude discrimination against candidates because of gender, race, ethnicity, sexual orientation, or disability. Violation of any of these guidelines can be the grounds for major legal actions by candidates that may be quite costly in funds, time, and institutional reputation.

The search process typically involves a thorough review by the search committee of all the relevant information provided by applicants for a position as they relate to the requirements of academic preparation, professional experience, or other criteria stated in the position description circulated to potential applicants. As a result of the intensive review of applicants' dossiers, the search committee may follow up by telephone or letter with persons who have been identified as references—persons who know the professional background of the applicant sufficiently well to give an accurate and comprehensive evaluation of their ability to perform the tasks assigned to the vacant position. As a result of these processes, a pool of five or so candidates may be identified as a short list of those persons most likely to perform with excellence in the available position. At this point in the search process, the short list of candidates is usually recommended to the department administrator as persons to invite for interviews. Depending on available resources and university guidelines, three or so of the candidates may be asked to come to the department for interviews by members of the search committee, current faculty, students, department administrators, faculty in other departments or agencies with whom they might work, and institution-level administrators.

Following the interview period, the search committee members will likely convene and make a decision about which candidate they would recommend to the department administrator. Before making their recommendation, search committees will frequently hold meetings with current faculty, students, or other groups to hear their perspectives on the candidates and whom these persons perceive as the best fit with the department mission and its needs.

Ordinarily, the department administrator will forward the search committee's recommendation of a candidate to the dean of the college in which the department is located, and the department administrator will indicate his or her support of the candidate recommended by the search committee or his or her support for another candidate. Before indicating a split in support for a candidate between a search committee and a department administrator, the latter would be wise to meet with the search committee to reconcile the differences in the perception of a candidate so that the person whose name goes forward is a unanimous choice. If differences between the department administrator and search committee cannot be resolved and the disparity in judgment about the suitability of a candidate is large, the dean may meet with the search committee and the department administrator and either bring the matter to closure, keep the search process open and ask the search committee to look for new candidates, or declare the search to be ended until a time in the future when it will be reinstituted.

Assuming a successful search instead of a split decision, it is typically the dean of the college who actually makes the job offer to a candidate and negotiates any types of benefits the candidate wants (e.g., a certain amount of moving expenses, a particular type of computer system, etc.).

In general, the employment of support staff members is somewhat less complex than that used when a faculty member is being hired in a full-time tenure-track position. For example, rather than national recruiting advertisements and contacts, support staff in many instances may "bid" for a job elsewhere in a college or university, which would be an upgrade in salary or responsibility for which they are qualified or persons in the local community may apply for the position. Within the academic department, several current support staff members may be empowered to serve as a panel to evaluate the experience, training, and references of candidates for open positions. As a result, they may recommend to the department administrator a short list of persons who should be interviewed by the search committee and department administrator. When these interviews are conducted and a candidate is chosen, the department administrator will likely work with the human resources or employment specialists of the college or university to process the appointment of the individual.

RETENTION AND PROFESSIONAL DEVELOPMENT OF FACULTY AND STAFF

Retention of faculty and staff is always an important goal because it is often an expensive fiscal situation to recruit and replace a faculty member or support staff member. It takes valuable time to do so, and replacement of staff members may mean a loss of institutional memory, the breaching of important collaboration across networks, and psychological discomfort.

Yet, it is important for purposes of retention to have a frame of reference that guides a department's efforts to retain faculty and staff and provide an environment that nurtures them. One such perspective is that of human capital theory (Davenport, 1999). In this view, any candidate for employment has control of his or her personal human capital and how and for what purposes it is used. The components of personal human capital are variously described by researchers, but Davenport, in a useful way, identifies these components as ability (knowledge, skill, talent), behavior, effort, and time. In essence, these components are interactive as human capital that can be invested in a job or withheld. For example, one can have great ability but not use it in a focused way, or one may display behaviors that are arrogant, self-absorbed, or negative to such an extent that they destroy interpersonal relationships and inhibit this person's ability to engage in teamwork and collaboration with others. Similarly, a person may have great ability, but be unwilling to put forth the effort to complete a task or otherwise not apply the effort required to make the contributions to a department or other organization that his or her ability would be capable of doing. Time is another element under individual control. As Davenport (1999) contended, "The most talented, skilled, knowledgeable, and dedicated worker will produce nothing without investing time in the job . . . jobs have become more autonomous. . . . Consequently, time allocation strategies make an increasingly important difference in how much a worker effectively invests in a job" (p. 21). Thus, as search committees or administrators consider candidates for faculty or support staff positions, they need to think about and make judgments about the candidates' human capital that they would bring to the department, what it would contribute, and how likely it is that they would engage in the behavior, effort, and time commitment that would maximize the application of their ability, knowledge, skill, and talent.

In a sense, retaining faculty or support staff members requires opportunities for these persons to use the components of their human capital in ways that are satisfying and yield the type of return on their human capital investment that they desire. Return on investment of personal human capital incorporates several issues. One is that people work for different reasons or combinations of reasons—economic, psychological, and affiliation, among others. Davenport identified these as intrinsic fulfillment, financial rewards, growth opportunities, and recognition. Second, although administrators often assume that people's motivations derive from high wages and job security, workers indicate that what really is important to them is interesting work, appreciation, feeling "in on things," recognition that they are valued, making an important contribution, and earning the respect of their supervisors and colleagues. These are returns of investments that an increasing proportion of workers, particularly in learning organizations, want to experience if they invest their human capital in their department.

There are many important responses a department administrator can initiate and nurture to create an environment that gives substance to faculty members' need for intrinsic fulfillment, growth opportunities, and recognition. They include providing funds to support travel to professional meetings and organizations for purposes of grant-seeking; providing group opportunities to participate in bag lunches or other forums devoted to hearing about and discussing trends in the field, new methods of research, new techniques of practice; providing encouragement to sit in on seminars or courses of interest to individual faculty and staff; providing equipment, seed money, and encouragement to help faculty initiate and carry out research projects; acknowledging the good work of individual faculty member; granting individual faculty members and support staff respect and accolades for excellent work; showcasing professional recognitions; nominating faculty and staff for incentives and awards provided by a college or university; and communicating with faculty and support staff routinely about new initiatives in which the department might engage or other information (program or financial) about the status of the department in which faculty and staff would be interested.

Retention and professional development of faculty and support staff are frequently interactive. They complement each other. Perhaps most important, they incorporate a state of mind, a psychology of who we are, what we are about, and how important our contribution is in this mix of processes that make up our department.

RECRUITMENT AND RETENTION OF STUDENTS

In any academic department preparing counselors and related specialists, the recruitment and retention of students is a paramount issue. If student demand does not support the offering of courses or programs housed in a particular department, that department is likely to be placed under significant scrutiny as to its continuation or elimination by institutional-level administrators. If the students recruited by a department are not well qualified and intellectually capable, compared with the students in other departments in a university, questions about the quality of a program's instruction are raised both in the university and among similar departments in other universities. If students in Counselor Education or Counseling Psychology are not accepted into top-flight internships or placed in excellent positions when they graduate, potential applicants or referral sources often begin to choose other programs for which the history of such placements is more positive.

Within such contexts, then, students represent many contributions to an academic department. They provide tuition funds; they are the recipients of student credits generated by the courses offered by the department; as graduate students, many participate in graduate assistantships in which they assist with research studies or teaching; as representatives of the programs in which they are being trained, they demonstrate the knowledge and skills they have acquired in off-campus settings, internships, and full-time employment following graduation; and as graduates, they develop reputations as excellent or mediocre counselors, as outstanding or poor teachers, as productive or casual scholars or researchers. In student performance in the program and after graduation, students are presumed to mirror the quality of knowledge, clinical skills, and ethics that they learned as counselors-in-training.

Every department administrator must be attentive to the recruitment of students and to their retention. Like the recruitment of faculty or support staff, the recruitment of students needs to maximize the fit of the students' aspirations, professional goals, and ability to the goals and instructional foci offered by a department. If there is too much disparity between what the student expects to learn and do and what the department can provide, the student will likely leave the program voluntarily or be dismissed. Thus, the department administrator must constantly work with faculty to examine the mechanisms by which students are recruited, admitted, evaluated, and taught during their matriculation.

Although universities may have explicit policies regarding the recruitment and retention of students, Departments of Counselor Education or Counseling Psychology may need to augment such policies with other policies and procedures unique to counselors-in-training. For example, before admission, it is useful to include in the information packet provided to all students policies dealing with student conduct, ethics, and the need for counselors-in-training to recognize that not only is there an expectation that students will be successful in their academic coursework, but that they will also demonstrate behavior that is professionally appropriate in their contacts with clients, other students, and professors. At admission and other points in their training, students need to be informed of the competencies they are expected to acquire in their didactic and clinical training and how evaluation of these competencies will occur. Counselors-in-training need to be provided and to learn from manuals describing practicum and internship procedures, how clients will be scheduled, how to use recording equipment, the forms and reports to be prepared and to whom and when they will be provided, who will supervise them, and the therapeutic and ethical environment they are expected to create.

Evaluation of students for admission needs to be systematic and based on explicit and defined criteria. Retention needs to be based on clear communication of expectations for performance. For many students, particularly but not exclusively graduate students, both recruitment and retention rest on the availability of financial aid. For undergraduates, this may mean work-study opportunities, Pell grants, and other resources; for graduate students, this may mean graduate assistantships, instructorships, student loans, and other relevant sources of aid (e.g., endowed scholarships). The department administrator needs to be on a continual search for financial aid for students, including sources of support for dissertation research, computer time, statistical consultation, seed grants for research, funds for travel to professional meetings, funds to bring potential doctoral students to campus for interviews, and orientation to the department.

Recruitment and retention of students for programs of Counselor Education or Counseling Psychology also hinge, in many instances, on the types of credentials for which students are eligible following graduation and whether a particular academic program is accredited. Examples of both individual credentialing (e.g., state licensure as a psychologist, an LPC, a state-certified school counselor, a national certified counselor, as a certified rehabilitation counselor) and program credentialing or accreditation (CACREP, CORE, APA) have been discussed at some length earlier in this chapter and will not be reiterated here. However, such issues are important in attracting students and maintaining their retention. As such, they deserve, if not demand, the leadership of the department administrator to initiate and ensure that the department programs continue to meet the criteria for accreditation.

Clarity of communication with students, financial and psychological support, accreditation, and credentialing availability are all-important aspects of the department climate or environment. Yet there are other important issues related to recruitment and retention of students. One of these is ensuring that the student body of the department is culturally diverse and representative of the larger society. Students of color, multiple ethnicities, alternative sexual orientations, and disability need to be included in the recruitment and retention processes for at least three reasons. The first is that the populations from which these students come need to have access to counselors who share their cultural traditions and experiences. This is not to say that White counselors cannot effectively counsel persons of color, persons of different sexual orientations, or those experiencing disabilities. Yet research studies indicate that there are many counselees who prefer to work with counselors from their own cultural background. The second issue is that having a culturally diverse student population of counselors in training means that these students will get to know each other on an intimate basis in classes and clinical experience that will likely break down cultural barriers. As a result, counselors being trained in a multicultural environment are likely to be more able to communicate and be empathic across cultural boundaries.

A third reason for recruiting students from culturally diverse and underrepresented populations is a pragmatic one. Programs that do not seek to recruit students of color or of culturally different backgrounds will find difficulty with accreditation or other teams engaged in evaluation of their academic program to prepare counselors. Increasingly organizations that provide accreditation standards and conduct accreditation processes expect departments to aggressively seek students of culturally diverse backgrounds, recruit them, support them, and ensure that their academic and clinical experiences are conducted in welcoming, positive, and informed environments. Such criteria are reflected as expectations and standards by the American Psychological Association, the American Counseling Association, the Council for the Accreditation of Counseling and Related Education Program, and other organizations engaged in evaluating the quality of counselor preparation programs.

The recruitment and retention of students whose aspirations are to become LPCs, LCPs, or other types of mental health providers imposes on an academic department preparing counselors a seriousness of purpose as they engage in recruiting students. Although such academic departments preparing counselors have a gate-keeping role to exclude persons who are obviously unsuited to be effective counselors, they also have a role in capacity-building—developing a body of counselors who possess multicultural counseling competencies as well as those who are members of underrepresented groups for whom mental health services have been limited in availability and often lacking in sensitivity to the particular needs of persons in these groups.

Clearly, one of the major challenges of department heads of academic departments preparing counselors is that of giving direction to and ensuring a comprehensive and sensitive search for students who can effectively serve culturally different and needy groups of clients. Achieving such goals requires commitment to these issues by a department head, leadership to faculty about recruitment, and aggressiveness in using all possible recruitment processes that identify and support aspiring counselors who can learn about and offer state-of-the-art counseling interventions.

USE OF TECHNOLOGY

For much of the last third of the 20th century and continuing into the 21st century, technologies of a variety of forms and structures have been designed to complement individual counseling between a counselor and a client; planned programs for groups that are designed to provide a guidance curriculum for clients or illustrations of desired behaviors used in psychoeducational programs; test administration, scoring, and interpretation; and scheduling of clients and related management processes. Depending on the specific point in time that is being discussed, emerging counseling technologies have included games, audio-video processes, simulations, films, problem-solving kits, assessment centers, self-directed inventories, programmed resource material, computer–person interactive systems designed to facilitate client behavior rehearsal and exploration, information retrieval, assessment, planning, simulation of likely outcomes of action, and treatment. The latest technology to either augment counseling or provide a medium by which counseling at a distance can take place includes the Internet and such elements as e-mail, chat rooms, bulletin boards, video conferencing, and related functions (Sampson, Kolodinsky, & Greeno, 1997).

As new technologies are incorporated into the counselor's repertoire of tools and techniques, they cause ethical guidelines to be revised or formulated with specific attention to the use of computers and the Internet. They also have an impact on how counselors function. Herr (1999) suggested that among the counselor roles that are becoming increasingly prominent are those times when the counselor must be a technologist, briefing, monitoring, and debriefing clients as they prepare to use computer-mediated assessments or career development programs and the Internet and explore how to use the results of these explorations in decision making or planning. In such instances, counselors need to know which software is appropriate for which client, whether particular clients will be able to use technologies successfully, and related issues. Most research studies (Bolles, 1997; Gati, 1994; Niles & Garis, 1990) indicate that technologies, particularly computer-mediated systems or the Internet, do not replace the counselor, but do alter the ways counselors interact with clients and particular content.

Given this brief context about the importance of technology as an adjunctive technique in counseling, it becomes an important issue in academic programs preparing counselors, counselor educators, or counseling psychologists. This is true for didactic, researcher, and management purposes.

From a didactic standpoint, a department administrator must plan for the availability of computers, access to the Internet, or other technologies for instructional purposes. Classrooms must be available that are technology-rich, in which faculty members can use their laptop computers, Power Point equipment, LD panels for projection, and other peripheral equipment to present information. Counselors-in-training can no longer simply be taught with computers. Software relevant to the use of computers or the Internet must be taught about and taught with to demonstrate that technology needs to be incorporated into programs, counselor roles, and counseling just as is true of less advanced technologies; paper-and-pencil tests, directories, and so on. Such technologies can no longer be treated as some exotic novelty, but as a contemporary tool that is pervasive in its uses. Instruction about and with computers or the Internet must acknowledge the increasing use of online counseling and how this process is being presented to clients. It also needs to reflect the placing of syllabi, course notes, examination, and other didactic material on the Internet as routine processes.

From a research perspective, computers and the Internet have become critical tools. Sophisticated analyses of research problems can now be accomplished rather easily on the computer, using various software packages, which were only dreamed about 20 years ago. Databases can be put on the Internet for students to use in practicing research methods. Surveys and other instruments can be placed on the Internet to collect relevant research data. The use of computers and the Internet can be used to generate graphic portrayals and analyses of data and expand the geographic scope of research samples at far less cost then using conventional postal services.

From a management viewpoint, computers and the Internet have myriad uses. They include sending and receiving documents to and from prospective students or applicants relevant to program admissions; managing class scheduling; making client, student, or faculty appointments; monitoring course enrollments; ordering textbooks for courses; preparing reports for institutional-level administrators; conversing by e-mail among faculty and students, as well as faculty colleagues elsewhere at the university or other universities; maintaining and processing financial records; processing travel requests; and engaging in many other administrative processes that support recruitment of students, monitoring of student progress, record-keeping and preparation, and communications within the departments and with colleagues nationally and internationally.

There is much more to say about the use of technology in an academic department preparing counselors. Suffice it to say here that the department administrator must make technology a vital part of his or her planning and fiscal procedures. Students expect to have access to computers and the

Internet as part of their instructional and research activities. Faculty members expect to have their own computer and peripheral equipment in their office for didactic, research, and management purposes. The department administrator needs to provide computers and necessary software for each faculty member and computers accessible to students as a continuing expenditure. Because both computers and software have a relatively short life before they become obsolete and replaced by more powerful hardware and software, the purchase of computers and other technology must be included in a constant replacement cycle in planning documents.

EVALUATION OF PROGRAMS

As suggested throughout this book, human services, including counseling programs in any setting, are affected by the expectations for accountability that are major issues to policymakers, legislators, and institutional-level administrators. These persons are constantly concerned with what returns they are receiving from the programs to which they have allocated resources. Depending on the institution and fiscal circumstances that are operational, policymakers and legislators may be concerned about many questions: Is this program or department generating sufficient tuition income or student credit hours to justify its continuance? What is the demand for departmental programs by applicants? What is the ratio of applicants to those accepted? What is the faculty–student ratio? Does this department or individual program bring in external funds for research, scholarship, and instruction? How productive is the department in publications, books, and grants compared with other departments in the college or university? What kind of respect does this program or department receive from other universities? What are the national ratings of the programs in this department? By whom have they been rated and on what criteria? Do students finish their degrees in an appropriate time period (e.g., undergrads, 5 years; master's students, 2 years; doctoral students, 8 years)? What is the placement rate of students graduating from the various departmental programs? Where are students placed? Do they obtain positions that are related to their training? Is this academic department or specific programs within it central to the mission of the college or university? Do program faculty receive prestigious awards? How many and from what sources? What credentials do faculty members possess?

These and many other questions are constantly being asked of department administrators, and answers are expected in periodic reports, end-of-year reviews, or other forms of feedback. Some of these questions are judgment calls, and many of them require a data system by which to monitor information about inquiries, admissions applications submitted, number of students selected by program per year, student progress toward degree, internships and jobs obtained by students at the end of course work or on graduation, and performance of students after graduation (e.g., books and articles published, jobs obtained, awards received, etc.). In these cases, evaluation of programs are primarily a matter of tallying numbers related to each of these questions, making calculations of faculty–student or other ratios, and aggregating such data into forms that allow them to be reported and understood by the recipients.

Evaluative questions related to the ratings of programs or the awards faculty members receive from professional organizations or learned societies, and so on can be answered with tallies and calculations as well. However, for programs that engage in the processes required to become accredited by APA, CACREP, CORE, NCATE, and State Departments of Education, the answers become self-evident. The program either meets the accreditation requirements or it does not. If the program does meet accreditation criteria, the assumption typically is that, as a result of the self-studies and evaluative processes that are inherent in accreditation reviews, this program can be considered professionally acceptable, if not among the elite programs in the nation. Further, there are often surveys published in professional journals or news magazines—*U.S. News and World Report*—that publish annual rankings of specific academic programs, including counseling programs, graduate schools, higher education institutions by faculty peers, and administrators in other universities. Although there is always controversy about the validity of rankings of programs or institutions, usually related to different forms of bias or political dynamics, the fact is that such rankings do receive both public and professional attention. It is hard to deny that institutions or programs care about the rankings they receive in various polls or surveys. These rankings obviously influence recruitment of faculty and students. For programs that receive high rankings, there are likely to be announcements and stories about these honors within university publications, local newspapers, and other media. They become a source of pride and achievement to college deans, university presidents, members of boards of trustees, and legislators.

Individual faculty honors are also seen as important and highly desirable because the assumption is often made that faculty members who receive prestigious awards must, then, be excellent teachers, researchers, and so on. The connection is an arguable one, but widely held. In any case, faculty members who are elected as Fellow, Distinguished Scholars, or similar designations by the American Psychological Association, the American Counseling Association, the National Career Development Association, or other major professional organizations or receive awards for scientific achievement, quality of research, or other contributions to their profession are, like programs of high ranking, regarded highly by institutional-level administrators, policymakers, and others. Having faculty members who receive prestigious awards on one's faculty is often taken as an indication that the program or department in which they work is also of high quality. Again this is an arguable assumption, but one that is used to recruit faculty, recruit students, obtain research grants, and engage in other processes valued in academe.

If one thinks in terms of formative and summative evaluations of academic programs and departments, the most prevalent type of information sought by institutional-level administrators or policymakers tends to be summative. In other words, What outcomes did you achieve? What rankings or honors did you acquire? How many students graduated on time? How many faculty wrote books, refereed articles, or obtained research grants? In essence, these questions are primarily about what are the results of a program or department, rather than what were the major factors or processes that were present in the program and led to these results? The latter question is a formative one. Summative evaluation is essentially concerned with the aggregate effects of the program in terms of its goals or mission compared with earlier assessments of results, rather than how well specific components of a program contributed to the results achieved.

As suggested in the description of summative evaluation, formative evaluation asks somewhat different questions. Among them are which components of the program (specific faculty members, particular courses, didactic versus clinical experiences, practica or internship) are most effective in achieving the outcomes or goals achieved? Formative evaluation, then, really implies that some persons or processes are more effective than other persons and processes in achieving the goals established for the program. Implied in such a perspective is that there may be other ways to structure the program or departments that may be more powerful, effective, and cost-beneficial than the program components now in place. Another implication of a formative process is that we need to eliminate those program components that are not as effective as others, thus reducing costs and increasing the efficiency of the program components to achieve the outcomes assessed in summative evaluation.

Formative evaluation in the terms just discussed is rare in the evaluation of academic programs or departments. Probably the closest to any type of formative analysis that most departments or programs use is the promotion and tenure process for faculty or the course evaluation process. How these evaluative processes are carried out varies from college to college and university to university. Typically, however, faculty members who are on the tenure track—that probationary track that over approximately a 6-year period, if successfully completed, leads to permanent employment—face comprehensive annual evaluations. These annual evaluations usually include the faculty members' publications and research, ratings by students of courses taught, and service performed (e.g., committee membership, leadership positions) for their program, college, or profession. Usually these annual evaluations are interspersed at 2-, 4-, and 6- year points, with increasingly more rigorous evaluation of the faculty members' progress. In many universities, there are department-based promotion and tenure committees comprised of faculty members elected to these committees by other department faculty who also evaluate the chronological progress of the faculty members. These annual and biennial recommendations accumulate in faculty members' promotion and tenure dossier until, at the end of a sixth year, if not before, judgments are made by the promotion and tenure committee, the department administrator, a college promotion and tenure committee, and the dean of the college about whether faculty members will be retained or terminated. This process does not really compare faculty member x to faculty member y to determine which of these faculty members is most effective in contributing to the goals of the program or department—a process that would qualify more fully as a formative process of evaluation. One can make the same observations in evaluations of faculty members' teaching of specific courses. Students evaluate their instructors, and periodically peer faculty members may observe a class of the faculty member being evaluated and rate it. However, in general, these courses are treated as a single entity being evaluated, not in terms of its contributions to the quality of student performance or graduation, nor are ratings of didactic courses typically compared with the ratings of other faculty members on didactic courses or with clinical experiences.

There are, of course, other forms of evaluation of specific courses or comparisons of courses in achieving particular behaviors or attitudes. Frequently, these are the subject of students' doctoral dissertations or other specific research processes. The findings of such studies can help the department administrator, but depending on their likely evaluation of a single instructional process form, not comparisons of multiple instructional forms, their value in formative evaluation terms is limited.

In summary, department administrators must be constantly attentive to the variety of evaluation questions that arise from institutional-level administrators—from accreditation groups, promotion and tenure processes, and other functions. The department administrator must give leadership in how and for what reasons these different evaluations will be undertaken, ensure that they are carried out with quality, and see that the processes used are well managed.

SUMMARY

In this chapter, the complex tasks required of the administrator of a department preparing counselors have been discussed. The role of the department administrator requires considerable attention to planning that is relevant to the larger institutional planning process. It also requires the department administrator to manage the fiscal resources of the department with integrity and wisdom. The allocation of such resources fairly and without favoritism to individual faculty or programs requires clear policies or standards that guide fiscal allocations. In addition to managing resources efficiently, many department heads are increasingly expected to seek funds from internal and external resources to augment the operational funds provided by the college housing the counseling department. In addition, department administrators must be conscious of the program accreditation and individual credentialing processes that affect department programs so that departmental curriculum content and clinical experiences are aligned with accreditation requirements.

7

Administration of Counseling in Government, Nonprofit, and Professional Organizations

CONTEXT

Two or three decades ago, virtually every state department of education in the United States and the federal government had program administrators and technical staff who were professional counselors. Their responsibility was to provide support to counseling, guidance, and testing programs as well as pupil personnel programs in local schools, often in community colleges, and sometimes in higher education. In the latter settings, these counseling specialists were concerned about the preparation and state certification of counselors and, in some cases, other members of pupil personnel teams—school psychologists, school social workers, home and school visitors, school nurses, and school psychiatrists. It is no longer true that every state department of education has a "Director of Guidance, Counseling, and Testing" (or related title) who oversees a staff of specialists who support the professional counseling function in schools and other settings. However, there are still many state departments of education that provide excellent leadership and technical support to schools and other settings in implementing, strengthening, and expanding counseling, testing, guidance, and related services. Among the finest offices of counseling support in state departments of education in the United States are those in such states as Maryland, Ohio, Georgia, California, Missouri, Minnesota, and Texas. There also are many state governments in which responsibility for certification or licensing of professional counselors, counseling psychologists, or rehabilitation counselors and specific funding for particular counseling emphases is decentralized among various departments and agencies.

Unfortunately, the U.S. government no longer has a distinct office providing leadership and technical support to counseling and guidance in the schools and other settings. However, there are specialists in the Departments of Defense, Education, Health and Human Services, and Labor, the Veterans Administration, and the Rehabilitation Services Administration, who have roles specific to the support of counseling and related processes. Such roles may have to do with implementing the provisions of legislation, which include specific support for counseling, assessment, and career guidance related to such topics as child abuse or neglect, the early identification of and intervention in special needs and at-risk populations, career development, workforce education and development, welfare reform, the transition from military service to civilian life, substance abuse, rehabilitation of persons with disabilities, among other emphases. These roles also may have to do with coordination among federal agencies; communication with state agencies relevant to the legislation or public policy of a particular federal agency; ensuring that grants of funds to state or local agencies from the federal government are appropriately applied for, meet legal guidelines, and are used for their intended purposes; collaboration with professional organizations to monitor public policy and amend it as necessary; to develop research initiatives related to important national goals; and to learn about trends in the field.

Before speaking more specifically to the roles on behalf of counseling and related services played by professional counselors working in government, state, or federal offices, it is useful to consider the roles of professional counselors acting as administrators of counseling-related programs in nonprofit organizations, primarily foundations, and in professional organizations.

ROLES OF COUNSELING ADMINISTRATORS IN NONPROFIT ORGANIZATIONS

As the number of staff in state and federal agencies decrease and their roles become less distinct, it can be argued that nonprofit foundations have sometimes filled these gaps by providing funds to support professional conferences, implement and evaluate program models, and prepare "White Papers" or task force reports devoted to needs for counseling, guidance, assessment, and related processes, the ways by which they can be expanded and strengthened, or relevant public policies that need to be implemented. In the absence of government employees sufficient to carry on many of these roles, foundations have often provided important papers and forums designed to influence public policy or to demonstrate effective practices. Indeed in many cases, foundations have received subcontracts from government agencies to carry out public meetings, conferences, research studies, and other initiatives of importance to a government agency for which sufficient staff do not exist inhouse in the agency.

Many of the recommendations that have come from foundations and "the Blue Ribbon panels," which they have supported, have, in fact, been accepted by government agencies and been incorporated into public policy and, subsequently, legislation. Foundations frequently have more limited priorities for counseling and related processes than do government agencies. For example, rather than be concerned with the total array of issues associated with the implementation of counseling services, a particular foundation may be primarily concerned with counseling in middle schools, preparation of counselors, planning for counseling programs, role of parents in counseling programs, impact of specific legislation on the provision of counseling, prevention programs that can be implemented in schools to diminish substance use and abuse, or provision of counseling in developing nations around the world.

Although foundations typically have several major priorities for expenditure of their funds, and counseling is only one of these priorities, they nevertheless are extremely important for their fiscal and policy support of counseling to address different problems in specific settings. At the least, foundations have complemented or augmented government action in these areas, been able to concentrate their staff on a particular problem with far less restrictions on their activities than governmental agencies, and provided an independent and informed voice in many issues concerning counseling. Foundations change their priorities for funding or research on an annual or multiyear basis, but there continue to be a number of foundations that have made significant contributions to the advancement of counseling. They include such examples as Carnegie, Ford, Lilly, Pew, the Robert Wood Johnson, the Russell Sage, and the W. T. Grant Foundations, among others. Although these foundations may receive some government funds to carry out tasks of importance to government agencies, their ability to function in examining particular counseling needs or practices comes from the large amount of funds donated to the foundation by corporate or individual donations.

Counseling Administrators in Professional Associations

A final category of professional counselors who serve as administrators of projects and programs are those who serve on the staffs of professional organizations such as the American Counseling Association, the American Mental Health Counselors Association, The American School Counselors Association, the National Career Development Association, the American Psychological Association, and many other professional organizations focused on mental health, child development, parenting, specific groups of at-risk populations, or those with special needs or disabilities. In this latter group of professional organizations, the focus of the professional organization is not on counseling per se, but on the multiple needs of a particular constituent group (e.g., the hearing or visually impaired, abused children, those experiencing mental disorders) for whom counseling is one of several important treatment approaches.

The roles of professional groups vary in their focus, although they may use similar methods to achieve their purposes. For example, several of the professional organizations named (e.g., the American Counseling Association, the American Psychological Association, the American School Counselor Association, etc.) have as their primary mission to provide advocacy and other forms of support for counselors, counseling psychologists, and the counseling process in different settings and with different populations. Advocacy can take many forms: providing testimony and lobbying in state and federal legislatures on behalf of or against legislation that may enhance access or opportunities for counseling to become more comprehensive in its coverage, receiving funds to increase counselor capacity and skills, or supporting counselor training to address specific individual problems—career, emotional, behavioral. In such cases, professional organizations, in addition to testimony and lobbying activities, may produce newsletters, "White Papers," or reports that address critical needs for counseling and demonstrate by research summaries or other media that counselors deserve to be provided fiscal support or acknowledgment of their contributions to national goals for mental health, for productivity and purpose in career development, and for the promotion of well-being. Such professional organizations may hold conferences for counselors addressed to advocacy and provide training in government relations, preparing and providing testimony and information about impending legislation and related topics.

Professional organizations on behalf of counselors, counseling psychologists, and other related personnel engage in many other processes designed to support the skills and continuing education of counselors. Among them are the administration of national or regional professional conferences; the provision of courses, online and conventional, designed to increase the professional development of counselors; the development and refinement of ethical guidelines in general and as specifically focused on the use of technology in counseling, the use of assessments, and counseling within a culturally diverse context; the management, acquisition, and production of professional journals and books; and the support of organizational governance structures, committees, and task forces to continuously examine trends and issues of importance to counseling.

Professional organizations also engage in or spawn organizations that accredit counselor or counseling psychology preparation programs and credential individual counselor competence. The previous chapters addressed some of these guidelines and mechanisms related to program accreditation and individual competence. Such credentialing has, in turn, led to various forms of national certification of counselors and to state licensure of psychologists and professional counselors.

Professional organizations typically engage as well in providing other forms of support to counselors, such as the availability of professional liability insurance, research grants, continuing education units, and awards that signify important professional achievements in the counseling profession.

AUTHORITY AND INFLUENCE ON COUNSELING BY GOVERNMENTAL AND NONPROFIT ORGANIZATIONS

It is fair to suggest that professional counselors who work in state and federal government offices or programs supporting counselors, professional organizations, and foundations do so with varying degrees of authority and influence. For example, in most situations, state governments can be considered the most powerful in terms of authority. This is true, among other reasons, because they have the power to (a) define the scope of work for licensed professional counselors, counseling psychologists, and other mental health specialists; (b) determine the eligibility requirements for such licensure; and (c) impose legal sanctions on persons who call themselves counselors or counseling psychologists, but who have not qualified for such roles or hold licenses that are not currently valid. State government agencies also certify counselors to work in schools and other settings and often accredit preparation programs that provide training for persons seeking certification to work in schools as school counselors, school psychologists, school social workers, or other mental health capacities, including private practice, as psychologists or rehabilitation specialists. In addition, state government agencies provide state funds to support counseling in different settings or they serve as a conduit for federal funds in support of counseling that are given to state agencies to disburse to local community agencies, schools, or other programs. In such cases, state departments are charged with processing grant proposals or otherwise validating the eligibility of local recipient agencies for such counseling funds and/or to ensure that the funds received are being used appropriately.

Thus, state departments of education, labor, human services, among others, have the power to give or withhold the credentialing of individuals to perform certain counseling functions; initiate or accredit programs to train counselors and other specialists; and identify local agencies to receive funds by which to implement counseling and related programs to serve particular constituent groups. These state agencies also have the power to penalize individuals, preparation programs, or programs that deliver services that violate the standards or regulations that are designed to address such activities. By having such powers of fiscal support and regulation, state departments and specific agencies within them can directly or subtly shape the form and purpose of counseling programs (e.g., who provides what services to whom, under what conditions). State departments can also shape the provision of counseling in a particular state by the type of technical assistance that is offered and the counseling program designs that are advocated as they provide consultation to local agencies. Such power can be enhanced when state departments provide workshops or other forums to introduce or advocate for particular techniques or processes or to advance such perspectives in state newsletters or other media.

In contrast with state departments, the influence on counseling of federal departments and foundations is usually less direct. Indeed these entities are limited in sanctions they can apply to individuals or programs. For example, if a school or other local counseling agency decides that it does not want to comply with federal regulations or guidelines in a particular area, they can choose not to apply for or accept federal funds. There are, however, some exceptions to such choices. For example, support at the local level for counseling of persons with disabilities or for persons who need assistance in obtaining employment is provided, respectively, through local bureaus of vocational rehabilitation from the Rehabilitation Services Administration and through one-stop centers, career links, and related local entities that are funded by the U.S. Employment and Training Administration. These funds that "flow through" state agencies are, in fact, federal funds allocated for these purposes by federal legislation. Less directly, foundations have no sanctions that can be applied to individual counselors or programs of counseling. Rather the impact of foundations is one of influence by selectively providing funds for demonstration of best practices in counseling, by invitational forums designed to address a specific issue in counseling, or by releasing major reports that are substantive in recommendations for public policy or other important directions in the provision of counseling.

The place of professional associations or organizations on a continuum of authority and power is somewhat less clear-cut than the other organizations discussed. Because professional associations are volunteer organizations, not all professional counselors or counseling psychologists hold membership in professional associations or are directly influenced by the various processes involved. For those counselors who do belong to and participate in the variety of activities provided by a professional association, they can pick and choose those to which they pay attention. They can read the professional journals they receive with their membership or ignore them; they can attend professional meetings or not; or they can participate in available skill training or continue to use skills that they have functioned with since graduate school. In other words, professional skill development, books, journals, and newspapers that discuss emerging trends or best practices in counseling; the provision of ethical guidelines; the organization and implementation of professional conventions; and the opportunity to purchase liability insurance and other supportive initiatives are the content developed and made available to members by professional organizations, but if members choose not to use these resources there are few sanctions that can be leveled against them. A major exception is if a particular counselor is alleged to have violated an ethical standard by a client or did not secure enough continuing education credits to retain a certification or license. In such cases, a member may be removed from membership or, in some cases, stripped of certification to practice as a counselor. At a macrolevel, professional associations can and do represent the needs of counselors to government agencies, the news media, employers, and other professional associations emphasizing best practices, contributions of counselors to national goals, and research findings about the areas in which counselors have been successful. Although these latter forms of advocacy and testimony help to shape positive images of counseling and create consumer guidelines for the use of counselors, methods of accessing counselors, and the importance of such roles, these effects on counseling are subtle and difficult to link to major changes in the profession.

SIMILARITIES AND DIFFERENCES IN THE ROLES OF COUNSELING ADMINISTRATORS IN NONCLINICAL SETTINGS

In a sense, the common thread that describes the role of professional counselors who work as administrators or technical staff in state or federal government agencies, foundations, and professional associations is that they do not provide direct clinical experiences to clients nor are they regularly involved in conducting research studies. Rather they provide indirect support of professional counselors by, in some cases, purchasing services or contracting with universities or counseling programs to provide particular research analyses or conduct training for counselors. In other instances, they process "flow through funds" to applicant agencies or programs to respond to the clinical needs of particular client groups, purchase tests and other resources to augment counseling, and support the skill development of counselors in such programs. The purpose for which these "flow through funds" are made available is typically defined by a particular piece of legislation or a public policy designating the allocation of funds for counseling; in the case of foundations, institutional priorities typically do not deal with "flow through funds," but rather specific purposes for which applicant university departments or counseling agencies compete to execute particular research studies, hold professional conferences on topics of priority concern to the foundation, or participate in writing professional reports about counseling, client concerns, or the context of counseling that are intended for use with the counseling community, the general public, or legislators and policymakers concerned about counseling. In the case of professional counseling associations, there is unlikely to be a major emphasis on "flow through funds" to counselors, although there may be some small grants for particular research or demonstration projects. Rather, the emphases are likely to be on advocacy in behalf of counselors, providing professional development opportunities, supporting a governance structure for the association and its component structures, producing publications, providing liability insurance, and working directly or indirectly with programs that train counselors and organizations that accredit such programs or credential individual counselors.

Another thread that cuts across the organizations discussed in this chapter is that professional counselors working within them have multiple roles. In many cases, professional counselors administer the organization at issue (a professional association, state department, or bureau responsible for counseling services). More frequently, the professional counselors involved in a federal government agency or a foundation administer programs within the organizational context. For example, in a government agency, a professional counselor may be assigned to administer the provisions of a particular piece of legislation that addresses support for a particular emphasis in a counseling program. In such legislation, typically there are guidelines that talk about how much money is allocated to specific purposes, the criteria by which they will be expended, and the procedures to be followed for applicants to apply for grants or for the government agency to dispense the funds allocated to eligible recipients. In some cases of federal legislation, state agencies must apply, through a procedure specified in the legislation, to obtain the funds allocated to their state, which are then disbursed to recipients who meet the eligibility criteria. In many cases, such legislation allocates a certain percentage (e.g., 5%) to the state agency for administrative costs that will likely include some portion of the salary of the professional counselor or other staff members administering the funds, postage and communications, travel, and other relevant costs.

Within a foundation, a professional counselor might administer a particular program dealing with counseling research or advocacy. The professional counselor administering such a program may supervise a small staff of persons who do the detail work related to the purposes of the program:

preparing requests for proposals (RFPs) by individuals, university programs, or counseling agencies to undertake specific research studies, conduct training, or serve in a consultative capacity to the foundation program as it pursues its purposes. In a professional association, a professional counselor may administer a particular department—professional affairs, interorganizational relationships, convention services, government relationships, publications, or continuing education.

In state and federal government agencies, foundations, and professional associations, the professional counselor administering a department, program, or legislative initiative is likely responsible for both the substantive content of the function and the logistical support for that effort. Ordinarily, each of these organizational entities receives an annual budget from the institution of which they are a part, including the funds allocated for the professional content (costs of research, costs of contracting experts or agencies in the field to actually conduct research, training, or drafting of position papers, etc.), as well as the costs of travel, housing, postage, communications, supplies, and other related expenditures to achieve the purposes of the department, program, or legislative initiatives.

As suggested in earlier chapters, the actual goals to be pursued within a state or federal agency, foundation, or professional association are typically closely aligned with the strategic plan for the larger organization, its mission, its objectives, and the nature of its constituents. Thus, planning and continuous monitoring of the activities carried out by any particular department, program, or other initiative are important tools to ensure that the entity under review is carrying out its assigned responsibilities efficiently and effectively.

The professional counselor serving as a program administrator within the types of organizations described here needs to plan, budget resources, recruit and supervise staff, implement the use of technology, conduct program evaluations, and perform in an ethical manner just as is required of the head of a university academic department preparing professional counselors or counseling psychologists, the director of a university counseling center or a career service, a director of guidance or counseling in a school district, or a professional counselor in private practice. Thus, the concepts and processes described in the first two chapters of this book are applicable within the organizations described in this chapter, although the entities involved are not providing direct clinical services to counseling clients, but rather indirect support to such clients by supporting the skills, professional development, preparation, and acceptance of professional counselors and their services to clients.

A further thread that tends to characterize the professional counselors serving in the organizational entities discussed in this chapter is a lack of empirically based information about their roles. There are, of course, position descriptions that tend to be organizationally specific, anecdotal perspectives on these roles, and personal experiences that accrue from interacting with professional counselors occupying positions within state and federal agencies, foundations, and professional associations. There are, however, virtually no research studies that directly examine the roles of professional counselors in such roles. The exception to these statements are some classic studies of the roles of directors of guidance or counseling in state departments of education. These studies, although several decades old, are nevertheless instructive in considering the nature of such roles.

SELECTED STUDIES OF STATE DIRECTORS OF COUNSELING

One of these studies (Duncan & Geoffroy, 1971) is a factor analysis of the role of the state directors of guidance services. Based on a questionnaire sent to 280 state directors and state supervisors of guidance services in the 50 states, 15 factors were found to emerge to describe the role of the State Director of Guidance Services. These 15 factors were grouped into three major categories: Service, Administration, and Nonservice. These findings were buttressed by examining the role-function statements for Directors of Guidance Services in 34 states and analyzing the more than 200 role-function items available in these statements. A selective and abbreviated summary of the 15 role factors subsumed under the three categories of service, administration, and nonservice include the following:

Service

Research and Certification

Included under this factor are interpretation/presentation of research results to various groups of policymakers relative to the needs for and status of guidance services; development and implementation of counselor certification requirements for certifying counselors to serve in public schools; accreditation of public schools in the areas of guidance, counseling, and testing; pilot and demonstration programs of counseling and related guidance techniques; and research for evaluating state guidance services.

Selection and Approval

Certify counselors for public schools and assist in the selection of recipients for federal scholarships and fellowships. Work with state institutions of higher education in providing strong programs of counselor education.

Testing Service

Organize and coordinate the statewide testing program, enter into contracts with testing companies, and prepare test summaries for the State Board of Education.

Information Service

Publish scholarships and student loan information. Supervise the preparation and distribution of newsletters. Serve as a liaison with associations and organizations on a statewide level for community referral services at the local level.

Field Service

Assign field visits to members of the guidance service staff. Review reports of visits to schools by guidance service staff. Establish a professional reference service to help schools at the local level secure materials of assistance in addressing counseling problems. Establish pilot projects at the local school level relative to various aspects of counseling or guidance services.

Counselor Education Service

Serve as liaison between guidance services and counselor education programs and other professional educational organizations.

Record-Keeping Service

Develop forms for reporting and recording guidance, counseling, and testing information from the local school districts. Maintain accurate records concerning the guidance, counseling, and testing program as provided by the State Department of Education.

Leadership

Serve as chairman of the state advisory committee for guidance, counseling, and testing. Develop a philosophy of guidance services within the State Department of Education. Participate with the State Board of Education in an annual review of the state's program in guidance, counseling, and testing.

Administration

Administration of Department

Make all decisions pertinent to the effective operation of programs and activities undertaken by the State Office of Guidance Services. Establish all office and personnel policies relative to the operation of the State Office of Guidance Services. Participate in federally-sponsored in-service programs. Recommend state standards for counseling and guidance services in terms of personnel, functions, facilities, equipment, training, and research.

Intra- and Interdepartmental Communications

Cooperate with other State Departments of Education. Conduct periodic staff meetings. Carry out necessary correspondence. Prepare reports on the activities of guidance services for the State Board of Education. Supervise expenditures for guidance services at the state level. Provide orientation for all new staff members of guidance services. Represent the guidance services of the state at meetings and conferences called by the U.S. Office of Education. Maintain accurate records concerning the guidance, counseling, and testing program as provided by the State Department of Education. Supervise the work of other state personnel assigned as specialists or consultants to guidance services-sponsored programs. Provide demonstrations of pilot programs. Recommend state standards for guidance services in terms of personnel, functions, facilities, equipment, testing, and research. Serve as liaison between guidance services and professional educational or other relevant organizations. Prepare budget for guidance services. Cosponsor yearly workshops with state higher education institutions preparing counselors.

Public Relations

Speak about guidance services to various local and statewide conferences. Represent guidance services, counseling, and testing at professional meetings and conferences. Conduct research and report the findings on the evaluation of guidance, counseling, and testing services in the state.

Cooperation With Counselor Educators

Coordinate the efforts of the State Guidance and Counseling Advisory Committee with professional organizations. Recommend state standards for guidance, counseling, and testing services. Cosponsor workshops and other initiatives with counselor educators in state higher education institutions preparing counselors.

Nonservice

Financial Management of Funds

Approve reimbursement of funds from federal sources for local systems. Devise forms for reimbursement of funds. Prepare budget for guidance services. Be responsible as the administrator on a state level for federal programs providing funds for guidance, counseling, and testing. Prepare operational outlines for guidance, counseling, and testing programs for various purposes at local and statewide levels. Supervise the work of other state personnel assigned as specialists or consultants to guidance services-sponsored programs.

Department Personnel

Evaluate guidance services professionals on an annual basis. Recommend for promotion or other personnel actions (e.g., dismissal, suspension) of any employee in the guidance services office. Keep accurate records of all travel, travel expenses, and vacation for members of the guidance staff.

Administrator

Evaluate clerical personnel on the staff. Assist local systems to establish a job analysis for counselor positions. Provide orientation for all new staff members. Keep accurate records on personnel.

Before commenting specifically on the contemporary meaning of Duncan and Geoffroy's important study, there is one other that is useful for discussion purposes. Herr (1971) sampled every 10th counselor educator, a random sample of 1,000 persons who held membership in the American School Counselor Association, and 137 state directors, state supervisors of guidance, and state guidance specialists in 37 states. A 30-item questionnaire was used to collect data on the most appropriate functions of the state guidance office as reported by school counselors, counselor educators, and state supervisors of guidance. The criterion for inclusion was 75% or greater agreement among the three groups that a particular item was a needed and appropriate function. The following information is divided into those functions for which there were 90%, 80%, and 75% agreement.

90% or More Agreement

The development and dissemination of statistical, narrative, or special reports describing the status of guidance programs in the state.

The development and conducting of regional in-service programs for the upgrading of practicing counselors.

The preparation and dissemination of publications pertaining to guidance designed to upgrade the competence of practicing counselors.

The stimulation of the development of pilot demonstration projects in local districts.

The provision of liaison with other agencies of state government concerned with programs serving youth.

The provision of liaison and consultative support to professional organizations outside of state government concerned with youth (e.g., professional education associations, counselor organizations, etc.)

80% or More

The development of certification requirements for school counselors in all educational settings from K through 12.

The review of local guidance programs for adherence to standards developed consistent with the state plan.

The development of and participation in activities designed to acquaint the public with services available in local guidance programs.

The development of joint projects with other agencies of state government designed to evaluate or demonstrate guidance services.

The provision of liaison and consultative support to lay organizations concerned with youth.

The provision, in combination with counselor education programs, of regional in-service activities.

The reviewing of state needs for and programs of guidance in cooperation with representatives of the U.S. Office of Education.

The development and conducting of statewide school dropout studies.

75% or More

The conducting of pilot/demonstration projects in guidance in local districts.

The supervision and evaluation of pilot demonstration projects in guidance in local districts.

The development and dissemination of occupational and educational information for use in guidance programs.

The development of statewide data retrieval systems in support of local guidance programs.

These studies, although relatively old and primarily school-based, are reflective of the multitasking activities in which State Directors of Counseling or Guidance engage. Studies of the State Office for Rehabilitation Services, or substance abuse, would show similar processes, although the specific content of the activities would be different.

Any study of a professional counselor's roles as an administrator obviously changes over time as the counseling profession changes in the needs for support from state-level offices. Today, for example, most role studies would show state directors of counseling, guidance, testing, or pupil personnel services assigned to projects that have to do with safe schools, reduction of violence in the schools, a resurgence of concern about preventing dropouts, and renewed emphasis on career counseling in schools and across the lifespan.

In essence, whatever the role of a state director of counseling—whether dealing with schools, rehabilitation services, career services, prison populations, persons in transition from military to civilian life, dislocated workers, and so on—there are several givens. One is that professional counselors serving as state directors of counseling or counseling specialists must be credible as counselors. They must know their field, its history and trends, as well as its best practices. They must also be excellent and efficient administrators with the ability to be responsible for a wide range of tasks— from supervising professional and clerical staff to managing records and large fiscal allocations and ensuring that they are expended in a legal and appropriate manner.

It is also accurate to suggest that state directors of counseling and related processes are the public face for these professional endeavors. This person is the contact for news media about the importance of counseling, guidance, testing, rehabilitation, and so on with regard to contemporary social problems, whatever they may entail (e.g., homelessness, substance abuse, violence, academic competence, welfare reform, cultural diversity, preparation for work, etc.). In these instances, directors of counseling at the state level must be able to communicate intelligently and knowledgeably.

It also needs to be reinforced that state directors of counseling and related processes must be able to work within a network of persons and agencies. Facilitating and participating in interorganizational discussions and collaborations and representing one's constituency—counselors, counseling psychologists, rehabilitation specialists—and its contributions to state goals and social issues are significant parts of the job.

It is not inaccurate to suggest that many of the tasks engaged in by professional counselors functioning as administrators in state agencies overlap with those in which their federal counterparts engage. Obviously, the geographic spread, regional difference, and scope of problems dealt with may be wider than those at the state level, but certainly state and federal issues overlap and interact. One can make similar comparisons to the roles of the professional counselor employed in foundations and professional associations. Those working in foundations are likely to have a more limited range of processes to administer or provide leadership for and, likely, a more focused set of professional problems to address, but, again, many of the processes used by professional counselors in administrative posts in foundations are the same as those used by state and federal administrators of counseling-related programs or agencies. Much the same could be said of professional counselors administering programs within professional associations. Although the constituencies may be national or international, many of the problems at issue require responses by professional counselors in administration that emphasize networking, providing a public face, information management, and other skills similar to those required of a state or federal counseling administrator.

PLANNING

It has almost become a litany or mantra in this book that counseling agencies or programs rarely plan independent of the institution in which they are housed and to which they are expected to contribute. That is not to say that planning is not an important matter in state and federal departments, bureaus, or programs; foundation programs; or professional associations. Planning is necessary and essential both to (a) demonstrate connections to the institutional mission and goals of the larger institution, and (b) identify the priority of expenditures for cost centers that reflect the agency or program's responsibilities. The plans that are made must be done within the context of institutional policies and deadlines and with respect to the tasks assigned to the state or federal office, foundation program, or professional association unit that is assigned responsibility for overseeing, supporting, or providing advocacy and technical assistance to counseling programs.

The seminal documents that are important in planning in the organizations discussed in this chapter may overlap with those documents of importance to department heads of academic programs preparing counselors or counseling psychologists, directors of guidance or counseling in a school district, and directors of university counseling centers or centers for career services. In other words, counseling-related organizations in state and federal agencies, foundations, and professional associations must be aware of the seminal documents pertinent to schools, universities, or community settings in which they are supporting counseling services. Unless an administrator of counseling programs in a relevant state or federal office, foundation program, or professional association is cognizant of the scope of work, policies, and documents that influence such organizations, and the goals to which they aspire, the plans of state and federal agencies, foundation programs, or professional association offices may, in fact, be serving as an impediment, rather than an asset, to the counseling programs being supported. Having knowledge of the planning processes and influences that affect constituent counseling practices and counselor preparation also allows a support agency to target those funding policy, research, advocacy, or communication issues to which support efforts should be directed as plans for a year or multiple years are developed.

It must also be said that, in addition to understanding the plans, influences, and aspirations of constituent professional organizations, it is likely that state and federal departments, foundation programs, and professional association units will have additional or more specific tasks to address within the institution in which they are housed. Professional counselors serving in administrative roles in federal departments of defense, education, human services, or labor may be expected to take responsibility for managing a particular piece of legislation and overseeing its specific purposes (e.g., providing funds to support counseling services directed to state agencies for distribution to counseling programs in schools, universities, or community settings or directly to the local recipients; creating clearinghouses of data about best practices or other counseling-relevant topics; setting up professional meetings and invitees to these meetings; consulting about counseling with officials in other departments within one's institutional setting; producing newsletters and other publications that are available to counselors for their professional development; coordinating interorganizational meetings of agencies and professional associations that have responsibility for counseling in different venues and with different populations; providing state or national leadership in behalf of counseling; and making recommendations to institutional superiors about needed legislation or providing critiques to policymakers of existing legislation).

Administrators of bureaus or departments and their professional counselor staff may engage in many similar processes to those active in federal agencies, but the setting will likely be focused on counseling within a given state rather than nationally. In such cases, plans must be made to process funds that come from federal sources on a "flow through" basis to local counseling agencies or university departments. They must also manage any initiatives in which state funds are available for direct allocation or for the support of research or instructional projects to be competitively based on recipient proposals. State-level counseling administrators may also be expected to consult about counseling with other departments or with policymakers and legislators about the status of counseling; the preparation, certification, or licensure of counselors; and the needs of programs. A major task will likely be to serve in a liaison relationship with state-level professional associations concerned about counseling, with representatives of local counseling programs and university academic departments in counselor preparation, and, perhaps with a statewide advisory committee on counseling.

PLANNING ISSUES IN NONCLINICAL COUNSELING-RELATED SETTINGS

A major planning issue at the state department level, but less so for federal counseling-related administrators, is whether a state office for counseling, guidance, testing, rehabilitation, or other related processes will focus on regulation, technical assistance, advocacy, all of these, or other purposes. For example, it is possible to visualize a state office in which the staff is primarily concerned with upholding the state standards for counseling programs in schools and other settings and investigating instances of potential violations (e.g., inadequate counselor–client ratios, uncertified or unlicensed counselors, misuse of counseling funds, and penalizing programs in which violations have been established). One also can visualize a state or federal office that is primarily oriented to providing technical assistance to schools, institutions of higher education, or community agencies. Technical assistance in such circumstances could mean having professional counselors employed in the state or federal office who can work directly with local administrators of counseling programs or heads of academic departments in efforts to evaluate their programs, incorporate best practices, and examine the best organizational structures for their program, methods of obtaining external funding for particular counseling initiatives, and related program improvement purposes. In such circumstances, the state or federal office professional staff are seen as collaborators, not overseers, engaged in helping local programs make decisions about improving their program, using their staff most effectively, or assessing their program. A third scenario could visualize a state or federal office as primarily committed to advocacy for counseling programs. In such an emphasis, the professional counseling staff of the state or federal office would emphasize their role of championing the needs for counselors; the contributions they make to state or federal social, political, and economic goals; the personnel, facilities, and equipment required to operate an excellent program; and the expanding client concerns to which counseling can be addressed in various settings and with diverse populations. Depending on the institutional mission and the goals established for its individual units, it is conceivable that the administrator of the state or federal counseling program will have to lead the planning for, implementation of, and evaluation of any one or all three of the counseling office or department emphases: regulation, technical assistance, and advocacy.

In contrast, foundation programs in counseling are not likely to be regulatory; they may offer some technical assistance, but probably in a less direct form than that of state or federal offices. Foundation technical assistance is likely to take the form of research, summaries of research on particular counseling-relevant topics, and the development of position papers analyzing particular social, economic, political, or mental health problems, the theoretical frames of reference in which they can be understood, and evidence-based best practices found to effectively address such problems. In an important sense, the products of the technical assistance offered by foundation programs that are counseling-relevant overlap with advocacy for counseling. Advocacy is not just sharing opinions with policymakers, institutional administrators, employers of counselors, or counselors. Advocacy involves well-reasoned and factually-based arguments presented in a coherent, thoughtful manner in written and oral forms. Advocacy requires a professional analysis of problems and needs that is credible to policymakers, their staff members, institutional members, and others. In some instances, policy papers may be placed into monograph or book form as the core content for professional symposia or conferences integrating policymakers, theorists, researchers, and practitioners.

Professional associations, as volunteer organizations, take on many forms. To some extent, they overlap with some of what foundations do in advocacy, but they are not likely to have the staff to do technical assistance to counselors in a direct way. Rather, they bring to bear the critical mass of professional counselors whom they represent as the credibility from which they speak in testimony on counseling or client-related topics in state legislatures and in the U.S. Congress. In their government relations activities, they lobby policymakers and legislators on behalf of legislation supporting counselors and granting them access to third-party payments to pay client fees within particular populations. They bring to policymakers and legislators the "best thinking" on a particular topic from the professional literature or from professional members of the counseling professions who work with, do research on, and can serve as important spokespersons for a particular topic of concern. Professional associations also engage in regulation, but usually in limited and specific ways. For example, professional associations typically offer mechanisms to adjudicate ethical complaints about members. Or they manage individual eligibility for membership in the professional association. They may provide for accreditation of professional preparation programs. Often, however, professional associations provide the facilitation of processes to achieve such purposes, rather than use the professional counselors serving as administrators in the professional association. For example, the American Psychological Association does accredit/approve doctoral programs preparing counseling, clinical, and school psychologists. However, the teams that visit the programs onsite are comprised of volunteers selected and trained to conduct visits to programs to assess the degree to which they meet the standards for such preparation programs. Professional counselors or psychologists employed in the professional association administer all of the logistics of identifying and bringing an evaluation team to a site visit and to processing the recommendations from the site visit by committees of volunteer professional counselors within the professional association who ultimately decide whether a given preparation program has effectively met the standards for such programs.

In summary, the counseling-related offices within state and federal agencies or departments, foundation programs related to counseling, and professional associations are all vital elements of the counseling profession. Their missions and specific goals vary, but their roles are different from those of counseling units providing direct clinical services to clients or academic departments in universities preparing professional counselors. Thus, the administrative roles of directors of state or federal counseling offices, foundation programs, or units within professional associations are different from those programs offering direct clinical services to clients in schools, university counseling services or career centers, or community agencies or teaching and socializing students to assume positions as professional counselors. The functions of the counseling administrator in settings that offer direct clinical services or student preparation as counselors are different from those of administrators in support organizations (e.g., state and federal offices, foundations, and professional associations). The former administrative roles are direct, whereas the latter are indirect. The administrator of counseling programs and academic preparation programs must ensure that the clinical services and teaching of students are state of the art, consistent with professional program accreditation standards and ethical guidelines, based on the "best practices" identified in the professional literature, and planned in accord with the institutional mission of which the program is a part.

In state and federal offices, foundation programs, and professional association units, the administrator must ensure that the programs and services offered are what the professional counselors in settings delivering clinical services to clients or teaching students to become professional counselors need. The administrator must ensure that his or her staff of professional counselors are credible, informed, and respectful of those whom they regulate; provide technical assistance; or represent in advocacy initiatives. In this sense, the administrator of any of the counseling support organizations must work within a network of roles played by administrators of programs providing clinical services or the teaching of students learning to become professional counselors, of policymakers and legislators, and of intra- and interorganizational colleagues in other professional associations or agencies that employ professional counselors or view them as relevant to the client populations they represent. They must know the missions of the organizations other administrators direct. They must know the national trends and professional literature so they can talk about the history, issues, and promise of the counseling profession. They must be able to lead by influence and persuasion, not by mandate or regulation. They must be able to work with volunteer professional counselors whom they do not employ, but who are vital to achieving many aspects of the organization's goals. They must know how to work without mandated authority to intervene in the work of professional counselors in direct clinical settings.

INTELLECTUAL CAPITAL AS A FUNCTION OF NONCLINICAL SETTINGS

As a final perspective on the professional counselor as administrator of a counseling-related office, bureau, department, or program in the organizations discussed in this chapter, there is the matter of *intellectual capital*. Typically, it is thought that the research and scholarship (the intellectual capital) that undergirds the identification of evidence-based best practices, the best models of counselor preparation, the analysis of public policy, and related influences on the counseling process emanates from university academic departments in counselor education, counseling psychology, rehabilitation, and programs in the behavioral and social sciences. Although such departments are major, if not the major, contributors to the creation of intellectual capital—concepts, theories, research findings, hypotheses, scholarly treatises—these efforts can be augmented by the various projects sponsored or facilitated by foundation programs, professional association units, and state and federal offices representing counseling services. Each of these organizations has the potential to facilitate the production of intellectual capital by awarding contracts to address specific research questions or preparing scholarly analyses of particular problems of importance in counseling. Their organizations typically have the capability to store and retrieve such information in data banks, in various forms of information repository, or as books, journals, or newsletters. They also serve in many cases as clearinghouses of information classified into information categories (e.g., counseling, assessment, technologies, counselor preparation, client groups, psychoeducation or curriculum models, computer-assisted systems, emerging trends in counseling). It can be argued that, within such functions, foundations, professional associations, and state and federal offices that are counseling-oriented, by the nature of their responsibilities, must keep in mind the "big picture"—the status of national and international trends affecting the expansion or changes in the support for professional counselors and counseling. In this sense, professional counselors working as administrators or staff members in foundations, professional associations, and state and federal offices with responsibility for counseling must do environment screens and serve as futurists constantly analyzing and reporting on new issues for counselors to address, new processes, and new research findings that need to both be reported to professional counselors served by these organizations and integrated into the planning and goals of the organization. In this sense, the administrator of the organization must be able to provide leadership to and a rationale for facilitating the creation of intellectual capital as a service to the counseling profession and as the content by which advocacy on behalf of counseling is credible.

BUDGETING

As discussed in each of the chapters preceding this one, planning and budgeting must ultimately come together as a major administrative task. It is fair to suggest that planning helps an administrator decide on priority actions and new initiatives that must guide the organization in meeting its mission. Yet great plans without the resources necessary to bring them to fruition can be, at best, window dressing or a frustrating or demoralizing situation. In an overly simple-minded perspective, in such a case, the great plans must be amended and downsized or the resources necessary to achieve the plan specified must be acquired in some fashion.

One can argue that budgeting is budgeting regardless of the setting. That is, in many ways, accurate. Many of the issues and processes focused on budgeting in earlier chapters are relevant here, although the content of the funding priorities and the sources of revenues are likely to differ from organization to organization. In other words, the investments in people, resources, and facilities needed to accomplish the mission follow from the mission and goals specified for the organization. The precise expenditures, cost centers, and investments in people and resources that need to be budgeted if the mission is to be achieved depend on many different variables. As an example, if an organization owns its own facility and can accommodate the mission needs within it, there is no need to budget facility rental, although budgeting still needs to include custodial care and maintenance of the facility. If much of the governance and professional work is done by volunteers from among the membership ranks of the association, with the exception of salaries for core professional counseling and clerical staff, there is no need to pay or budget salaries for the volunteers engaged in professional relations, government relations, convention planning, or other initiatives, but there are still cost centers associated with these activities. The volunteers staffing different committee and action activities must be reimbursed for travel expenses, lodging, per diem, and perhaps clerical support or special resources. In the organizations discussed here (state and federal agencies, foundation programs, professional associations), rather than add core professional staff members, the alternative is to contract or subcontract with professional counselors, in university academic departments or from other settings, who have particular forms of expertise to draft a position paper or engage in some other activity that essentially becomes a product of the organization. The point is that planning goals rarely come free; they involve professional effort, which, whether produced by volunteers, contracted personnel, or core staff, cost money and must be budgeted.

Another budgeting factor that differentiates organizations is the source of funds or revenue streams from which monies for budgeted items are obtained. For state or federal offices with oversight responsibility for counseling services, it is likely that funds will come primarily from state or federal funds allocated to the larger organization of which the counseling office is a part. Each year it is likely that the departments of defense, education, human services, labor, or other will propose a budget through its institutional-level administrators to a legislative committee for all of the entities and budgets located in the department. By sequence, theoretically, there would first be a strategic plan produced with the general mission, goals, and objectives of the institution-level organization specified. Ultimately, the counseling-related office would need to project its own proposed plans and a rationale for them, which must be seen as contributing to the overall strategic plan of the institution/department and any subadministrative units of which the counseling oversight office may be a part. As this planning process unfolds and the basic mission goals and objectives are accepted, the financial implications of these goals must be transformed into cost centers and budget items. Thus, in state and federal offices, a line item budget specifying the costs of the office to meet the planning goals and objectives must be proposed, negotiated, and probably revised until final approval is given by institutional decision makers. In one sense, these governmental budgeting processes are more rigid and complex than in foundations or professional associations, in part, because there are more restraints, legislative mandates, and specific policies focused on how funds are proposed and allocated.

The budgets for state or federal offices in which professional counselors serve as administrators are those in which the primary budget allocations are from the state or federal funds allocated to the institution of which the office is a part. In addition to these budgeted funds, there are also other limited, but possible, revenue streams. For example, in the cases where federal or state counseling-related offices manage funds allocated by specific legislation, either as flow through funds to be processed and passed on from federal to state agencies for disbursement or from state-level offices to local counseling units, or as targeted funds for a specific purpose (e.g., welfare reform, child abuse, dislocated workers, etc.), these funds can only be provided to specific agencies that have met the eligibility criteria to receive the funds if they submit an appropriately executed proposal. The point is that, typically, legislation authorizing funds for either flow through or targeted purposes also includes a provision providing 5% (or something in that range) to the agency or office providing the processing of such funds to help defray the management and staffing costs to implement this process. From a budgeting standpoint, we have now identified two revenue streams: (a) the primary budget from state or federal funds, and (b) an amount to reimburse some of the costs of managing or processing legislative allocations. There may be some others. For example, a state or federal office overseeing counseling-related issues may be contracted by a foundation to plan and implement a conference focused on a particular conceptual priority of the foundation. A state office may be funded by a federal office to run a conference or be a partner in a research study. These processes are also revenue streams, although the likelihood is that the state or federal offices of counseling services will be primarily limited to the first two revenue streams noted.

A foundation's budgeting process tends to be less restricted, but no less important, than government offices or agencies. In most foundations, funds are made available from corporations or individuals for philanthropic purposes—not to make a profit, but to engage in the use of funds to solve local, state, national, or international social, economic, and political problems. Although the donors of these funds typically receive tax benefits from doing so, with effective management these funds augment those of academic departments and state and federal agencies in supporting the development of intellectual capital on behalf of whatever problems are the focus of a particular foundation. Although there is a certain mythology that foundations exist to give money away, such give aways are not random. Indeed the allocation of funds by foundations is usually related to a planning process that defines the general priorities of the foundation or those which are specific for a particular year or several years. In many foundations that have been established and monies donated for specific purposes, the mission is proscribed by those processes. In other foundations, the priorities are established in response to changing social, economic, and political questions that have triggered problems that need to be understood and possible solutions identified. In some foundations that deal with social and economic problems, counseling becomes cited as one of the possible treatments or interventions that should be addressed to the priority problems. In other words, neither a particular foundation nor its programs may be focused entirely on counseling. Yet because counseling has become increasingly comprehensive in its applications to a wide range of problems, populations, and settings, it becomes a priority issue for many foundations to consider as they study the social, economic, or political problems that are the prime focus.

Ordinarily, the budget processes in foundations are less complex than in government agencies. Therefore, the applications for funds related to some analysis, research, or demonstration about counseling are likely to be less complex. For example, rather than preparing a huge proposal with all sorts of legal affidavits appended, applications for funds to foundations frequently begin with a letter or a 3- to 5-page paper that addresses the research or theoretical ideas that the author proposes. If that idea is sufficiently well formulated and of interest to the foundation, the author may be invited to prepare a full proposal or come to the foundation to discuss it. Before doing so, the administrator of a counseling program seeking funding for research, scholarly, or demonstration activities needs to obtain as much information from directories of foundations or Web sites to identify those foundations of most relevance to counseling-related issues.

To return to issues of revenue streams in foundations, a major one is interest that accrues from the foundation's endowment. Spending only the interest or dividends that accrue annually from the foundation's endowment or principal is often that which is allocated among the priorities of the foundation as established by its strategic planning. A further revenue stream may be funds from the federal government for which the foundation is an applicant and a recipient. In such cases, the foundation may be subcontracted by a federal government agency to conduct a research study, plan and execute a conference, prepare "White Papers" on a particular problem, or bring together a "Blue Ribbon Panel" to study and make policy recommendations of importance to the federal government. Flowing from such activities, many foundations actually publish books or occasional papers, which of course represent another revenue stream.

As stated earlier, foundations are, in large measure, producers of intellectual capital on major social problems. They are frequently organized around specific problems and the programs that address them. Therefore, the professional counselor as administrator is likely to be heading up a program devoted to addressing a social problem within which counseling is a treatment of preference. The program administrator may have his or her own professional staff, but is likely to network with experts in a particular subject field with whom a research proposal may be funded or a contract to engage in certain scholarly activity may be implemented. In either case, the program administrator must know the profession of counseling; manage funding processes related to planned priorities; network with experts, government officials, and others; and create a learning organization (Senge, 1990).

It can probably be argued that professional associations have the most diverse revenue streams. Among these are membership dues, sales of books and other publications, possible grants and contracts from government sources or foundations, convention registration fees, fees for continuing education credits, and donations to particular professional initiatives by members or other interested people. All of these revenue streams must be kept separate, tracked, and allocated to particular cost centers within the professional associations. Given these multiple revenue streams, professional associations tend to be the most complex of the organizations discussed here in the programs they provide to advance members' professional development (e.g., conventions, continuing education, books, and other publications), advance the profession's intellectual capital (e.g., contracts from government agencies and foundations, donations from members for research and scholarly practices), and provide support to members (e.g., liability insurance, provision of advocacy for counseling, consumer guidelines for choosing a counselor, advertising, lobbying for counseling with legislators, and policymakers).

Because professional associations are comprised of both professional and support staff, as well as a larger number of volunteers or elected officers within the organization, the typical budget process is to have the professional staff draft the annual budget for the organization, submit it for review by a financial affairs committee, and then submit the final budget to the governing council, board of directors, or whatever term describes the administrative group with policy and fiscal oversight. The latter typically provides final approval and adopts the budget for the organization as a whole and for its components. In such a context of a complex budget and review process, the professional counselor as administrator needs to understand and be a credible representative of the counseling profession and also be adept in strategic planning, managing and creating operational budgets, networking among members and volunteers serving in governance capacities in the association, and presenting budgets to the committees that comprise the approval mechanisms for budgets, new initiatives, and future plans.

As an aside, of the organizations discussed in this chapter—government offices with responsibilities for counseling and related processes and foundations with counseling as a priority commitment among its strategic plans—professional associations representing professional counselors as its principal constituency are the only organizations in which counseling is the raison d'etre for the association. Therefore, professional associations are stand-alone organizations that can create their own strategic plans, mission statement, goals, financial systems, and implementation processes. Thus, professional associations are not subsets of universities, government agencies, or other institutions, but rather they are their own entity with full authority to shape their culture, commitments, and political, professional, and fiscal processes. This is not to say that professional associations function in a vacuum. They do not. Their leadership must be attentive and responsive to the needs of the membership, to the dynamics and challenges that comprise the range of counseling services across settings and populations, and to the opportunities for networking with related professional associations and government agencies.

STAFFING

The size and composition of the professional and clerical staffs that carry out the counseling-related responsibilities in state and federal agencies, foundations, and professional associations vary widely. Professional associations may have as many as 100 professional and clerical staff members plus volunteers or as few as 8 or 10 employees. Depending on the number of counseling-related initiatives or programs being undertaken, foundations may have several persons assigned to each such initiative or program. Government agencies, state or federal, with responsibilities for leadership, advocacy, professional development, or management of legislation allocating funds to counselors and counseling programs again are likely to have as many professional counselors as there are particular programs being offered in support of counseling. In most cases, each initiative will have several support or clerical staff assigned as well.

Credentials Required

Whatever the particular oversight responsibility, the legislative process, the technical assistance provided to local counseling units, and professional counseling staff, as far as possible, need to have had experience as counselors in settings similar to those to whom they are offering assistance, and they need to have credentials similar to those persons delivering counseling services or the preparation of counselors in local settings. Depending on the organization at issue, it is common to have a person with a doctorate in counselor education or counseling psychology administering each program initiative as well as the specific state government or federal office, the foundation program, or the professional association. Depending on the settings and populations with which specific offices or programs work, the staff may comprise some persons with doctoral degrees and a greater number of persons with master's degrees and experience in counseling. To add credibility with their constituents, it is important to have staff members who have achieved certification as National Certified Counselors (NCC), as certified school counselors or rehabilitation counselors, as licensed professional counselors (LPC), or licensed counseling psychologists. These credentials affirm that the staff members have met important standards of knowledge and experience as well as continuously engaged in professional development efforts to be aware of best practices in the fields they represent.

RECRUITMENT, RETENTION, AND SUPERVISION OF PROFESSIONAL STAFF

Professional counselors as administrators of government, state, and federal counseling-related offices; foundation counseling program initiatives; and professional association units must place high on their leadership and management priorities the recruitment, retention, and supervision of professional staff. In terms of recruitment, the counseling-related organizations discussed in this chapter are likely to compete for professional counseling staff members with academic departments in universities to find professional staff members who have a large sense of the history of the counseling profession, its trends and issues, its practices, and its needs. Therefore, these organizations will likely need to provide the incentives and support systems available in academic departments if they are to be successful in attracting the most able persons, the professional counselors with potential for leadership in counseling, who are available. It would be useful for the reader to review the section of chapter 6 that pertains to recruitment, retention, and supervision of professional staff. There is much of relevance in chapter 6 to the organizations discussed in this chapter.

Whatever the specific recruiting process (e.g., a search committee comprised of other professional counseling and support staff members), it is important that, before recruitment of additional professional or support staff members begins, the administrator of the counseling office, program, or unit be clear about the actual skills needed in the new position. Such analyses take into account the strengths and weaknesses inherent in the current staff and the emphases, values, and skills that need to be added. In a sense, this means considering whether current staff need to be reassigned in ways that capitalize on their skills, promoted, or otherwise redeployed. Thus, before moving to recruit new staff members, it is important to ensure that current staff members understand the purpose for which new staff members are going to be employed and how such additions will affect their roles and responsibilities. In this context, it is useful to outline to current staff members the factors involved in the decision to recruit new staff members and any anticipated changes that such employment will occasion in the assignments of current staff members (Heller & Hindle, 1998).

When new professional counseling or support staff members are employed, it is important to make every effort to ensure that they are fully integrated into the existing staff, oriented to their specific responsibilities and their expected interactions with others, and provided any necessary training. Pursuing such goals is extremely important as part of the retention effort that will immediately begin on employment of new staff members.

Although recruitment processes may be similar in the organizations discussed in this chapter to the processes discussed in chapter 6, one difference in retention between academic departments in universities and the organizations in this chapter is the issue of tenure. Typically, academic departments can offer tenure, which approximates secure, life-long employment if a candidate successfully negotiates the 6-year process of probation, review, and productivity preceding a tenure decision. Chapter Six discusses this process. However, government offices, foundations, and professional associations typically do not have the ability to offer tenure as a reward for persons who have performed in a highly effective manner over a period of years of what is essentially probation. Instead the organizations discussed in this chapter may offer other alternative methods of providing relative security for their professional staff. Sometimes these alternatives may be labeled *continuing appointments, civil service seniority, long-term contracts* (5 years or so) with the possibility of renewal, or another method. Although not ordinarily as secure or permanent as tenure, these processes offer substantial protection from being dismissed arbitrarily, abruptly, or for political reasons. As such they do offer a retention incentive for many potential or actual professional counseling staff members.

Beyond these methods of providing for employment security with which the professional counselor serving as an administrator must be familiar, there are other matters of the professional climate or organizational culture that have much to do with retention. These include having available a variety of interesting work, done in a collegial and collaborative environment, where staff members and the administration of the organization respect and support each other. Embedded in such organizational cultures are efforts by the administrator to acknowledge excellent work by a staff member through additional pay, awards, paid continuing education courses, or other forms of recognition.

Retention is frequently a direct result of the interaction between the professional counselor serving as administrator and his or her staff. Trust and respect for members of the professional counseling or support staff by the administrator is frequently reflected in the administrator's willingness to listen, support, help, delegate responsibility, or train staff in a manner that conveys their value to the organization. The leadership role is one of not showing favorites, treating all staff members fairly and as important contributors, ensuring that they know how to (have been trained to) do the tasks to which they have been assigned, informed about any changes contemplated by the organization, and treated as persons of dignity who deserve respect. A particularly important issue is not confronting professional or support staff members for a mistake or error in a public forum, but privately in a way that focuses on the issue to be corrected, not a personal attack. Such meetings should be one on one, and free from interruption, allowing for frank discussion of the issues at hand. Reprimands should be communicated sensitively, without anger, and with a clear focus on what is to be corrected.

Supervision can take many forms described in other chapters, but certainly one important aspect of retention and supervision is an individual appraisal of staff member performance. When an administrator is preparing an appraisal of individual staff, he or she can use such processes as a way to motivate professional or support staff to do well, to be stakeholders in achieving the mission of the organization, and to have pride in the work they do. Before such appraisals are held, the administrator should engage in planning to ensure that the individuals' strengths are clearly identified so they can be complimented and weaknesses can be discussed for improvement's sake. In that sense, an appraisal is a feedback mechanism and, indeed, the substance for a "personal development plan" or similar constructive future-oriented improvement process. Whether held annually or more frequently, the counseling administrator should plan to follow up on any items that need to be strengthened or implemented. Frequently, appraisals are conducted in relation to developing a career path or career plan. Thus, new responsibilities or specific training may be decided on as next steps and to which the professional counseling or support staff may have given agreement. Such agreements clearly need to be pursued, identified, and made to occur.

To the degree possible, in doing performance appraisals, it is best to have measures of staff performance. It may not be possible to measure all the types of performance required in a particular position, but where possible such measurement makes appraisal of performance more concrete. The measures take many possible forms: the actual expenditure versus approved budget for the period of appraisal, accuracy of communications, actual results of performance outcomes from collaborating with target populations, performance as assessed by coworkers, by team members, by customers, contributions of the staff member to the goals of the organization beyond specific assigned duties. In essence, any measures used to assess the performance of individual professional and support staff members must be meaningful and accurate, and they should be defined in terms of the standards established for the various processes and components of importance to the office, programs, and goals. At a minimum, supervision and performance appraisal should be relevant to the roles that the individual staff members are assigned. Thus, although there may be some general standards—communicate clearly, meet deadlines, and treat other staff members with civility and respect—that apply to all professional and support staff, whatever their role, performance appraisal in a substantive sense must be tailored to the expectations and content of the individual's particular role in the organization. When thinking about such roles, the reader might find it useful to reread the first 10 or 15 pages of this chapter to discuss the types of roles that professional counselors play as administrators or technical staff members in state and federal offices relevant to counseling, in foundations, and in professional associations. The reader should recognize that such roles are diverse and span a wide range of programs and processes, including such examples as:

- The preparation of newsletters, "White Papers," books, and journals;
- The creation and maintenance of a Web site providing pertinent information about the mission of this office, program, or unit; the status of the counseling profession; trends and issues in the field; currently active legislation relevant to counseling; and requests for collaboration or for proposals for research (RFPs);
- The planning and delivery of workshops on specific counseling problems and practices;
- Collaborative planning with other organizations for statewide, regional, or national conferences;
- The processing of and negotiations about applications for "flow through" funding of specific counseling-related functions with eligible recipients;
- The specification of RFPs that identify research studies to be funded by the office, unit, or program;
- The coordination of or serving as a staff liaison to persons on advisory committees or "Blue Ribbon Panels" to examine particular topics of concern to the application of counseling; and
- The preparation and delivery of testimony to legislators and policymakers on behalf of advocacy for resources and recognition of counselors or counseling psychologists, including certification and licensure.

The point here is that these roles are different in the skills and tasks involved and deserve different performance appraisals and supervision. The professional counselor serving as the office, program, or unit administrator needs to understand and prepare to implement these processes related to recruitment, retention, and supervision.

USE OF TECHNOLOGY

As is true in the many other settings discussed in this book, the counseling administrator in government offices, foundation programs, and professional association units related to counseling must be attentive to how technology needs to be integrated into the organizational content and processes. This includes securing appropriate technologies—computers, Internet access, telecommunication equipment, and related software and hardware. It also involves planning how to most effectively use technology to meet mission objectives.

At the very least, technology has become a prime medium for communication between the organizations represented in this chapter and their constituents. In a growing proportion of organizations, the Internet has become the method of dispersing information about conferences, workshops, the availability of RFPs, grant applications, and other items reflecting the organization's activities. Often this information is first posted on the organizational Web site. Negotiations and clarifications about such information are frequently conducted on e-mail or online bulletin boards, chat rooms, or via video conferences.

Because all of these organizations are learning organizations, they are also likely to need to be technologically enriched: capable of permitting professional and support staff to do much of their work on laptop and desktop computers, PowerPoint equipment, LD display panels, and searching the Internet for relevant or posting information.

The professional counselor who serves as an administrator in any of the organizational units cited in this chapter must ensure that appropriate technology is available to professional and support staff, that such technology is fully integrated into the processes that are used to meet the goals of the organization, that all staff are trained to use the technology available to them, and that the periodic needs to upgrade technology are included in the annual budget for the organization.

SUMMARY

The provision of counseling services can be provided directly or indirectly. The indirect provision of counseling services can be associated with state and federal offices, foundations, and professional associations (such as the American Counseling Association and the American Psychological Association) that produce public policy, legislation, governmental "flow through" money, training, and advocacy on behalf of the needs for counseling related to specific personal, social, and career concerns. Such indirect provision of counseling services can also be manifested in analyses and publications of best practices in counseling, consumer guidelines for selecting a counselor, and effective training and capacity-building of trained, competent, and ethical counselors, counseling psychologists, and related professionals.

The chapter depicts the contexts in which such indirect support of counseling services occur, the roles of professional counselors in offices, programs, and units in organizations that address the needs for and the importance of counseling within states or national arenas. Such perspectives address the types of challenges faced by the professional counselor serving as administrator in such organizations.

8

Leadership and Management of Counseling in the Community and Workplace About Work

CONTEXT

Virtually every community has counseling services directed to those choosing, preparing for, adjusting to, readjusting to, or dealing with employment, unemployment, and related issues. Several of these services are government sponsored, and often they are mandated by specific legislation. Other services are embedded in human resource management programs in workplaces, subcontracted to counselors in independent practice, or provided by independent practitioners on a fee-for-service basis.

In most communities, then, counseling services directed to the choice of and adjustment to work are a mosaic provided by a mix of agencies, workplaces, and independent practitioners. In each of these cases, it is likely that professional counselors will serve as administrators of these agencies, practices, or workplace services. Because of the differences in the settings providing these services, it is likely that the administrative functions will vary to some degree.

Two of the most prominent of government agencies concerned with employment and related work issues in a community are the U.S. Department of Labor's Employment and Training Administration (www.doletz. gov) and the U.S. Department of Education's Rehabilitation Services Administration. The Employment and Training Administration administers federal government job training and worker dislocation programs, federal grants to states for public employment service programs, and unemployment insurance benefits. These services are primarily provided through state and local workforce development systems. Among the programs administered by the

Employment and Training Administration are the Job Corps and Apprenticeship training. Most visible in most communities, however, are the One-Stop Career Centers, employment counselors, and specific programs of customized training of workers related to the needs of new industries moving into a particular community, retraining of workers who have been dislocated by local jobs being transferred overseas or who have left their jobs through international competition, and the administration of unemployment benefits.

COUNSELING IN PUBLIC EMPLOYMENT CENTERS

The One-Stop Career Centers are current methods of combining the various services provided by the Employment and Training Administration at the local level that result from federal support and direction. One-stop Career Centers offer different kinds of assistance to persons seeking jobs and developing their careers. A wide array of job seeking and employment development services are offered, including the initial assessment of worker skills and abilities, self-help information relating to career exploration and the skill requirements of different occupations, information on local education and training providers, and comprehensive labor market information. An important aspect of the One-Stop Career Centers is the use of technology to explore labor market information, match personal characteristics and available jobs or training opportunities, and access Internet Web sites identifying job vacancies across the nation. Centers provide both technological and staff-facilitated activities that are focused on providing a seamless approach to service delivery in relation to employment, training, and educational programs. From a counseling perspective, services provided include career assessment; career counseling; prevocational services including assistance with resume writing, interviewing, and other necessary job search skills (e.g., assistance with posting resumes on America's Talent Bank and America's Job Bank—a nationwide listing of job openings); staff matching of job seekers to existing job openings; and arranging interviews with those local businesses that have job openings. Related services include providing information to eligible individuals by which to meet child-care and transportation needs, as well as providing for short-term courses in computer skills; literacy; academic coursework required for the GED; self-employment assistance for these persons interested in starting their own businesses; and services for older workers including employment counseling, job-related training programs, and job placement assistance.

The Department of Labor administers and enforces more than 180 federal laws that cover many workplace activities and issues. Among major emphases in these laws are such examples as the Fair Labor and Standards

Act, which prescribes standards for wages and overtime pay, and the Occupational Safety and Health Act (OSHA), which regulates safety and health conditions in most private and public workplaces. Other major laws are also included. The Labor-Management Reporting and Disclosure Act of 1959 (the Landrum–Griffin Act) deals with the relationship between a union and its members. The Uniformed Services Employment and Reemployment Act and Veteran's preference deal with the employment rights of those called to active duty from the National Guard or the Reserves and those former active duty personnel applying for federal positions. The Migrant and Seasonal Agricultural Worker Protection Act regulates hiring and employment practices, wage protection, housing and transportation safety standards, and related concerns for migrant and seasonal agricultural workers. The National Apprenticeship Act of 1937 (the Fitzgerald Act) identifies the criteria by which apprenticeship programs are developed and evaluated, the standards related to job duties, wages, related instruction, and health and safety regulations that must be met if an apprentice program is to be registered with the federal government.

The federal laws described before and the remaining 180 federal laws for which the U.S. Department of Labor is responsible are monitored by and frequently acted on by personnel based in One-Stop Career Centers. However, the most important piece of legislation that has stimulated and shaped the concept of One-Stop Career Centers is the Workforce Investment Act, which in 1998 replaced the Job Training Partnership Act with block grants to states requiring the delivery of workforce development services through a system of One-Stop Career Centers. Basic to the expectations of the workforce Investment Act of 1998 were the provision by One-Stop Career Centers of such core services as:

- Initial assessment of worker skills, aptitudes, abilities, interests, and needs for services.
- Job search and placement assistance, including career counseling when appropriate.
- Labor market and other information to support decision making, including job listings and the skills necessary to obtain these jobs, local occupations in demand and their skill requirements, the availability of support services, and information on the performance of authorized training providers.
- Follow-up services, including counseling, for individuals placed in employment.

One-Stop Career Centers, like their counterparts in other nations (e.g., Japan), have provided what is analogous to a triage approach in emergency medicine. The issue is how many services and with what intensity clients of a center need. After their initial intake interview, do they primarily need to work on self-directed exercises and information resources with minimal staff support? Do they need some staff assistance, perhaps through participation in selected groups or support activities? Or do they need extensive individual counseling? Such an approach attempts to use the resources of a One-Stop Career Center most effectively, providing clients the services they need, but not committing personnel or other resources to them that they do not need.

THE LOCAL COUNSELING ADMINISTRATOR AS PLANNER

The professional counselor as administrator within a One-Stop Career Center, or within other aspects of the U.S. Employment and Training Administration, needs to be familiar with the philosophy and specific content of the legislative acts that essentially define the purposes and practices of the activities in which he or she and various staff members engage and that provide the resources by which to carry out specified activities. Further, the administrator must be informed about the strategic plan to which his agency contributes. Within this context, strategic planning is typically a function of the central Employment and Training Administration (ETA) that must specify the changing missions of the ETA as legislation assigned to it is modified or newly approved. Because the ultimate delivery of these services sponsored by the federal government occurs at the local community through One-Stop Career Centers and related venues, the strategic plan must define and document how these local offices will accomplish or are carrying out their legislative mandates. Because the ETA is an agency within the U.S. Department of Labor, its strategic plan must be reported to and approved by the U.S. Secretary of Labor and by Congress. Although the directors of a local One-Stop Career Center may not be required to prepare a strategic plan per se, they must prepare planning documents that describe the constituents with whom they work, the local mandates and legislation in force, the distribution of resources and services, and the effectiveness of the various programs offered.

COUNSELING IN PUBLIC REHABILITATION AGENCIES

A similar situation prevails within the local offices implementing the various legislative and regulatory activities of the federal Rehabilitation Services Administration (RSA). The RSA oversees programs that help individuals with physical or mental disabilities obtain employment through the provision of such supportive processes and practices as counseling, medical and psychological services, job training, and other services. RSA, like the ETA, provides grants to states and, ultimately, local public vocational rehabilitation agencies to provide employment-related services for individuals with disabilities, giving particular priority to persons who are severely disabled.

Administratively, the RSA is one of the three major agencies in the Office of Special Education and Rehabilitation Services within the U.S. Department of Education. The other two agencies are the Office of Special Education Programs and the National Institute on Disability and Rehabilitation Research. Collectively, these agencies within the Office of Special Education and Rehabilitation Services provide funding and other types of support to programs that assist in educating children with special needs, provides for the rehabilitation of youth and adults with disabilities, and supports research to improve the lives of individuals with disabilities.

Although there is other relevant and important legislation undergirding rehabilitation services and, more specifically, rehabilitation counseling, three of the most prominent pieces of legislation are the Rehabilitation Act of 1973, the Rehabilitation Act of 1998, and the Americans With Disability Act of 1990.

As a function of these legislative actions, earlier legislation, and related legislation, rehabilitation counseling has become increasingly professionalized, with many practitioners earning the standard certification in the field: Certified Rehabilitation Counselor. In many of the states that offer licensure for professional counselors, rehabilitation counselors also seek such licensure.

As the education and professional statutes of rehabilitation counselors have evolved through legislative mandates on behalf of persons with disabilities, professional organizations, such as the American Rehabilitation Counselors Association and the National Rehabilitation Counseling Association, have come to a consensus about the scope of practice for rehabilitation counselors that is used to define the coursework and education they need to implement the expectations of rehabilitation legislation in public agencies or to practice in the private sector for fees for service. This statement also defined the roles rehabilitation counselors play in the community.

The scope of Practice Statement for Rehabilitation Counseling found in the Web site www.nchrtm.okstate.edu, which the National Rehabilitation Counseling Association maintains for itself and for the American Rehabilitation Counselor Association, is as follows:

> Rehabilitation Counseling is a systematic process which assists persons with physical, developmental, cognitive, and emotional disabilities to achieve their

personal, career, and independent living goals in the most integrated setting possible through the application of the counseling process. The counseling process involves communication, goal-setting, and beneficial growth or change through self-advocacy, psychological, vocational, social, and behavioral interventions. The specific techniques and modalities utilized within this rehabilitation counseling process may include, but not be limited to:

- assessment and appraisal;
- diagnosis and treatment planning;
- career counseling;
- individual and group counseling treatment interventions focused on facilitating adjustment to the medical and psychosocial impacts of disability;
- referral;
- case management and service coordination;
- program evaluation and research;
- interventions to remove environmental, employment, and attitudinal barriers;
- consultation services among multiple parties and regulatory systems;
- job development and placement services, including assistance with employment and job accommodations;
- providing consultation and access to rehabilitation technology.

As suggested by the scope of practice statement, rehabilitation counselors must engage in a wide array of functions and interventions on behalf of their clients. In addition to their knowledge of their counseling procedures, rehabilitation counselors must be aware of the factors that cause and accompany disabilities: physical, mental, developmental, cognitive, and emotional. Further, although counseling and related interventions are at the core of the rehabilitation process, counselors involved must be familiar with the provisions of the legislation under which they are performing their duties, the philosophies and values underlying such legislation, eligibility requirements for service to clients, the medical and psychosocial impacts of specific disabilities, and how to coordinate all of the services for which a particular client is eligible and requires. So, too, must the professional counselor serving as administrator of a rehabilitation agency be knowledgeable about these matters as well as about planning, budget allocation, recruiting and supervising staff, implementing technology within the agency's program, evaluation, and the other types of managerial and leadership roles discussed throughout this book.

In a comparative sense, much of the planning, budget allocation, descriptions of staff positions, and use of technology occurs at levels beyond the local rehabilitation agency or One-Stop Career Center. Federal legislative mandates and state policies related to application for state block grants or other "flow through" funds from the federal government for allocation to local rehabilitation offices or One-Stop Career Centers tend to dictate, to a large degree, what is to exist at the local level and, in this sense, what the administrator will manage and give leadership. Such is not likely to be the case for other practitioners and administrators involved with the provision of work, employment, and career-related services in workplaces or in independent practice in a community. The exception to this point is in the case of independent practitioners in a community who may subcontract with a local office of rehabilitation counseling or, possibly, a One-Stop Career Center to provide assessments and/or counseling of specific clients of these agencies. In such cases, subcontractor hourly fees for service or fees for particular tasks (e.g., administering and interpreting tests) are likely to be established, and the subcontractor, as a surrogate for the agency, must function within the legislative purposes and policies of the agency.

COUNSELING IN NONGOVERNMENTAL LOCAL SETTINGS

The nongovernment work-related counseling services in a community are likely to include a mix of persons with a range of education, credentials, experience, and focus on work-related issues. They may include school counselors; counselors in career services centers in community colleges or universities; clinical mental health or licensed professional counselors in independent practice; counseling or clinical psychologists in independent practice; career coaches in independent practice; or persons who work within or who contract with employers and work organizations to provide outplacement counseling, conduct employee assistance programs, or engage in specific tasks (e.g., assess workers, consult on career development of employees, do research on workers' morale, advise on succession planning, provide workshops for workers on particular topics of interest to the employers or the workers, etc.). In most states, there are no regulations barring persons from calling themselves career counselors or career coaches. There are, however, regulations, certifications, or licensure for persons identifying themselves as licensed psychologists or licensed professional counselors. However, many of these persons have little experience or education related to work-related, employment, or career issues, although they may be highly trained in dealing with behavioral, emotional, and mental disorders. Several of these groups have been discussed in earlier chapters.

Rather than talking further in this chapter about the professional counselor or administrator of government agencies, One-Stop Career Centers, rehabilitation counseling agencies, or counselors who have been discussed in other settings (e.g., schools), the remainder of this chapter focuses on the director of counseling services in workplaces or in relation to workplaces.

COUNSELING IN WORKPLACES

In workplaces, many of the functions related to the recruitment, adjustment, and mobility of workers are incorporated under entities entitled *human resource development* or *human resource management*. Sometimes these terms are subsumed under the personnel function in a workplace, and sometimes these terms subsume the personnel function under them. As typically used, *human resource development* and *human resource management* are umbrella terms that include such activities as training, education, appraisal, recruitment, selection, career development, succession planning, workforce planning, employee assistance programs, job enrichment, and organizational development. Although corporate headquarters may encompass all of these functions within human resource management, local plants under a particular corporate banner may be somewhat more limited in how they conceive of this function. Small individual firms, not part of a large corporate structure, may be limited in the functions that are undertaken by staff members in human resource management within the firm and subcontract to various independent providers in the community responsible for such activities as employee assistance programs, outplacement counseling, and so on.

Human resource development or management is potentially a wide-ranging concept. Conceptually, it can encompass virtually anything that has to do with human activity in the workplace, including a whole range of services and support systems provided to employees. In a given firm, these may include how new employees are oriented to their jobs, to the culture of the workplace, and to their contributions to the mission of the enterprise and the degree to which new, younger, and older workers receive employer-provided training or educational benefits to attend courses relevant to their work in the community. Human resource development may include support groups for minority workers or women in technical fields; classification of worker skills and their placement in positions that promise the best person–job fit; the counseling of troubled workers or workers contemplating new assignments or a geographical transfer; the assignment of senior employees as mentors to new employees; and the development of career ladders, posting of vacant positions, and availability of seminars relating to mobility within the firm or preparation for supervisory positions or management. Other foci may include terminating workers and supervising the process of severance, advising workers considering retirement about their pension plan and related benefits, and referring workers to employer assistance programs or outplacement counseling.

Human resource management is not confined to providing counseling services for employees. Indeed human resources management is a mix of responsibilities for advisement, classification, recruitment, placement, organizational development, mentoring, training, and counseling. Human resource development is not intended to be the setting for psychotherapy for employees or counseling for its own sake. Rather the intent is to staff a work organization with personnel who are motivated, purposeful, and productive. Within this context, however, there are likely to be an array of procedures and issues that relate to the motivation, purpose, and productivity of workers that can be dealt with through accurate information, mentoring, and advice. Sometimes good workers are suddenly confronted with family problems, substance abuse issues, or other concerns that are eroding the quality of their work. Human resource specialists, often in consultation with a worker's supervisor, must determine whether the worker should be referred to an employee assistance program (if there is one), terminated, and possibly offered outplacement counseling.

Employee Assistance Programs

Employee Assistance Programs (EAPs) typically exist outside of a workplace and outside of the direct staffing by human resource specialists in the firm. Many firms subcontract with local psychologists or counselors to provide counseling to troubled employees who may decide to use the confidential services of an EAP or they may be referred by a human resource management specialist. The fundamental role of EAPs is to assist workers who have been productive and effective to return to that status by confronting their current mental and physical health problems (e.g., stress, alcoholism, chemical dependency, family conflicts, interpersonal difficulties, or financial pressures).

Originally EAPs began in response to employee alcohol problems. More recently, such programs have expanded to address other forms of employee or family problems. The expectation is that such programs do reduce absenteeism, stress, and the incidence of accidents, and thereby increase the productivity of workers who use them. They tend to be seen as cost-efficient methods of handling problem employees (Palmo, Shosh, & Weikel, 2001). Although there is not a large volume of studies, those that do exist suggest that EAPs do add value to the organization (Gladding & Ryan, 2001; Herr, Cramer, & Niles, 2004). In one study of EAPs, the top five services offered were found to include: (a) training of managers and supervisors to use EAP services, (b) evaluation and referral (internal or external) of substance abusers, (c) case consultation for supervisors, (d) crisis intervention, and (e) assessment (Hosie, West, & Mackey, 1993).

Outplacement Counseling

Outplacement counseling, or job separation counseling as it was earlier known, has a different set of goals than that of an EAP. Where outplacement counseling exists, it is intended to assist an employee who is to be terminated

> to find new employment, sharpen their job search and access skills, deal with the psychology of job loss, and otherwise make the transition from employment to unemployment and back to employment more successfully than they would if they were cut off abruptly without specific attention to their economic and psychological needs during such a difficult time in their lives. (Gray & Herr, 1998, p. 286)

Mirabile (1985) made the point concisely and powerfully by suggesting that Outplacement counseling "is a process that enables management to deal with the sensitive and often traumatic problem of the employee who must be released or the staff that must be reduced" (p. 40).

Often outplacement counseling is conducted by personnel or human resource specialists within a firm. However, frequently employers or human resource management specialists will subcontract with consulting firms or individual counseling practitioners who specialize in outplacement counseling to conduct group workshops and/or individual counseling to help workers who are to be terminated to deal with the effects associated with being terminated, to do self-assessments of interests and skills, to set goals and identify next steps, to engage in the development of strategies by which to reach their goals, and to implement action.

For the professional counselor serving as the administrator of an EAP, a consulting firm specializing in outplacement counseling or a human resource development program, a first step would be to identify the mission of these entities as defined by the corporation or work organization strategic plan. As suggested here, the extent of the activities and purposes of human resource development can be wide ranging or limited. Such status is a function of the resources allocated to human resource development as well as the culture of the workplace. Are workers in this organization seen in holistic terms—as persons who have outside lives that are not left at the door of the workplace, but are part of their daily focus and productivity? In some cases, these outside lives, including family issues, abuse of chemical substances, and so on, erode work performance and productivity. Therefore, are workers valued for their potential contributions to the firm and as deserving support to deal with the current dilemma or behavior at issue? Or are workers in this organization viewed as persons who perform a particular set of tasks for a specified period of time each day? Therefore, they are expected to separate whatever occurs in their lives outside of the workplace from their work role. This is their problem, and if they cannot keep it from interfering with their work performance, they should be terminated. Although these are caricatures of how workers may be viewed by employers, there are elements of reality in both views. As such, they represent the contexts, the culture, in which the administrator of counseling services must shape the human resource management process and make decisions about what management tasks and leadership opportunities exist.

PLANNING

In chapter 7, there was considerable discussion about professional counselors as administrators serving in state and federal offices who have responsibility for the oversight, leadership, advocacy, funded contracts, and selected policies affecting counseling services. Many of the same planning issues that pertain to serving in state and federal offices also arise in managing and providing leadership to One-Stop Career Centers or Rehabilitation Counseling Agencies at local or community levels. The reader is encouraged to re-read the sections on context and planning in chapter 7 before reading the next sections of this chapter because there are many parallels to be drawn for the planning to be done. For example, whether at federal, state, or local levels, administrators' planning within government-sponsored agencies must be cognizant of the legislative mandates of direct relevance to funding of the office or agency and to its directions.

We previously mentioned that much of counseling in general, and specifically work-related counseling, is a creature of public policy. Without the resources and requirements of legislation and policy directing that there be assistance provided to persons seeking employment and to persons with disabilities, it is unlikely that the current national network of government-sponsored local agencies and centers addressed to such issues would exist. Thus, the seminal documents for planning and One-Stop Career Centers and rehabilitation agencies are the legislative acts that mandate these entities, provide them resources, and define the boundaries and purposes within which they are to work. In this chapter, we have talked in the previous section about the importance of the Workforce Investment Act of 1998, the Rehabilitation Acts of 1973 and 1998, and the Americans With Disability Act of 1990 as examples of such seminal documents. Because legislation virtually always includes sections about the expressed processes and actions supported—specific types of actions or interventions to be taken, for whom, for what purposes, and the resources available to support such initiatives—this information and its pertinence to federal, state, and local agencies become major input to the planning process.

A second seminal document for local One-Stop Career Centers and public rehabilitation agencies is the Strategic Plan, for example, of the U.S. Employment and Training Administration or the Rehabilitation Services Administration that provides insight into the connections among federal, state, and local agencies, the coordination expected among them, the services for which each are responsible, who the primary constituents are, the outcomes sought, and the reporting required at each level. Although local agencies of a federal- or state-supported network of employment and rehabilitation counseling services are not likely to have to complete a strategic plan per se, they are likely to be required to complete a mission statement, goals, program plans by which to meet legislative mandates, descriptions of personnel needs, collaboration with other agencies, budget requirements, and related structural and process elements of the local agency by which various constituencies (e.g., employers, unemployed workers, new entrants to the labor force, persons with disabilities, etc.) will be served. Such agency plans may include the elements by which local marketing or promotion of the One-Stop Career Center or Rehabilitation Services agency will communicate with potential referral or user populations to ensure that persons who are eligible for services know about them and how to access them.

Planning Differences Across Settings

The planning process for nongovernment counseling services in workplaces, in EAPs, and in firms specializing in outplacement counseling is likely to be less prescribed or clearly defined in form and substance than is true of the plans of government agencies. Although planning is no less important, the specifications of what content will be included in planning documents will tend to be largely a function of the particular context in which the counseling or career development services are to operate, whom they are to serve, and for what purposes.

A major difference in planning between local government agencies and counseling services in workplaces, contracted EAPs, and contracted outplacement counseling firms is that the nongovernmental, private sector services are not likely to engage in planning related to salient documents, like legislative mandates that give direction, indeed requirements, for the services offered. Having said this, however, does not mean that there are no salient documents that should affect the planning at a local firm level. For example, if counseling services are being offered within the purview of a human resources management system and the local workplace is one location in a large corporation that has multiple locations, it is likely that corporate headquarters and the central office at headquarters overseeing human resources management will have a strategic plan. Such a plan includes within it values and expectations related to the corporation's human resources, the functions of human resource management in general and, perhaps, specifically at local plants or other workplaces, the gross human resource budget, pertinent information about the goals and directions of the corporation over the next several years, the importance of human resource management, the general outcomes expected of such processes, and the roles played by specialists in the area. If the corporation is a public company, is listed on one of the stock or security exchanges, and has investors who buy the company's stocks, it is likely that many of the general corporate goals and dynamics affecting them will appear in the corporation's annual or semi-annual reports to their stockholders. Although the latter are useful documents to identify the corporation's values, goals, and aspirations, and the current economic and social dynamics affecting its directions, annual or semi-annual reports do not talk in specific terms about the internal functions (e.g., human resource management) that the corporate goals will pursue. These occur within the strategic or local plans by which the overall expectations of the strategic plan are implemented.

The professional counselor as administrator of a human resources development department, or a subset of career development services under the oversight of the human resources department, must be aware of whatever strategic plans or other salient corporate documents exist that will affect the programs for which he or she is responsible. They also need to know about the information describing the economic and policy directions set by or forecast for the state, region, or local community in which they are located. They also need to know the potential roles and functions of human resource management groups in corporate settings, the types of services they offer to workers, what functions they perform in-house and what they contract with outside specialists to perform, and what assistance local government agencies (e.g., One-Stop Career Centers, rehabilitation agencies) can provide in the recruitment of workers, in job design for persons with disabilities, and in operating within the federal or state legislation on such emphases as discrimination, fair standards, compensation safety, and so on. Although it was suggested that counseling and related services in the workplace are not specified by legislative mandate, when performed they must ensure that the federal laws pertaining to treatment of workers and the quality of the conditions in which workers function are observed and implemented. The professional counselor as administrator may not need to be an expert in the 180 or so federal laws that the U.S. ETA administers, but he or she must know who, in local One-Stop Career Centers or rehabilitation counseling agencies, has the expertise to advise about specific federal laws that have direct pertinence to human resource management.

With regard to the roles that human resource management specialists, counselors, and counseling psychologists play in different workplace settings, there are many descriptive articles about their emphases and roles in the professional counseling literature. What counselors do in business and industrial settings depends in many cases on effective advocacy of the roles these professionals play by the administrator of their unit, department, or programs and on the degree to which counseling and related services are viewed as providing added value to the mission of the workplace. Thus, there is much variance in what counselors and other human resource specialists do in addressing work-related issues. For example, in one large-scale study of career development services offered with Canadian corporations, it was reported that the key goals for these services were to promote job satisfaction, enhance employee productivity, reduce employee turnover, and increase employee motivation (Bernes & Magnusson, 1996). The researchers found that the array of services offered in the 30 organizations studied, with a range of employees from 1,000 to 18,000, could be classified into three major categories: career planning, career management, and life planning. Under each of these categories of services were many individual services that were used by different organizations to serve either individual worker or organizational needs. *Career management services*, typically focused on the needs of the organization, included such functions as performance appraisal, promotion and transfer procedures, educational assistance programs, recruitment procedures, management succession and replacement planning, communications on equal employment opportunities, affirmative action policies, job requirements, career paths or career ladders, training and development options, and new employee orientation. *Career planning or life planning* was more directly related to individual needs. Career planning services included such examples as informal counseling by personnel (or human resource management staff), career exploration or support groups, psychological testing, assessment, feedback regarding aptitudes, interests, and other work-related attitudes and skills, career counseling by professional trained staff counselors, referrals to external counselors and resources, career planning workshops, informal or formal mentorship programs, and teaching of advancement strategies. *Life planning services* included such examples as personal financial planning, family/marital counseling, alcohol/drug counseling, formal employee assistance programs, interpersonal skills training, and workshops on a variety of subjects—retirement planning, time management, stress reduction, smoking cessation, and general wellness.

No work organization offered all of these services, nor did they offer them for the same purposes. In some organizations, there is an integration of career services that meet the needs of both individuals and organizations. In many organizations, the provisions of career development services are intended to negotiate or reduce the tension that exists among the needs, aspirations, and goals of the worker, on the one hand, and the organization's needs and requirements, on the other hand.

However defined, counselors in business, industry, and human resource management can potentially be involved in a wide range of activities that, in a broad sense, are work-related, but often bridge the gap between work and other life roles. Counselors in business and industry might consult with managers about job satisfaction and job stress, advise and support for external training, lead or initiate support groups for minority group members or women in work specialties in which they are traditionally underrepresented, lead seminars designed to help selected workers prepare to become supervisors, counsel plateaued workers, initiate mentorship programs, teach workshops on nutrition and health wellness, and provide job separation or outplacement counseling.

The professional counselor as administrator in a human resource management department or career services program must be aware of the types of functions that counselors and related specialists can and do perform within work organizations. He or she must also understand the culture of their particular work organization and the expectations of the central administration relative to support for counselors functioning with a human resource management or career development perspective. Given such information, when coupled with a corporate strategic plan or other relevant documents, the professional counselor as administrator must include within the mission plan for the areas for which he or she is responsible— those activities and functions most likely to integrate worker and organizational needs and expectations.

Within such plans, where appropriate the administrator will want to include those functions that can be contracted to professional counselors or other specialists in the community rather than done in-house. Examples of such contracting could include EAPs; outplacement counseling; teaching of workshops on stress reduction, wellness, nutrition, smoking cessation, stress management, or educational options; and how to prepare for them. To the degree that these functions can be contracted or outsourced, rather than performed by in-house personnel, it is likely that budget savings can be demonstrated in the department or unit plan. Contracting for these functions on an as-needed basis reduces the need for core staff and the costs for those staff members' salaries, health, retirement, and social security benefits. Indeed in recruiting staff or advocating for increased functions to be informed by in-house staff, the administrator must recognize that currently many work organizations are attempting to reduce the number of core staff and increasing the number of part-time and outsourced staff to attain quality services. Such personnel planning attempts to reduce staff whose specialties will not be used on a daily basis and can be purchased as the need for such services occurs.

Finally, for the counselor who serves as the administrator of an EAP or outplacement firm with which workplaces contract, the planning issue is to provide services that are directly related to the contract negotiated to ensure in one's planning process that the services provided to workers who are referred to or, where so designed, can refer themselves are confidential. In many cases, the names of workers who use the EAPs are not reported to the administrator of the human resources management unit. Rather, the number of workers using such services and the number of hours to be billed to the human resources management unit per month are provided. Such procedures need to be clarified at the outset when contracts are being negotiated so that confidentiality between workers using external EAPs and their work organizations can be maintained, and that labels such as *troubled employees* or *misfits* can be avoided on their records.

Contracted outplacement counseling is somewhat different, in the sense that the persons referred to outplacement counselors or firms specializing in this process are known by human resource management. They have already been identified by their supervisors or others for termination and have been told that they are being terminated on a particular date. Outplacement counseling is seen as part of a severance package to ease their transition to unemployment and, hopefully, to reemployment as quickly and smoothly as possible. Although the names of the persons referred to outplacement counselors are known, the content of what they discuss with outplacement counselors should remain confidential. Their anger, feelings of betrayal and being treated unfairly, and their plans should remain confidential between the outplacement counselors and the worker. Again the professional counselor as administrator of an outplacement counseling unit needs to negotiate that proviso in contracts that are negotiated with human resource management personnel in workplaces.

The plans of EAPs or outreach counseling firms or groups need to identify the values of such groups (including confidentiality), who they see themselves serving primarily (the worker or the organization), the services they can provide, and the costs of such services.

BUDGETING

In the previous section, some of the planning differences that differentiate federal-supported local government counseling agencies concerned with work-related issues from the counseling services that are part of human resource development units in work organizations have to do with revenue streams. As suggested in chapter 7, and in this chapter, federal, state, or local offices or agencies have revenue streams that emanate from legislative mandates and the resources allocated to such purposes. They may be "flow through" funds or "targeted funds," but they typically come only from federal or state budgets. These federal, state, and local government agencies (e.g., those sponsored by the U.S. Employment and Training or Rehabilitation Services agencies) do not charge fees for their services, although they may charge for the costs of a particular publication. Thus, government agency budgets are relatively straightforward in the available funds allocated to support their services. As budget resources increase or erode, services in local agencies tend to increase or decrease in parallel with this ebb and flow. Even so, planning and the provision of budgets for the personnel and fiscal resources needed to achieve the local agency's mission effectively are the annual procedures necessary to obtaining funds, advocating for the funds needed to provide quality services, and connecting plans and resource priorities.

Although other chapters have discussed budgeting in some depth, it may be useful here to reiterate several points about budgeting that deserve reinforcement in this chapter. For example, for those agencies at the local or state levels that are supported by federal funds on a flow through or direct basis, they are at the end of a long tail of budget processes. In a major sense, budgeting begins with the Secretary of Labor or Education identifying priorities to which departmental administrators at the federal level and related administrators at the state or local levels can prepare budget submissions. To a greater or lesser degree, these budget submissions are negotiated and fine-tuned at each governmental level and assimilated into the Secretary's overall budget package to be presented to Congress and the staff of the president of the United States.

At the federal secretarial level, the strategic plan created to define the strategic objectives and priorities for the major entity (e.g., the Department of Labor, the Department of Education) and all of its related subdivisions at state and local levels is what leads then to the strategic or overall strategy for the budget. Inherent in the overall budget are the strategic priorities and targets for spending, the attainment of revenues, and related matters such as budget surpluses or deficits, public debt incurred to meet budget priorities, and so on.

A federal department's strategic plan and strategic budget, when completed, are incorporated into the total federal government budget and submitted to the U.S. Congress for its review and action. From a federal government standpoint, the various budgets for different government departments—defense, education, labor, and so on—are assigned to specific congressional committees in the U.S. House of Representatives and the Senate, which individually hold hearings on the strategic priorities and strategic budget reflected in the federal government's submission to Congress. Where the House of Representatives and Senate committees disagree on the goals to be pursued or the costs involved, these committees come into a conference process where they try to resolve the disagreements and bring the federal budget and its parts to a vote. In many instances, professional counselors serving as administrators within federal, state, or local departments or agencies delivering work-related services will be asked to testify on behalf of congressional committees to clarify particular strategic priorities or costs for legislators. In many ways, the activities in state legislatures are a microcosm of the federal process as the federal allocation to states and other state funds are combined into a state budget that is ultimately allocated to local agencies. Although oversimplified here, this sometimes complicated budget process at federal and state levels allows the government to (a) establish and adjust its fiscal objectives in relation to its anticipated revenues, expenditures, debt repayment requirements, and other fiscal obligations; (b) maintain effective fiscal control and project its fiscal status for the coming year and the several years beyond; (c) allocate the available resources, including those coming from legislative mandates, consistent with the government's strategic objectives and priorities; (d) fulfill legislative requirements; and (e) implement congressional or legislative oversight of spending.

Regardless of the fiscal magnitude or complexity of a budget at the federal, state, or local level, there are commonalities. All budgets itemize the projected costs and, in most cases, the income or revenue that is expected to cover these costs in relation to a defined set of activities. In other words, budgets are not random requests for funds that are not tied to particular activities or priorities. Rather budgets are itemized in relation to a single activity, like a workshop, program, project, or organization. Regardless of which of these levels of magnitude a budget is prepared, a budget is both a political document and a financial management tool. It is a political document in the sense that it emphasizes and is intended to fund some activities and not others. It is a financial tool because it quantifies the organization, project or program's goals, and objectives by guiding the allocation of financial and human resources. As we suggested in previous chapters, the budget can be used in combination with expenditure reports to compare actual spending with expected costs for specific budgeted activities, to determine which programs are more or less cost-effective, to predict needs for additional resources, to identify where and what costs need to be cut, and, in the worst-case scenario, to determine what programs should be discontinued.

In a major sense, as suggested previously, budgets are political statements about what goals are priorities. To arrive at such decisions means that there are alternative priorities and alternative scenarios that might have been chosen, and that would have resulted in different activities, costs, and, perhaps, revenues.

Budgets, then, have different uses and content. They allow an administrator to monitor and control daily operational costs and to allocate available resources as effectively as possible. Within such a context, budgets help administrators make decisions about the likely costs of different scenarios and the probability that different budget items will be needed. Budgets help administrators to differentiate between essential and nonessential activities and the priorities for funds that each deserves. Thus, the exercise of preparing a budget causes administrators at any level to think through each activity as completely as possible before committing these thoughts to paper. The exercise of monitoring a budget that is constantly updated allows the administrator to anticipate shortfalls in the available resources for a particular activity and either reallocate available resources or change the vulnerable activity to keep it within budget or terminate the activity.

In an earlier chapter, we discussed the concept of cost centers. These accounting constructs are ways to assess all of the costs related to a particular activity. For example, the cost of putting a counselor in place is not confined to the individual's salary; also included are the organization's costs for health and retirement benefits, social security supplies, workman's compensation, travel, office furniture, and technology. In this sense, each counselor is a cost center, and the costs attributed to each counselor can be added together and considered the total cost of providing the activity—counseling. Each activity provided by an organization can be seen as a separate cost center (e.g., communications, printing, rent, technology maintenance, data analysis, workshops, etc.). All of these cost centers collectively reflect the work plan, which is the operational budget by which the implementation of the strategic plan occurs.

When preparing a budget, an administrator must begin by identifying what activities will be itemized in the budget, their costs, and the sources of funding available to pay for these activities. In doing so, the administrator must be aware that in broad terms there are two categories of costs: *fixed costs* and *variable costs*. Fixed costs are those that are going to occur regardless of the amount of service offered. Fixed costs might include the salaries of the professional and support staff, rent of the facility, electricity, heat, and so on. *Variable costs* are those that vary with the amount of service or range of activities provided. Thus, the administrator who monitors his or her budget closely may be able to stay within the budgeted resources by reducing the amount or type of services offered and thereby reducing the variable costs, although the fixed costs remain static. An additional way to think of costs is to consider them direct and indirect. Direct costs are things like rent, equipment, telephone lines, and salaries—the obvious costs of maintaining the agency. Indirect costs are those less obvious, such as fringe benefits (e.g., health insurance, sick leave, social security, pensions), overhead (e.g., general and administrative costs), the costs associated with maintaining buildings (e.g., custodial care), accounting, legal services, and so on. Overhead is figured in different ways, but is usually a percentage of the total budget or of the direct costs.

Budgeting can be a complicated process depending on the magnitude and complexity of the services offered, the size of the staff, and other factors. To accomplish budgeting well means that the professional counselor serving in an administrative role must work in collaboration with program staff as well as with the administrator to whom he or she reports to ensure that costs and revenues are constantly and accurately reported; that the organization's policies, practices, and procedures are understood and followed; and that the budgeting process is efficiently conducted and useful as a management tool.

The Interaction of Planning, Budgeting, Management, and Leadership

In summary, the professional counselor as administrator needs to engage in at least three broad functions. One is to select a course of action or a set of directions that will achieve the mission of the organization. This is the *planning process*. While creating a work plan, strategic or mission plan, or other major planning document once a year is important, in reality managers are engaged in planning virtually every day. The second broad management function is making sure that the plan is carried out. This is the *supervision process*. A third broad function is analyzing the results, monitoring and adjusting budgets, and communicating about and clarifying the tasks of professional and support staff members. This is the *control process*. Embedded in how these functions are executed is *leadership*—the role modeling, vision, and ability to motivate others and to treat them fairly.

We have extended this discussion of budgeting here because it is a vital management role in government-sponsored organizations as well as in the corporate workplace. Although these settings vary in how the budgeting process occurs, the professional counselor as administrator needs to be aware of the fundamentals of planning, budgeting, control, and supervision and imbue these functions as fully as possible with leadership. He or she has to recognize that in all public agencies and, to a large extent, in the private sector, administrators operate within a budget that has been approved and allocated by some authorized group of individuals or board of overseers.

Planning and budgeting for resource needs in human resource management departments or related units in corporations and single workplaces is somewhat analogous to that of government agencies. Human resource management groups do not charge workers for their services. Whatever services are provided to workers—career counseling, assessment, training, mentoring, and so on—are viewed as a cost of doing business—as procedures that add value to the work organization's support for workers to be productive and loyal. Thus, the counselor as administrator in corporate work settings must know how to plan and deliver services that are basic to maintaining the organization—recruiting new workers, classifying them, making provisions for compensation and other benefits, orienting new employees, and so on—and services that provide for individual needs to be successful and mobile within the organization—training, EAPs, workshops on advancement and preparing to be a supervisor, wellness programs, and seminars on stress or anger management. The professional counselor as administrator must be aware of the outcomes likely to occur as a result of services that go beyond those necessary to maintain the organization to those that are likely to create more effective work identification with the organization, motivate the workers to prepare to advance and manage others, give incentives to learn new skills and engage in lifelong learning, and help them learn the interpersonal behaviors that improve the interaction and cooperation among workers.

In essence, from a conceptual and budgetary standpoint, the professional counselor/administrator must be aware of alternative services that are evidence-based—that have had their effectiveness in affecting certain types of worker behavior demonstrated. Being aware of alternative services also means being aware of the likely costs of different services and their likely impact on worker behavior for each dollar of cost. Armed with such knowledge, the counseling administrator can attempt to maximize the likely gain from particular alternative services with the need to limit their costs. For example, Oliver and Spokane's (1988) review of the effectiveness of career interventions has indicated that individual counseling, although more costly than other approaches, is the most efficient intervention in terms of amount of gain per hour of effort. They have also reported that longer (at least 10 sessions) and more comprehensive sessions, although they require much more time from the counselor and the client, yield roughly twice the beneficial effects of briefer interventions. Reviews that have extended the findings of Oliver and Spokane have also demonstrated the effectiveness of career counseling for a variety of concerns, including indecision (Whiston, Sexton, & Lasoff, 1998). The point here, from a budgetary standpoint, is can we afford to provide individual counseling for every worker who needs assistance? Although individual career counseling may be the most effective, can we afford its costs and can we find an alternative service (e.g., group counseling, workshops) that may be somewhat less effective, but also less costly? These are pragmatic issues of budgeting the services necessary and also answering the likely questions from central administration. To wit, what are the results of the services for which I am providing resources? What am I buying if I invest resources in in-house activities, EAPs, or outplacement counseling? What are the costs of these services and what are the likely benefits?

In formulating budgets for human resource management, career counseling services, EAPs, or outplacement counseling, the counseling administrator must be an advocate for the programs he or she represents and express this advocacy in the budget presented. As such, however, the counseling administrator must be clear about how new services can be integrated with ongoing services and how they can add to the services required to maintain the organization—the services that advance the workers' view of the organization as supportive and concerned about their individual needs. The counselor administrator must be aware that the cost of every new service added to the budget ultimately increases the costs of each unit of production or service of the parent organization. Thus, to not offer costs that will increase the costs of the work organization in ways that make it less competitive, the counseling administrator must recognize such realities and plan and budget judiciously.

As suggested in other chapters, budgeting is not a random act or one that occurs in a vacuum. Rather it must be tied to goals to be achieved, it must reflect accountability, and it must be based on allocating resources to best practices—the most efficient and cost-effective ways to meet the goals for which human resource management, career development services, EAPs, or outplacement counseling are put in place.

STAFFING

Whether in government-sponsored local agencies (One-Stop Career Centers or rehabilitation agencies—Office of Vocational Rehabilitation) or in Human Resource Management departments in business and industry, staffing becomes a critical issue. However talented or effective as a leader or manager a professional counselor may be, he or she must have professional or support staff that are competent and enthusiastic to take on the tasks assigned to them.

As the professional counselor as administrator considers identifying and selecting staff members, he or she must recognize that there is a movement away from a random deployment of professional counselors or support staff to an increasingly planned approach to defining the roles of these persons and to identifying their responsibilities for implementing selected activities or achieving personal, academic, and career outcomes that are part of the mission for the Human Resource Management or Career Services department.

Beyond defining the types of activities or outcomes to be achieved (Herr, Cramer, & Niles, 2004) under the aegis of Human Resource Management (HRM), and the general staffing requirements, the administrator must decide whether to use independent contractors (outsourcing) or hire professional counselors as employees to conduct the activities assigned to the counseling unit. In either case, it means recruiting and training the employees or the contractors to whom certain tasks have been outsourced, ensur-

ing that they have the necessary support and clarity of task to be high per-
formers and they understand the culture that the HRM unit intends to
foster among its employees and those whom it serves.

Human Resource Management (HRM) is sometimes used as a synonym
for Human Resource Development (HRD). However, some observers would
argue that Human Resource Management is really a major management activity that is subsumed under the title Human Resource Development,
which is a profession (McNamara, Carter, Human Resources Management,
www.mapnp.org/library/ht-mgmt/hr-mgmt.html. In such a view, Human Resource Development is viewed as including a broad range of activities designed to develop personnel inside of organizations, which would include
such areas as career development, training, organizational development,
and so on. In any case, it seems clear that both HRM and HRD have become
significant aspects of corporate environments, often replacing traditional
personnel departments. In a caricatured way, it can be argued that traditional personnel departments emphasized personnel management—hiring,
classifying, and firing workers. Now HRM or HRD may do those activities,
but are also into personnel development, finding ways by which to increase
the purpose and productivity of workers. On the Web site identified earlier,
it is argued that overviews of HRM suggest the following emphases: getting
the best employees (workforce planning; specifying jobs and roles; recruiting, outsourcing, and screening applicants; selecting and hiring new employees); paying employees and providing benefits; training employees (career development, employee orientation, leadership, management,
personal and supervisory development, training); ensuring compliance to
regulations; ensuring safe work environments (diversity management, dealing with drugs or HIV/AIDS in the workplace, personal wellness, preventing
violence in the workplace, supporting spirituality in the workplace); and
sustaining high-performing employees.

This wide array of complex activities suggests that staffing should include professional counselors, counseling psychologists, or professional
career counselors who are trained and experienced in helping employees
resolve career problems, make adjustments in the workplace, and find
ways to achieve their career aspirations and remain employable.

Within this context, Ginac (2004) suggested that career counselors can
make important contributions to HRD and employers in several ways:

- Administer and interpret assessments and inventories to assess work
  values, interests, skills, and competencies.
- Identify alternative internal career options for people in transition that
  capitalize on individual knowledge, skill, and ability profiles.
- Develop specific career paths with experience, knowledge, abilities, and
  skills defined.

- Create career development plans to help employees grow and learn.
- Maximize person–job–organizational fit.
- Explore and prepare employees for internal job searches, including resume preparation, in-house interviewing, and networking.
- Identify and cultivate internal mentor and career advisor networks for personal career development.
- Link employees with internal and external training programs based on performance improvement needs.
- Provide unbiased, objective career counseling intervention/mediation/ facilitation for people experiencing job stress, job loss, or transition during corporate reorganizations, mergers, or downsizing.
- Teach internal career advisors and mentors how to be more effective in guiding employee development.
- Facilitate employee training and development initiatives. (p. 6)

Although there are other examples of what counselors and counseling psychologists can do in HRD, these suffice to illustrate some of the activities to which counselors can contribute. The question then becomes: Should these people be permanent members of staff or independent contractors? Many organizations employ counselors on a retainer fee. These rates are negotiated based on the number of days and/or hours the career counselor is engaged in career or work-related activities for the corporation. According to Ginac, hourly fees vary between $85 and $200 per hour. Often these counselors function on-site in an office that can provide confidentiality. In some cases, however, employees are referred directly to the counselor's office off-site.

The professional counselor serving as an administrator of counseling services in workplace-oriented settings must decide what functions must be performed and who is best prepared to perform these functions. To an increasing degree, counselors and counseling psychologists have become professionalized and credentialed. Thus, if the counseling administrator wants professionally trained staff, he or she will want to consider employing persons whose training and experiences have qualified them to be Licensed Counseling Psychologists, Licensed Professional Counselors, Certified Rehabilitation Counselors, National Certified Counselors, or National Certified Career Counselors. Although business and industry HRD programs are not under any mandates to hire licensed or certified counselors, it is nevertheless true that if such a program has a mission to provide the best support and assistance to their workforce, it is important to employ professionals who bring a wide range of skills, training, and experience to these roles. In some ways, such a stance may be even more important in subcontracting with independent contractors to provide EAPs, outplacement counseling, or related services. For example, it is possible in some circumstances for employees' health benefits to pay for workers who are receiving psychological counseling within an EAP that is external to the workplace. However, only agencies that employ Licensed Professional Counselors, psychologists, or social workers are eligible to receive third-party payments, health insurance reimbursements for a specified number of counseling sessions. In such cases, counselors and others who are certified but not licensed are unlikely to be eligible to receive health insurance payments for their services. The case for Licensed Professional Counselors and psychologists can also be related to their knowledge of referral and community resources, and, in the cases of particularly troubled employees, admission to mental health and psychiatric facilities.

One of the critical factors in recruiting staff for HRD departments in workplaces or, indeed, local government One-Stop Career Centers or Rehabilitation Counseling agencies is their knowledge of the language of the workplace. As HRD specialists assist workers in their career problems and aspirations, it is important that they can communicate in a common language about career paths, job classification, mobility in the firm, educational and training opportunities, worker–supervisor difficulties, relationships with coworkers, job/family conflicts, apprehension about unemployment and underemployment, and benefits and other policies relating to workers.

Recruiting individual counselors is likely to be different than identifying potential independent contractors. Depending on whether the professional counselor as administrator is conducting a search for staff that is nationwide, statewide, or local, there are professional organizations and newsletters that can be used to list position descriptions and solicit possible candidates for these positions. There are also Web sites (e.g., America's Job Bank; www.ajb.dni.us) from which resumes of possible candidates can be obtained. In addition, university departments preparing counselors and psychologists can be contacted to post position descriptions or provide nominations of graduates who may be seeking such positions.

In the case of the need to employ independent contractors to conduct an EAP off-site or to do other tasks such as conducting workshops for workers, it would be useful to ask for individual or groups of counselors or psychologists in private practice to submit a proposal describing their credentials, experience, proposed organization, and costs related to their delivery of services. Such contracts can then be negotiated as appropriate.

A final concern in staffing is supervision. Decisions will need to be made about who will conduct supervision, what the supervisory process will be and how often it will be conducted. In a small HRD department of 5 to 10 employees, it is likely that the professional counselor serving as administrator will provide the supervision of each staff member, professional or support staff. In larger offices, there may be assistant administrators or senior employees who will conduct the supervision. As suggested in several previous chapters, supervision may be very formal, with the staff members maintaining data about their performance, how many employees they serve, for what purposes, and so on. Feedback about the quality of their services may be provided periodically by those whom they serve, with all of this information being synthesized and ratings applied to it by the supervisor. In some instances, supervision takes place whenever it appears necessary to correct a particular procedure or teach a new technique. Sometimes staff members are asked to complete an annual report of their activities and identify their goals and proposed new initiatives for the forthcoming calendar year. In summary, there are many ways to do supervision. Those discussed in other settings in this book can be applied to the settings discussed in this chapter or folded into the general policies regarding supervision in the corporate setting in which HRD is a part or, in the case of local government agencies, defined by personnel policies created for use by all such agencies. In summary, supervision is a vital element of staffing, retention of staff, and facilitating quality service. As such, it is a vital management task.

THE USE OF TECHNOLOGY

One of the important roles of either government-sponsored, local, work-related counseling agencies (e.g., One-Stop Career Centers, Rehabilitation Counseling Agencies) or HRD programs in business and industry is the provision of relevant information about job openings, mobility, advancement, career paths, education and training, the availability of EAPs, employee benefits, the company mission, and other important topics. This distribution of information is accomplished in many ways: brochures, workshops, newsletters, bulletin boards, copies of the firm's annual report, and career resource centers.

Increasingly, however, the distribution of information to workers is done using advanced technology: videotape presentations, Power Point presentations, computer-assessed data and reports, and Web sites on the Internet. In some cases, these are national databases and, in other cases, they are locally created Web sites that include the posting of job vacancies, the training opportunities available to prepare for advancement to supervisory positions or gain remedial basic academic skills, clarifying what career ladders are available in particular workplaces, or considering self-improvement, wellness, networking, or retraining for totally new job functions.

In the case of both local, government-sponsored, work-related agencies and HRD agencies, there are national databases on the Web that are helpful to employees and counselors. Although there are many such possibilities, among the most useful is one of the largest job databases in the world. America's Job Bank (www.ajb.dni.us) provides job openings and resumes for workers seeking particular jobs across the United States. On this site, workers or unemployed persons seeking new jobs can look at constantly updated job vacancies classified by geography, field, and other dimensions. Once relevant vacancies are located, these persons can place their resumes on the Web relative to a specific vacancy or for more general perusal by employers. This site is also linked to other occupational, educational, and labor market information databases such as America's Career InfoNet, O*Net, and so on.

Another important Web site is O*Net, the Occupational Information Network, the Department of Labor's comprehensive database of worker attributes and job characteristics. The O*Net (http://www.doletz.gov/programs/onet) is intended to replace the Dictionary of Occupational Titles by providing either online or CD-Rom information that can be readily updated in a timely manner. The O*Net database contains information about knowledge, skills, abilities (KSAs), interests, general work activities (GWAs), and work content related to 1,172 occupations. The content model for O*Net (http://www. onetcenter.org/content.html) is organized into six major domains: (a) work characteristics, (b) worker requirements, (c) experience requirements, (d) occupational characteristics, (e) occupational requirements, and (f) occupation-specific requirements. Embedded in the vast amount of information in these six domains is the opportunity for workers, HRD specialists, career counselors, and employers to compare occupations, worker requirements, and the elasticity of worker skills across occupations—what is important in effective job performance and many other significant topical areas? As such, O*Net standardizes the language by which workers, employers, career counselors, providers of education and training, and HRD specialists can communicate about jobs, employment statistics, work requirements, training, and so on.

Most, if not all, states also have their own state career information systems online (e.g., Pennsylvania Career Link). These are, in many ways, microcosms of the kind of information and action that are available on America's Job Bank, O*Net, or other databases. Their content, however, is focused on the occupations available in a particular state, job vacancies, the types of training and educational opportunities available, the opportunity to put resumes online, tips on job searches, and related information. Some states have purchased and adapted to state needs relevant occupational and educational information in the more general career guidance systems such as DISCOVER, SIGI Plus, GIS, CHOICES, and so on. Such databases are accessible in local One-Stop Career Centers and Rehabilitation Counseling Centers and to HRD programs to reinforce worker career planning as applicable to the mission and functions of such programs.

For the professional counselor serving as administrator, the uses of technology provide many sources of information for planning purposes, for career planning, and for the distribution of firm-specific career information to workers. The administrator of a One-Stop Career Center, other government-sponsored, work-related counseling centers, and HRD programs must embed such technologies in the program for which he or she provides management and leadership. In doing so, the administrator must be creative, aware of the information needs of the workforce and the best forms of technology to address its needs, and planful in integrating technology into the other activities and functions of his or her program.

EVALUATION

A final management topic to be discussed is that of evaluation. Although considered last in this chapter, evaluation plans should be considered at the beginning of any new initiative or program and integrated with the planning process. In other words, systematic planning at any level (e.g., strategic planning, project planning, etc.) requires deliberation about how to assess whether the particular plan is yielding the results intended. Thus, evaluation is not something independent of the planning process, but rather a process critical to determining the effectiveness of the planning process.

For many administrators and professional counselors, evaluation is seen as a threatening process. Some persons view evaluation as a highly sophisticated and esoteric process that requires skills beyond their ability to implement or administer or to comprehend the results. Such a perspective is widely held, but generally inaccurate. Evaluation occurs at many levels of complexity and detail, not all of which are difficult to administer. At the least, "evaluation is conducted in the context of the assessed needs, the program design, and the implementation plan" (Henderson & Gysbers, 1998, p. 59). In essence, evaluation is conducted to determine whether the work-related needs of the counseling programs' constituents are being met, whether the program design is adequate, and whether the program is being implemented as designed.

In local governmental settings, there are frequently protocols about how evaluation designs are to be done or what information is to be assessed. In some instances, there are personnel assigned to central offices whose primary role is to design and conduct evaluations. In nongovernmental programs, such as corporate HRD independent contractors can be employed to work with planners and administrators to identify what should be evaluated and how.

However evaluation is done and by whom, effective evaluation cannot occur unless it is effectively planned and unless the program or agency's goals are clear and measurable. This, then, means that the persons doing the evaluating need to be clear about what evidence will be accepted by the central administrators to demonstrate that planned goals or behavioral objectives have been met. These forms of evidence vary with the goals to be assessed. They include:

- judgments by experts of whether program goals have been met;
- follow-up studies of how employees are able to do career planning, apply decision-making skills, and identify career paths related to their skills and interests after they have been exposed to career counseling;
- supervisor reaction sheets describing how and whether employee work behavior has changed after exposure to counseling or other career services;
- employee opinions about how relevant or accurate the career information they are provided has been;
- changes in employee absenteeism; vandalism; use of sick leave following exposure to career counselors or other career services; the productivity gains from such changes in employee behavior;
- audits of how career counselors or other HRD specialists are spending their time by area of function or responsibilities and the comparative costs of these functions;
- the appropriateness of fit of employees to particular training opportunities as measured by posttraining supervisor ratings;
- changes in attitude or performance of employees after exposure to EAPs for different periods of time or number of sessions;
- overall changes in productivity or turnover of workers after use of career counseling services or other HRD initiatives; and
- changes in stress levels and work-related accidents after participation in wellness programs provided by the firm.

Although there are many other types of evaluation and methods of identifying the information about worker behavior or professional staff performance related to the planned goals for the government agency or corporate department, a fundamental point is that the type of evaluation and the data to be collected will differ in accordance with the setting and type of behavior being assessed. These things depend on what the program goals are; what types of energy, competencies, and personnel time can be committed to evaluation or what assistance from independent contractors can be purchased; what fiscal support is available to support evaluation processes; and the types of evaluation questions that most need to be answered. Evaluation is not free. It costs time and money to plan evaluations, gather data, and analyze the results. Therefore, evaluations must be carefully designed and implemented with the goal to obtain results that are directly useful in future planning.

A system of evaluation is usually concerned with one or two major approaches. The first and probably most likely in the context of the current chapter is concerned with whether the total program is meeting its goals, typically referred to as a *summative* or *product evaluation*. The second form of evaluation is designed to determine whether the individual processes or activities intended to accomplish particular goals or stimulate certain worker behavior are doing so effectively or more effectively than other possible processes or activities. This form of evaluation is typically referred to as *formative* or *process evaluation*. Put simply, summative or product evaluation is essentially concerned with the aggregate effects of all of the program elements and processes related to the goals to be achieved; formative or process evaluation is concerned with how effectively specific techniques or activities contributed to such goals.

Process or formative evaluation is typically concerned with more experimentally oriented questions than is product evaluation. Process or formative evaluation seeks answers to whether individual behavioral objectives are being met effectively by the specific techniques related to them (e.g., individual group counseling, group lectures, workshops, employee assistance programs, etc.), whether particular techniques or activities are more effective with some subgroups rather than others, and which program techniques or activities are most cost-effective for what purposes and with what groups.

Regardless of the intent of the evaluation to engage in product or process evaluation (summative or formative), there are several logical steps to be pursued. They include:

1. *Identifying goals and stating objectives.*

2. *Choosing criterion measurements.* The question here is what data or measurements we can use to collect pertinent information on the goals the program is to achieve. It is likely that these goals will differ in the precision of the measurements chosen. In some cases, commercially published instruments can be used to collect pertinent data; in other cases, locally devised rating scales, self-reports, observations, and questionnaires will suffice.

3. *Establishing levels of performance or standards.* Although there is no magic formula that can be applied here, within the planning process, it is necessary to decide at an individual or a group level what is an acceptable performance for each of the goals to be assessed.

4. *Specifying program elements.* In summative evaluation, the boundaries of the program to be assessed need to be specified, and the elements that are considered to comprise the career development or other work-related programs must be isolated. In essence, the task here is to identify those ele-

ments that are distinct from other parts of the agency or the workplace and are the subject of this evaluation.

5. *Designing the evaluation.* In this step, who will be involved is evaluated, who will be sampled to obtain the information needed is defined, and what will be the timing of the information collected and of the evaluation process itself is determined.

6. *Collecting data.* How will the desired information be collected?

7. *Analyzing data.* How the information collected will be analyzed depends on the type of information collected and the evaluative questions asked.

8. *Interpreting data.* Who will make such judgments and for what purposes?

9. *Reporting and using data.* Who will be apprised of the outcomes of the evaluation? What are the central findings? What, if any, are the needs for improvement or change? How much support should the program receive in the future? How will the findings be fed back into the strategic planning process? What are the cost–benefit implications of the evaluation findings? (Herr, Cramer, & Niles, 2004).

Clearly, the role of the counselor as administrator is data-driven in governmental or corporate settings which expect that the roles of counselors will add value to the purpose and productivity of the workforce, both directly and indirectly. Evaluation, in its multiple forms, represents a significant tool for management and leadership. Although the administrator of counseling services in the settings discussed in this chapter may not be the person to conduct evaluations of program quality and performance, it is likely that he or she will have to ensure that such evaluative studies are undertaken, and the findings of such studies can be interpreted and used as an integral part of the ongoing planning process.

SUMMARY

This chapter has discussed a number of governmentally supported and private-sector settings in which counseling takes place and in which professional counselors serve as administrators. Within these settings, as in the others discussed in this book, the counseling administrator will be engaged in planning, budgeting, recruitment and retention of staff, use of technology, and evaluation. However, it is likely that the policies that govern these activities in different settings will vary in their complexity and intent.

9

The Professional Counselor as Manager in Independent Practice

CONTEXT

For a large segment of clinical and counseling psychologists, as well as for many other licensed or certified counselors, independent practice affords the opportunity to enjoy the freedom to practice in one's area of specialization, to cultivate new and interesting opportunities for service, to forge professional associations with colleagues from various professions throughout the community, and to earn a comfortable living. Regarding the latter, according to the salary surveys provided by the American Psychological Association (2003), private practitioners average the highest incomes vis-à-vis practitioners in other settings.

Prior to the emergence of the managed care culture, private practitioners were free to set fees that were "usual and customary," consistent with community standards. In the current context, however, there have been a number of factors impacting the fee for service. In general, rates for services have been driven down as a result of a highly differentiated and complex system of managed care, including preferred provider organizations (PPOs), health maintenance organizations (HMOs), Employee Assistance Programs (EAPs), and myriad other hybrids that have emerged to mediate the needs of client consumers. The purported purpose of the managed care industry is to provide efficient cost-effective services in the best interest of client consumers, arguably the same intentions of the independent practitioner. In reality, however, managed care has created numerous challenges for the solo or group practitioner to manage the various plans, to understand and abide by myriad requirements, and to stay abreast of the ever-changing nuance of managed care systems. Thus, the cost to providers, in addition to lowered fees, is exacerbated by an increasing load of administrative demands that have moved a traditional practice that required limited overhead expenses to one that, in many instances, requires the need for part- or full-time administrative and clerical support. Spiraling costs for the same have caused many solo practitioners to gravitate toward group practices in an effort to share the administrative expenses of the practice. Couple that with the challenges inherent in running a business and it is not surprising that many professionals prefer the ease and convenience of the standard practice in a clinic or other setting, which offers a predictable salary, benefits, and a relatively hassle-free professional existence.

Irrespective of the changing expectations for private practice, one thing remains the same—to run an effective service, independent practitioners must not only be good clinicians, they must also be good administrators. A recent report in the *Journal of Clinical Psychology* on "the competent clinician" (Spruill et al., 2004) cited the compelling need for clinicians to be managers as well:

> Whatever the setting, it is necessary to manage available resources to achieve the desired intervention outcome. Management skills are needed to recruit, train, and supervise other professionals, paraprofessionals and support staff Even solo practitioners may employ one or more office staff, such as a clinical assistant or a receptionist. Office policies and procedures should be written in a manner consistent with state and federal laws pertaining to privacy, electronic transmission of protected health information, and record keeping. Knowledge of Medicare, Medicaid, and other third-party reimbursement mechanisms is highly desirable and, in some settings, it is essential. Psychologists who anticipate contracting with managed-care companies need to understand how to apply for provider panels, submitting their credentials for review, interpret contract provisions, interact with care managers, prepare treatment plans for review, and explain benefits to their clients. Specific clinical privileging may be required by managed-care panels, hospitals, and other forms of institutional practice. Effective psychological intervention depends upon learning and negotiating the culture and requirements of diverse practice settings. (p. 750)

It is not an overstatement to suggest that if one does all of this—remains competent and current in clinical practice, and sensitive to the needs of the community of consumers, then a successful practice will follow.

Despite the sometimes formidable challenges, private practice remains attractive to many practitioners. Those who remain in private practice are affirmed in their belief that the benefits of flexibility, income, and the freedom to choose areas of specialization outweigh the burden of increased administrative effort. After decades of successful independent practice, there are many templates for establishing and maintaining a practice. Moreover, there are increasing opportunities for assistance to counselors to reduce the fear of flying blind into the maze of practice requirements. For instance, the American Psychological Association Web site (APApractice.org), endorsed by APA's Division 42 (Psychologists in Independent Practice), provides the practitioner with numerous practical strategies and helpful hints to build and maintain one's private practice. A review of Web site postings offers illuminating topics such as, "Give Your Practice a Financial Checkup," outlining key financial ratios to consider (e.g., profitability ratios, liquidity ratios, debt management ratios, asset management ratios), "HIPAA for Psychologists" (an online course on the Privacy Rule Compliance), "Developing a Professional Image that Reflects Your Strengths," and "Networking: Are You Connected?" (developing professional and community connections that benefit your practice). Ready access to resources like these can be reassuring to the practitioner concerned about the viability, sustainability, and profitability of his or her practice.

ON BECOMING AN INDEPENDENT PRACTITIONER

Private practice is not for everyone. Among other things, an individual must be prepared to practice in relative isolation, compared with colleagues in an agency or university settings where a readily available cadre of professional colleagues abounds. Self-employment may not offer the advantage of regular and recurrent contacts with colleagues as one would find in multidisciplinary agency settings. Moreover, because every working hour is conceivably a "billable hour," vacations, professional development, conferences—indeed phone calls and coffee breaks—now "cost" the professional in terms of lost potential income. Moreover, overhead costs become palpable, real, and recurrent. Marketing and administration—qualities that are rarely taught in graduate preparation programs—become on-the-job mandates if the practice is to survive and thrive. Finally, the challenges of managed care requirements, empanelment on managed care organization (MCO) provider lists, and the attendant endless paperwork can be daunting. Be that as it may, many of our best professionals see fit to pursue private practice as a way to a satisfying and fulfilling professional career. Being your own person, pursuing your own interests, building a practice, establishing meaningful collegial relationships, and enjoying the flexibility of the application of time and energy are fitting rewards for those with the creativity, ingenuity, confidence, and energy to engage in private practice.

As with any business, management becomes critical to the success of the enterprise. Among the areas required for managing an independent practice are planning and budgeting, marketing, organization and staffing, directing, and evaluating. Ideally, the practice administrator must be a self-starter who can initiate contacts, seek referrals, develop niche markets, and promote the practice. Regardless of one's technical clinical expertise, failure to adequately market and support a practice can be the death knell of any potentially good practice.

Hanging your shingle on the door comes only after a considerable amount of preparation and start-up activity has been pursued. Many practices have failed or floundered far longer than was necessary due to failure on the part of the practitioner to adequately plan and prepare to enter the psychological service marketplace. In planning for an independent practice, there are a number of factors to be considered. Size and organization of staff, location and configuration of the office, marketing of the practice, and budgeting of expenses are prerequisites to consider in establishing any practice. Finally, in any community, it is incumbent on the private practitioner to determine what services are currently available, the need for an expansion of those services, or, if expedient, the development and maintenance of expertise to allow the provider to offer those services.

Variations of Private Practice: Legal Considerations

According to the *Law and Mental Health Professionals* (Bersoff, Field, Anderer, & Zaplac, 1999), a mental health provider who is not employed in a salaried position essentially has three options for establishing a private practice: sole proprietorships, professional corporations, and partnerships.

The simple structure of a *sole proprietorship* eliminates consideration of any formal corporate structure. Individuals practice alone, and not under the umbrella of any corporate structure. Any and all assets are the property of the owner of the proprietorship. Ultimately the sole proprietor is responsible for all legal liabilities assigned to the practice, and the owner's personal assets are subject to the same liabilities (Bersoff et al., 1999).

A second private practice entity, the *professional corporation*, may provide the practitioner with a number of benefits, including tax benefits. Unlike the sole proprietorship, the liability for the shareholders of a professional corporation are limited to the assets of the corporation and not the individual's personal assets. In addition, members of the corporation commonly receive tax breaks on their health and retirement plans. The corporation also promotes (indeed requires) that the shareholders meet regularly to review business practices, records, and other corporate activities, thereby encouraging a continuing interest in the business among the stakeholders. Similar to the sole proprietorship, individuals within the corporation are ultimately liable for their own practices. However, in the corporation, individual liability for others in the practice is limited to the assets of the corporation, thus protecting them against any encroachment on their personal resources if a fellow practitioner in the practice is sued (Bersoff et al., 1999).

In addition to sole proprietorships and professional corporations, independent practitioners may elect to establish a *partnership* with one or more colleagues. When two or more persons come together to establish a practice, a partnership is formed. All partners are considered owners of the business, and the partnership is established as a legal entity. Unlike the sole proprietorship, the shared expertise present in a partnership allows for a more comprehensive array of services. In forming a partnership, however, it is important to consider that the partners are now liable to one another and the actions of any one of the partners presents liability concerns for each other partner (Bersoff et al., 1999).

SIZE OF PRACTICE AND ITS ORGANIZATION

Most communities have an array of independent providers of services ranging from individual solo practitioners to large and comprehensive group practices employing multidisciplinary professionals, including psychiatrists, psychologists, social workers, and counselors. In some respects, the issues for any practice may be the same, but in terms of management there are a number of factors that vary contingent on the size and scope of the practice.

Solo Practices

A solo practice has the advantage of a contained infrastructure, although it lacks the benefits of size and scale to provide comprehensive services or cost-sharing advantages. Quite simply, a solo practice consists of a professional, in an office, providing services to clients while managing the business aspects of the operation. In reality, a full-time practice usually consists of far less than 40 face-to-face clinical hours per week. In fact, few would argue with the common notion that a full-time practice consists of approximately 20 ongoing clients. This norm aside, however, the volume of clinical activity varies depending on such things as income needs, the economy and the client marketplace, as well as therapist energy and lifestyle preferences. A solo practitioner may buy office space in which to practice, although most choose to rent or share space as the more cost-effective option. A major time drain for any practitioner is the paperwork and administrative activities that go along with the practice. Although some solo providers contain costs by doing their own clerical activity, most hire part-time receptionists/secretaries, telephone answering services, and other forms of ancillary assistance necessary for running the business. In any case, it is important to seek out support services that are tried and true and that allow one to remain confident that the day-to-day business operation is being managed. Be that as it may, the solo practitioner must remain on top of the business, checking and reconciling business operations, ensuring that collections are being made in a timely fashion and no important deed is left unattended. Irrespective of size, consumer confidence, but also legal liability, requires that any practice be run efficiently and responsibly. Finally, it is important that the solo practitioner establish a network of support services, from legal advisors to psychiatric providers, as well as other referral sources for services that fall outside one's area of specialization (e.g., physicians, hospitals, community agencies, and colleague providers with specializations).

Group Practices, Professional Corporations, and Partnerships

A *group practice*, a popular form of private practice, may range from formal corporate or partnership entities to a simple assemblage of providers sharing the costs of space and secretarial services. A clear advantage of the group practice is the opportunity, through shared resources, to employ a broader range of support personnel to manage routine activities, including secretarial, accounting, legal, management, and additional specialty services. In addition, having many counselors associated with the practice provides the advantage of conveying a more comprehensive, full-service image.

Professional Corporations. Mid- to large-sized practices organized around the corporate model have a select number of primary shareholders who essentially manage the organization and are ultimately responsible for all operating expenses, capital expenditures, promotion, and marketing of services. In forming a corporate entity, it is assumed that there will be a chief operating officer and an elected or appointed president of the organization. The shareholders, who represent the core body of managers, are responsible for voting on any and all managed care contracts, expansions, service offerings, overhead expenditures, policies and procedures, approvals of contracts with associate providers, strategic planning, and the management of day-to-day operations. The chief operating officer becomes the point person who is ultimately responsible for initiating the agreed-on policies and procedures and serves as the information conduit back to the partners on emerging issues of concern to the practice. The corporation is formally established, legally defensible, and registered as a professional corporation for tax purposes and benefits.

Larger corporate practices may secure a secondary layer of clinical staff, commonly referred to as *contract associates*. These professionals, fully qualified to practice independently in their domain of expertise, prefer not to bear the expense, time, and energy of running a business. Ordinarily, associates are expected to yield a percentage of their income generated from the practice to the corporate practice partners. This exchange typically provides the revenue required to reduce business expenses. In exchange, the associates receive a steady stream of referrals, the use of furnished offices, secretarial services, and other administrative prerequisites that would otherwise be expenses of their own. In most cases, this becomes a win–win situation, with the practice accruing discretionary dollars to maintain or improve the practice while the associates are relieved of any of the headaches involved in the maintenance of a business.

Partnerships. Consideration of a partnership involves the manner of sharing profits and losses of the partnership, including formulas for time and involvement vis-à-vis percentages of profit and loss. In many instances, areas of responsibility are delegated, although record keeping, business activities, and all other activities are shared and open to scrutiny among the partners. Thus, it is important to keep in mind that when any one partner signs a contract, offers a service, expresses an opinion, or engages in unethical practices, then, unlike the professional corporation, each of the partners is considered personally liable. Similar to the corporate practice, the advantages of a partnership are that it conveys the comprehensive nature of the practice, allows for a more differentiated public offering of services, and encourages both fiscal and collegial sharing.

MANAGEMENT CONSIDERATIONS

Location/Configuration of Office

In initiating a practice, the practice manager must make important decisions aside from the services offered. Among them are the place-and-space issues that influence access and ambience—two critical variables related to the success of the practice. Simply put, if potential clientele believe that a resource is difficult to access and not comfortable or pleasing to the eye, all other things being equal, they will opt for another resource to pursue their services.

One might assume that, in our mobile society, location becomes less of an issue for access to one's service. Be that as it may, there are some practices that, depending on their specialty and primary source of clientele, may choose to locate close to client market sources that provide referrals to their practice. For example, a psychologist with expertise in health psychology may choose to locate near a hospital setting or within a comprehensive medical office building that allows for easy access and consultation with referral sources. Likewise, practitioners who provide specialized services to a young adult population may choose to locate near a university setting, providing services within walking distance of the campus, or on easily accessed public transportation routes.

The prototypical office arrangement for a private practice is simple: an administrative office/reception/waiting area with easy access to counseling offices. Beyond that, space requirements will vary with the size of the professional staff, as well as with the unique programs, services, and activities offered. Those practices limited to individual treatment can manage on single offices per member, with each room providing space for an individual or couple. If a practice offers group or family therapy, self-help classes, and the like, a designated group room, or classroom area, or occasional access to the same will be considered essential. Obviously, larger practices with a mix of full- and part-time providers need not require an office for each staff, but must work out a system of sharing space that meets the mutual needs of the practice and the providers.

Regardless of size and location, the aesthetics of the setting convey an important image to any potential client. Thus, warm colors, a comfortable and well-appointed reception area, and offices that reflect a professional image are essential. In the final analysis, creating the right ambience for the counselor and client is not only important for the comfort of each, but contributes in subtle, but tangible, ways to the facilitative ingredients of counseling. Conversely, if a client does not feel drawn to a setting and physically comfortable within it, the setting may serve as a potential barrier to the establishment and maintenance of a productive therapeutic relationship.

Marketing of the Practice

Any practice, irrespective of size, must grapple with the formation of a focus or area(s) of specialization. In today's competitive service marketplace, many providers are finding that the development of at least one specialization (beyond general practice) enhances one's practice and opens up new opportunities for practice growth and development. Whereas in most markets it is essential to maintain the image of a general practitioner, the hooks provided by specializations can be the enduring piece that ensures continuing business for the practice during the lean times of flagging referrals. In truth, whereas virtually every provider is trained as a generalist, there are few opportunities to specialize beyond the pre- and postdoctoral internship or training experiences. Thus, it behooves independent practitioners to remain flexible and open to continuing education and retooling if they are to capitalize on emerging markets. Be that as it may, as competition increases, practitioners are seeing increasing value in pursuing a number of niche markets such as behavioral health specialist, consultant to business and industry, executive coaching, group therapy, and forensic psychology, to name a few. Indeed a recurrent theme in the primary publication of the American Psychological Association, *Monitor on Psychology*, has been the unique and heretofore atypical application of psychology, such as designing psychologists who create living and working spaces, life, retirement and executive coaches, and consultants to attorneys (American Psychological Association, 2004).[1] Of course in group practices, the cultivation and promotion of ancillary specialties may be shared across professionals, making a credible case to the community that the practice offers comprehensive services. All other things being equal, if the group offers a broader spectrum of services, it is more likely that a client seeking any particular service is likely to be accommodated by contacting this group. Thus, an association of psychiatrists, psychologists, social workers, and counselors, each of whom may offer general as well as specialized services, may ensure a steady stream of clients and broaden community awareness of the group. The downside, of course, is that sizable practices require the creation of a business infrastructure and the increased costs associated with it.

Because the insular nature of counseling dictates privacy and a low profile, independent practitioners must seek other opportunities to become visible to the community of potential consumers. To do so, providers are encouraged to offer workshops, seminars, and public lectures; to volunteer time; and to offer public service to the community. Although attendees at these various offerings may not have an immediate need for services, they or someone known to them may have a need for services in the future, and they now have a name and a face to associate with an array of potential services.

Beyond efforts to be present to the community at large, the wise independent practitioner will be mindful of the range of services offered and consider the most likely sources of referral to those services. Thereupon, a list of gatekeepers to clients in need of these services may be compiled, and direct contact can be established and maintained. Establishing a referral

---

[1]As a cautionary note, it is important to be mindful of the state regulations regarding the establishment of practice specialties. In general, state laws require that licensed professionals only provide services for which they have "sufficient training and experience." It is incumbent on each professional, but also the community of ethically responsible professionals, to ensure that safe, quality services are being offered to the public. When economic realities drive practice differentiation, continuous monitoring of practice standards must be ensured. For a summary of information on legal requirements for entry into the field of psychology, see *Entry Requirements for the Professional Practice of Psychology: A Guide for Students and Faculty* (The Association of State and Provincial Psychology Boards [ASPPB], 2004).

network in service to the practice may be the single most important effort pursued by the independent practitioner.

Establishing Collegial Relationships and Support

One of the major limitations of a private practice, particularly a small or solo practice, is the absence of colleagues across the hall or in the break room, immediately accessible to them as they would be if they were practicing in a community clinic or university setting. Thus, it is imperative that the practice manager encourage the continuing education and professional development of each practitioner. To be driven exclusively by the generation of revenue, to the exclusion of nonrevenue time dedicated to continuing education and consultation, is unacceptable by any professional standard. Moreover, it is unethical to rely on clinical experience alone to retain currency in one's profession. For these reasons, many states now require continuing education for all forms of helping professionals as a prerequisite to the retention of one's license or certification. However, even when it is not imposed by a licensing board, ethically responsible professionals seek opportunities to extend knowledge and information about their area of expertise, to remain current with the professional literature and the emerging trends in treatment, and to establish ready access to other professionals with whom they might consult.

In the absence of regular and recurrent professional development opportunities, such as those found in a university setting, independent practitioners must seek it elsewhere. In such cases, local, regional, and national associations become prime sources of the collegial support and continuing education that would otherwise be unavailable. For instance, a review of the membership of most local psychological associations will yield a high percentage of individuals in private practice. These organizations provide regular opportunities for social and collegial exchange that keeps the independent provider professionally robust and well informed. Indeed in the absence of such organizations, it is incumbent on private practitioners to establish the means for this form of exchange by seeking workshops and professional development opportunities, informal meetings, luncheons, and other opportunities to discuss professional matters, as well as for informal consultation, and support.

Finally, in our litigious society, it is inadvisable to proceed with high-risk clients without consulting other professionals. The worst-case scenario is to have pursued a course of action with a high-risk client and to have legal action taken against one's practice as a result. For providers to admit in a legal proceeding that it was their judgment and theirs alone that may have led to an untoward outcome is to place oneself in serious jeopardy. The best defense in a legal situation is to be able to certify that two or more colleagues agreed that the course of action pursued was well considered as well as expedient under the circumstances. It behooves the practice administrator to be informed about potentially risky clinical situations, to consult on the best course of action, and to facilitate a referral to legal counsel when indicated.

Credentialing

In considering associates for one's practice, it is critical for the practice manager to ensure that the practice is staffed with qualified, well-credentialed members. Licensing and certification regulations vary from state to state; before any agreement is reached with colleague providers for association with one's practice, a review of those credentials must be undertaken. Licensed professional counselors, licensed psychologists, certified addictions counselors, and others must meet standards of practice unique to their specialty to ethically and responsibly, but also legally, practice in any jurisdiction. Whereas certification and licensure are essential to establish one's ability to practice independently, of additional importance currently are the requirements imposed on one's private practice by managed care organizations, preferred provider organizations, and the like. A provider who fails to have the minimum credentials required will be of limited value to the group practice, and most likely they will not be viable in a solo practice because private-pay clients (those who do not rely on managed care organizations or health insurance to underwrite expenses) are increasingly rare.

Health Insurance Portability and Accountability Act (HIPAA)

In addition to managed care considerations, the enactment of the Health Insurance Portability and Accountability Act (HIPAA) exemplifies other important mandates to which the independent practitioner must respond. Signed into law in 1996, the implementation of the law became effective beginning on April 14, 2003. According to the materials available through the American Psychological Association (APApractice.org, 2004), the act is broken into three categories: the transaction rule, the privacy rule, and the security rule. The transaction rule provides guidelines for electronic billing, including the technical aspects and requirements for submitting health care claims electronically. The privacy rule establishes standards for practitioners in view of patients' rights vis-à-vis the use and disclosure of confidential information. Finally, the security rule addresses the physical maintenance and delivery of confidential client information. On the surface, all three rules would appear to create major hurdles for the independent practitioner. Be that as it may, professional associations such as the American

Psychological Association Practice Organization have provided clear-cut and easily applied procedures for conforming to HIPAA regulations.

Managed Care

Increasingly, managing a private practice has become an exercise in understanding and applying the ever-changing rules and regulations of myriad forms of managed care. For nearly two decades, managed care has been the engine driving the private practice marketplace. The profession's more senior private practitioners yearn for "the good old days," when they could charge a fair fee for service in view of market considerations, collect from indemnified insurers, and earn a comfortable living while engaging in the professional activities they enjoy. In an effort to reduce burgeoning medical costs, however, the norm has shifted dramatically toward the imposition of limits to the length of treatment, reduced fees for service, and client eligibility standards. Because of its continuing importance to the world of private practice, a brief review of the primary forms of managed care organizations (MCOs) follows. (For an excellent source of expanded descriptions of the various MCOs, see Lowman & Resnick, 1994).

Managed care organizations can be traced back to 1978 when the Health Maintenance Organization Act Amendments were promulgated. Since then there was a slow but growing expansion of HMOs leading to a virtual explosion over a decade ago (Lohman & Resnick, 1994). Throughout its history, there has been tension between mental health providers (as well as our medical counterparts) and the managed care entities. The complaints of private practitioners revolve around contracted fees for service that are below the usual and customary fees, perceived unrealistic limits to treatment placed on the provider by the MCO, and sluggish systems for treatment authorization and reimbursement. For instance, the standard MCO use of general medical primary care providers (PCPs) as gatekeepers may limit or slow client access to mental health services. Given good working relationships and a thorough understanding of mental health services on the part of the PCP, this system may work to the benefit of the consumer. When that is not the case, however, it may lead to slow or inappropriate responses for individuals who are in need of timely services. Finally, because the private practitioner is affected by the industry's efforts to reduce the length of treatment, it behooves the provider to become adept at brief, contained therapy (e.g., see Budman & Gurman, 1988) and other short-term treatment approaches to common client concerns. Unfortunately, the reality is, when the services and fees offered by an MCO to qualified providers are too marginal to be justified, many providers opt out of the network, forcing the MCO to seek less qualified and less experienced individuals who are nonetheless willing to accept the depreciated rates for service.

In their most generic forms, MCOs may be categorized as health maintenance organizations (HMOs) or preferred provider organizations (PPOs). In
brief, MCOs reflect systems of health care that enlist professional providers
as salaried service providers, contracted individually, or as groups to provide services to a select consumer population on a reduced fee-for-service
basis. An MCO is likely to employ or contract with a wide range of professionals and settings, beginning with the individual provider, but expanding
to hospital-sized entities. Ultimately, it is the desire of the MCO to provide
clients with all forms of health care for a given patient population (Lowman
& Resnick, 1994).

Irrespective of nuance or title, MCOs are established to provide the consumer with an array or network of individuals in private practice who,
while remaining independent providers, contract with the MCO to offer reduced fees for service to a restricted MCO consumer group. Often the consumer is free to select other providers outside of the network, but there is
usually a cost penalty for doing so. The negotiated fee to the provider is
typically below the usual and customary rate for the services provided.

The main consideration for the manager of a private practice and his or
her staff is to decide on what the service is worth in view of what he or she
stands to gain or lose from a source of referrals. Because MCOs are established to limit and control the costs associated with medical and mental
health services, the manager of a private practice can assume that the established rate for a service outside of an MCO plan would be generally
higher, and in some cases much higher, than what the MCO plan offers the
provider. In general, MCOs and other variants of the same offer the provider a contract that requires them to see, within a reasonable period of
time, any referrals from the organization's patient population at the prees-
tablished and contractually agreed-on fee and for the authorized length of
treatment.

The challenge for the practice administrator is to winnow through the
variety of contracts offered to the practice and to select, on the basis of the
potential number of referrals and the contracted fee for service, while
weighing the cost to them in terms of reduced fees for service, and the administrative load for processing treatment authorizations, billing, and collection. Ultimately, the manager and members of any practice need to make
strategic decisions about when or if to be contractually associated (or *pan-
eled* to use the popular jargon) with MCOs, to negotiate a range of acceptable fees per MCO, to limit to a few select or to multiple MCO contracts, and
to accept, reject, or negotiate restrictive practice covenants. Most practitioners would agree that this has proved to be a somewhat unpleasant task
that requires their constant vigilance, their assertion of treatment recommendations in the best interest of their clients, and their ability to keep up
with regular change in the form of buyouts and/or carveouts of mental

health services (*carveouts* refer to the contractual separation of the mental health service component from the other health-related service offerings). Many providers assume that they must be locked into the fee-for-service offer from a given MCO. What is often not understood is that this fee may at times be negotiable (S. Ragusea, personal communication, 2004) if the practice administration is willing to take a stand and make a case. Depending on the marketplace for qualified professionals and the need for the MCO to provide specific services to the community, negotiations often yield a better return on the professional's investment.

In establishing one's practice, the manager/administrator needs to bear in mind what forms of practice and practitioners would be most attractive to potential MCOs shopping for providers. Thus, whereas the larger, more comprehensive private practices may be viewed as more desirable by managed care companies, in that these organizations can offer one-stop, comprehensive services in a competitive market, any individual provider or small group may offer a unique specialty, accept a lower fee, or have practice guidelines more suitable to the MCO requirements.

Despite the prevalence of the managed care culture, a few private practitioners have elected to avoid any and all managed care contracts. Indeed some larger communities allow for a limited number of well-established providers to enjoy the luxury of a contract-free professional existence, which allows them to set their usual and customary fee, with the client being exclusively responsible for that fee. A robust marketplace generally allows for a few individuals to operate a practice at this level, although it is risky in the event that there is a significant downturn in the economy or if potential consumers recognize that competitive sources of service are more cost-effective in providing services of comparable quality.

In any case, it would appear that, despite the hue and cry for reform of the current system, HMOs, PPOs, and their variants are here for the foreseeable future. Although the appeal for revision of health care policy appears to be increasing, it may be years before real reforms are realized. The astute manager of an independent practice will remain attuned to the vagaries of the managed care system while readying the practice to capitalize on systemic changes.

Employee Assistance Programs

Finally, Employee Assistance Programs (EAPs) are worth considering in a comprehensive business plan for one's practice. EAPs offer large and midsized practices ready referral for services related to employee personal concerns. The typical EAP contract usually provides the employee with intake and assessment, crisis intervention, and brief counseling (usually up to three cost-free sessions), with subsequent referral to other resources, both private and community based. The provider is given a negotiated annual fee sufficient to provide services to employees seeking EAP services. Employees and their families are eligible to receive EAP services by calling a local or toll-free number that links the individual privately and confidentially to the counseling service that has contracted with the organizational entity. Practitioners who agree to be EAP providers agree to accept any and all EAP contracts for the minimum service required. In some cases, the professional is then expected to refer an individual requiring more than the minimum to other providers and, in some cases, to their own private practice. At that juncture, the patient's managed care plan or insurance would "kick in" to underwrite the continuing cost of services.

When contemplating the value of an EAP contract, the practice administrator must consider the ability of the practice to readily respond to all of the requests for service from the covered entity. For instance, if the contract calls for a capitated plan, the practice is given a one-time fee to cover the costs of all employee EAP usage for the contractual period (usually 1 year). Thus, the per-use fee to the provider varies depending on the number of contacts requested during the course of the year.

Sliding Scale and "Pro Bono" Work

The previous discussions of income production aside, most individuals in private practice maintain a belief in the value of what they have to offer to all individuals irrespective of their ability to pay. It is, after all, a safe assumption that most professionals select and persist in the counseling profession due to an inherent and/or cultivated desire to help others, and to extend their efforts in a reasonable way to all who might profit from a course of therapeutic treatment. Thus, caring and responsible private practitioners are committed to serving the broader population of clients irrespective of their ability to pay. Often sponsored by local and regional professional associations, independent providers volunteer their time to those in the greatest need. Most providers reserve a segment of their practice to include individuals who cannot afford services, who may feel blocked temporarily from receiving timely treatment from community resources, or whose unique need for specialized services may not be satisfied in community-based clinics. The provision of "pro bono" services or sliding scale fees to persons who cannot secure services otherwise is an important contribution to the community to which the provider belongs, and the practice manager is often the party responsible for highlighting the need among the practice providers and arranging policies and procedures to implement the program.

Consultation

For some, an interesting ancillary activity associated with their practice is the opportunity to provide consultation to a variety of individuals and organizations. Consultation at the organizational level with administrators and executives allows the experienced and appropriately qualified provider to offer wisdom and advice and to share knowledge with others who would profit from their area of expertise.

Other forms of consultation include program evaluation of community organizations, organizational analysis and development, training programs, appraisals of employees and candidates for hire, and consultation regarding specific problems such as alcohol and drug abuse, employee absenteeism, poor morale, mid-career life planning, reentry into the world of work, outplacement, retirement and preretirement planning, and in-service training for professional and paraprofessional staff.

Evaluation

To determine the success of the practice, to monitor client progress, and to provide the basis for alteration of the business plan, client and gatekeeper surveys prove to be invaluable. Whether utilizing available, over-the-counter evaluation instruments or tailoring an instrument to the unique needs of the practice, it is incumbent on each practice manager to keep a finger on the pulse of the practice, monitoring efficacy and progress per the business plan.

In addition to the focused, practice-based evaluations, private practitioners are challenged to be supportive of and cooperative in the more rigorous academic research pursued by the profession. As an example of a well-contrived and valuable study of clinical efficacy of services, the Pennsylvania Practice Research Network (Borkovec, Echemendia, Ragusea, & Ruiz, 2001, 2004) undertook a large and comprehensive study of symptom improvement among clients seen in private practices. The results of studies such as these, derived from broad-based practices in cooperation with private practitioners, remain an essential tool in evincing the value and efficacy of the services provided by independent practitioners.

SUMMARY

The opportunity to be in control of one's time, to tailor a practice that matches one's primary interests, and to enjoy the flexibility of self-employment attracts many of our best professionals to independent practice.

Given these incentives, matched with a well-contrived business formula and careful plan for continuing education and collegial support, the pursuit of a private practice can be among the most rewarding options for many counseling professionals.

As this chapter illustrated, private practice is not without its challenges. In today's marketplace, being a good psychologist means far more than providing effective treatment planning and delivery for clients. Whether a solo practitioner or the chief operating officer of a large comprehensive practice, the practice manager must have a solid business sense as well as broad knowledge of the nuances of running a professional practice. Reducing the exposure to legal risk, responding to the vagaries of the marketplace, remaining open to new opportunities, while addressing the need for continuing education and professional development make independent practice a particularly challenging prospect. A return to the simplicity of private practice that existed over a decade ago is not likely. Instead the simple fee-for-service concept has been eroded, spun, and modified to conform to the complex sets of guidelines promulgated in today's managed care climate. Irrespective of one's professional specialization, length of experience, and reputation, today's independent practitioner is necessarily an administrator and a manager. Business knowledge and savvy, coupled with professional expertise, now represent the standard for viability in today's complex independent practice marketplace.

10

The Professional Counselor as Administrator

EPILOGUE

In reality, all books end. However, for many, if not most, the content with which they deal is ongoing and in a constant state of change. So it is with leadership, management, and administration of counseling services. The professional counselor who becomes an administrator of counseling services, in whatever setting she or he functions, will be, like books, always chasing a moving target—a frequently changing context in which the counseling service is located. In many ways, the administrator must understand the context in which the counseling service operates or he or she becomes a captive of the context. In this sense, the epilogue for this book accents that the context of any organization is dynamic; it is the place where trends, policies, pressures, and challenges occur and affect, if not shape, the counseling services for which the administrator is responsible. Contexts are different from one counseling setting to another, and they each demand different responses from counseling administrators. In this book, we have tried to discuss such issues and the tools that the professional counselor as administrator needs to use to give leadership to how the context of a counseling program is understood and its implications for action implemented.

Thus, this book is intended to be a reference guide for those counselors, counseling psychologists, and related mental health professionals who find themselves in leadership and management roles or who aspire to such roles. We believe it provides generic administrative, management, and leadership knowledge as well as specific practical suggestions for successful management in a wide range of counseling settings. In the next section, we summarize the major emphases of each of the preceding nine chapters.

1. Leadership, Management, and Administration in Perspective

In chapter 1, we discussed leadership, management, and administration and identified the subtle but important distinctions among them. We pointed out that management and administration tend to be more technically oriented, drawing heavily on organizational and analytical skills to ensure that processes are running smoothly and achieving the desired results. Leadership, in contrast, has more to do with vision, mission, and goals; setting the values of the organization and ensuring that the organization is delivering the right programs, moving in the appropriate direction, and effectively utilizing resources. Writings from business and higher education are cited in an attempt to enhance the readers' understanding of the meaning and nature of administrative, management, and leadership roles.

2. Fundamental Processes of Leadership, Management, and Administration

Chapter 2 examined the tools, concepts, and processes used by the professional counselor serving as an administrator. Concepts like strategic planning, systems thinking, and budget management are examined as they relate to such business- and accounting-related concepts as cost centers, revenue streams, cost–benefit analysis, grant-seeking, and external funding. This chapter also included generic discussions of staff recruitment, retention, supervision, and professional development and concluded with a discussion of the increasing importance of the use of technology to acquire, store, manage, analyze, and disseminate information in support of counseling services.

3. The School Counselor as Program Administrator

Chapter 3 delineated the unique challenges confronted by the school counselor who is asked to become a program administrator. Perhaps the foremost of these challenges is establishing the counseling role as a major part of the school's mission, as opposed to being marginalized or viewed as unimportant or ancillary. An extensive section on context pointed out that the school counselor's role is increasingly determined by external forces, including federal, state, and local legislation. These external forces, together with the following four overarching societal challenges, shape the context in which the school counselor must work: (a) the shifting economy and occupational structure, (b) changing family structures and the gender revolution, (c) the growing pluralism of contemporary society, and (d) the changing definitions and increasing magnitude of at-risk populations. In addition, the chapter contained sections addressing planning, staff recruitment and retention, supervision, performance evaluation, program evaluation, and cost–benefit analysis. The chapter concluded by providing the elements of a school counseling program audit as recommended by the American School Counselor Association.

4. University Counseling Centers

Chapter 4 focused on the role of the director of the university counseling center, pointing out that this role has rarely been studied in any systematic way, and thus there is little research to guide or support those who aspire to direct counseling centers. Further it pointed out that, to be effective, the modern-day director must be integrally involved at a variety of levels within the student affairs operation because often the goals of the counseling center are dictated by faculty committees, or central administrators. Thus, an important part of the director's role is to be wired to these policymaking bodies and decision makers—"managing up" may be as important as other aspects of the job. Maintaining high-quality staff is cited as a particular challenge given the competition to move into private practice.

The chapter included sections on the role of the director; the internal organization of staff professionals; budgeting and financial considerations; staff recruitment, retention, and professional development; staff morale; training and supervision; use of technology; diversity issues; assessment and evaluation; program accreditation; and concluded with a section on the administration of data banks and surveys.

5. University Career Services

Chapter 5 examined the unique character of the challenges confronted by those who function in a leadership role in college and university career centers. A large section is devoted to planning and the strategic factors that have an impact on planning, including: institutional mission, impact of theory, professional standards, ethical guidelines, institutional structure, behavioral expectations, and management style/philosophy. Particular emphasis is placed on these factors and their implications for leadership. Other sections include: budgets and budgeting; staff recruitment, retention, and professional development; the use and impact of technology; organizational structure; outreach; diversity issues; program evaluation; accreditation; marketing and public relations; and a summary of the most pressing leadership/management issues.

6. Chair, Academic Department

Chapter 6 described the demanding nature of chairing an academic department of counselor education or counseling psychology and concluded that one of the most challenging issues is the management of the ever-shifting and changing responsibilities within the dynamic, committee-driven, academic environment. Other compelling issues included the ever-increasing pressure to generate external resources, and the generally low esteem accorded departmental chairs by faculty. The chapter identified and explored several key challenges, including the establishment and maintenance of academic partnerships and interdisciplinary collaborations; meeting external professional standards imposed by accrediting agencies; and the press to recruit, support, and retain high-quality, diverse graduate students. The chapter concluded by addressing the issues of facilities management, budgeting, faculty and staff recruiting and retention, professional development, and evaluation.

7. Government, Nonprofit, and Professional Organizations

Chapter 7 discussed a range of counselor/administrator positions that exist within governmental agencies, nonprofit organizations, and various professional associations. A considerable portion of the chapter is devoted to describing the administrative functions performed by counselor administrators in these organizations, including: advocacy and support, conference administration, journal editing and management, credentialing and certification, grant proposal administration, membership management, financial management, information management, enforcement of professional ethics, and imposition of member sanctions. The range of administrative and management opportunities in these organizations is extensive, but differs from other counselor administrator roles in that no direct clinical services are being delivered, managed, or supervised. The later sections of the chapter explore the topics of planning, budgeting, staffing, recruitment and retention, and supervision as they relate to these unique work environments.

8. Counseling in the Community and Workplaces About Work

Managing counseling services in the community and within the workplace is the subject of chapter 8. A large portion of this chapter was devoted to understanding the highly variable context, which may be determined by federal, state, and local legislation as well as by the vagaries of the organizational goals within which the counseling services are being delivered. A broad range of counseling services are represented, including rehabilitation services, EAPs, career management services, life planning services, human resource management, human resource development, and so on. The chapter offered a broad discussion of planning within the context painted in the first section and drew particular attention to the likelihood that in these contexts counseling strategic plans are guided by legislation, relevant law, and salient corporate and organizational plans. An extensive discussion of the challenge of balancing the needs of the individual with those of the organization and the possibility of outsourcing certain counseling functions was offered.

The importance and power of budgeting within business environments was discussed, emphasizing that private organizations as well as governmental agencies utilize budgets as both financial and political tools to facilitate and control the implementation of strategic plans. A section on staffing explored the difficult issues of staff roles and definitions given the broad range of organizations served, the issue of credentialing, and again the issue of whether to outsource. The chapter included a discussion of the use of technology in workplace counseling settings and concluded that the main functions of the professional counselor as administrator in this environment are (a) the planning process both strategically and on a daily basis, (b) the supervision process to make sure the plans are carried out, and (c) the control process, including analyzing results, monitoring and adjusting budgets, and clarifying and adjusting staff tasks.

9. Private Practice

Chapter 9 delved into the opportunities and challenges of managing a private practice. The early section of the chapter explored the many advantages of private practice (freedom, flexibility, higher income) versus some common disadvantages (working in relative isolation, third-party payment hassles, and escalating administrative and overhead costs). Later sections addressed such practical matters as the development of a business plan, building a practice, staffing, location and configuration of the office, marketing, professional development, credentialing, and managed care and fee issues. The chapter closed with a discussion of the advantages of various types of business structures (incorporation vs. proprietorship, etc.), evaluation, and consultation.

SOME MAJOR THEMES

Several major themes cut across all nine chapters and emerge as being particularly salient. First, it is increasingly apparent that the successful counselor/manager must be capable of responding rapidly and positively to an ever-changing contextual climate. Each chapter of this book began with an emphasis on understanding the unique character of the work environment and how to function effectively in it. Today's rapidly changing climate demands that a director be adept at conducting ongoing environmental scans and managing perceived change. Second, all counseling environments now require directors to take on increased budgetary responsibility, including the ability to raise external funds through a broad range of fundraising strategies. Indeed fundraising will almost certainly comprise a substantial portion of the successful director's time. Third, the successful counseling director must be capable of representing the goals and values of the counseling enterprise to those within the greater organization in positions of power (central administration), in terms they understand. The ability and willingness to *manage up* in this way has become increasingly important if counseling agencies are to maintain their resource base. Fourth, counselors must learn to effectively harness technology to enhance efficiency and free counselor time for those tasks that require human sensitivity. Huge strides have been made in the development of administrative and management software for the counseling profession in recent years, and the effective director must embrace and integrate its use. Finally, directors of counseling agencies must adopt a healthy bias for action. A great challenge within the counseling profession is the tendency for counselors to engage in endless process—a sort of paralysis by analysis. A core value in virtually all of the best-run organizations, whether they are a business or educational institution, manufacturing or service organization, is a strong bias for action (Peters & Waterman, 1982). Although counselors can resist this trend, the counselor as manager must embrace it.

COUNSELOR AS DIRECTOR: THE LEADERSHIP CHALLENGE

Throughout this book, it should be clear to the reader that the leadership, management, and administration of counselors, counseling agencies, and counselor training programs are highly complex and challenging enterprises. Although management within each of the different counseling environments represents unique challenges, there are certain overarching issues that are common to successful management within these varied counseling environments.

First, many of the skills and values that have utility for the process of counseling also have utility for administration and management. Notable here are the ability to empathize—to put oneself in another's place (empathic understanding)—and the listening and process facilitation skills that one hones in counselor training. Clearly empathy and facilitation skills are critical for the successful leadership of nearly any enterprise. Employees at every level want to be respected, heard, and treated with dignity, and that is the very essence of the counseling relationship. These highly developed counseling skills are tremendous assets to the leader/manager of any enterprise, but especially a counseling organization.

Just as the previously mentioned counseling skills translate well to the task of administration, others may be a deterrent to successful administration and management. Although it is essential for a counselor to be process-oriented and to value process above some arbitrary goal, the administrator/manager must be goal-oriented and must not allow protracted process to deter personal or organizational goal attainment. Indeed the highly developed process orientation of many counselors is in direct opposition to the strong bias for action and goal orientation that scholars of organizational behavior regard as essential to dynamic leaders and organizations (Peters & Waterman, 1982). Similarly, a skilled counselor must be nonjudgmental and possessed of unconditional positive regard for the client, whereas the administrator/manager spends much of his or her energy critically evaluating clients, staff, facilities, budgets, political situations, personnel, colleagues, organizational structures, strategic plans, and nearly every element of the work environment. Indeed critical thinking skills, sometimes called *shrewdness*, are the very essence of skillful leadership and management. Put crudely by Lee Iacocca (1984) in his book, "A Good Manager Must Be Able to Distinguish the Difference Between a Dip of Ice Cream and a Dip of Bullshit." Admirable as it is to be nonjudgmental and possessed of unconditional positive regard, it is essential for effective managers to be judgmental, critical thinkers and to confront destructive, inappropriate, and unprofessional behavior when it is exhibited by employees.

Yet another highly desirable quality in a manager/administrator is superior organizational skill as opposed to the sometimes whimsical, artistic approaches that often prove productive in the art of counseling. If, as some organizational scholars say, "management is more art than science," it is also more about being organized than it is about being artistic.

If we look at our own literature—the literature of career counseling—we note that the prominent personality characteristics of counselors are those that Holland (1973) defined as being principally social and artistic. Indeed a high percentage of counselors have Holland codes of SAE (*S*ocial, *A*rtistic, *E*nterprising) or SIA (*S*ocial, *I*nvestigative, *A*rtistic). In contrast, the Holland code of good managers, administrators, and leaders tends to be ESC (*E*nterprising, *S*ocial, *C*onventional) or ECS (*E*nterprising, *C*onventional, *S*ocial). It should not be surprising to us that counselors often struggle in the role of leader because their personality codes as a group are incongruent with the codes we would expect for success in an enterprising/organizational environment. In short, there is a naturally poor person—environment fit. To function effectively in leadership and administrative roles, many counselors must acknowledge this incongruence and take positive steps to overcome it. Perhaps one of the first necessary steps is to identify those qualities that distinguish a leader.

In the introduction to *The Leader of the Future* (Hesselbein, Goldsmith, & Beckhard, 1996), Peter Drucker pointed out:

All effective leaders I have encountered—both those I worked with and those I merely watched—*knew* four simple things:

1. The only definition of a *leader* is someone who has *followers*. Some people are thinkers. Some are prophets. Both roles are important and badly needed. But without followers, there can be no leaders.
2. An effective leader is not someone who is loved or admired. He or she is someone whose followers do the right things. Popularity is not leadership. *Results* are.
3. Leaders are highly visible. They therefore set *examples*.
4. Leadership is not rank, privileges, titles, or money. It is *responsibility*.

Regardless of their almost limitless diversity with respect to personality, style, abilities, and interests, the effective leaders I have met, worked with, and observed also *behaved* much the same way:

1. They did not start out with the question, "What do I want?" They started out asking, "*What needs to be done?*"
2. Then they asked, "*What can and should I do to make a difference?*" This has to be something that both needs to be done and fits the leader's strengths and the way she or he is most effective.
3. They constantly asked, "What are the organization's *mission* and *goals*? What constitutes *performance* and *results* in this organization?"
4. They were extremely tolerant of diversity in people and did not look for carbon copies of themselves. It rarely even occurred to them to ask, "Do I like or dislike this person?" But they were totally—fiendishly—intolerant when it came to a person's *performance, standards*, and *values*.
5. They were not afraid of strength in their associates. They gloried in it. Whether they had heard of it or not, their motto was what Andrew Carnegie wanted to have put on his tombstone: "Here lies a man who attracted better people into his service than he was himself."
6. One way or another, they submitted themselves to the "mirror test"—that is, they made sure that the person they saw in the mirror in the morning was the kind of person they wanted to be, respect, and believe in. This way they fortified themselves against the leader's greatest temptations—to do things that are popular rather than right and to do petty, mean, sleazy things.

Finally, these effective leaders were not preachers; they were doers. . . . Effective leaders delegate a good many things; they have to or they drown in trivia. But they do not delegate the one thing that only they can do with excellence, the one thing that will make a difference, the one thing that will set standards, the one thing they want to be remembered for. They do it. (pp. xii–xiv)

We believe that aspiring leaders of counseling organizations would do well to heed Drucker's advice as well as the contents of this volume. We hope that this book makes a contribution to the counseling profession and to those who aspire to lead.

References

American Counseling Association. (1995). *The American Counseling Association Code of Ethics and Standards of Practice.* Alexandria, VA: Author.

American Educational Research Association. American Psychological Association and National Council on Measurement in Education. (1999). *Standards for educational and psychological testing.* Washington, DC: Author.

American Psychological Association. (2003). *The American Psychological Association Ethical Principles of Psychologists and Code of Conduct.* Washington, DC: Author.

American Psychological Association. (2003). http://www.research.apa.org/salsburv.html

American Psychological Association. (2004). *Monitor on Psychology, 35*(7).

American School Counselors Association. (1998). *Ethical standards for school counselors.* Alexandria, VA: Author.

American School Counselors Association. (2000). *Ethical standards for school counselors.* Alexandria, VA: Author.

Archer, J., & Cooper, S. (1998). *Counseling and mental health services on campus: A handbook of contemporary practices and challenges.* San Francisco: Jossey-Bass.

Association for Counselor Education and Supervision. (1989a, Spring). ACES adopts standards for counseling supervisors. *ACES Spectrum,* pp. 7–10.

Association for Counselor Education and Supervision. (1989b). *The Association for Counselor Education and Supervision Standards for Counselor Supervision.* Alexandria, VA: The Author.

Association for Counselor Education and Supervision. (1995). Ethical guidelines for counseling supervisors. *Counselor Education and Supervision, 34,* 270–276.

Association of State and Provincial Psychology Boards. (2004). *Entry requirements for the professional practice of psychology: A guide for students and faculty.* Montgomery, AL: ASPPB: www.asppb.org.

Association for University and College Counseling Center Directors. (2005). Elements of Excellence Task Force. http://www.aucccd.org/boardinfo/eofe.htm.

Astin, A. W. (1977). *Four critical years: Effects of college on beliefs, attitudes, and knowledge.* San Francisco, CA: Jossey-Bass.

Babbish, H. E., Hawley, W. W., & Zeran, J. (1986). The best of both worlds. *Journal of Career Planning and Employment, XLVII*, 48–53.

Bardwick, J. (1996). Peacetime management and wartime leadership. In F. Hesselbein, M. Goldsmith, & R. Beckhard (Eds.), *The leader of the future. New visions, strategies, and practices for the next era* (pp. 131–140). San Francisco, CA: Jossey-Bass.

Bechtel, D. S. (1993). The organization and impact of career programs and services within higher education. In J. R. Rayman (Ed.), *The changing role of career services* (pp. 23–26). San Francisco, CA: Jossey-Bass.

Bennis, W. E. (1989). *On becoming a leader.* Reading, MA: Addison-Wesley.

Bennis, W. G., Benne, R., & Chin, R. (Eds.). (1961). *The planning of change.* Troy, NY: Holt, Rinehart, & Winston.

Bernes, K., & Magnusson, K. (1996). A description of career development services with Canadian organizations. *Journal of Counseling and Development, 74*(6), 569–574.

Bersoff, D., Field, R., Anderer, S., & Zaplac, T. (1999). *The law and mental health professionals.* Washington, DC: American Psychological Association.

Bolles, R. N. (1997). *Job hunting on the Internet.* Berkeley, CA: Ten Speed Press.

Bolt, J. F. (1996). Developing three-dimensional leaders. In F. Hesselbein, M. Goldsmith, & R. Beckhard (Eds.), *The leader of the future. New visions, strategies, and practices for the next era* (pp. 161–173). San Francisco, CA: Jossey-Bass.

Borders, L. D., & Drury, S. (1992). Comprehensive school counseling programs: A review of policymakers and practitioners. *Journal of Counseling & Development, 70,* 487–498.

Borkovec, T., Echemendia, R., Ragusea, S., & Ruiz, M. (2001). The Pennsylvania Practice Research Network and Future Possibilities for Clinically Meaningful and Scientifically Rigorous Psychotherapy Effectiveness Research. *Clinical Psychology: Science and Practice, 8*(2), 155–167.

Borkovec, T., Echemendia, R., Ragusea, S., & Ruiz, M. (2004). Research in training clinics and practice research networks: A route to the integration of science and practice. *Clinical Psychology: Science and Practice, 11*(2), 211–215.

Bornstein, S. M., & Smith, A. F. (1998). The puzzles of leadership. In F. Hesselbein, M. Goldsmith, & R. Beckhard (Eds.), *The leader of the future. New visions, strategies, and practices for the next era* (pp. 281–292). San Francisco, CA: Jossey-Bass.

Bowers, J., & Hatch, T. (2003). *The ASCA national model. A framework for school counseling programs.* Alexandria, VA: American School Counselor Association.

Boyd, V. T. (2004). *Annual Counseling Center Survey.* College Park, MD: University of Maryland Counseling Center.

Boyd, V. T., Hattaner, E., Brandel, I. W., Buckles, N., Davidshoter, C., Deakin, S., Erskine, C., Hurley, G., Locher, L., Piorkowski, G., Simono, R. B., Spirack, J., & Steel, C. (2003). *Accreditation Standards for University and College Counseling Centers, 81,* 168–177.

Brinckerhoff, P. C. (2000). *Mission-based management. Leading your not-for-profit in the 21st century.* (2nd ed.). New York: Wiley.

Budman, S., & Gurman, A. (1988). *Theory and practice of brief therapy.* New York: Guilford.

Campbell, C., & Dahir, C. (1997). *The national standards for school counseling programs.* Alexandria, VA: American School Counselor Association.

Committee on Accreditation, American Psychological Association. (2004). *Guidelines and principles for accreditation of programs in professional psychology.* Washington, DC: Author.

Cook, W. J. (2001). *Strategic planning for America's schools.* Montgomery, AL: The Cambridge Group.

Council for the Accreditation of Counseling and Related Education Programs. (2001). *CACREP Accreditation Manual.* Alexandria, VA: The Author.

Council for the Advancement of Standards in Higher Education. (2003). *Counseling services standards and guidelines: Self-assessment guide.* Washington, DC: Author.

Covey, S. (1996). Three roles of the leader in the new paradigm. In F. Hesselbein, M. Goldsmith, & R. Beckhard (Eds.), *The leader of the future. New visions, strategies, and practices for the next era* (pp. 140–160). San Francisco, CA: Jossey-Bass.

Davenport, T. O. (1999). *Human capital. What it is and why people invest in it.* San Francisco, CA: Jossey-Bass.

Deming, W. E. (1986). *Out of the crisis.* Cambridge, MA: MIT Press.

Deming, W. E. (1993). *The new economics for education, government, and industry.* Cambridge, MA: MIT Press.

Duenwald, M. (2004, October 26). The dorms may be great, but how's the counseling? *The New York Times,* pp. D1, D6.

Dumaine, B. (1994, December 26). Why do we work? *Fortune,* p. 1996.

Duncan, J. A., & Geoffroy, K. E. (1971). A factor analyses of the role of the State Director of Guidance Service. *Counselor Education and Supervision, 10*(3), 251–260.

Erford, B. T. (2003). *Transforming the school counseling program.* Upper Saddle River, NJ: Merrill Prentice Hall.

Ford, D. H. (1987). *Humans as self-constructing living systems. A developmental perspective on behavior and personality.* Hillsdale, NJ: Lawrence Erlbaum Associates.

Friedman, M. B. (1992). *The leadership myth.* Pittsburgh, PA: Dorrance.

Gallagher, R. (2004). *National survey of counseling center directors.* Alexandria, VA: International Association of Counseling Services.

Gati, I. (1994). Computer-assisted career counseling: Dilemmas, problems, and possible solutions. *Journal of Counseling and Development, 73*(1), 51–56.

Ginac, L. (2004). Career counseling is a valuable benefit for employees. *Career Developments, 20*(2), 6–7.

Gladding, S. T., & Ryan, M. (2001). Community counseling settings. In D. C. Locke, J. E. Myers, & E. L. Herr (Eds.), *The handbook of counseling* (pp. 343–354). Thousand Oaks, CA: Sage.

Goodman, A. P., Rayman, J. R., & Ferrell, D. (2001). The commercialization of career services: Ethical considerations for practitioners. *Journal of Career Planning and Employment, LXI*(2), 21–27.

Gray, K. C., & Herr, E. L. (1998). *Workforce education: The basics.* Boston, MA: Allyn & Bacon.

Gysbers, N. C., & Henderson, P. (1994). *Developing and managing your school guidance program* (2nd ed.). Alexandria, VA: American Counseling Association.

Handy, C. (1989). *The age of unreason.* Cambridge, MA: Harvard Business School Press.

Handy, C. (1996). The new language of organizing and its implication for leaders. In F. Hesselbein, M. Goldsmith, & R. Beckhard (Eds.), *The leader of the future. New visions, strategies, and practices for the next era* (pp. 3–10). San Francisco, CA: Jossey-Bass.

Harris, W. G. (1987). Computer-based test interpretations: Some development and application issues. *Applied Psychology: An International Review, 36,* 237–247.

Hart, G., & Nance, D. (2003). Styles of counselor supervision as perceived by supervisors and supervisees. *Counselor Education & Supervision, 43,* 146–158.

Heitzmann, D., & Nafziger, K. (2001). Assessing counseling services. In J. H. Schuh, & M. L. Upcraft (Eds.), *Assessment practice in student affairs: An applications manual.* San Francisco: Jossey-Bass.

Heller, R., & Hindle, T. (1998). *Essential manager's manual.* New York: DK Publishing.

Henderson, P., & Gysbers, N. (1998). *Leading and managing your school guidance program staff.* Alexandria, VA: American Counseling Association.

Herr, E. L. (1971). National perspectives on state guidance office functions. *Counselor Education and Supervision, 10*(3), 209–218.

Herr, E. L. (1999). *Counseling in a dynamic society: Contexts and practices for the 21st century.* Alexandria, VA: American Counseling Association.

Herr, E. L. (2002). Costs/benefits of career development. In L. Bezanson & E. O'Reilly (Eds.), *Making waves: Connecting career development with public policy* (pp. 25–30). Ottawa, Canada: Canadian Career Development Foundation.

Herr, E. L., Cramer, S. H., & Niles, S. G. (2004). *Career guidance and counseling through the lifespan. Systematic approaches* (6th ed.). Boston, MA: Pearson/Allyn & Bacon.

Herr, E. L., Rayman, J., & Garis, J. (1993). *Handbook for the college and university career center.* Westport, CT: Greenwood.

Hesselbein, F., Goldsmith, M., & Beckhard, R. (1996). *The leader of the future.* San Francisco, CA: Jossey-Bass.

Holland, J. L. (1973). *Making vocational choices: A theory of careers.* Englewood Cliffs, NJ: Prentice-Hall.

Hoover, E. (2003, December 5). More help for troubled students. *The Chronicle of Higher Education,* pp. A25–A26.

Hosie, T. W., West, J. P., & Mackey, J A. (1993). Employment and roles of counselors in employee assistance programs. *Journal of Counseling & Development, 71,* 355–359.

Iacocca, L. (1984). *The autobiography of Lee Iacocca.* New York: Bantam.

International Association of Counseling Services, Inc. (2000). *IACS accreditation standards for university and college counseling centers.* Alexandria, VA: Author.

International Association for Educational and Vocational Guidance. (1996). *IAEVG Ethical Standard.* Berlin, Germany: Author.

Kadison, R., & DiGeronimo, T. (2004). *College of the overwhelmed: The campus mental health crisis and what to do about it.* San Francisco: Jossey-Bass.

Keeling, R., & Heitzmann, D. (2003). *Financing health and counseling services.* In J. H. Schuh (Ed.), *Contemporary financial issues in student affairs* (pp.). San Francisco: Jossey-Bass.

Kennedy, K., Moran, L., & Upcraft, M. L. (2001). In J. H. Schuh & M. L. Upcraft (Eds.), *Assessment practice in student affairs: An applications manual.* San Francisco, CA: Jossey-Bass.

Kotter, J. P. (1999). *What leaders really do.* Cambridge, MA: Harvard Business Review Book.

Kuh, G. D. (1985). What is extraordinary about ordinary student affairs organizations. *NASPA Journal, 23*(2), 31–43.

Kuh, G. D., & Andreas, R. E. (1991). It's about time: Using qualitative methods in student life studies. Using qualitative methods in student life studies. *Journal of College Student Development, 32,* 397–405.

Ladany, N., Walker, J. A., & Melincoff, D. S. (2001). Supervisory style: Its relation to the supervisory working alliance and supervisor self-disclosure. *Counselor Education and Supervision, 43,* 146–158.

Lavoritano, J., & Segal, P. B. (1992). Evaluating the efficacy of a school counseling program. *Psychology in the Schools, 29,* 61–70.

Levine, A., & Cureton, J. (1998). *When hope and fear collide.* San Francisco: Jossey-Bass.

Littrell, J. M., & Peterson, J. S. (2001). Transforming the school culture: A model based on an exemplary counselor. *Professional School Counseling, 4*(5), 310–319.

Lowman, R., & Resnick, R. (Eds.). (1994). *The mental health professional's guide to managed care.* Washington, DC: American Psychological Association.

MacDonald, J. (2004, December 6). Reaching out to students. *USA Today.*

McNary, L. D. (1999). Leadership in the new economic age. Quality management and the revival of leadership in organizational America. *Proteus. A Journal of Ideas, 16*(2), 19–28.

Miller, T. K. (Ed.). (2003). *CAS. The book of professional standards for higher education* (3rd ed.). Washington, DC: Council for the Advancement of Standards in Higher Education.

Mirabile, R. J. (1985). Outplacement as transition counseling. *Journal of Employment Counseling, 22*(1), 39–45.

MonsterTrak. (2004). http://www.monstertrak.monster.com/intro/terms.html.

NaceLink. (2004). http://www.nacelink.com/

Naisbitt, K., & Aburdene, P. (1990). *Megatrends 2000.* New York: Simon & Schuster.

National Association of Colleges and Employers. (1998). *Principles for Professional Conduct for Career Services and Employment Professionals.* Bethlehem, PA: Author.

National Association of Colleges and Employers. (2004). *State of the profession: Results from NACE's 2004 career services benchmarking survey.* Bethlehem, PA: Author.

National Career Development Association. (2003). *The National Career Development Association Ethical Standards.* Washington, DC: Author.

Niles, S., & Garis, J. W. (1990). The effects of a career planning course and a computer-assisted career guidance program (SIGI Plus) on undecided university students. *Journal of Career Development, 16,* 237–248.

Oliver, L. W., & Spokane, A. R. (1988). Career intervention outcome: What contributes to client gain? *Journal of Counseling Psychology, 35,* 447–462.

Ouchi, W. (1981). *Theory Z.* Reading, MA: Addison-Wesley.

Paisley, P. O., & Borders, L. D. (1995). School counseling: An evolving specialty. *Journal of Counseling and Development, 74,* 150–152.

Palmo, A. J., Shosh, M. J., & Weikel, W. S. (2001). The independent practice of mental health counseling. Past, present, and future. In D. C. Locke, J. E. Myers, & E. L. Herr (Eds.), *The handbook of counseling* (pp. 653–667). Thousand Oaks, CA: Sage.

Peters, T. J., & Waterman, R. H. (1982). *In search of excellence.* New York: Warner Books.

Rayman, J. R. (1993). *The changing role of career services.* San Francisco, CA: Jossey-Bass.

Rayman, J. R. (1999). Career services imperatives for the next millennium. *Career Development Quarterly, 48*(2), 175–184.

Rayman, J. R. (2001). Assessing career services. In J. H. Schuh & M. L. Upcraft (Eds.), *Assessment practice in student affairs: An applications manual.* (pp. 365–389). San Francisco: Jossey-Bass.

Ripley, V., Erford, B. T., Dahir, C., & Eschbach, L. (2003). Planning and implementing a 21st century comprehensive developmental school counseling program. In T. Bradley & Erford (Eds.), *Transforming the school counseling profession* (pp. 63–119). Upper Saddle River, NJ: Merrill Prentice Hall.

Ritenour, J. P. (1934). *Annual report on health service.* Unpublished manuscript, The Pennsylvania State University, University Park, PA.

Sampson, J. P., Kolodinsky, R. W., & Greeno, B. P. (1997). Counseling on the information highway: Future possibilities and potential problems. *Journal of Counseling and Development, 75*(3), 203–212.

Sampson, J. P., & Reardon, R. (Eds.). (1990). *Enhancing the use and design of computer-assisted career guidance systems.* Alexandria, VA: National Career Development Association.

Schoenberg, M. (Ed.). (1978). *A handbook and guide for the college and university counseling center.* Westport, CT: Greenwood.

Schuh, J. H., & Upcraft, M. L. (Eds.). (2001). *Assessment practice in student affairs: An applications manual.* San Francisco: Jossey-Bass.

Senge, P. M. (1990). *The fifth discipline.* New York: Doubleday.

Spruill, J., Rozensky, R., Stigall, T., Vasquez, M., Bingham, R., & DeVaney Olvey, C. (2004). Becoming a competent clinician: Basic competencies in intervention. *Journal of Clinical Psychology, 60*(7), 741–754.

Super, D. E. (1957). *The psychology of careers.* New York: Harper & Row.

Townsend, R. (1970). *Up the organization.* New York: Knopf.

U.S. Office of Personnel Management. Center for Leadership and Executive Resource Policy. (1998). *Guide to the senior executive service.* Washington, DC: Author.

Vailli, P. B. (1989). *Managing as a performing art: New ideas for a world of chaotic change.* San Francisco: Jossey-Bass.

Vailli, P. B. (1996). *Learning as a way of being. Strategies for survival in a world of permanent white water.* San Francisco, CA: Jossey-Bass.

Whiston, S. C., Sexton, T. L., & Lasoff, C. L. (1998). Career intervention outcome: A replication and extension of Oliver and Spokane (1988). *Journal of Counseling Psychology, 45*(2), 150–165.

Author Index

Subject Index

A

Accreditation bodies for counseling programs, 46, 86, 184, 186, 192
American Psychological Association, 51, 86, 196–199
Council for the Accreditation of Counseling and Related Educational Programs, 51, 86, 192–194
Council for the Advancement of Standards in Higher Education, 125, 190
Council on Rehabilitation Education, 195, 200–203
International Association of Counseling Services, 124
Administration, 3–5
administrator as statesperson, 35
combining managerial and leadership skills, 23
defined, 5, 320
American School Counselor Association
national model for school counseling programs, 67, 78, 80, 190
Association for University and College Counseling Center Directors, 107

B

Budgeting, 34, 114, 209–219, 288
academic departments, 209

cost centers, 39
direct costs, 40, 289
expenditures, 39
facilities and administrative costs, 40
fixed costs and variable costs, 289
flow through funds, 243
fringe benefits, 40
indirect costs, 40, 289
federal budgeting process, 287
government, nonprofit, and professional organizations comparisons, 259–264
nongovernmental workplaces, 290–292
revenue streams, 37–39, 149, 210, 260–264
creative funding sources for counseling centers, 115
legislative mandates, 286
supplementing the career service budget, 150
university career services, 147
university counseling centers, 114

C

Certified rehabilitation counselor, 46, 203, 294
Community counseling agencies
context, 271
planning differences between local government agencies and workplaces, 282
public employment centers, 272–274